Superconducting Qubit Design Using Qiskit Metal

Subhojit Halder • Kinjal A. Chauhan •
Muhamad Bagher Barfar • Srinjoy Ganguly •
Shalini Devendrababu

Superconducting Qubit Design Using Qiskit Metal

Engineering of Superconducting Quantum Architecture

Apress®

Subhojit Halder
Pune, Maharashtra, India

Kinjal A. Chauhan
Ahmedabad, Gujarat, India

Muhamad Bagher Barfar
Karbala Governorate, Iraq

Srinjoy Ganguly
Ghaziabad, Uttar Pradesh, India

Shalini Devendrababu
Tiruppur, Tamil Nadu, India

ISBN-13 (pbk): 979-8-8688-1503-4 ISBN-13 (electronic): 979-8-8688-1504-1
https://doi.org/10.1007/979-8-8688-1504-1

Copyright © 2025 by Subhojit Halder, Kinjal A. Chauhan, Muhamad Bagher Barfar, Srinjoy Ganguly and Shalini Devendrababu

This work is subject to copyright. All rights are reserved by the Publisher, whether the whole or part of the material is concerned, specifically the rights of translation, reprinting, reuse of illustrations, recitation, broadcasting, reproduction on microfilms or in any other physical way, and transmission or information storage and retrieval, electronic adaptation, computer software, or by similar or dissimilar methodology now known or hereafter developed.

Trademarked names, logos, and images may appear in this book. Rather than use a trademark symbol with every occurrence of a trademarked name, logo, or image we use the names, logos, and images only in an editorial fashion and to the benefit of the trademark owner, with no intention of infringement of the trademark.

The use in this publication of trade names, trademarks, service marks, and similar terms, even if they are not identified as such, is not to be taken as an expression of opinion as to whether or not they are subject to proprietary rights.

While the advice and information in this book are believed to be true and accurate at the date of publication, neither the authors nor the editors nor the publisher can accept any legal responsibility for any errors or omissions that may be made. The publisher makes no warranty, express or implied, with respect to the material contained herein.

Managing Director, Apress Media LLC: Welmoed Spahr
Acquisitions Editor: Smriti Srivastava
Development Editor: Laura Berendsom
Editorial Assistant: Jessica Vakili

Cover designed by eStudioCalamar

Distributed to the book trade worldwide by Springer Science+Business Media New York, 1 New York Plaza, New York, NY 10004. Phone 1-800-SPRINGER, fax (201) 348-4505, e-mail orders-ny@springer-sbm.com, or visit www.springeronline.com. Apress Media, LLC is a Delaware LLC and the sole member (owner) is Springer Science + Business Media Finance Inc (SSBM Finance Inc). SSBM Finance Inc is a **Delaware** corporation.

For information on translations, please e-mail booktranslations@springernature.com; for reprint, paperback, or audio rights, please e-mail www.bookpermissions@springernature.com.

Apress titles may be purchased in bulk for academic, corporate, or promotional use. eBook versions and licenses are also available for most titles. For more information, reference our Print and eBook Bulk Sales web page at http://www.apress.com/bulk-sales.

Any source code or other supplementary material referenced by the author in this book is available to readers on GitHub. For more detailed information, please visit https://www.apress.com/gp/services/source-code.

If disposing of this product, please recycle the paper

To my late grandfather—whose memory continues to inspire me every day.
To my parents—for their unwavering love, guidance, and support.
To my brother—for his constant motivation and encouragement.
And to my friends and family—for always believing in me, even when I struggled to believe in myself.
—*Subhojit Halder*

To my beloved family, friends and mentors.
—*Kinjal Chauhan*

To my parents, for their endless love.
To my wife, Noor, for her unwavering support.
To Zahra and Roya, for their boundless joy.
To my siblings, my lifelong friends.
And to my teachers, for their invaluable guidance.
—*Muhamad Bagher Barfar*

To my beloved family, mentors, students, and the omniscient power that guides me in my life.
—*Srinjoy Ganguly*

To my late mother, whose love and wisdom continue to guide me from beyond the stars.
To my dear father, whose strength and support are my constant anchors.
To my cherished fiancé, the heartbeat of my soul and the joy of my life.
To my beloved sibling, my lifelong friend and confidant.
To my dear niece, who represents the promise of our family's future.
And to my other family members.
This book is a tribute to each of you, the pillars of my life.

—Shalini Devendrababu

Contents

About the Authors xi
About the Technical Reviewer xv
Acknowledgments xvii
Introduction xix

1 Introduction: Superconducting Qubits and Their Realizations 1
- 1.1 Quantum Computing and History 1
- 1.2 Introduction to Qubits 3
- 1.3 Timeline of Quantum Computing and Superconducting Circuits ... 4
- 1.4 Quantum Computing Fundamentals 5
- 1.5 Classical and Quantum Circuits 9
- 1.6 Lagrangian Models 13
- 1.7 Pauli Matrices 16
- 1.8 Hamiltonian Model 16
- 1.9 Superconducting Circuits 17
    - 1.9.1 What Is Superconductivity? 18
- 1.10 Terms and Definitions of Some Important Concepts 19
- 1.11 Superconducting Qubits 26
- 1.12 Advantages and Disadvantages of Superconducting Systems 31
- 1.13 Realizing Superconducting Circuits 34
- 1.14 Conclusion 35

2 Theory of Superconducting Qubit 37
- 2.1 Harmonic Oscillator 37
    - 2.1.1 Classical Harmonic Oscillator 38
    - 2.1.2 Quantum Harmonic Oscillator 40
    - 2.1.3 Can a Harmonic Oscillator Serve As a Qubit? 42
- 2.2 Classical Electrodynamics of an LC Oscillator Circuit 43
    - 2.2.1 Generating Hamiltonian of the Circuit 46
- 2.3 Quantum Hamiltonian of an LC Oscillator Circuit 48
- 2.4 Superconducting Qubits 53
    - 2.4.1 Basic Types of Superconducting Qubits 54
- 2.5 Transmon Qubit 60

		2.5.1 Classical Hamiltonian of Transmon Qubit	63

        2.5.1   Classical Hamiltonian of Transmon Qubit 63
        2.5.2   Quantum Hamiltonian of Transmon Qubit 64
  2.6   Other Refinements of Superconducting Qubit 69
        2.6.1   Xmon Qubit 69
        2.6.2   Quantronium Qubit... 70
        2.6.3   Fluxonium Qubit 71
        2.6.4   Gmon Qubit 72
        2.6.5   Coaxmon Qubit... 73
  2.7   Conclusion 74

3 Qiskit and Introduction to Qiskit Metal 77
  3.1   Writing Basic Code.. 77
  3.2   Logic Gates 84
  3.3   Important Quantum Circuits 94
  3.4   Qiskit Metal.. 105
        3.4.1   Designing Quantum Chips 106
        3.4.2   Typical Quantum Processor Structure 106
  3.5   Qiskit Metal Installation Steps 108
  3.6   Conclusion 114

4 Qiskit Metal and Introduction to Chip Design 115
  4.1   Qiskit Metal and Python... 115
  4.2   Quantum Pins: QPins.. 126
  4.3   Routing Between the Qcomponents 130
        4.3.1   Straight Routing 131
        4.3.2   Any Direction Routing 133
        4.3.3   Routing at Bent Angles 136
        4.3.4   CPW Route Meander.. 139
  4.4   Types of Qubit 142
        4.4.1   Xmon Qubit 142
        4.4.2   Concentric Transmon 145
        4.4.3   Interdigitated Transmon Qubit................................. 149
  4.5   Designing a Full-Fledged Chip in Qiskit Metal 153
  4.6   Josephson Junction 158
        4.6.1   Manhattan Style 160
        4.6.2   Dolan Style 161
  4.7   Qubit Coupler.. 163
        4.7.1   Direct Coupler (Transmon-Transmon) 166
        4.7.2   Tunable Couplers... 168
        4.7.3   Bus Resonator Coupler (Transmon-Transmon).............. 170
  4.8   Electromagnetic Analysis and Quantization and Qiskit Metal 173
  4.9   Conclusion 179

5 Lumped Oscillator Model Analysis 181
  5.1   Elements in Classical Lumped Model 182
        5.1.1   LC Tank Circuit 182

		5.1.2	Amplifier	184

     5.1.2 Amplifier 184
     5.1.3 Oscillator Frequency and Stability Response 185
5.2 Lumped Oscillator Model Analysis (LOM) 186
5.3 Matrices 187
     5.3.1 Capacitance Matrix 188
     5.3.2 Resistance Matrix 191
     5.3.3 Impedance Matrix 193
     5.3.4 Admittance Matrix 197
     5.3.5 Mutual Inductance Matrix 199
     5.3.6 Inverse Inductance Matrix 200
     5.3.7 Scattering Matrix (S-Matrix) 201
5.4 Capacitance Matrix and Lumped Oscillator Model Analysis 202
5.5 Two Transmons Coupled by a Direct Coupler 210
5.6 Advantages of Lumped Oscillator Model Analysis 219
5.7 Conclusion 219

6 Energy-Participation Ratio Method for Quantization and Analysis ... 221
6.1 The EPR Method for Quantization of Superconducting Circuit..... 222
     6.1.1 Simple Circuit Quantization: Coupled Qubit and
            Cavity System 222
     6.1.2 Quantization of the General Josephson System............... 229
6.2 EPR Analysis of Quantum Circuit in Qiskit Metal 234
     6.2.1 Step 1: Design the Circuit Layout in Qiskit Metal........... 234
     6.2.2 Step 2: Perform Eigenmode Analysis in Ansys HFSS 235
     6.2.3 Step 3: Run EPR Analysis and Construct the
            Quantum Hamiltonian.. 235
6.3 EPR Examples in Qiskit Metal....................................... 235
     6.3.1 Example of Single Transmon Qubit 235
     6.3.2 Example of CPW Resonator 242
     6.3.3 Example of the Combined System of Transmon Qubit
            and CPW Resonator 247
     6.3.4 Example of a Combined System of Two
            Transmon Qubits 251
     6.3.5 Double-Hanger Resonator (S Param) 257
6.4 Conclusion 263

7 Modelling the Hamiltonian Transmon Qubit Cooper Pair Box
in the Charge Basis 265
7.1 Cooper Pair Box to Transmon Qubit 266
7.2 Hamiltonian Model Cooper Pair Box (Hcpb) Class 267
7.3 Modeling of a Transmon Qubit 269
     7.3.1 Energy Level Computation 269
     7.3.2 Comparison with the Analytic Expressions for Energy 271
     7.3.3 Wave function Plotting 272
7.4 Additional Analysis 275
     7.4.1 Charge Dispersion 275

		7.4.2 Energy Level Differences	278

- 7.4.2 Energy Level Differences ... 278
- 7.4.3 Anharmonicity ... 279
- 7.4.4 Dephasing Time (T2) ... 281
- 7.5 Qutip Simulation ... 283
- 7.6 Back-Calculation of E_J and E_c ... 286
- 7.7 Conclusion ... 287

8 Manufacturing: Fabrication and Packaging of Qubits ... 289
- 8.1 Sputtering ... 289
  - 8.1.1 Ion Beam Sputtering ... 291
  - 8.1.2 Gas Flow Sputtering ... 293
- 8.2 Evaporation ... 295
  - 8.2.1 Shadow Evaporation ... 298
- 8.3 Creation of Unwanted Josephson Junctions and Generation of Supercurrents ... 299
  - 8.3.1 Phonons ... 301
  - 8.3.2 Supercurrents and Magnetism ... 304
- 8.4 Flip Chip ... 306
- 8.5 Chip Fabrication Parameters ... 308
  - 8.5.1 Inter-Chip Spacing ... 309
  - 8.5.2 Chip Tilt ... 310
  - 8.5.3 Transition Temperatures ... 312
- 8.6 Conclusion ... 315

References ... 317

Index ... 319

About the Authors

Subhojit Halder is a graduate from India with a bachelor's degree in Electronics and Telecommunication Engineering. He is a published author in quantum technologies and has contributed several research articles in this field. His research focuses on astronomical simulations using quantum computing and integrating quantum technologies with existing classical systems. He has been awarded multiple patents and copyrights for his innovations, including a unique backend kernel for Android devices that temporarily replicates quantum computations in cached memory, allowing for complex quantum circuit simulations with minimized noise errors. He has also developed software and apps deployed on the Google Play Store. His hobbies include astronomy and quantum simulations in the technical domain. In his free time, he enjoys playing football and badminton, and he loves to travel as much as possible. His current work focuses on bridging Python-based quantum computing technologies, which require special kernels and computational techniques, with hardware systems primarily built on Java and C + +. He aims to make quantum technologies more accessible by enabling seamless integration with existing Java- and C + +-based software.

About the Authors

Kinjal A. Chauhan is a researcher specializing in quantum technologies with a strong foundation in solid-state physics, computational physics, and quantum information. She holds a dual degree in Engineering Physics (BTech) and an MS in Solid State Physics from the Indian Institute of Space Science and Technology (IIST), Trivandrum. Kinjal has contributed to several cutting-edge research projects and published work in reputed journals like *Journal of Physics D: Applied Physics* and *Optical and Quantum Electronics*, including studies on magnonic and photonic sensors. Currently a Junior Research Fellow at the Indian Institute of Technology, Delhi, she is focused on designing a quantum dot-based single-photon source and CNOT gate. Her research experience spans renowned institutions, including IIT Delhi, NIT Delhi, and ISRO Ahmedabad, focusing on advanced topics such as magnonic and photonic systems, single-photon generation, and plasmonic sensors. As an adept user of various computational tools such as COMSOL, Ansys Lumerical, and Qiskit Metal, Kinjal deeply understands quantum device design's theoretical and computational aspects. Beyond her research, Kinjal is developing educational resources on quantum device design and simulation, reflecting her passion for making complex quantum concepts accessible. With her dedication to advancing quantum technologies, Kinjal aims to make complex problems more accessible through open source software and hands-on experience.

Muhamad Bagher Barfar is a researcher specializing in Quantum Technologies and SQUIDs (superconducting quantum interference devices), particularly with a background in Solid-State Physics (BSc). He holds a double master's in Optic-Laser and Theoretical Physics from Tarbiat Modares University, Tehran. He is also a QML researcher at Tarbiat Modares University in Iran and a founding member of PlancQ group working on Superconducting Quantum Chip Design. He has been a part of multiple projects such as A Survey on Quantum Hardware Tools Using Open-Source

Packages for Designing Qubit Technology, QWorld 2022, Quantum Machine Learning for Conspicuity Detection in Production, Womanium + Fraunhofer ITWM and published work in Quantum Computing Based on Superconducting Circuits, The International Conference on Quantum Technologies & Industrial Applications, Shahid Beheshti University (SBU), Tehran. Bagher has specialized in quantum hardware design using open source software and packages, Qiskit Metal, KQcircuits, and QuTip, as well as in simulation and modification of superconducting quantum circuits using computational tools such as Ansys Lumerical, Elmer FEM, and Gmsh and in quantum computing and programming with Python and R using Anaconda. With his experience, he is working on a program to inspire physics students to solve real problems using quantum technologies through events, courses, and workshops.

Srinjoy Ganguly is a PhD researcher in quantum technologies at University College London focusing on heterogeneous neutral-atom-superconducting quantum architectures and an IBM Qiskit Advocate with 7+ years of experience in different aspects of quantum technologies (software and hardware). Formerly, he was a Lead Quantum AI Research Scientist at Fractal Quantum AI Lab, a Clinical Professor of Practice for Quantum Technologies at Woxsen University, and an Associate Supervisor at the University of Southern Queensland supervising a PhD student in quantum machine learning. He is an author of multiple quantum books and research papers across quantum chemistry, quantum machine learning, quantum NLP, and materials science. He holds triple master's degrees in Quantum Technologies, Quantum Computing Technology, and AI, respectively, and a bachelor's in Electronics and Communications Engineering. He has published two Udemy courses—Quantum Computing Ultimate Masterclass (14,600+ enrollments globally) and QNLP using the Lambeq Toolkit (3000+ enrollments globally). Srinjoy has delivered expert talks at IITs, IEEE SPS, and faculty development programs on QML, QNLP, and Quantum Computing. His QNLP talk at IIT Madras earned praise from Bob Coecke (QNLP Pioneer and Chief Scientist at Quantinuum) and Ilyas Khan (Vice Chairman of the Board and Chief Product Officer of Quantinuum). He leads the global QOSF mentorship program, serves on program committees for international conferences, and is an editor of a De Gruyter quantum computing book.

Shalini Devendrababu holds a master's in Quantum Technologies from CSIC-UIMP, Spain. She is currently the lead Quantum AI Researcher at Fractal Quantum AI Lab. She authored a bestselling and highly rated Udemy course on Qiskit and has published research works on quantum materials science with Springer and IEEE. She also wrote the world's first book exclusively dedicated to Product Managers in the field of quantum computing. She was featured in Times Square, New York Billboard, as a part of mentoring and providing career guidance on Topmate in Quantum Computing. She is a seasoned speaker on quantum computing at various academic institutions as well as a writer on Medium. She has been recognized internationally as a finalist in a summit for Women in Quantum Awards for her contributions in the field of quantum technologies.

About the Technical Reviewer

Sultana Begum is a semiconductor product management expert and AI technology enthusiast with 12+ years of experience at Intel and Accenture. She is a quantum computing enthusiast with a deep understanding of quantum mechanics and physics principles of Qubits. She is the lead author of the book *Competitive Semiconductor Product Management*. Sultana held critical roles in technical product marketing and hardware and software product management to gain a broad and deep-rooted expertise in the semiconductor technology industry. With deep technical expertise and a keen eye for strategic thinking, her expertise spreads widely across semiconductor design development to define and execute a competitive product strategy, with hands-on experience in launching multiple software and hardware products.

Sultana holds both bachelor's and master's degrees in electronics and an MBA in product management and has completed the Stanford LEAD Executive Management Education Program from Stanford University.

Acknowledgments

This book would not have been possible without the invaluable contributions of various individuals, organizations, and resources that have supported and inspired this work. We extend our heartfelt gratitude to the following:

- We would like to thank the QResearch Department, QWorld, for organizing QIntern 2023 and for sponsoring our research project. Special thanks to Adam Glos and Aritra Sarkar for coordinating this program.
- The Qiskit Metal team and contributors, for their dedication to advancing open source tools for quantum hardware design. Their work, hosted on GitHub (https://qiskit.org/metal)
  and the informative YouTube Channel https://www.youtube.com/playlist?list=PLOFEBzvs-VvqHl5ZqVmhB_FcSqmLufsjb, has been instrumental in shaping the content of this book.
- Zlatko Minev, for his pioneering contributions to the field and his exceptional work on Qiskit Metal, which has provided the foundation for many concepts explored in this book.
- The Qiskit website and IBM Quantum Cloud, for providing comprehensive resources and access to cutting-edge quantum computing tools, enabling deeper understanding and hands-on learning.
- Elmer FEM, the open source multiphysical simulation software, and Gmsh, the three-dimensional finite element mesh generator, both of which have proven invaluable in simulating and visualizing complex systems described in the book.
- Adityan Arumuganainar and Mukta Hulyalkar, for their outstanding effort in creating the graphics and illustrations that bring clarity and visual appeal to the book's concepts.

We are deeply grateful for the collective effort and innovation that have made these resources and contributions accessible to the global quantum computing community. This book is a humble reflection of their impact.

Introduction

Quantum computing is one of the most exciting technological advancements of the 21st century, with the potential to revolutionize fields such as cryptography, optimization, and materials science. As the field progresses, different types of qubits have been developed, with superconducting qubits emerging as one of the most promising implementations. These qubits leverage quantum mechanics to process information in ways that classical computers cannot, opening new possibilities for computation. However, designing and analyzing superconducting qubits require a deep understanding of superconducting circuits, quantum mechanics, and specialized computational tools.

This book explores superconducting qubit design and analysis using Qiskit Metal, an open source framework developed by IBM to simplify quantum hardware design and simulation. Qiskit Metal provides an intuitive, Python-based interface that allows researchers and engineers to create, simulate, and optimize superconducting qubit architectures with greater ease.

Through a step-by-step approach, this book will guide you from writing the first lines of Python code in Qiskit Metal to building and analyzing complete qubit chips. It will break down complex concepts, explain the functionality of each code snippet, and provide a hands-on learning experience to ensure a smooth and practical introduction to superconducting qubit design.

By the end of this book, readers will have a solid foundation in superconducting qubits, the ability to use Qiskit Metal for qubit design, and the skills to analyze, fabricate, and optimize quantum circuits. Whether you are a researcher, student, or enthusiast, this book aims to make superconducting qubit design more accessible, helping you contribute to the future of quantum computing.

Introduction: Superconducting Qubits and Their Realizations 1

1.1 Quantum Computing and History

For a long time, classical computers have been used to realize complex systems, but with time, the complexity of the circuits increased. We started to witness the limitations of this type of computing, resulting in a lack of appropriate analysis and a vast runtime for the running code. Most of all, there are inaccurate results for a massive data pool. Classical computers, which rely on bits to represent data as 0 or 1, have been the foundation for handling complex applications like artificial intelligence, GPS tracking, and large-scale simulations. However, as the complexity of problems increases, especially in areas such as AI, climate modeling, and drug discovery, classical systems face limitations in processing power and efficiency with the increase in data pool and for faster processing time with more accuracy, a new method sought after a method which can provide parallel computation of data and can handle large pool of data at ease handling the unique exceptions keeping these concerns in mind many pioneers started to look after alternative to classical computation methods. In contrast, many believed in the power of classical computation and tried to improve its efficiency and usage, while others started looking into alternatives.

During the 1980s, there came two pioneers who presented the idea of how the computers would look like if they can encode or represent in state of 0, 1, and the superposition state of both 0 and 1, and that's how the idea of the first quantum computer came to light, and it was hypothesized by none other than Dr. Richard Feynman and Yuri Manin. In 1982, Dr. Richard Feynman presented this idea at a conference, stating how different the world would be if computers could do quantum simulations, a computer that can do and process the information of the quantum world, giving birth to the first idea of quantum computing. The introduction of this idea was initially heavily critiqued by many other pioneers; critics argued that building a practical quantum computer would be nearly impossible due to the challenges of controlling quantum states, such as superposition and entanglement,

© Subhojit Halder, Kinjal A. Chauhan, Muhamad Bagher Barfar, Srinjoy Ganguly and Shalini Devendrababu 2025
S. Halder et al., *Superconducting Qubit Design Using Qiskit Metal*,
https://doi.org/10.1007/979-8-8688-1504-1_1

in a stable environment. Others wondered whether quantum computers would offer a significant advantage over classical computers for most real-world problems, particularly given the technological and theoretical hurdles in developing quantum algorithms. Despite all the skepticism and criticism the idea initially received, it soon became a paradigm-shifting revolution.

The concept of quantum computing revolves around principles of quantum mechanics with the states of 0, 1 and the superposition of both states 0 and 1. Quantum computers, compared to classical computers, take advantage of the strange and powerful properties of quantum mechanics. They use qubits, which can represent both 0 and 1 at the same time, thanks to superposition. This property allows quantum computers to explore many possible solutions simultaneously, making them potentially much more powerful for certain types of problems.

Quantum computers hold the potential to outperform classical computers in specific applications, such as factoring large numbers (important for cryptography), simulating quantum systems, searching unsorted databases, and solving optimization problems. The representation and visualization of a quantum computer that we use currently is displayed in Figure 1-1. However, building and controlling stable qubits to harness these properties effectively is one of the primary challenges in realizing the full potential of quantum computing. Among other types of qubits such as quantum dots, trapped ions, and topological qubits, we will be learning about superconducting qubits, methods to realize them, their basic uses in the modern era of quantum computing, and how they affect us.

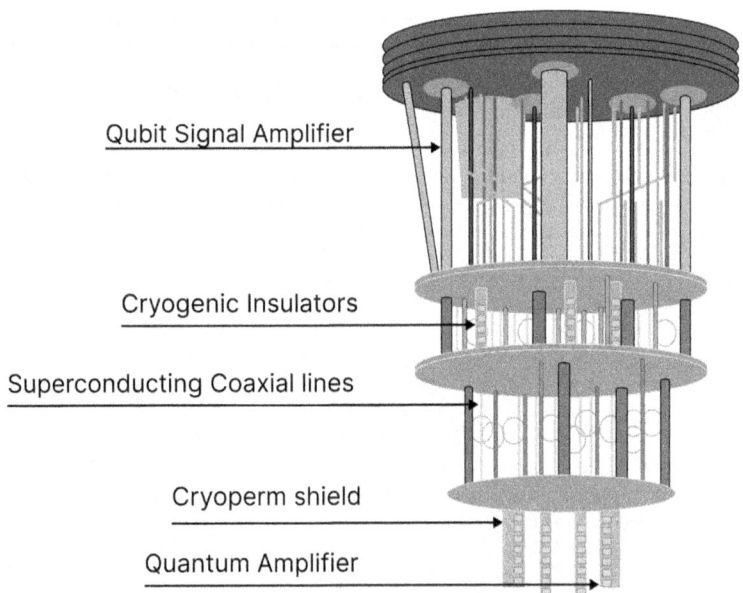

Figure 1-1 Representation of a quantum computer

Before moving on to superconducting qubits, we will have a quick discussion about what qubits are, the properties of quantum computing, and some classical circuits to provide a better and wider scope for us to understand the depths of superconducting qubits.

1.2 Introduction to Qubits

The introduction of qubits is a fundamental concept in the field of quantum computing and quantum information theory. The term **"qubit"** stands for **"quantum bit,"** and it is the basic unit of quantum information, analogous to the classical bit in classical computing.

The concept of qubits was first introduced in the early 1980s by physicist Paul Benioff and computer scientist David Deutsch. Paul Benioff was one of the first to introduce the idea of a quantum mechanical model of a Turing machine in 1980, which laid the groundwork for quantum computing. However, he did not specifically introduce the concept of qubits. David Deutsch formally introduced the concept of qubits in 1985 in his work on the universal quantum computer, where he described how quantum systems could be used to perform computations more efficiently than classical systems. So, while Benioff and Deutsch contributed significantly to the early development of quantum computing, the explicit concept of qubits is more closely associated with David Deutsch. Coining of the term qubit is attributed to Benjamin Schumacher. However, the real breakthrough came in the mid-1990s when researchers, including Peter Shor and Lov Grover, demonstrated specific algorithms that could be more efficiently solved using quantum computation than classical computation.

In classical computing, bits are the basic units of information, and they can represent either a 0 or 1. These bits are the foundation of all classical computations and form the basis of digital technology. On the other hand, qubits take advantage of the principles of quantum mechanics. Unlike classical bits, qubits can exhibit the superposition principle, which means they can be in a linear combination of both 0 and 1 simultaneously. This property of superposition enables quantum computers to perform certain calculations much faster than classical computers for specific types of problems. For example, if there is only one qubit, then there are two quantum states 0 and 1 because of 2^n states, while if there are two qubits, then there exist four quantum states $|00\rangle$, $|01\rangle$, $|10\rangle$, and $|11\rangle$.

Additionally, qubits have a unique property called **entanglement**. When qubits become entangled, the state of one qubit becomes intrinsically linked with the state of another, regardless of the distance between them. In a famous thought experiment illustrating the properties of entanglement, imagine two electrons that are entangled. Now, place these two electrons at opposite ends of the universe. If you measure the state of the first electron (such as its spin), the measurement of the second electron's state is instantly determined, no matter how far apart they are. However, it is essential to note that while measurement outcomes are correlated, actively changing the state of one electron (e.g., by applying electromagnetic fields) does not directly influence the other in the same way. This phenomenon highlights the non-locality of quantum mechanics without violating the principles of relativity.

Entanglement is a crucial property in quantum computing and allows for even more powerful computations. Entanglement enables quantum computers to perform powerful computations by allowing qubits to process information in parallel and exploit quantum correlations. Entanglement leads to significant speedups in tasks like database searching, factoring large numbers (as in Shor's algorithm), and simulating complex quantum systems. Entanglement also plays a crucial role in quantum error correction, ensuring computations' reliability and enabling quantum teleportation, which has implications for secure communication. These capabilities make quantum computers exponentially more efficient than classical systems for solving some complex issues.

The introduction of qubits has opened up a whole new realm of computing and information processing, promising groundbreaking applications in cryptography, optimization, simulation of quantum systems, developing a quantum hardware for specific applications, and more. However, building and controlling stable qubits is a significant challenge, and researchers continue to explore new ways to harness the power of quantum mechanics for practical computing tasks. As the field of quantum computing advances, it has the potential to revolutionize various industries and contribute to solving some of the most complex problems in science and technology.

1.3 Timeline of Quantum Computing and Superconducting Circuits

Quantum computing had many steps and developments along the way. It started with an ambitious and unimaginable idea, with few of the century's most remarkable minds endorsing it. We now see black hole images and stimulation because of it. Quantum computing may have started as something that cannot be understood or visualized. Still, it ended up being one of the most significant accomplishments that have made us extremely close to understanding the fundamental concepts of the universe. There have been many landmarks, instances, growths, and developments. Before starting the journey with superconducting qubits, let us look into how the pioneers designed the idea and how we have reached the present stage of quantum computing:

- **Theoretical Foundations**: During the early 1980s, Nobel laureate Richard Feynman proposed quantum computing to simulate quantum systems efficiently. David Deutsch introduced the concept of a quantum Turing machine, laying the theoretical groundwork for quantum computation. These early developments sparked the foundation of quantum computing, providing a new framework for solving complex problems in physics, cryptography, and optimization that classical computers struggle to handle efficiently.
- **Shor's Algorithm and Early Quantum Gates**: In the 1990s, Peter Shor developed Shor's algorithm, demonstrating that a quantum computer could factor

large numbers exponentially faster than classical computers, posing a potential threat to classical cryptography. IBM and Stanford University demonstrated the first two-qubit quantum computer using liquid-state nuclear magnetic resonance. This experiment was done in 2001 to test Shor's algorithm. The number 15 was factored using 1018 identical molecules, each containing seven active nuclear spins. Lov Grover devises Grover's algorithm, which can search an unsorted database quadratically quicker ($O(\sqrt{N})$ where N is the number of elements in the database) than classical algorithms.

- **Superconducting Circuits Take Center Stage:** In the early 2000s, several approaches to quantum computing are explored, including trapped ions, linear optics, and superconducting circuits. IBM introduced the concept of "**superconducting qubits**" using Josephson junctions, which have become a leading candidate for scalable quantum computing.
- **Rise of Quantum Hardware and Quantum Supremacy**: During the early and late 2010s, significant advancements in quantum computing took place. The D-Wave One, a quantum annealing processor, is released as the first commercially available quantum computer. In collaboration with NASA and the Universities Space Research Association, Google launches the Quantum Artificial Intelligence Lab, aiming to develop quantum algorithms for machine learning. Google announces the Quantum AI team's development of a superconducting qubit that significantly reduces errors. Google claims to achieve "quantum supremacy" with its Sycamore processor, performing a calculation in 200 seconds that would take the most powerful supercomputers over 10,000 years.

1.4 Quantum Computing Fundamentals

In quantum computing, the main property that we consider care is the dual nature of the matter, which states that all properties exist in both waves and particle nature, which De Broglie first introduced. Wave-nature duality is the fundamental principle of quantum mechanics. In quantum computing, the main properties we consider are superposition, entanglement, and quantum interference. While wave-particle duality is a foundational concept in quantum mechanics, it is not the main property used in quantum computing. Instead, quantum computing focuses on how quantum bits (qubits) can exist in multiple states simultaneously (superposition) and how they can be correlated with each other (entanglement).

The quantum state of a system, often represented by a wave function $|\psi\rangle$, describes the state of the entire system, including all qubits involved. This quantum state is not just the "sum" of individual wave functions; instead, it is described as a superposition of the basis states of the system. The quantum state can be represented as a tensor product of the individual qubits' states for a system of multiple qubits. The tensor product helps to combine the state vector of individual qubits to form the state vector of the entire system. The quantum state cannot be separated into individual qubits' wave functions if the qubits are entangled. The overall wave function of the system describes all possible configurations (basis states) and their corresponding amplitudes. The significant properties that make qubits exciting can help explore many domains that classical computers can never comprehend. Diving into them, they are

- **Superposition**: Superposition is the most fascinating concept and property of quantum computing, and it makes quantum computing different from classical computation. As we have previously discussed, the property of superposition makes quantum computing interesting. So basically, as the name suggests, superposition is the phenomenon where a qubit can exist in a combination of both the $|0\rangle$ and $|1\rangle$ states simultaneously. However, it is not that the qubit is literally in both states at once in a classical sense, but instead that it has a probability amplitude for being in each state. The qubit state is represented as $|\psi\rangle = \alpha|0\rangle + \beta|1\rangle$ where α and β are the complex numbers that represent the probability amplitudes for the qubit being in states $|0\rangle$ and $|1\rangle$.
  Together, without any issue, this unique nature creates multiple possibilities for the computation as it increases the possible outcomes and helps channel the route faster. Superposition is technically achieved by a specific quantum gate known as the Hadamard gate or the H gate. In quantum computing, the corresponding state $|0\rangle$ and state $|1\rangle$ are termed as the computational basis states, so when the Hadamard gate is applied to this state, it results in the translation to the superpositional states that are + and - states, respectively, as $H|+\rangle = |0\rangle$ and $H|-\rangle = |1\rangle$. The transformation to superpositional states makes it easy for us to do manipulation to the state of the qubit and helps in achieving the goal set.

$$H|0\rangle = |+\rangle = \frac{|0\rangle + |1\rangle}{\sqrt{2}} \tag{1-1}$$

$$H|1\rangle = |-\rangle = \frac{|0\rangle - |1\rangle}{\sqrt{2}} \tag{1-2}$$

  The concept of superposition makes the fundamentals of major work such as cryptography, encoding quantum simulations and many others making it one of the most powerful tools that differentiates it from classical computers.
- **Entanglement**: Entanglement can be understood in simpler terms, for example, assuming that you have two electrons, and they are entangled with each other, so the core properties of these electrons are mutually dependent on each other. Now, you somehow managed to place one of the electrons at one end of the universe and the other one at the other end of the universe, so now when you record the measurement of one of the electrons and change one of its properties like changing the spin or phase of that electron, it can be understood that the other electron's corresponding phase or spin will also alter based on the value that you have changed the previous one. This property where two different objects are mutually dependent on one another is called entanglement.
  In quantum entanglement, the properties of the particles are interdependent in a way that goes beyond classical intuition. This "spooky action at a distance,"

1.4 Quantum Computing Fundamentals

as Einstein called it, is an essential resource in quantum computing, enabling certain algorithms and communication protocols that are not possible in classical systems. The best example of entanglement is the **Bell states**, which represent maximally entangled quantum states. These states demonstrate the highest possible degree of entanglement between two qubits, meaning that the measurement outcomes of one qubit are perfectly correlated with the other, regardless of the distance between them.

Bell states are fundamental in quantum information theory, as they illustrate the non-local nature of quantum mechanics and are used in quantum teleportation, superdense coding, and testing Bell's theorem to show the violation of classical hidden variable theories. A simple Bell state can be created by entangling two qubits using a Hadamard gate followed by a Controlled-NOT (CNOT) gate. The Hadamard gate creates a superposition in the first qubit, and the CNOT gate entangles it with the second qubit, resulting in one of the four Bell states. After applying these gates, the two qubits will be in one of the four Bell states, depending on their initial states, where an entanglement is created between the two qubits, which are named as Bell states. There are four Bell states in total, represented as $|\phi^+\rangle, |\phi^-\rangle, |\psi^+\rangle$, and $|\psi^-\rangle$ and represented as -

$$|\phi^+\rangle = \frac{|00\rangle + |11\rangle}{\sqrt{2}} \quad |\phi^-\rangle = \frac{|00\rangle - |11\rangle}{\sqrt{2}} \qquad (1\text{-}3)$$

$$|\psi^+\rangle = \frac{|01\rangle + |10\rangle}{\sqrt{2}} \quad |\psi^-\rangle = \frac{|01\rangle - |10\rangle}{\sqrt{2}} \qquad (1\text{-}4)$$

Bell states exhibit non-local correlations, meaning that the measurement outcomes of one qubit are instantly correlated with the measurement outcomes of the other qubit, regardless of the physical separation between them. When two qubits are in a Bell state, measuring one qubit will instantaneously determine the measurement outcome of the other qubit, even if they are far apart. Entanglement can be done with more than two qubits too; entanglement helps in the preparation of states as required for an application. When more than two qubits are involved in a process of entanglement, it is termed as the GHZ state, or the Greenberger-Horne-Zeilinger state.

- **Interference**: The idea of interference arises from the knowledge of classical wave physics and quantum mechanics, and it suggests that if two waves interfere, they will result in constructive interference, leading to an increase and peak in amplitude by the addition of the two wave amplitudes, or destructive interference where they generate zero amplitude as they cancel each other out. The idea of interference arises in quantum computing too with the same concepts following that of quantum mechanics, Interference is a quantum phenomenon that arises from the property of superposition. When qubits are in a superposition of states, they can overlap and interfere with each other, just like waves in physics. This interference allows quantum computers to amplify the correct answers to a problem while canceling out the incorrect ones, leading to more efficient and faster computations.

When two or more quantum states, represented by qubits, overlap and combine, they can interfere with each other. This interference can be constructive or destructive, depending on the phase relationship between the states. The interference concept for quantum computing can be understood easily by imagining a simple scenario. Imagine you are standing in front of a pond, and you throw a rock into it—it will create ripples. Now, if you throw two rocks at the same time or after a specific interval, then you can see the amplitude of the ripples increasing; this phenomenon is called constructive interference. Similarly, when two qubits share the same phase or are $2n\pi$ phase apart from each other, this results in the interfering of the qubits constructively and increasing the amplitude of the system. The waves effectively "**add**" each other, leading to an increased or a maximum probability of finding the quantum system in a particular state. In other words, certain outcomes become more likely or even guaranteed to observe. Now imagine if you throw two rocks that are out of sync; this causes the ripples to die off. This phenomenon is called destructive interference. Similarly, if two qubits that are out of phase or are out of phase by $(2n+1)\pi$, then they interact destructively, reducing the amplitude of the qubit combination. The waves effectively "**subtract**" from each other, leading to a reduced or zero probability of finding the quantum system in a particular state. In other words, certain outcomes become less likely or even impossible to observe. The interference of quantum states plays a crucial role in quantum computing algorithms. By cleverly arranging the quantum states, quantum algorithms can amplify the correct solutions (constructive interference) and reduce the incorrect ones (destructive interference). This interference phenomenon is what gives quantum algorithms their power and efficiency in solving certain types of problems. One famous example of interference in quantum computing is Grover's search algorithm. It can search an unsorted database exponentially faster than classical algorithms, thanks to constructive interference, which amplifies the required answer and reduces the incorrect ones. Mathematically, suppose we want to check the time taken by both the computation methods. In that case, we observe that the classical search takes linear time $O(N)$. Grover's algorithm offers a quadratic speedup, taking only $O(\sqrt{N})$, for N entries in the database, showcasing the power of quantum interference in solving specific computational problems more efficiently.

- **Quantum Gates**: The very basic and fundamental unit of building and realizing quantum circuits are the quantum gates. Quantum gates manipulate the state of qubits, enabling operations like superposition, entanglement, and interference. By combining quantum gates in specific ways, quantum algorithms can be designed to solve various problems more efficiently than classical algorithms. Some important quantum gates that are used are shown in Figure 1-2. Quantum gates can be classified based on the number of qubits they operate on: single-qubit gates and multi-qubit gates. As the name suggests, a single-qubit gate has one input and one output, performing transformations on the state of a single

1.5 Classical and Quantum Circuits

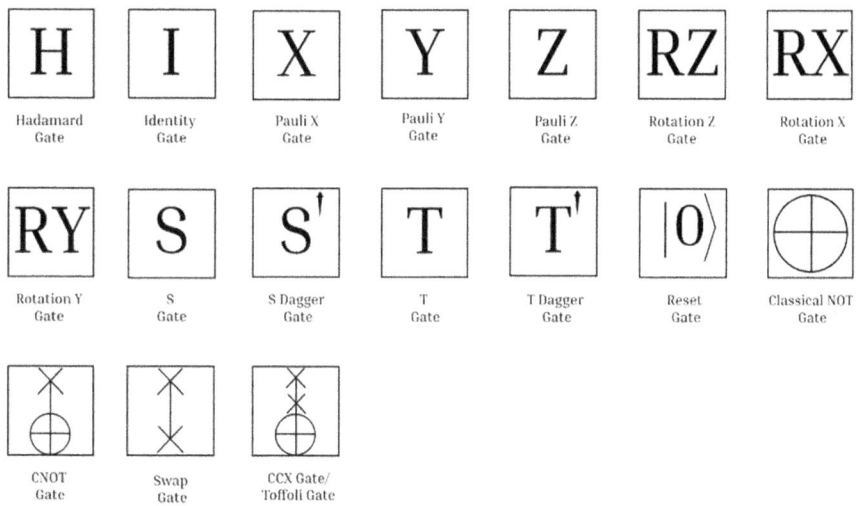

Figure 1-2 Single- and multi-qubit gates

qubit. In contrast, a multi-qubit gate acts on multiple qubits, modifying their states collectively. Examples of single-qubit gates include the Hadamard gate (H), Pauli gates (X, Y, Z), and rotation gates (RX, RY, RZ). Common multi-qubit gates include the CNOT gate (CX) and the Toffoli gate (CCX). We will be learning more about these quantum gates in Chapter 3 Section 3.2.

1.5 Classical and Quantum Circuits

In quantum computing, there are two important things to remember, that is, classical circuits and quantum circuits.

- **Classical Circuits**: In simpler terms, classical circuits are basic entities that use basic logic gates as their building blocks and only work with bits 0 and 1. You may have heard of some of these basic logic gates before. For example, the AND gate provides an output 1 if both inputs are 1; otherwise, it provides an output 0 for all cases. The OR gate provides an output 0 only when both inputs are 0; otherwise, it provides an output 1 for all the remaining cases. The bit inversion gate, also known as the NOT gate, flips the input bit from state 0 to 1 and vice versa. These basic gates are examples of logic gates and form the building blocks of the classical circuits that we know of. The information of the basic logic gates used in classical circuits is given in Figure 1-3.
These logic gates are built using transistor technology. Bipolar junction transistor (BJT) technology, used in the olden days of electronic circuit building, was used

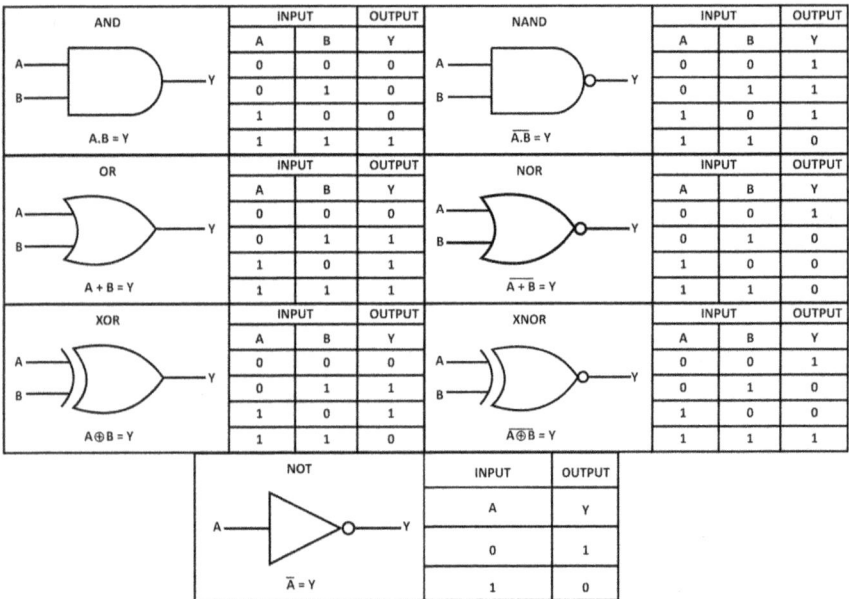

Figure 1-3 Universal logical gates

to create many of these logic gates; current transistor technology uses MOSFETs (Metal-Oxide-Semiconductor Field-Effect Transistors) to build such logic gates and realize classical circuits.

- **Quantum Circuits**: Similar to classical circuits, quantum circuits also require basic building blocks to build and realize them, known as quantum gates. So, in quantum computing, the gates manipulate the quantum state of quantum bits (qubits) to perform quantum computations. Quantum circuits are governed by the laws of quantum mechanics, which allow for the fascinating properties of superposition, entanglement, and interference. Quantum gates manipulate the state and the phase of qubits to achieve the desired results for users by applying the unitary transformation of phases or by changing the probability of occurrence in that state; more about quantum gates is mentioned in Section 1.3. Quantum gates together form quantum circuits, which are the critical components of quantum algorithms, and they exploit the unique properties of qubits to solve specific problems more efficiently than classical algorithms. Quantum circuits can perform tasks such as factoring large numbers, searching unsorted databases, simulating quantum systems, and more.

Classical circuits and quantum circuits differ fundamentally due to the unique properties of classical and quantum bits (qubits). Here, we'll use a classical harmonic oscillator shown in Figure 1-4 as an analogy to illustrate the differences and why quantum circuits have certain advantages over classical circuits.

1.5 Classical and Quantum Circuits

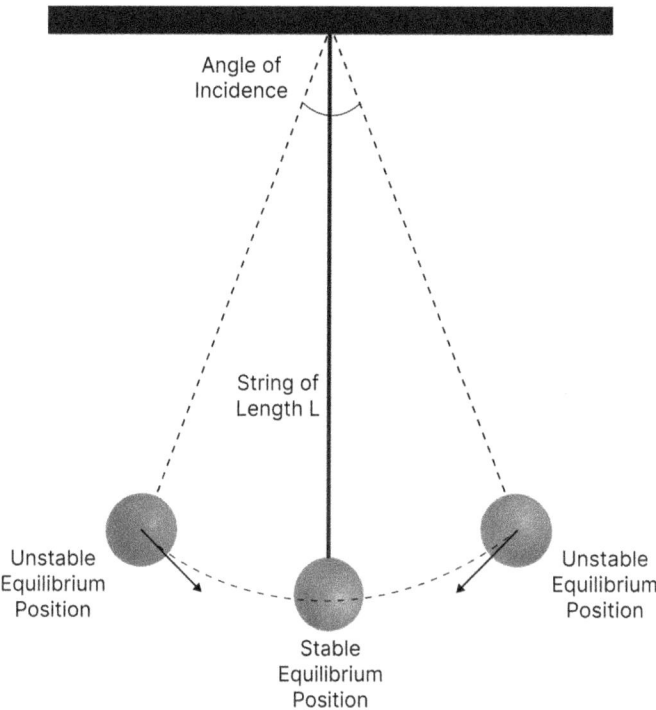

Figure 1-4 A simple harmonic pendulum demonstrating the stable and unstable states of equilibrium in classical mechanics

A classical harmonic oscillator is a simple physical system, like a pendulum or a mass attached to a spring, that exhibits oscillatory behavior. The basic concept of a simple harmonic oscillator can be understood through an analogy. Imagine you have a bead, and you have tied one side of it to the rope and hanged it vertically still with the length of the rope as its maximum elongation. When the system is stationary, the bead will be at its vertical downright position or the stable equilibrium position; when a tiny displacement is provided to this stable system, then the pendulum starts oscillating from its unstable equilibrium, and at the long distance traveled between the two end points, the velocity of the bead becomes zero momentarily before being pulled down by the force of gravity. The position of the oscillator can be described using a classical variable, like the angle of the pendulum or the displacement of the mass from its equilibrium position. This is the concept of a simple harmonic oscillator.

- **Classical Circuits and Classical Oscillator**: In a classical circuit, information is processed using classical bits (0s and 1s), and the operations are based on classical logic gates. Just like in a classical harmonic oscillator, the state of each

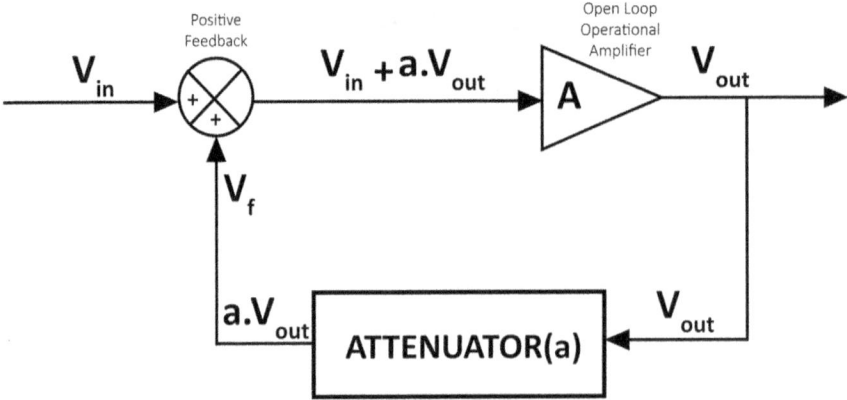

Figure 1-5 Representation of a classical feedforward circuit with amplifier and feedback configuration acting as a classical oscillator

bit in a classical circuit can be precisely determined at any given time. Figure 1-5 explains how a classical circuit works.

Imagine a classical circuit as a set of interconnected pendulums, and you can observe the position (angle) of each pendulum at any moment. The circuit's behavior is entirely deterministic, and each bit follows definite paths based on the input and operations applied. The most common examples of classical oscillator circuits are an LC/RC oscillator and a feedback open-loop amplifier circuit as shown in the figure. There are several types of oscillators deployed and currently used that are built using basic logic gates and transistors such as ring oscillators.

- **Quantum Circuits and Quantum Oscillator**: In contrast, a quantum circuit processes information using quantum bits (qubits), which can exist in superpositions of states. Quantum operations are performed using quantum gates, taking advantage of quantum properties like superposition and entanglement. Now, let's think of a quantum oscillator as a "quantum pendulum" that can be in a superposition of different positions. Instead of precisely knowing the angle of the pendulum, the state of the quantum oscillator (qubit) can be in a combination of multiple states at the same time, just like the qubit's superposition. Unlike classical harmonic oscillators, which can have any energy, quantum harmonic oscillators have quantized energy levels. The energy levels are discrete and evenly spaced, with each level corresponding to a specific quantum state. Quantum oscillators can exhibit tunneling, a quantum effect where a particle can pass through an energy barrier even if it does not have enough classical energy to overcome it. This phenomenon has significant implications in quantum mechanics and is essential in various quantum devices.

Advantages of Quantum Circuits over Classical Circuits:

- **Parallelism**: Quantum circuits can process many possibilities in parallel due to superposition. This gives them the potential for exponential speedup in certain computations compared to classical circuits, which can only process one specific state at a time.
- **Quantum Interference**: Quantum circuits can exploit interference between quantum states, leading to the amplification of correct answers and reduction of incorrect ones. Classical circuits lack this phenomenon, making some algorithms, like Grover's search, more efficient on quantum computers.
- **Quantum Communication and Cryptography**: Quantum circuits enable secure communication and cryptographic protocols leveraging entanglement and the no-cloning theorem, which are not achievable in classical circuits.
- **Quantum Encoding**: Quantum encoders can encode the corresponding data with respect to amplitude and phase, making it extremely hard to decrypt it without Quantum Key Sharing (QKS). This concept of QKS makes the transmitted data highly reliable and secure. Data encryption and security is still an issue faced by classical circuits due to the linear encryption patterns which be easily decoded without a security key; whereas quantum encrypted circuits, due to the superposition of states makes it really hard to determine the final output state without the correct decryption algorithm.

1.6 Lagrangian Models

The Lagrangian model is derived from classical physics and stationary action principles. So, the Lagrangian model is based on the principle of the energies of the system which is extremely different from the classical Newtonian model that takes force into consideration rather than energy. The Lagrangian model is based on one of the most simple ideas and a central quantity that summarizes the dynamics of the entire system, namely, the "Lagrangian"; the Lagrangian has units of energy, but no single expression for all physical systems. The fundamental principle of Lagrangian mechanics is the principle of stationary action, also known as the principle of least action. This principle states that the true path taken by a system between two points in space and time is the one that minimizes (or maximizes) a quantity called the action. The action is defined as the integral of a quantity called the Lagrangian over a certain path taken by the system.

While representing the Lagrangian model mathematically, we represent it in the format of the action of the system denoted by "S," and it is equal to the integral of the Lagrangian over a time interval from time t_1 to t_2 and given as

$$S = \int_{t_1}^{t_2} L(x, x^{\cdot}, t)\, dt \tag{1-5}$$

In this equation, x represents the spacial coordinates. These are variables that define the configuration of the system, and they can be positions, angles, or any other parameters that describe the system's state. $x^{\cdot}$ denotes the first derivative of the generalized coordinates with respect to time "t," and the Lagrangian "$L(x, x^{\cdot}, t)$" in itself is a function that encodes the kinetic and potential energies of the system as a function of the generalized coordinates, their time derivatives, and time itself and can be obtained as

$$L(x, x^{\cdot}, t) = T(x, x^{\cdot}, t) - U(x, x^{\cdot}, t) \tag{1-6}$$

where the functions $T(x, x^{\cdot}, t)$ and $U(x, x^{\cdot}, t)$ denote the kinetic energy and the potential energy of the system, respectively.

As much as we can see, the application of the Lagrangian model is in Cartesian coordinate systems defining the motion of the subsystem, but we are working on quantum computing and electronic circuits, so how do the implications of a model that defines motions guide us in developing electronic circuits and subsystems?

Well, this model is also used in electrical subsystems and in circuit theory applications. In circuit theory, the Lagrangian method provides an alternative way to analyze electrical circuits. It is based on applying the principles of Lagrangian mechanics to electrical systems. This approach is particularly useful for dealing with circuits involving energy storage elements like capacitors and inductors. Let's dive into a step-by-step approach to find out how Lagrangian models are used in circuit theory:

- **Generalized Coordinates**: Generalized coordinates are a concept primarily used in the field of classical mechanics to describe the configuration or state of a mechanical system. They are a set of independent parameters that fully specify the position and orientation of a system in a way that is more general and flexible than using Cartesian coordinates (x, y, z) or other fixed coordinate systems. In circuit theory, generalized coordinates are used to represent the voltages across energy storage elements (like capacitors) and the currents through inductors. These are chosen because they represent the fundamental variables associated with energy storage in the circuit. The number of generalized coordinates required for a system is equal to its degrees of freedom.

  Degrees of freedom represent the number of independent ways a system can move or change configuration. The primary purpose of using generalized coordinates is to simplify the analysis of complex mechanical systems. They allow you to describe the system's configuration in a more compact and intuitive manner. Considering the fact that, in the case of electronic subsystems, voltage and current are the basic measures for understanding the depth of the entire circuit, the storage criteria for each are hence considered the basis for the generalized coordinates in Lagrangian systems.

- **Lagrangian Function**: The Lagrangian function, denoted as L, is constructed based on the electrical elements in the circuit and their associated energies. The Lagrangian typically has the form $L = T - U$. T represents the kinetic energy term. In circuit theory, this corresponds to the energy stored in inductors and is given by $T = \frac{1}{2}LI^2$ where L is the inductance, and I is the current through the inductor. U represents the potential energy term. This corresponds to the energy stored in capacitors and is given by $U = \frac{1}{2}CV^2$ where C is the capacitance, and V is the voltage across the capacitor. The primary use of the Lagrangian function in circuit theory is to deal with circuits that contain energy storage elements, such as capacitors and inductors. Traditional circuit analysis techniques, like Kirchhoff's laws, are well suited for circuits with resistors and ideal voltage or current sources, but they are less convenient for circuits with energy storage elements. The Lagrangian method provides a systematic way to incorporate these elements into the analysis.

- **Lagrangian Equations**: To derive the equations of motion for the circuit, apply the Euler-Lagrange equation, which is a generalization of Newton's second law to the Lagrangian framework:

$$\frac{d}{dt}\left(\frac{\partial L}{\partial \dot{q}}\right) - \frac{\partial L}{\partial q} = 0 \qquad (1\text{-}7)$$

q represents the generalized coordinates (voltage and current in this case). $\dot{q}$ represents the time derivatives of these coordinates. This helps in providing a unified relation for the motion of the charge and current through the storage units in the electrical circuits. Lagrangian equations help in providing the idea that the system's movement of current through the components is unified or not after the interval of time and how much current is flowing through at any certain instance.

The thing to look after is that the Lagrangian model is especially used for the understanding of mechanical subsystems but its implications can be observed in building classic electronic circuits too. Similarly, the Lagrangian model is used to build superconducting circuits too. Superconducting qubits are a promising candidate for building quantum computers, and the Lagrangian model can offer valuable insights and assistance in their development. Superconducting qubits operate based on the manipulation of energy levels and quantum states. The Lagrangian can be used to analyze the energy levels, transitions, and couplings between different energy states in a qubit. This understanding is crucial for designing qubit gates and ensuring coherence. Quantum gates are fundamental to quantum computing. The Lagrangian can help in designing and optimizing gate operations in superconducting qubits. It can be used to model the dynamics of the qubit under the influence of control pulses, external fields, and coupling to other qubits or resonators. Superconducting qubits are often integrated into circuit-QED (Quantum Electrodynamics) systems, where they interact with microwave resonators or other electromagnetic modes. The Lagrangian can be used to describe the interactions between qubits and resonators, enabling the design and analysis of hybrid quantum systems. We will learn about the further mathematical derivations and applications of superconducting qubits and their applications in Quantum Electrodynamics in the coming chapters.

1.7 Pauli Matrices

Before delving into the Hamiltonian model, it is essential to understand a fundamental concept in quantum mechanics: the Pauli matrices. These are a set of three 2 × 2 complex matrices that are Hermitian (equal to their own conjugate transpose), involuntary (equal to their own inverse, meaning squaring them results in the identity matrix), and unitary (their inverse equals their conjugate transpose). There are three Pauli matrices used in quantum mechanics, and they are

$$\sigma_x = \begin{pmatrix} 0 & 1 \\ 1 & 0 \end{pmatrix} \tag{1-8}$$

$$\sigma_y = \begin{pmatrix} 0 & -i \\ i & 0 \end{pmatrix} \tag{1-9}$$

$$\sigma_z = \begin{pmatrix} 1 & 0 \\ 0 & -1 \end{pmatrix} \tag{1-10}$$

In the world of quantum mechanics, Pauli matrices specifically apply to quantum states of spin-1/2 particles, such as electrons, describing how their spin interacts with external fields like electromagnetic fields. For light polarization, Jones or Stokes vectors are used instead to describe interactions between different polarization filters, such as horizontal/vertical, 45-degree, and circular polarization. The Pauli-X matrix flips the qubit state from $|0\rangle$ to $|1\rangle$. The Pauli-Y operator combines a phase flip and a bit flip operation on the qubit's state. The Pauli-Z operator introduces a phase change without flipping the qubit state.

1.8 Hamiltonian Model

Hamiltonian is the basis of the entire quantum mechanics. The Hamiltonian of a system is defined as the operator corresponding to the system's total energy. It includes the total kinetic as well as the total potential energy of the system. When we plot the energy spectrum of the Hamiltonian or set of energy eigenvalues, the output is the set of possible outcomes that can be obtained from measuring the system's total energy. Hamiltonian represents the total energy in the system. However, Hamiltonian can still take other forms. It can be written and understood in a simplified equation in many instances by considering several defined characteristics, such as single or several particle systems or time-dependent or time-independent systems.

Hamiltonian is represented as $\hat{H} = \hat{T} + \hat{U}$ where T and U represent the kinetic energy function and the potential energy of the functions, respectively. In quantum mechanics, the potential energy operator is mentioned as $\hat{U} = U(r, t)$, and the kinetic energy operator is defined as $\hat{T} = -\frac{\hbar}{2m}\nabla^2$ where $\hbar$ is the reduced Planck constant and ∇^2 is the Laplacian operator. It is denoted as

$$\nabla^2 = \frac{\partial^2}{\partial x^2} + \frac{\partial^2}{\partial y^2} + \frac{\partial^2}{\partial z^2} \quad (1\text{-}11)$$

Hence, combining the results of these two, the final Hamiltonian equation presented above yields

$$\hat{H} = -\frac{\hbar}{2m}\nabla^2 + U(r,t) \quad (1\text{-}12)$$

This equation is the Schrodinger's equation. Although this is not the technical definition of the Hamiltonian in classical mechanics, it is the form it most commonly takes. The Hamiltonian model is crucial for understanding and designing superconducting qubits, which are the building blocks of quantum computers. The general Hamiltonian for a superconducting qubit can be expressed as

$$\hat{H}_{qubit} = -\frac{\hbar}{2}(\omega_p \sigma_z + \Omega_{Rabi}(t)\sigma_x) + \hat{H}_{relax} + \hat{H}_{deph} \quad (1\text{-}13)$$

The Hamiltonian model looks extremely complex but is rather simple to understand. ω_p represents the qubit's energy splitting, which is determined by its transition frequency. $\Omega_{Rabi}(t)$ is the time-dependent Rabi frequency, which controls qubit rotations. $\hat{H}_{relax}$ represents relaxation processes, and $\hat{H}_{deph}$ represents dephasing processes. The applications of this equation will be discussed in depth in the coming chapters.

The Hamiltonian model allows for the manipulation of qubit states through the application of external fields and control pulses. By adjusting the Rabi frequency and other parameters, you can perform various quantum gate operations, such as X, Y, and Z rotations. Superconducting qubits are often coupled to resonators (microwave cavities) to facilitate quantum state readout and control. The Hamiltonian describes the interaction between the qubit and the resonator, enabling quantum information transfer. The Hamiltonian model is used to study the effects of noise and decoherence on superconducting qubits. By modeling these processes within the Hamiltonian framework, researchers can develop error correction techniques and improve qubit coherence times.

1.9 Superconducting Circuits

We have understood the need for quantum computing and how it makes computation better from the classical circuits present, but then what is the need for superconducting circuits? What are superconducting circuits? We will be answering these questions in the following chapters, and we will be seeing how superconducting qubits and circuits make our jobs easier than before and what problems are associated with realizing such circuits.

In classical computing, we use machines based on classical mechanics to perform calculations. However, when we deal with very small particles, like atoms and electrons, we need a different approach called quantum mechanics. Quantum computing explores this fascinating world of small particles and uses their unique properties to perform tasks that regular computers cannot. In quantum computing, we use tiny units called qubits instead of classical bits. These qubits are like magical coins that can be both heads and tails at the same time. To build qubits, we use special materials called superconductors, which have amazing properties at very low temperatures. These materials can conduct electricity without any resistance, making them perfect for creating qubits. We make qubits using circuits with capacitors and inductors, which act like tiny tanks that store and release energy. These circuits are super cool because they can store information without losing any energy as heat, which is crucial for preserving quantum information.

However, building quantum circuits is challenging, and they must meet certain conditions to work correctly. Theoretical physicist David P. DiVincenzo proposed some criteria for making quantum computers, ensuring they follow the rules of quantum mechanics and can communicate information effectively. Overall, quantum computing is a thrilling area of research that uses the magical world of quantum mechanics to explore new possibilities in processing information and solving problems that classical computers can't handle.

1.9.1 What Is Superconductivity?

Superconductivity is a phenomenon where, when a material is cooled below its critical temperature (which is often much higher than absolute zero), it allows electricity to flow with zero electrical resistance and zero energy loss. When compared to the classical conductor and insulator circuit, we can observe that when electricity flows through the material, it will exhibit a loss in electrical energy due to the presence of resistance, as the name suggests. Conductors have low resistance, which leads to some energy loss during electrical conduction, whereas insulators prevent current flow and, therefore, do not exhibit energy loss through conduction.

In 1911, Dutch physicist Heike Kamerlingh Onnes made a groundbreaking discovery. He found that their electrical resistance suddenly dropped to zero when he cooled certain materials, specifically mercury, to very low temperatures near absolute zero (around 4.2 K or $-268.95\,°C$). The mercury became a superconductor. This phenomenon was wholly unexpected and marked the first discovery of superconductivity. The transition into a superconducting state was characterized by a sudden drop in electrical resistance, which was a completely unexpected phenomenon.

This discovery fundamentally changed our understanding of how certain materials can conduct electricity at low temperatures and led to decades of further research

1.10 Terms and Definitions of Some Important Concepts

into the properties of superconductors. Later, it was discovered that the property of zero resistance is incurred due to a unique property known as the generation of Cooper pairs; we will be learning more about them in the upcoming chapters. Each superconducting material has a critical temperature (Tc), below which it becomes superconducting. Above this critical temperature, the material behaves as a regular conductor. When the temperature drops below Tc, the material transitions into a superconducting state, implying its electrical resistance vanishes.

1.10 Terms and Definitions of Some Important Concepts

Well before diving deep into superconducting circuits, we have to have our fundamentals prepared, so let's dive into some of the basic and crucial information regarding superconducting circuits:

- **Cooper Pairs**: The concept of Cooper pairs is fundamental to understanding superconductivity. Cooper pairs are formed when two electrons, despite their natural repulsion, become weakly bound due to interactions with the material's crystal lattice at temperatures below the material's critical temperature. This pairing allows electrons to move through the lattice without scattering, resulting in zero electrical resistance, but this occurs at temperatures **above** absolute zero. It is stated that when two electrons travel through the physical metallic lattice, even with small electron attraction, it can make two electrons form a pair, and this results in the net energy of the pair having energy less than the Fermi energy. The generation of such a pair is due to electron-phonon interactions. An electron in a metal behaves typically as a free particle. The electron is repelled from other electrons due to their negative charge, but it also attracts the positive ions that make up the rigid lattice of the metal. This attraction distorts the ion lattice, moving the ions slightly toward the electron and increasing the positive charge density of the lattice in the vicinity. This positive charge can attract other electrons. At long distances, this attraction between electrons due to the displaced ions can overcome the electrons' repulsion due to their negative charge and cause them to pair up, as shown in Figure 1-6. The rigorous quantum mechanical explanation shows that the effect is due to electron-phonon interactions, with the phonon being the collective motion of the positively charged lattice. Phonon is an excited state in quantum mechanics and can be thought of as quantized sound waves, similar to photons as quantized light waves.

    As a result of the attractive electron-electron interaction mediated by **phonons** (phonons are quantized vibrations or collective oscillations of atoms within a crystal lattice; they represent the quantum mechanical description of sound or heat waves propagating through a solid material), two electrons with opposite spins can pair up and become tightly bound together. These pairs of electrons are called Cooper pairs. These interactions and formation of pairs can only take in extremely low temperatures as the pair will have energy of 1mev, and any thermal excitation can break these pairs, and the electrons will not be able to move or

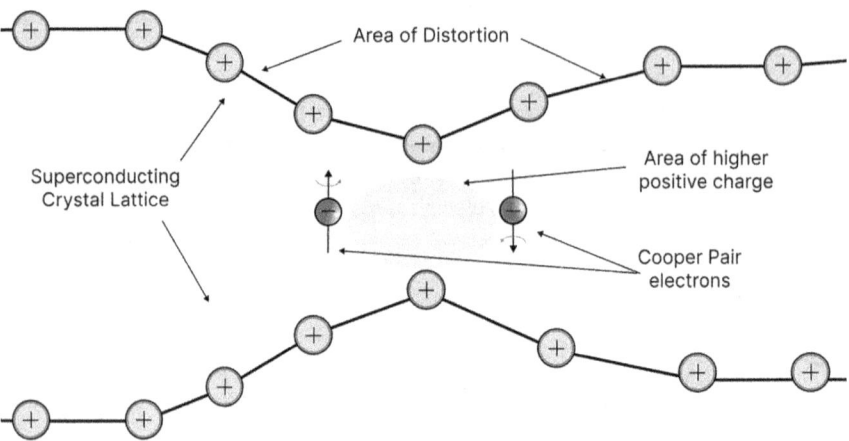

Figure 1-6 Visualization of formation of Cooper pairs in a crystal lattice structure

stay close to each other. The formation of Cooper pairs opens up an energy gap between the lowest and higher energy states, leading to a gap in the electronic energy spectrum. This gap prevents low-energy excitations, contributing to the stability of the superconducting state.

The formation of these pairs inside the crystal lattice allows them to move through the lattice without scattering, which prevents energy loss through resistance. This movement of Cooper pairs gives rise to the phenomenon of superconductivity, where electrical current flows with zero resistance. Diving into quantum mechanics, we find that two types of baryonic matter are observed in the universe: "**fermions**" and "**bosons**." Fermions are those subatomic particles that have a half-integer spin, such as $+/-$ $1/2$, such as protons and electrons, whereas bosons are those that have a whole integer spin as 0, 1, 2, and the best example of a boson is a photon. Cooper pairs are considered a particular type of boson known as a composite boson, which has a total spin of either 0 or 1; that means a pair of electrons will have a net quantum spin of 0 if individual electrons have opposite quantum spins of $+1/2$ and $-1/2$ and 1 if both the electrons have similar quantum spins. This means the wave functions are symmetric under particle interchange. Therefore, unlike electrons, multiple Cooper pairs are allowed to be in the same quantum state, which is responsible for the phenomenon of superconductivity.

- **Josephson Junction**: The Josephson effect is one of the most important phenomena in quantum mechanics. It is complex but can be understood in very simple terms. Assume that you have two superconductors placed next to each other separated by a thin insulating object between them and the movement of the Cooper pairs through this region is due to the Josephson effect. This region generated is known as the Josephson junction; it can be visualized in Figure 1-7.

1.10 Terms and Definitions of Some Important Concepts 21

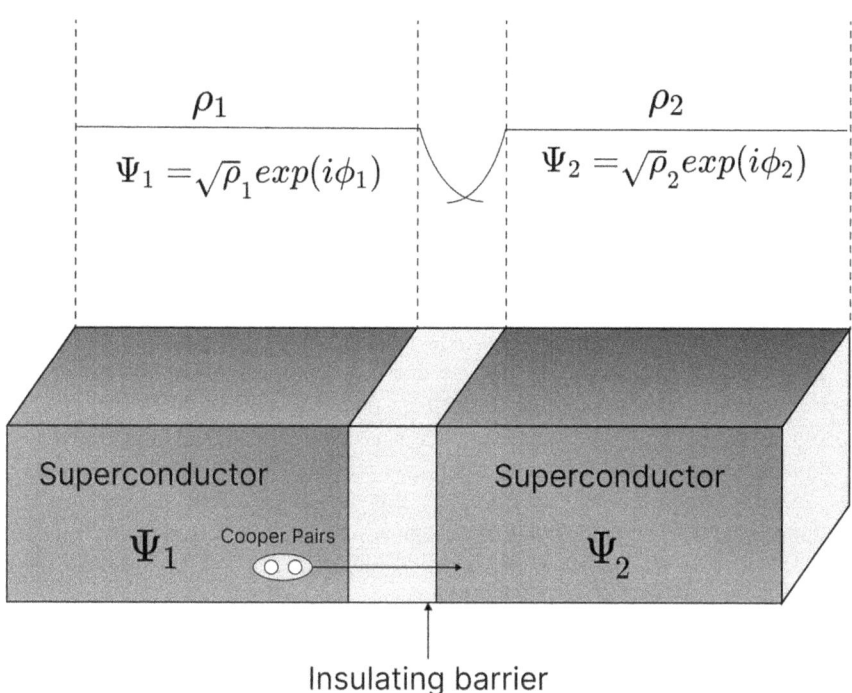

Figure 1-7 Illustration of the generation of the Josephson junction and how Cooper pairs traverse through this junction between two superconductors

It is a fundamental building block of superconducting qubits and has numerous applications in quantum computing, metrology, and sensing. When the Josephson junction is cooled below its critical temperature, Cooper pairs can tunnel across the barrier, despite the insulating nature of the barrier. This is known as Cooper pair tunneling. The key quantum mechanical phenomenon in a Josephson junction is the Josephson effect. When a voltage is applied across the junction, a supercurrent can flow through the barrier without any resistance. This supercurrent is directly related to the phase difference (ϕ) between the superconducting wave functions on both sides of the barrier. Quantum mechanics is a domain where all the effects take place on an atomic scale despite the fact that the Josephson effect can be observed in the real world on a non-atomic scale. Let us dive into the mathematical understanding of the Josephson junction and explore how energy is stored in it.

The **Josephson energy** is the energy required by Cooper pairs (pairs of electrons) to tunnel across a Josephson junction. It represents the maximum energy stored or transferred through the junction due to this effect and is given by

$$E_J = \frac{\hbar I_c}{2e} \quad (1\text{-}14)$$

where E_J represents the Josephson energy and I_c represents the critical current of the Josephson junction with $\hbar$ as the reduced Planck constant and e as the basic electronic charge. Josephson energy plays a crucial role in determining the energy levels of a qubit and helps in determining the anharmonicity for the qubits. The Josephson junction is determined by two important relations, the current phase and voltage phase relationships:

$$I = I_c \sin\phi, \quad V = \frac{\hbar}{2e}\frac{d\phi}{dt} \tag{1-15}$$

where ϕ is the phase difference of the wave function in that junction. The current phase relationship describes how the phase difference ϕ modulates the current through the junction, whereas the voltage phase relationship describes the **rate** of change of the phase difference ϕ that is proportional to the voltage across the junction. Using these two relationships, we can calculate the power stored in the junction by the forumla $P = IV$ where P is the power, I is the current, and V is the voltage; replacing the value of voltage with the value obtained from Equation 1-15, we obtain the power in the Josephson junction as

$$P = I \cdot V = I \cdot \frac{\hbar}{2e}\frac{d\phi}{dt} \tag{1-16}$$

As we know that the total work done by a system is calculated as the integral of power over time, we get the potential energy stored in the junction as

$$U = \int P \cdot dt = \int I \cdot \frac{\hbar}{2e}\frac{d\phi}{dt} \cdot dt \tag{1-17}$$

We obtain the equation of the potential energy by replacing the value of power obtained from Equation 1-16. By substituting the value of current obtained from Equation 1-15 and canceling dt from the numerator and denominator, we get the new value of integral as

$$U = \int I_c \sin\phi \cdot \frac{\hbar}{2e} d\phi \tag{1-18}$$

From Equation 1-18, we can simplify the equation by removing the constants out of integral and solving the integral over a phase difference of ϕ starting from 0, so we get

$$U = \frac{\hbar I_c}{2e}\int_0^\phi \sin\phi \cdot d\phi = \frac{\hbar I_c}{2e}(-\cos\phi) \tag{1-19}$$

1.10 Terms and Definitions of Some Important Concepts

By replacing the value of the Josephson energy from Equation 1-14, we get the value for the potential energy stored inside the junction as

$$E_J(\phi) = -E_J \cos \phi \tag{1-20}$$

The current phase relation obtained from Equation 1-15 determines the shape of the Josephson potential energy, and the Josephson potential energy obtained from Equation 1-20 acts as the potential well for the superconducting qubits. As we have studied earlier, anharmonicity refers to the uneven distribution of energy level for a qubit and can be calculated by the first and second transition frequencies for a qubit. Hence, we can represent anharmonicity (α) as

$$\alpha = \frac{E_{21} - E_{10}}{E_{10}} \tag{1-21}$$

where E_{10} represents the energy difference between the first excited state and the ground state, and E_{21} represents the energy difference between the second excited state and the first excited state. In order to figure out the rest, let's first define the Hamiltonian of a Transmon Qubit and try to establish a relation between the Josephson energy and anharmonicity. The first step is to define the charging energy, or E_C, as the charging energy and the Josephson energy help in defining the Hamiltonian and calculating the eigenstates for the Hamiltonian for the qubit.

The charging energy, or the E_C, is the energy to add an electron into the capacitor and is represented as

$$E_C = \frac{e^2}{2C} \tag{1-22}$$

where C represents the capacitance of the qubit. The Josephson energy (E_J) and the charging energy (E_C) are important parameters that help in understanding the working of a superconducting qubit. We will explore these parameters in depth, along with their applications, in the later chapters.

- **Flux Quantum**: Magnetic flux is a concept that describes the amount of magnetic field passing through a closed loop and is calculated as the product of the magnetic field and the loop surface area. Now, when this concept is applied to superconductors, it is said that if there is a hole or loop in a superconductor, then the magnetic field traveling through that region is quantized, as shown in Figure 1-8.

  This quantized magnetic flux is represented as $h/2e$ where h is the Planck constant, and e is the charge of an electron (2e comes due to the Cooper pairs, which is twice of a normal electron charge), and when evaluated the value comes out to be equal to $2.067 \times 10^{-15} wb$. The inverse of the flux quantum, $1/\psi_0$, is called the Josephson constant and is denoted as kJ. It is the constant of proportionality of the Josephson effect, relating the potential difference across a

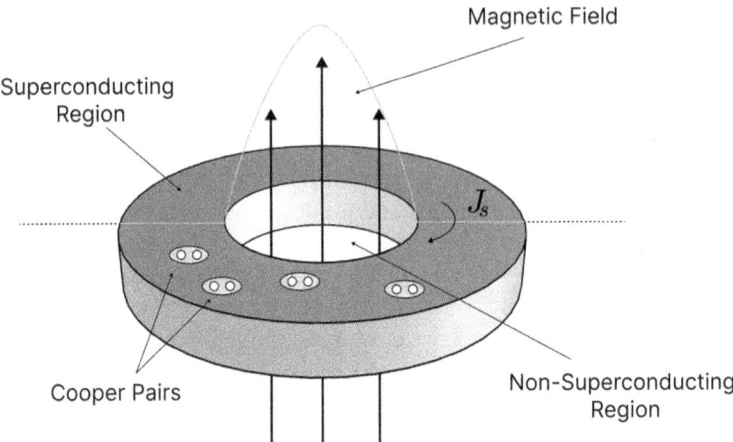

Figure 1-8 Visualization of the generation of magnetic flux quantum in a superconductor in the presence of a non-superconducting region

Josephson junction to the frequency of the irradiation. Due to the Meissner effect, a superconductor actively expels magnetic field lines attempting to penetrate it, ensuring that the magnetic induction B inside the superconductor is effectively zero. However, in practical scenarios, complete expulsion is not always achieved, and a weak magnetic field can penetrate slightly into the surface. More precisely, the magnetic field H penetrates the superconductor over a small distance known as the London penetration depth (λ_L), typically around 100 nm. This depth quantifies how far a magnetic field can enter a superconductor before being exponentially attenuated.

The screening currents also flow in this λ_L layer near the surface, creating magnetization M inside the superconductor, which perfectly compensates the applied field H, thus resulting in B = 0 inside the superconductor. The magnetic flux frozen in a loop/hole (plus its λ_L layer) will always be quantized. However, the value of the flux quantum is equal to ϕ_0 only when the path/trajectory around the hole described above can be chosen so that it lays in the superconducting region without screening currents, that is, several λ_L away from the surface. There are geometries where this condition cannot be satisfied, for example, a loop made of very thin ($< \lambda_L$) superconducting wire or a cylinder with a similar wall thickness. In the latter case, the flux has a quantum difference from ϕ_0.

- **Meissner Effect**: The Meissner effect is one of the most intriguing effects in quantum mechanics and plays an important role in understanding superconducting circuits. It states that when a conductor is cooled from a natural state to below that of its critical temperature, then it exhibits a unique property wherein it repels all the magnetic and electric fields passing through it; it can be visualized as represented in Figure 1-9. A superconductor with little or no magnetic field within it is said to be in the Meissner state.

1.10 Terms and Definitions of Some Important Concepts

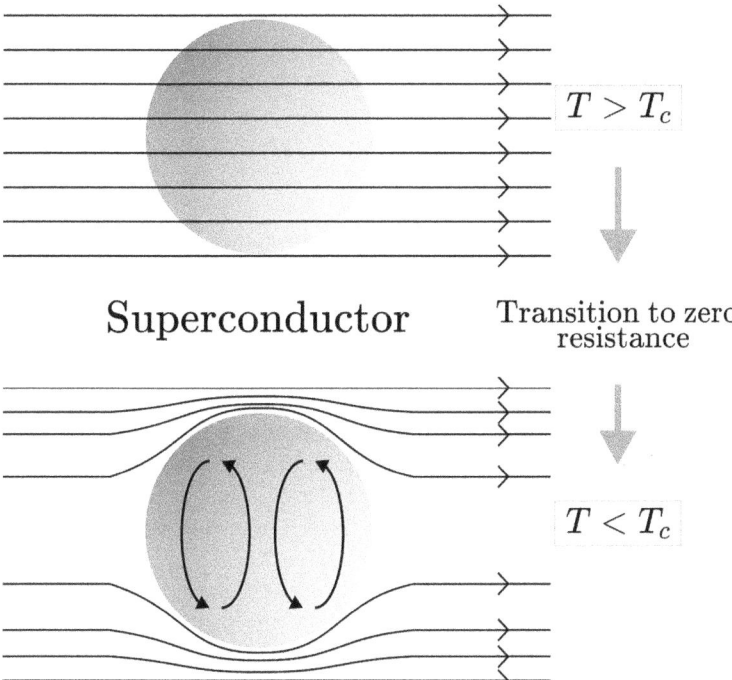

Figure 1-9 Demonstration of how the Meissner effect acts and expels all the magnetic field when the temperature falls below critical temperature for the superconductor

The Meissner state breaks down when the applied magnetic field exceeds a critical strength. Superconductors are divided into two classes based on how they respond to magnetic fields:

Type I superconductors completely expel the magnetic field (perfect diamagnetism) until a critical field is reached, at which point superconductivity is abruptly destroyed. They are typically composed of pure elemental metals like lead, tin, and mercury. Due to their limited ability to handle strong magnetic fields, type I superconductors are less commonly used in practical applications.

Type II superconductors, however, allow partial penetration of the magnetic field in the form of vortices between two critical field values, maintaining superconductivity in the presence of stronger fields. They are typically made from alloys or compounds, such as niobium-titanium (NbTi) and high-temperature superconductors (e.g., YBCO). Type II superconductors can handle much stronger magnetic fields and higher temperatures than type I superconductors, making them highly useful in practical applications such as MRI machines, particle accelerators, and magnetic levitation (maglev) trains.

Superconductors in the Meissner state exhibit perfect situations wherein the total magnetic field is very close to zero deep inside them. This property or phenomenon is known as diamagnetism or super diamagnetism, meaning their volume magnetic susceptibility equals −1. **Diamagnetics** is defined as generating a spontaneous magnetization of a material that directly opposes the direction of an applied field. However, the fundamental origins of diamagnetism in superconductors and standard materials are very different. In ordinary materials, diamagnetism arises directly from the orbital spin of electrons about the nuclei of an atom induced electromagnetically by applying an applied field. In superconductors, the illusion of perfect diamagnetism arises from persistent screening currents that flow to oppose the applied field (the Meissner effect), not solely the orbital spin. Meissner's effect is guided by a simple formula known as the "**London Equation**."

$$\nabla^2 H = (1/\lambda^2).H \tag{1-23}$$

A superconductor field (less than the critical field that breaks down the superconducting phase) expels nearly all magnetic flux by setting up electric currents near its surface, as the magnetic field H induces magnetization M within the London penetration depth from the surface. These surface currents shield the internal bulk of the superconductor from the external applied field. As the field expulsion, or cancellation, does not change with time, the currents producing this effect (called persistent currents or screening currents) do not decay with time. The persisting currents that exist in the superconductor to expel the magnetic field is commonly misconceived as a result of Lenz's Law or Faraday's Law. A reason this is not the case is that no change in flux was made to induce the current. Another explanation is that since the superconductor experiences zero resistance, there cannot be an induced emf (Electromotive Force) in the superconductor. The persisting current therefore is not a result of Faraday's Law.

1.11 Superconducting Qubits

Superconducting qubits are a type of quantum bit (qubit) that utilize the phenomenon of superconductivity to encode and manipulate quantum information. They are one of the leading qubit technologies in the field of quantum computing and quantum information processing. Superconducting qubits are typically made from superconducting circuits composed of Josephson junctions, which are weak links between two superconducting electrodes.

Superconducting qubits encode quantum information in the form of the quantum states of superconducting circuits. The qubit states are represented by different energy levels of the superconducting circuit, similar to how energy levels represent quantum states in atoms. To perform quantum computations, superconducting qubits are manipulated using microwave pulses and electromagnetic fields. These pulses cause transitions between different energy levels, enabling operations like superposition, entanglement, and interference. Superconducting qubits have made significant progress in recent years, with many technology companies and research institutions actively working on their development.

1.11 Superconducting Qubits

However, they face challenges such as coherence times (how long quantum information can be preserved) and error rates. Recent advancements in quantum hardware have extended coherence times significantly. For example, superconducting qubits in research labs have demonstrated coherence times on the order of **hundreds of microseconds**, with IBM reporting up to **350 microseconds** in their latest devices. These improvements are crucial as longer coherence times allow for more complex quantum computations to be performed before decoherence and errors occur. We will talk in depth regarding the hardware manufacturing process of these superconducting qubits in the coming chapters. Researchers are continually improving the design and fabrication techniques to overcome these challenges and scale up the number of qubits for practical quantum computation. There are several types of superconducting qubits, each with its unique properties and advantages. Some common types include

- **Transmon Qubit**: A variation of the Cooper pair box qubit with improved coherence times and robustness against certain types of noise. In its simplest form, the transmon consists of two islands interconnected by one junction.
The circuit diagram of the transmon qubit is represented in Figure 1-10. Those of you familiar with circuits, particularly electrical engineers, will recognize that the transmon looks, well, just like a parallel combination of one capacitor and one inductor—in other words, an LC oscillator! This gets us most of the way there, so let's take a look.
A direct correspondence can be made between this Hamiltonian and that of the simple harmonic oscillator by mapping the flux to the position of the mass and the charge to its momentum. Physics students will thus not be surprised to learn

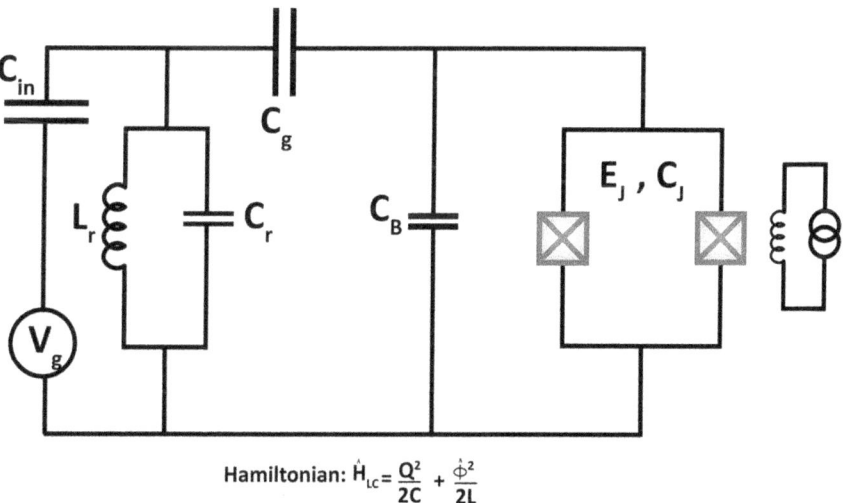

Figure 1-10 Classical circuit diagram of a transmon qubit

that the spectrum of the quantized LC oscillator is perfectly harmonic: levels are equally spaced in energy! This equal spacing is given by a familiar formula: one over root LC. But, unfortunately, a harmonic spectrum does not make a good qubit! It is very difficult to confine the dynamics to just two levels, so "**leakage**" out of the qubit subspace is a permanent threat. That is why the transmon differs from the LC oscillator in a fundamental way. In the transmon, the inductance is provided by a Josephson junction and not by a typical coil inductor. The inductive energy for the junction is not quadratic, but a cosine function of the generalized flux through it. This difference has important consequences for the spectrum: crucially, it disrupts the harmonic spectrum in ways that are very practical.

- **Xmon Qubit**: A version of the transmon qubit with an X-shaped circuit layout that enhances scalability. It was introduced by researchers at Google, and it has become one of the popular and promising architectures for building scalable and error-resistant quantum computers. The circuit diagram of a simple Xmon qubit is represented in Figure 1-11. The Xmon qubit is a transmon qubit with an X-shaped architecture, which is where it gets its name ("Xmon" stands for

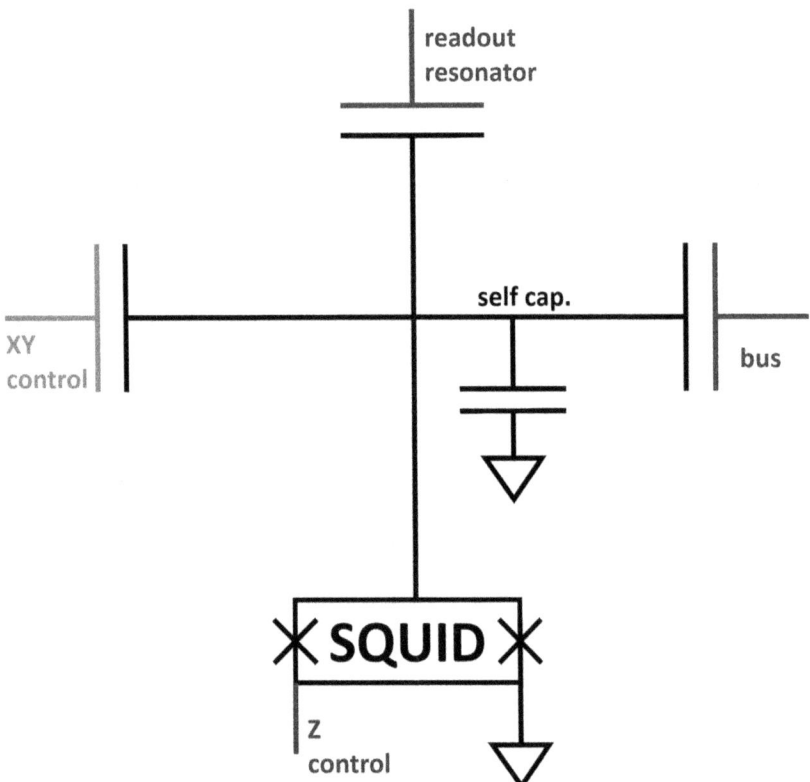

Figure 1-11 Classical circuit diagram of an Xmon qubit

1.11 Superconducting Qubits

"X-shaped transmon"). Transmon qubits are an enhanced version of the Cooper pair box qubit, designed to improve coherence times and reduce sensitivity to certain noise sources. The Xmon qubit's X-shaped design helps to mitigate certain noise sources that can cause decoherence (loss of quantum information). By using the X-shaped layout, the qubit can be made less sensitive to charge noise, which is one of the main sources of decoherence in superconducting qubits. Xmon qubits are operated using a set of quantum gates, such as single-qubit gates (e.g., X, Y, Z rotations) and two-qubit gates (e.g., CNOT gate). These gates are used to perform quantum computations and algorithms. The Xmon qubit architecture is well suited for scalability, which means it can be easily extended to larger arrays of qubits. This scalability is essential for building practical quantum computers capable of solving real-world problems. Xmon qubits, like other superconducting qubits, are used in quantum computing to perform various quantum algorithms. They have shown promise in solving optimization problems, simulating quantum systems, and breaking certain cryptographic algorithms (Shor's algorithm for factoring large numbers).

- **Phase Qubits**: A qubit type based on the phase difference across the Josephson junction. A *phase qubit* is a current-biased Josephson junction operated in the zero-voltage state with a nonzero current bias. A **Josephson junction** is a tunnel junction made of two pieces of superconducting metal separated by a fragile insulating barrier, about 1 nm thick. The barrier is thin enough that electrons are superconducting, and Cooper-paired electrons can tunnel through the barrier appreciably. Each superconductor that makes up the Josephson junction is described by a macroscopic wave function, as described by the Ginzburg–Landau theory for superconductors. The schematic of the phase qubit is displayed in Figure 1-12.

The difference in the complex phases of the two superconducting wave functions is the most important dynamic variable for the Josephson junction, and it is called the phase difference delta, or simply "phase." To manipulate the quantum state of a phase qubit, microwave pulses are applied to control the phase difference ψ. By adjusting the phase, the qubit can be put into superposition states (a combination of $|0\rangle$ and $|1\rangle$) and entangled with other qubits. While **phase qubits** were an early design in superconducting qubits, they generally exhibit **shorter coherence times** compared to other superconducting qubits like **transmon qubits**, due to

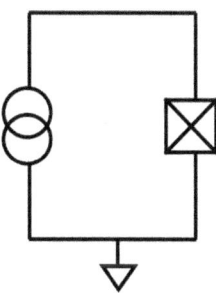

Figure 1-12 Classical circuit diagram of a phase qubit

Figure 1-13 Classical circuit diagram of a flux qubit

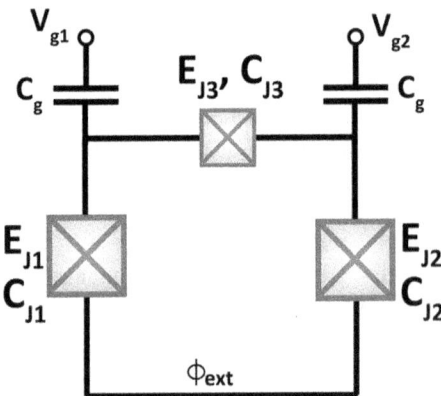

higher sensitivity to noise and decoherence effects. Transmons, a variant of phase qubits, were developed specifically to reduce sensitivity to charge noise and have demonstrated longer coherence times—often exceeding **100 microseconds**—compared to the typical **10–20 microseconds** for phase qubits.

- **Flux Qubit**: Flux qubits are a type of superconducting qubits used in quantum computing. They are designed based on the magnetic flux through a superconducting loop and exhibit unique properties that make them attractive candidates for quantum information processing. The circuit diagram of a basic flux qubit is shown in Figure 1-13. Flux qubits rely on the magnetic flux as the degree of freedom to encode quantum information. They are based on superconducting loops interrupted by one or more Josephson junctions. The Josephson junction is a weak link between two superconducting electrodes and is the critical element that allows the flux qubit to operate quantum mechanically. The magnetic flux threading the superconducting loop determines the qubit's energy levels in a flux qubit.

The loop's design and the presence of Josephson junctions allow for the quantization of the magnetic flux, leading to discrete energy levels analogous to the energy levels of an atom. The qubit's magnetic flux can be manipulated by applying external magnetic fields or microwave pulses, allowing it to exist in a superposition of different magnetic flux states. These superposition states represent quantum coherence, where the qubit simultaneously exists in multiple magnetic flux states. Like other qubits, flux qubits have two distinct quantum states, often denoted as $|0\rangle$ and $|1\rangle$. These states correspond to different magnetic flux levels in the superconducting loop. The qubit's information is encoded in the relative phase difference between these two states. The flux qubit design creates an energy gap between the $|0\rangle$ and $|1\rangle$ states, similar to the energy gap in other qubit types. This energy gap is determined by the Josephson energy, which depends on the properties of the Josephson junction and the loop's inductance. To perform quantum computations, researchers apply microwave pulses or magnetic fields to the flux qubit, allowing them to control its quantum state. These control techniques enable single-qubit rotations and two-qubit interactions for quantum gate operations.

1.12 Advantages and Disadvantages of Superconducting Systems

Superconducting circuits and applications in quantum computing are a relatively new branch in physics and modern electronics. Though theoretically superconducting circuits provide a logical solution to many problems during practical analysis, many new and unforeseen difficulties and problems came up. Let's look into some of the advantages and disadvantages of superconducting circuits before moving on ahead.

Advantages: Superconducting circuits offer several advantages that make them promising candidates for quantum computing and other quantum technologies. Let's delve into the details of these advantages:

- **Zero Electrical Resistance**: The most significant advantage of superconducting circuits is their ability to conduct electricity with zero electrical resistance when cooled below their critical temperature (Tc). This property allows superconductors to carry electric current indefinitely without any loss of energy due to resistance. In the context of quantum computing, zero resistance is crucial for maintaining the coherence and integrity of quantum information, leading to longer qubit coherence times.
- **Long Coherence Times**: Superconducting qubits have demonstrated coherence times in the range of **tens to hundreds of microseconds**, with some reaching up to **350 microseconds**. In comparison, **silicon spin qubits** have coherence times on the order of **milliseconds**, but qubits like **neutral atoms** and **photonic qubits** typically exhibit shorter coherence times, often below **100 microseconds**. Coherence time refers to the duration for which a qubit can maintain its quantum state before decohering (losing its quantum information). The low electrical resistance and reduced sensitivity to certain noise sources in superconducting circuits contribute to longer coherence times.
- **Scalability**: Superconducting circuits are well suited for scalability, which is essential for building practical quantum computers. They can be fabricated using established semiconductor fabrication techniques, allowing for the integration of multiple qubits and complex quantum circuits on a chip. This scalability is crucial for building large-scale quantum processors capable of solving complex problems.
- **Fast Quantum Gates**: Superconducting qubits can be manipulated and controlled using microwave pulses, allowing them to perform quantum gate operations essential for executing quantum algorithms. These qubits have demonstrated fast gate operations with **typical gate times of 20–50 nanoseconds**, significantly faster than other qubit technologies such as **trapped-ion qubits**

(with gate times around **10 microseconds**) and **neutral atom qubits** (with gate times on the order of **100 microseconds**), making them suitable for quantum information processing tasks.
- **Versatility in Qubit Types**: Superconducting circuits support various qubit types, each with its unique advantages and challenges. Some of the commonly used superconducting qubit types include transmon qubits, Xmon qubits, flux qubits, and phase qubits. This versatility allows researchers to explore different qubit designs to optimize performance and address specific quantum computing challenges.
- **Compatibility with Classical Electronics**: Superconducting circuits can be interfaced with classical electronics, making them potentially easier to integrate into existing computer architectures and hybrid quantum-classical systems. This compatibility enables researchers to leverage classical computing resources alongside quantum processing, facilitating hybrid quantum algorithms.
- **Accessible Temperature Range**: While achieving the ultra-low temperatures required for superconductivity is challenging, it is still more feasible compared to the extremely low temperatures required for some other qubit technologies, such as ion traps or certain topological qubits. This accessibility makes superconducting circuits more practical for implementation in current laboratory setups.
- **Broad Quantum Applications**: Superconducting circuits are not limited to quantum computing; they have applications in quantum simulation, quantum sensing, and quantum communication. This versatility makes them attractive for exploring a wide range of quantum technologies and scientific research.

Despite these advantages, superconducting circuits also face challenges, including noise sources, qubit crosstalk, and coherence times that can be affected by external factors. Let's look into some of the disadvantages of superconducting quantum circuits.

Disadvantages: While superconducting circuits offer many advantages for quantum computing and other quantum technologies, they also come with several disadvantages that present challenges to their implementation and practical use. Let's explore the details of these disadvantages:

- **Cooling Requirements**: Superconducting circuits require extremely low temperatures, typically near absolute zero (0 K or $-273.15\,°C$), to achieve the superconducting state. Cooling systems, such as dilution refrigerators or cryocoolers, are necessary to maintain these low temperatures. The cooling process adds complexity and cost to the quantum computing setup.
- **Energy Consumption**: Cooling superconducting circuits to such low temperatures consumes significant amounts of energy. The power consumption of the cooling system can be substantial, though not as substantial as other issues that can lead to the data being compromised. However, energy consumption causes severe issues while working with multiple superconducting qubits, leading to

1.12 Advantages and Disadvantages of Superconducting Systems

many design challenges and limiting the overall energy efficiency of superconducting quantum computers.

- **Decoherence**: Despite relatively long coherence times compared to some other qubit technologies, superconducting qubits are still susceptible to decoherence due to various noise sources. Noise from thermal fluctuations, magnetic fields, and charge fluctuations can cause qubits to lose their quantum information and reduce the overall accuracy of quantum computations.
- **Flux Noise**: Flux noise is a particular type of noise that affects superconducting qubits, especially flux qubits. It arises from fluctuations in the magnetic flux threading the superconducting loop. Flux noise can introduce errors and reduce the fidelity of quantum operations.
- **Complexity of Fabrication**: Building and fabricating superconducting circuits with high precision can be challenging. The Josephson junctions and other circuit elements need to be accurately controlled and fabricated to ensure qubits perform as expected. The complexity of the fabrication process can hinder large-scale production and limit the potential for mass-manufacturing quantum processors.
- **Qubit Crosstalk**: While creating quantum computing chips, we have to integrate multiple qubits in a single chip, leading to the issue with qubit crosstalk. This phenomenon refers to the unwanted interaction between neighboring qubits, leading to errors, and, in such cases, the data becomes corrupted, which reduces the performance. Controlling crosstalk is critical for scaling up quantum processors. One example of qubit crosstalk is seen in IBM's **Falcon quantum processors**, where qubit crosstalk is a severe problem. To mitigate this, IBM has implemented advanced calibration techniques. One of those methods is to reduce interference between qubits and improve gate fidelities, which is crucial for scaling up their quantum chips. This method is **crosstalk-aware pulse shaping**. Another widely researched method that can lead to the suppression of qubit crosstalk is dynamic coupling between qubits; this method is still researched upon and if successfully manufactured can lead to feasible and scalable quantum chips with multiple qubits in it. We will be discussing this method in detail in the following chapters.
- **Readout Errors**: Extracting quantum information from superconducting qubits without introducing errors can be challenging. Readout errors in quantum computing refer to inaccuracies when measuring qubit states, with current research focusing on reducing these errors through **quantum error correction techniques** and **machine learning models**. IBM recently reported improvements using **hidden Markov models** to lower readout error rates. A hidden Markov model (HMM) is a statistical model that represents systems with hidden states, where the system transitions between states probabilistically, and these hidden states influence the observed outcomes we will be talking regarding the HMM in the following chapters. The readout process may be sensitive to noise, leading to errors in the measurement of qubit states.
- **Limited Connectivity**: In certain superconducting qubit architectures, connecting qubits for two-qubit gate operations can be challenging. This limited

connectivity may restrict the types of quantum algorithms that can be efficiently executed on the quantum processor.
- **Complexity of Error Correction**: To build fault-tolerant quantum computers, error correction techniques are necessary. Implementing error correction for superconducting qubits can be complex and requires additional qubits and overhead, making fault-tolerant quantum computing a challenging task.

1.13 Realizing Superconducting Circuits

Well now after we have looked through the basics of superconducting circuits, we should also look at the basics of realizing these special circuits. Superconducting circuits are developed and stimulated using many open source and paid software available where one can realize their own superconducting qubits with the prior knowledge of the subject for their respective field of study. Among the many and most popular ones, we will be using and working on "Qiskit Metal" for the application.

Qiskit Metal is a software framework developed by IBM Quantum that is used for designing and simulating superconducting quantum circuits. It is an essential part of the Qiskit ecosystem, which is an open source quantum computing software development kit (SDK) developed by IBM. Qiskit Metal provides a powerful set of tools and capabilities to design and analyze quantum circuits based on superconducting qubits. Qiskit Metal allows users to design and construct quantum circuits based on superconducting qubits using a graphical user interface (GUI). Users can create and arrange qubits, couplers, and other circuit components to build complex quantum circuits. The framework provides visualizations that allow users to view and analyze the designed quantum circuits in a user-friendly manner. Users can inspect the layout, connectivity, and properties of the qubits and couplers in the circuit. Qiskit Metal supports the simulation of microwave signals and their interactions with the superconducting qubits in the circuit. This feature enables users to study the effects of microwave control and manipulation on the qubit states. Qiskit Metal allows users to design quantum circuits that can be mapped onto specific quantum chips or hardware architectures.

This feature is crucial for designing circuits tailored to specific quantum computing systems. The framework includes optimization tools to fine-tune quantum circuits for improved performance and error mitigation. It helps users optimize the qubit layout, connectivity, and other parameters to enhance the circuit's overall performance. Being part of the Qiskit ecosystem, Qiskit Metal seamlessly integrates with other Qiskit components. This integration allows users to simulate, execute, and analyze quantum circuits on real quantum hardware using Qiskit. Well for the entire literature ahead, we will be using Qiskit Metal and will be showing how to develop superconducting circuits using Qiskit Metal from the very basics so that anyone can develop the circuits. The proper guide and more information regarding the Qiskit Metal will be provided in Chapter 3 where we will be learning about the installation guide, and we will walk through how to use the framework.

1.14 Conclusion

In this chapter, we explored the fundamentals of superconductivity, beginning with the origins of quantum computing and its distinctions from classical computation. We explored key concepts essential for forming the groundwork required for understanding the subsequent chapters, including the mathematical frameworks of Lagrangian mechanics and Pauli matrices, as well as important theories in superconductivity like the Josephson junction and Cooper pairs. Additionally, we introduced various types of superconducting qubits, such as the transmon, Xmon, and flux, highlighting their unique characteristics and importance. This chapter set the stage for understanding the potential of quantum computing and established why superconducting qubits represent a promising frontier in the evolution of computational technology.

Theory of Superconducting Qubit 2

The fundamental requirement for a quantum mechanical system to function as a qubit is the presence of two well-defined states that can be precisely controlled and measured. In this chapter, we will explore how superconducting microwave circuits can be engineered to realize qubits. We begin with the harmonic oscillator, a system fundamental to both classical and quantum mechanics. Section 2.1 introduces the classical and quantum descriptions of harmonic oscillators, examining their energy quantization and limitations in quantum computing. Here, we address the question: Can a harmonic oscillator function as a qubit?

In Section 2.2, we extend this discussion to the quantum LC oscillator, a key system in superconducting circuit theory. We first outline the classical dynamics of an LC oscillator circuit, then derive its Hamiltonian, leading to its quantum description using ladder operators. This section highlights the bridge from classical circuits to quantum systems, providing a pathway to understanding superconducting qubits.

Sections 2.3 through 2.5 delve into various superconducting qubit types, starting with phase, charge, and flux qubits in Section 2.3. Each type has unique characteristics based on its operational principles and the parameters it encodes, such as magnetic flux or electric charge. We then focus on the transmon qubit in Section 2.4, detailing its classical and quantum Hamiltonians and exploring methods of control and measurement. Section 2.5 concludes with recent advancements and refinements in superconducting qubit designs, setting the stage for next-generation qubits.

2.1 Harmonic Oscillator

The harmonic oscillator is a cornerstone in both classical and quantum physics due to its fundamental nature and widespread applicability. In classical mechanics, it can be visualized as a mass attached to a spring that is fixed at one end. When the mass is displaced from its equilibrium position, the restoring force of the spring pulls it back, but the momentum of the mass causes it to overshoot the equilibrium. This overshooting sets up a repetitive motion, as the spring alternately pulls and pushes the mass back toward equilibrium. In an ideal system without damping or energy loss, this oscillatory motion, known as harmonic motion, would persist indefinitely. The simple harmonic oscillator is not only valuable as a model for practical systems, such as the suspension system in vehicles, but also because its principles extend to many other systems with similar dynamic behavior. A striking example is an electrical circuit comprising an inductor and a capacitor in parallel, where the voltage and current oscillations obey equations identical in form to the spring-mass system.

In quantum physics, the harmonic oscillator gains even greater significance. Any classical system modeled as a harmonic oscillator can also be described in terms of quantum mechanics, particularly when the system operates at small energy scales. For instance, in an LC circuit, while the voltage and current can take on a continuous range of values in the classical description, quantum mechanics constrains these quantities to discrete energy levels. This quantization is especially relevant in our context because we can use two of these discrete levels as the basis for a qubit. To lay the groundwork for understanding transmon qubits, we first examine the classical and quantum harmonic oscillators, which serve as the theoretical foundation for our discussion.

2.1.1 Classical Harmonic Oscillator

Let us analyze the dynamics of a classical harmonic oscillator using both Newtonian mechanics and the Lagrangian formulation. Consider a mechanical system consisting of a spring with a force constant K, fixed at one end, and a mass attached to the other. We define the position of the mass as x, with $x = 0$ representing the equilibrium position.

2.1.1.1 Newtonian Analysis

When the mass is displaced by x from equilibrium, the spring exerts a restoring force F directed toward the equilibrium. According to Newton's second law, $F = \frac{dp}{dt}$, where p is the momentum of the mass. Equating the restoring force to the rate of change of momentum gives

$$\frac{dp}{dt} = -Kx \tag{2-1}$$

By expressing the momentum in terms of x, where $p = mv = m\frac{dx}{dt}$, we can rewrite this equation as

$$m\frac{d^2x}{dt^2} = -Kx \tag{2-2}$$

2.1 Harmonic Oscillator

This is the standard equation of motion for a harmonic oscillator. A solution to this equation is $x(t) = A\cos(\omega t)$, where ω is the angular frequency, given by

$$\omega = \omega_0 = \sqrt{\frac{K}{m}} \tag{2-3}$$

The frequency ω_0 represents the natural oscillation frequency of the system. Alternatively, complex notation can be employed, where $x(t) = Ae^{-i\omega t}$, and the real part of this expression corresponds to the physical displacement over time.

2.1.1.2 Lagrangian Formulation
We now examine the system using the Lagrangian framework. The Lagrangian $\mathcal{L}$ for the harmonic oscillator is given by the difference between the kinetic and potential energies:

$$\mathcal{L} = \frac{1}{2}m\dot{x}^2 - \frac{1}{2}Kx^2 \tag{2-4}$$

The equation of motion is derived from the Euler-Lagrange equation:

$$\frac{\partial \mathcal{L}}{\partial x} - \frac{d}{dt}\frac{\partial \mathcal{L}}{\partial \dot{x}} = 0 \tag{2-5}$$

Substituting the expression for $\mathcal{L}$ obtained from Equation 2-4 into Equation 2-5 yields:

$$-Kx - m\ddot{x} = 0 \tag{2-6}$$

which is consistent with the equation derived using Newton's laws.

2.1.1.3 Hamiltonian Formulation
The canonical momentum associated with x is defined as

$$p = \frac{\partial \mathcal{L}}{\partial \dot{x}} = m\dot{x} \tag{2-7}$$

The Hamiltonian $\mathcal{H}$, representing the total energy of the system, is expressed as

$$\mathcal{H} = \frac{p^2}{2m} + \frac{1}{2}Kx^2 \tag{2-8}$$

Substituting $K = m\omega_0^2$, the Hamiltonian becomes

$$\mathcal{H} = \frac{p^2}{2m} + \frac{1}{2}m\omega_0^2 x^2 \tag{2-9}$$

2.1.2 Quantum Harmonic Oscillator

In classical mechanics, position (x) and momentum (p) commute, that is, $xp = px$. However, when transitioning to quantum mechanics, the corresponding operators do not commute. In quantum mechanics, commutation relation indicates

$$(xp - px)|\psi\rangle = i\hbar|\psi\rangle \tag{2-10}$$

This relationship is expressed using the commutator notation, defined as $[x, p] = xp - px$. The commutator quantifies whether two operators commute. In this case, we have

$$[x, p] = i\hbar \tag{2-11}$$

This non-commutation between position and momentum implies that these two observables can't be simultaneously known with absolute certainty. This is a foundational aspect of the Heisenberg uncertainty principle. The uncertainty in the simultaneous measurement of position and momentum is related by

$$\Delta x \Delta p \geq \frac{\hbar}{2} \tag{2-12}$$

Position and momentum are conjugate variables, connected through a Fourier transform. The Hamiltonian for the quantum harmonic oscillator can be formulated by replacing the classical position and momentum with their respective quantum operators. The time-independent Schrödinger equation for the harmonic oscillator then becomes

$$\mathcal{H}|\psi\rangle = \mathcal{E}|\psi\rangle \tag{2-13}$$

$$\left[-\frac{\hbar^2}{2m}\frac{d^2}{dx^2} + \frac{1}{2}m\omega_0^2 x^2\right]|\psi\rangle = \mathcal{E}|\psi\rangle \tag{2-14}$$

Although x and p are useful for describing the physical properties of a state, there are instances where it is more practical to use operators directly linked to the energy of the state. To achieve this, we define the annihilation operator a as

$$a = \sqrt{\frac{m\omega_0}{2\hbar}}\left(x + i\frac{p}{m\omega_0}\right) \tag{2-15}$$

2.1 Harmonic Oscillator

The Hermitian conjugate of this operator is

$$a^\dagger = \sqrt{\frac{m\omega_0}{2\hbar}} \left(x - i\frac{p}{m\omega_0} \right) \quad (2\text{-}16)$$

These operators act on the quantum states as follows:

$$a|\psi_n\rangle = \sqrt{n}|\psi_{n-1}\rangle \quad (2\text{-}17)$$

$$a^\dagger|\psi_n\rangle = \sqrt{n+1}|\psi_{n+1}\rangle \quad (2\text{-}18)$$

The operator a, which lowers the quantum state from n to $n-1$, is called the annihilation (or lowering) operator. On the other hand, $a^\dagger$ raises the state from n to $n+1$ and is referred to as the creation (or raising) operator. Together, these operators are known as ladder operators, as they allow transitions between energy levels.

When both operators are applied to a state, we expect to return to the same state due to their combined action:

$$a^\dagger a|\psi_n\rangle = a^\dagger \sqrt{n}|\psi_{n-1}\rangle = n|\psi_n\rangle \quad (2\text{-}19)$$

In terms of the ladder operators, the Hamiltonian of the system can be expressed as

$$\mathcal{H} = \hbar\omega_0 \left(a^\dagger a + \frac{1}{2} \right) \quad (2\text{-}20)$$

This results in the quantized energy levels:

$$\mathcal{H} = \hbar\omega_0 \left(n + \frac{1}{2} \right) \quad (2\text{-}21)$$

where $n = 0, 1, 2, 3, \ldots$ is the quantum number. Unlike in classical mechanics, the energy levels in the quantum harmonic oscillator are discrete.

The lowest energy state, known as the ground state, has a nonzero energy:

$$E_0 = \frac{1}{2}\hbar\omega_0 \quad (2\text{-}22)$$

This energy is called the zero-point energy, which arises due to the Heisenberg uncertainty principle. The wave functions $\psi_n(x)$ for different energy levels are solutions to the Schrödinger equation. These wave functions are associated with Hermite polynomials and exhibit oscillatory patterns, with each state corresponding to a specific probability of finding the particle at various positions. As the quantum number n increases, the wave function becomes more spread out, indicating a higher likelihood of the particle being farther from the origin.

The zero-point energy ensures that the particle cannot be at rest at $x = 0$. If the particle were at rest with zero momentum, it would violate the uncertainty principle:

$$\Delta x \cdot \Delta p \geq \frac{\hbar}{2} \tag{2-23}$$

Thus, the uncertainty principle implies that the particle must always possess some uncertainty in both position and momentum, preventing it from being perfectly localized at the origin.

2.1.3 Can a Harmonic Oscillator Serve As a Qubit?

Having gained some understanding of the quantum mechanical harmonic oscillator, let's now consider whether it could be utilized as a qubit. One of the essential characteristics of a qubit is the presence of exactly two discrete states. However, the harmonic oscillator, in its simplest form, has an infinite number of quantized energy levels, all separated by equal spacing. What happens if we attempt to use this system as a qubit?

Let's imagine preparing the harmonic oscillator in its ground state and then applying a π-pulse to move it into the first excited state. If we then want to return the system to its ground state, a second π-pulse would ordinarily suffice in a two-level system. However, in the case of the harmonic oscillator, the second π-pulse could equally drive the system to the second excited state ($n = 2$) instead of bringing it back to the ground state, due to the equally spaced energy levels.

In contrast, the spin systems we explore in later sections of this book are naturally suited for use as qubits because they only possess two distinct energy levels. While many physical systems, like the harmonic oscillator, exhibit more than two states, this doesn't preclude them from serving as qubits. The key requirement is that the energy gaps between the states are sufficiently large to allow us to selectively apply pulses that couple only two of these states. The difficulty with the harmonic oscillator arises from its equidistant energy levels, which makes it challenging to isolate just two states.

The energy of a system can be written as

$$\mathcal{E} = \langle \psi | \mathcal{H} | \psi \rangle \tag{2-24}$$

where the wave function is assumed to be normalized, that is, $\langle \psi | \psi \rangle = 1$.

Now suppose the Hamiltonian consists of a solvable part and a small perturbation, expressed as $\mathcal{H} = \mathcal{H}_0 + V$. The energy then becomes

$$\mathcal{E} = \langle \psi | (\mathcal{H}_0 + V) | \psi \rangle = \langle \psi | \mathcal{H}_0 | \psi \rangle + \langle \psi | V | \psi \rangle \tag{2-25}$$

2.2 Classical Electrodynamics of an LC Oscillator Circuit

For small perturbations, we can approximate the wave function using the unperturbed solution, leading to

$$\mathcal{E}'_n \approx \langle \psi_n | \mathcal{H}_0 | \psi_n \rangle + \langle \psi_n | V | \psi_n \rangle \approx \mathcal{E}_n + \langle \psi_n | V | \psi_n \rangle \qquad (2\text{-}26)$$

Here, $|\psi_n\rangle$ represents the nth eigenstate of the unperturbed Hamiltonian $\mathcal{H}_0$. Because the spatial extent of these wave functions increases with n, the effect of the perturbation grows larger as n increases. Consequently, the energy differences between adjacent states become unequal:

$$\mathcal{E}'_{n+1} - \mathcal{E}'_n \neq \mathcal{E}'_n - \mathcal{E}'_{n-1} \qquad (2\text{-}27)$$

If these differences are large enough to be experimentally resolved, we can focus on transitions between just the ground and the first excited states, neglecting the higher states for simplicity in the initial approximation.

For mechanical harmonic oscillators, such a perturbation might arise from deviations from the ideal spring force law, $F = -Kx^2/2$. In the next section, we will see that an LC circuit, which behaves like a harmonic oscillator, can introduce a similar perturbation. By incorporating a Josephson junction as a nonlinear inductor, we can create the necessary perturbation to form a viable qubit.

2.2 Classical Electrodynamics of an LC Oscillator Circuit

The LC oscillator consists of two metal pads connected by a very small path of non-metal on a substrate as presented in Figure 2-1. The connecting metal pad here plays the role of an inductor. The electric field between these pads causes positive and negative charges to move; it should be noted that there are no charge losses anywhere. Based on this displacement, charge (Q), electric current (i), voltage (v), capacitance (C), flux (Φ), and inductance (L) can be defined for this oscillator.

This elementary model, consisting of two metal pads and an inductor, is described using fundamental electrical equations that relate magnetic flux, charge, voltage, and current. The current through the inductor and the voltage are related by the expression:

$$v = L\frac{di(t)}{dt}, \qquad (2\text{-}28)$$

or assuming a time-invariant inductor:

$$v = \frac{d\Phi}{dt}. \qquad (2\text{-}29)$$

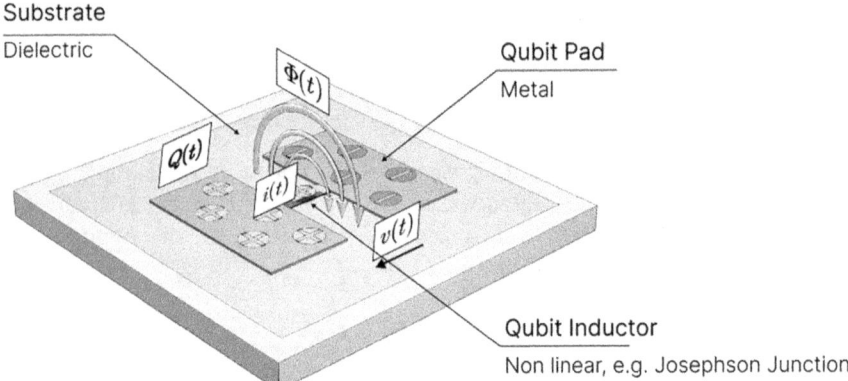

Figure 2-1 Physical layout of an LC oscillator

Integrating this equation yields the following expression for the flux Φ:

$$\Phi(t) = \int_{-\infty}^{t} v(t')\,dt'. \tag{2-30}$$

Here, we assume the voltage vanishes as $t \to -\infty$. These interrelations serve as the foundational elements for various constructs, ranging from qubits to readout resonators and amplifiers. Consequently, the foundation of the qubit oscillator relies on the interplay between an inductor and a capacitor.

The instantaneous, time-dependent energy of the circuit which oscillates between the inductor and capacitor is derived from its current and voltage:

$$E(t) = \int_{-\infty}^{t} v(t')i(t')\,dt' \tag{2-31}$$

This amount of oscillator energy is equal to the energy that is either stored or delivered in the capacitive and inductive elements. Following the previous formula, the energy of the inductor and capacitor can be defined in terms of the square power of the flux or charge and their derivatives as follows:

$$\mathcal{E}_{cap}(\dot{\Phi}) = \frac{1}{2}C\dot{\Phi}^2, \quad \mathcal{E}_{ind}(\Phi) = \frac{\Phi^2}{2L}$$

$$\mathcal{E}_{cap}(Q) = \frac{Q^2}{2C}, \quad \mathcal{E}_{ind}(\dot{Q}) = \frac{1}{2}L\dot{Q}^2 \tag{2-32}$$

In our analysis, the inclusion of a variable inductor, particularly relevant in the context of the Josephson junction, requires expressing the fundamental relationships in terms of magnetic flux. We can represent the physics layout of the LC oscillator in its lumped form as presented in Figure 2-2.

2.2 Classical Electrodynamics of an LC Oscillator Circuit

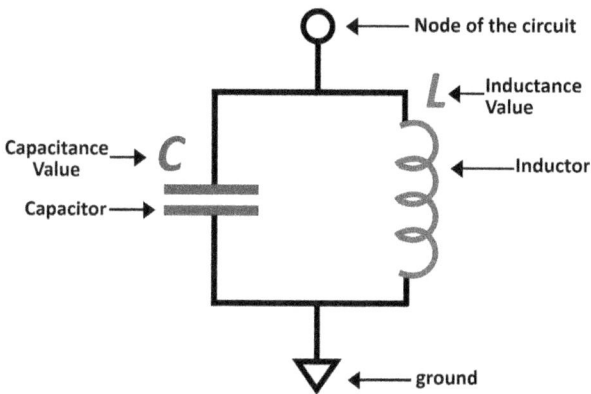

Figure 2-2 Lumped-element LC, the oscillator of inductance L and capacitance C

Leveraging the principles of charge conservation (Kirchhoff's current law) and Faraday's law of induction (Kirchhoff's charge law), we can formulate the following equation for this oscillator. The model includes both capacitors and inductors, effectively capturing their intricate interplay within the system. The corresponding equation of motion is given as

$$C \cdot \Phi + \frac{\Phi}{L} = 0 \qquad (2\text{-}33)$$

The above equation is analogous to those governing the harmonic motion of springs and masses and can be expressed as $\ddot{\Phi} = -\omega_0^2 \Phi$. This similarity shows the basic connection between harmonic oscillators and electromagnetic circuits. In the context of the spring problem, the equilibrium rests at $x = 0$, while in the magnetic scenario, equilibrium requires $\phi = 0$. Notably, the first derivative of flux in the spring problem corresponds to the initial derivative of x (analogous to velocity), and the second derivative of spring problem flux aligns with the second derivative of x (analogous to acceleration). In spring problems, oscillations center around the spring's position. However, in electromagnetic circuits, the focus shifts to fluctuations in the magnitude of electromagnetic flux. This duality helps us understand the underlying challenge. By comparing the oscillatory dynamics of a spring and its weight to the behavior of an electromagnetic circuit, which is characterized by flux fluctuations, a connection is made between mechanics and electromagnetic theory. The above discussion leads us to derive the LC oscillator's frequency and impedance as given in Equation 2-34.

$$\omega_0 = \frac{1}{\sqrt{LC}}, \quad Z_0 = \sqrt{\frac{L}{C}} \qquad (2\text{-}34)$$

By clarifying the connections within classical physics, we can gain a better understanding of the abstract Hilbert or bosonic space.

2.2.1 Generating Hamiltonian of the Circuit

With the help of Kirchhoff's laws, we arrived at an equation by which it is determined how the magnetic flux oscillates, and the obtained equation is similar to the oscillation of a spring in classical physics. For this reason, we can define this dynamic system using classical physics tools that will help us in the process of quantizing the electrical circuit further. The quantization process involves first writing down the classical Lagrangian of the circuit, which is equal to the kinetic and potential energy difference, and identifying generalized coordinates and momenta in the circuit.

$$\mathcal{L}(\Phi, \dot{\Phi}) = \mathcal{E}_{cap}(\dot{\Phi}) - \mathcal{E}_{ind}(\Phi)$$
$$= \frac{1}{2}C\dot{\Phi}^2 - \frac{\Phi^2}{2L} \qquad (2\text{-}35)$$

In the next step, we have to derive the Hamiltonian of the equation. From the Lagrangian in Equation 2-35, we can derive the Hamiltonian using the Legendre transformation. To do so, we first compute the momentum conjugate to the flux, which, in this case, corresponds to the charge on the capacitor.

$$Q = \frac{\partial \mathcal{L}}{\partial \dot{\Phi}} = C\dot{\Phi} \qquad (2\text{-}36)$$

The Hamiltonian of the system is now defined as

$$H = Q\dot{\Phi} - \mathcal{L} = \frac{Q^2}{2C} + \frac{\Phi^2}{2L} \qquad (2\text{-}37)$$

Based on the extracted Hamiltonian relationship, the energy diagram of the oscillator is shown in Figure 2-3.

In classical physics and according to the obtained relations, we can consider the particle as a point on a parabola whose energy is changing between kinetic energy and potential or, in the case of electromagnetism, between the energy of the inductor and the capacitor. We assume that in relation to oscillator energy, the value of $L = C = 1$. We write the oscillator energy as a quantum energy value, where $\hbar$ is Planck's constant and n is an ordinary number.

$$E = \frac{1}{2}(Q^2 + \Phi^2) = \hbar\omega_0\left(n + \frac{1}{2}\right) \qquad (2\text{-}38)$$

2.2 Classical Electrodynamics of an LC Oscillator Circuit

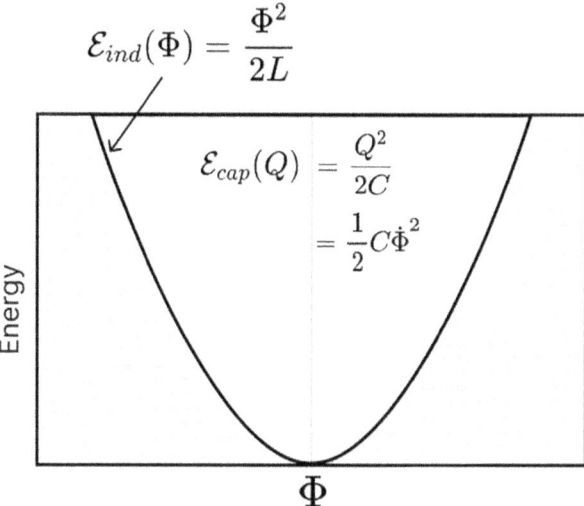

Figure 2-3 Harmonic energy $\mathcal{E}$ versus flux Φ for the LC oscillator

According to these relationships, the graph of Q in terms of Φ becomes concentric circles as shown in Figure 2-4. The smallest circle shows the oscillator's energy when $n = 1$, and the next circle shows the energy in the state of $n = 2$. In the same way, as the value of n increases, the amount of energy increases, and the point here is that the energy difference between two consecutive values of n is equal to $\hbar\omega_0$. If we want to express how the classical oscillator behaves with the help of this diagram, we place a point on one of the circles. The point shows the location and momentum of the particle.

Using Hamiltonian equations for motion, which provide an alternative way to express Kirchhoff's rules, we find that changes in magnetic flux depend on the position Q, and Q itself depends on Φ. This indicates that a positive charge initially creates a magnetic flux, which then leads to a current in the inductor. As the charge becomes negative, the polarity of the capacitor reverses, and this process repeats periodically (Figure 2-4).

Based on this process, a very useful variable α can be defined. Variable α is an imaginary variable that shows the location of a point in the phase space of the oscillator.

$$\alpha(t) = \sqrt{\frac{1}{2\hbar Z}}[\Phi(t) + iZQ(t)] \qquad (2\text{-}39)$$

$$\alpha^*(t) = \sqrt{\frac{1}{2\hbar Z}}[\Phi(t) - iZQ(t)] \qquad (2\text{-}40)$$

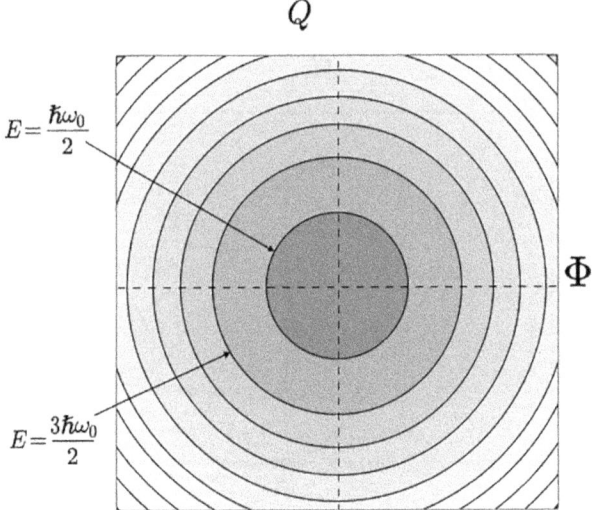

Figure 2-4 Phase space representation in the classical picture

with

$$\alpha(t) = \alpha(0)e^{-i\omega t} \tag{2-41}$$

These variables are very close to the creation and annihilation operators in quantum and act very similar to them. Therefore, we can write the Hamiltonian relation with the help of these variables.

$$\hat{H} = \frac{1}{2}\hbar\omega_0(\alpha^*\alpha + \alpha\alpha^*) \tag{2-42}$$

2.3 Quantum Hamiltonian of an LC Oscillator Circuit

The Heisenberg uncertainty principle is a fundamental concept in quantum mechanics that states there are inherent limits to how precisely we can simultaneously know certain pairs of physical properties of a particle, such as its position and momentum. The uncertainty principle is often described using the Heisenberg commutation relations, which mathematically express the limitations on our ability to measure these properties accurately.

The Heisenberg commutation relation involves two operators: the position operator ($\hat{x}$) and the momentum operator ($\hat{p}$). In quantum mechanics, operators are mathematical entities that represent observable quantities and how they act on

2.3 Quantum Hamiltonian of an LC Oscillator Circuit

quantum states. The Heisenberg commutation relation is given by

$$[\hat{x}, \hat{p}] = \hat{x}\hat{p} - \hat{p}\hat{x} = i\hbar \tag{2-43}$$

Dirac observed that in classical physics, there is a notion of the Poisson bracket, which relates classical variables x and p, which is analogous to the commutation relation. He connected classical mechanics with quantum mechanics through a systematic procedure that involved replacing classical variables (like position and momentum) with corresponding quantum operators. Dirac's approach was based on the principle that quantum observables should correspond to Hermitian operators, and the classical Poisson bracket $\{x, p\}$ should be replaced by commutation relation between these operators as $(1/i\hbar)[\hat{x}, \hat{p}]$.

The analogy discussed above can be used for our LC oscillator case where the classical variable $\Phi(t)$ and $Q(t)$ can be replaced by $\hat{\Phi}(t)$ and $\hat{Q}(t)$. Similarly, the following substitutions are made. The Hamiltonian operator $\hat{H}(\hat{\Phi}, \hat{Q})$ replaces the Hamiltonian function $H(\Phi, Q)$, and the commutation relation replaces the Poisson bracket. The Hamiltonian in the quantum regime is written as a sum of squares of two canonically conjugate variables.

$$\hat{H} = \frac{\hat{\Phi}^2}{2L} + \frac{\hat{Q}^2}{2C} \tag{2-44}$$

Further analogy needs to be made for $\alpha(t)$ and $\alpha^*(t)$ which are the phase space points. The classical description of $\alpha(t)$ and $\alpha^*(t)$ as mentioned in Equations 2-39 and 2-40 can be replaced by $\hat{a}$ and $\hat{a}^\dagger$ as follows:

$$\hat{a} = \sqrt{\frac{1}{2\hbar z}}(\hat{\Phi} + iZ\hat{Q}) \tag{2-45}$$

$$\hat{a}^\dagger = \sqrt{\frac{1}{2\hbar z}}(\hat{\Phi} - iZ\hat{Q}) \tag{2-46}$$

with the evolution of the operator in Heisenberg's picture described as

$$\hat{a}(t) = \hat{a}(0)e^{-i\omega t} \tag{2-47}$$

Conversely, following Equations 2-45 and 2-46, flux and charge operators can be written in terms of $\hat{a}$ and $\hat{a}^\dagger$ as

$$\hat{\Phi} = \Phi_{ZPF}(\hat{a}^\dagger + \hat{a}) \tag{2-48}$$

$$\hat{Q} = iQ_{ZPF}(\hat{a}^\dagger - \hat{a}) \tag{2-49}$$

where $\Phi_{ZPF} = \sqrt{\frac{\hbar}{2}Z_0}$ and $Q_{ZPF} = \sqrt{\frac{\hbar}{2}Z_0^{-1}}$. Here, Z_0 is circuit impedance as expressed in Equation 2-34.

By replacing $\hat{\Phi}$ and $\hat{Q}$ with Equations 2-48 and 2-49, Equation 2-44 becomes

$$\hat{H} = \hbar\omega_0(\hat{a}^\dagger\hat{a} + \hat{a}\hat{a}^\dagger) \qquad (2\text{-}50)$$

Using the commutation relation between $\hat{a}$ and $\hat{a}^\dagger$ in Equation 2-50, we get

$$\hat{H} = \hbar\omega_0\left(\hat{a}^\dagger\hat{a} + \frac{1}{2}\right) \qquad (2\text{-}51)$$

In quantum mechanics, the operators $\hat{a}$ and $\hat{a}^\dagger$ are known as ladder operators. The operator $\hat{a}$ acts as a lowering or annihilation operator, meaning it reduces the energy level of a quantum system. When applied to the lowest energy state $|0\rangle$, it yields a zero value since there's no lower energy state. When applied to a state like $|1\rangle$, it effectively lowers the state by one energy level, transitioning it to the state $|0\rangle$. This behavior is a fundamental property of ladder operators and is crucial in describing quantum systems and their energy states.

$$\hat{a}|0\rangle = 0$$

$$\hat{a}|1\rangle = \sqrt{1}|0\rangle$$

On the other hand, the adjoint operator $\hat{a}^\dagger$ is called the raising or creation operator and does the reverse operation:

$$\hat{a}^\dagger|1\rangle = \sqrt{1}|0\rangle$$

$$\hat{a}^\dagger|1\rangle = \sqrt{2}|2\rangle$$

The overall operation of the creation and annihilation operators can be summarized as

$$\hat{a}|n\rangle = \sqrt{n}|n-1\rangle$$
$$\hat{a}^\dagger|n\rangle = \sqrt{n+1}|n+1\rangle \qquad (2\text{-}52)$$

where, $n = 0, 1, 2 \ldots$.

In quantum mechanics, the Fock state or number state $|n\rangle$ represents a quantum system with a specific number n of quanta (particles or excitations). For instance, when $n = 0$, the state $|0\rangle$ corresponds to the lowest energy state, with no particles present. The operators $\hat{a}$ and $\hat{a}^\dagger$ are associated with annihilation and creation processes, respectively. The operator $\hat{a}$ removes one quantum from the system, effectively reducing the number of quanta by one. The operator $\hat{a}^\dagger$, on the other hand, adds one quantum to the system, increasing the number of quanta by one.

2.3 Quantum Hamiltonian of an LC Oscillator Circuit

The eigenvalues of these operators represent outcomes when measuring them on a specific quantum state. The eigenvalue of $\hat{a}$ is $\sqrt{n}$, where n is the initial number of quanta. Applying $\hat{a}$ on a state with n quanta results in a state with n quanta. Similarly, the eigenvalue of $\hat{a}^\dagger$ is $\sqrt{n+1}$, indicating that applying it on a state with n quanta yields a state with $n+1$ quanta. The matrix representations of $\hat{a}$ and $\hat{a}^\dagger$ demonstrate their actions on Fock states. For example, the matrix of $\hat{a}$ connects states with different quanta, reflecting the process of lowering the energy level by one quantum. These ladder operators and matrices are crucial in quantum mechanics, particularly for quantized harmonic oscillators and systems with discrete energy levels.

It's noteworthy that the multiplication of operators in quantum mechanics yields new operators. For instance, when we multiply the annihilation operator $\hat{a}$ and the creation operator $\hat{a}^\dagger$, we obtain the composite operator $\hat{a}\hat{a}^\dagger$. Similarly, the product $\hat{a}^\dagger\hat{a}$ is formed by multiplying $\hat{a}^\dagger$ and $\hat{a}$.

Consider the action of the operator $\hat{a}\hat{a}^\dagger$ on a quantum state $|n\rangle$, where $|n\rangle$ represents a state with n quanta. The sequence of operations involves the creation operator $\hat{a}^\dagger$ raising the energy level by one quantum, transitioning $|n\rangle$ to $|n+1\rangle$. Subsequently, the annihilation operator $\hat{a}$ acts on $|n+1\rangle$, returning the state to the original $|n\rangle$.

In the case of $\hat{a}^\dagger\hat{a}$, the order is reversed. $\hat{a}$ operates on $|n\rangle$, resulting in $|n-1\rangle$, followed by $\hat{a}^\dagger$ acting on $|n-1\rangle$, bringing it back to $|n\rangle$.

The eigenvalues of these composite operators can be determined. For $\hat{a}\hat{a}^\dagger$, the eigenvalue is $n+1$, indicating that applying this operator on a state with n quanta leads to a state with $n+1$ quanta. Likewise, for $\hat{a}^\dagger\hat{a}$, the eigenvalue is simply n, signifying that the operator maintains the number of quanta. These properties provide valuable insights into the dynamics and energy changes within quantum systems, particularly those described by ladder operators like $\hat{a}$ and $\hat{a}^\dagger$.

$$\hat{a}\hat{a}^\dagger|n\rangle = (n+1)|n\rangle$$
$$\hat{a}^\dagger\hat{a}|n\rangle = n|n\rangle \qquad (2\text{-}53)$$

We can use the eigenvalue of $\hat{a}^\dagger\hat{a}$ in Equation 2-53 and show that the quantum harmonics oscillator has energy as given below:

$$E_n = \left(n + \frac{1}{2}\right)\hbar\omega_0 \qquad (2\text{-}54)$$

where, $n = 1, 2, 3 \ldots$.

In the context of the harmonic oscillator, the variable n signifies the number of energy states within the system. When setting n to zero in the equation, a significant insight emerges. The outcome reveals the energy of the ground state as being equal to $\frac{1}{2}\hbar\omega_0$, where $\hbar$ represents the reduced Planck constant and ω_0 denotes the angular frequency. This discovery holds intriguing implications. It suggests that even when the quantum harmonic oscillator (QHO) lacks any excitations, there

Figure 2-5 Wave function of a quantum LC oscillator

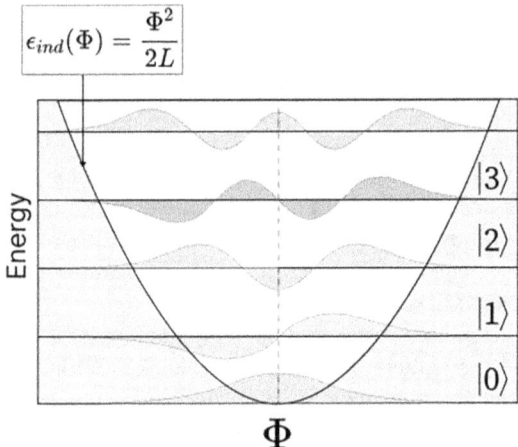

persists a presence of half the energy of a photon in the oscillator. This energy is known as zero-point energy (ZPE). This energy isn't rooted in classical mechanics and is a result of quantum fluctuations that exist even in the lowest energy state. These fluctuations, referred to as zero-point fluctuations (ZPF), underscore quantum systems' inherent uncertainty and dynamic nature.

We can further understand this by analyzing the mean value and variance of $\hat{\Phi}$ and $\hat{Q}$ in the ground state. We can show that the mean value of $\hat{\Phi}$ and $\hat{Q}$ is zero for any Fock state.

$$\hat{\Phi} = \langle n|\hat{\Phi}|n\rangle = 0$$
$$\hat{Q} = \langle n|\hat{Q}|n\rangle = 0 \qquad (2\text{-}55)$$

This observation implies that the average position of the quantum mechanical operators $\hat{Q}$ and $\hat{\Phi}$ in the phase space is always centered around zero. However, Equation 2-54 indicates that the quantum oscillator possesses energy even in its ground state, which seemingly contradicts this average zero position. This apparent discrepancy can be attributed to the presence of fluctuations. The fluctuations in the $\hat{\Phi}$ and $\hat{Q}$ operators are quantified by the variances of $(2n+1)$ times the zero-point fluctuations (Φ_{ZPF} and Q_{ZPF}, respectively). These considerations lead to the calculation of the root mean square deviations of $\hat{\Phi}$ and $\hat{Q}$, yielding $\sigma_{\hat{\Phi}} = \Phi_{ZPF}$ and $\sigma_{\hat{Q}} = Q_{ZPF}$.

Consequently, when attempting to measure $\hat{\Phi}$ as a function of time, the magnetic flux is observed to fluctuate around a value with an amplitude of Φ_{ZPF}. This highlights that even in the ground state, the electromagnetic oscillator exhibits perpetual motion due to these inherent fluctuations, akin to the behavior seen in atoms. This characteristic is also evident in the ground state's wave function in Figure 2-5, which takes the form of a Gaussian distribution with a mean value of zero and a variance of Φ_{ZPF}^2.

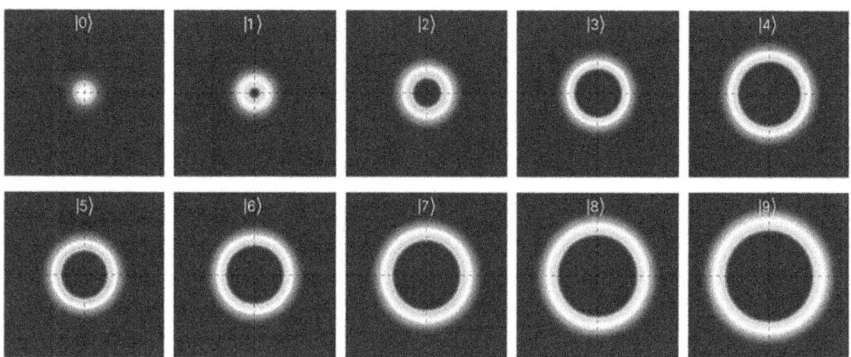

Figure 2-6 Quantum uncertainty cloud: phase space of $\hat{Q}$ and $\hat{\Phi}$ in the quantum picture

In Figure 2-5, the energy is plotted as a function of the magnetic flux. The quantum energy levels of the LC harmonic oscillator are determined by Equation 2-54. It starts from ground state $|0\rangle$ with its wave function or probability amplitude as a Gaussian function. It has a mean value of zero and variance of Φ_{ZPF}^2. We can observe in the figure that each energy level is separated by $\hbar\omega_0$, and each higher Fock level has an extra node.

To fully understand the behavior of the quantum picture of the LC oscillator, we need to analyze its phase space as well. As we saw in Figure 2-4, in the phase space of the classical picture, at constant energy it has a concentric ring centered at (0,0), and the particle will oscillate around the ring. In the quantum picture (Figure 2-6), the representation of phase space changes. The figure shows the Husimi Q function of various states in the phase space. The brighter the color, the more likely we are to find the particle or particular position in the phase space. In the ground state $|0\rangle$, we have a probability of finding a particle at (0,0). However, due to the non-commutativity of $\hat{Q}$ and $\hat{\Phi}$, we can't really measure the charge and magnetic flux simultaneously. There is a cloud of probability just like an atom. For higher excited states, the probability density looks like a donut shape. If we draw an analogy from the classical picture of Figure 2-6 here, we observe that each concentric ring is turned into a donut shape and gained a width of uncertainty.

2.4 Superconducting Qubits

In the LC quantum harmonic oscillator that we discussed, we saw that all the energy levels are separated by equal values. But, in order to achieve atom-like energy levels artificially, we need to have unequal energy differences between the states. Therefore, some degree of nonlinearity is required, and this can be made possible by using a nonlinear inductor element instead of a linear element between the two metal pads. This type of function can be achieved using a superconducting Josephson junction which acts as a nonlinear inductive element. Figure 2-7 shows the circuit

Figure 2-7 Nonlinear inductive element between two terminals

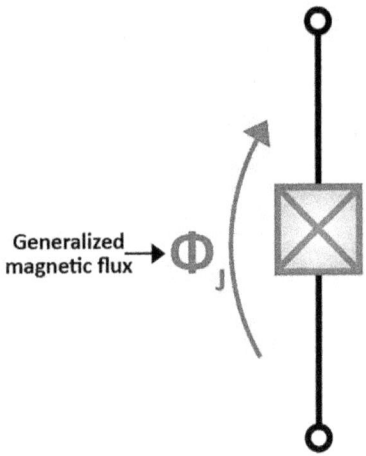

representation of a nonlinear inductive element between two terminals which has a change of magnetic flux Φ_j.

Josephson showed that a dissipationless current, that is, a supercurrent, could flow between two superconducting electrodes separated by a thin insulating barrier. Specifically, he established that this supercurrent can be described by the equation $I = I_c \sin \Phi$, where I_c represents the critical current of the junction, and Φ represents the phase difference between the superconducting condensates on either side of the junction. The critical current, dependent on factors like the junction's size and material properties, denotes the maximum current that can flow without breaking Cooper pairs. Beyond this point, dissipation occurs, resulting in the development of a finite voltage across the junction along with a resistive current. To operate in the quantum regime effectively, it is required to use currents well below this critical current threshold. Josephson also provided a crucial relationship between the time evolution of the phase difference, denoted as Φ, and the voltage across the junction. This relationship is expressed as $d\Phi/dt = 2\pi V/\Phi_0$, where $\Phi_0 = h/2e$ represents the flux quantum. It proves advantageous to express this equation as $\Phi(t) = 2\pi \Phi(t_0)/\Phi_0 \pmod{2\pi}$, where $\Phi(t)$ is the flux variable. The "mod 2π" term in these equations accounts for the fact that the superconducting phase Φ is a compact variable constrained to the unit circle, meaning $\Phi = \Phi + 2\pi$, while Φ_0 can take arbitrary real values.

2.4.1 Basic Types of Superconducting Qubits

The quantum state of the qubit can be manipulated through the application of electromagnetic pulses, which can control the magnetic flux, electric charge, or phase difference across a Josephson junction. One can insert additional inductors, capacitors, and Josephson junctions in the simple circuit of the LC oscillator as

2.4 Superconducting Qubits

Figure 2-8 (a) Schematic circuit diagram of a phase qubit consisting of a current-biased Josephson junction, (b) a non-linear potential plot of the phase qubit with two lowest qubit states $|0\rangle$ and $|1\rangle$

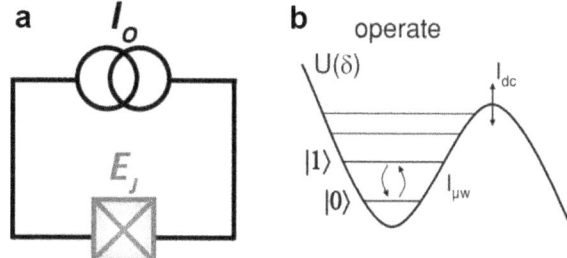

shown in Figure 2-2 to achieve certain design goals. The shape of the potential energy landscape and the nature of the encoding of the qubit states (charge, flux, etc.) depend on the relative strengths of the energies associated with these various circuit elements, including the Josephson energy E_J, the capacitive charging energy E_C, and the inductive energy E_L. One can tune the underlying circuit parameters and can engineer various qubit properties, including transition frequency, anharmonicity, and sensitivity to various noise sources. The three basic types of qubits are phase qubit, charge qubit, and flux qubit.

2.4.1.1 Phase Qubit

The phase qubit operates based on the phase difference across a Josephson junction and is arguably the first one explored in the family of superconducting qubits. In 1985, John M. Martinis, Michel H. Devoret, and John Clarke successfully demonstrated the quantization of energy levels associated with a microscopic variable: the phase difference across a Josephson junction subjected to a current bias (Martinis et al., 1985). This marked the pioneering development of an artificial electrical atom that harnesses the quantum properties of phase.

This qubit operates in the $E_J \gg E_C$ regime. It comprises a sizeable Josephson junction (with a ratio $E_J/E_C \approx 10^6$) regulated by an applied bias current I_b. The bias current skews the $\cos\phi$ potential with a linear term, resulting in the so-called tilted washboard potential (see Figure 2-8b). The bias determines the tilt of the potential and is usually tuned close to the critical current I_c. The Hamiltonian of the circuit is given by

$$H = \frac{2\pi}{\Phi_0} \frac{p^2}{2C_J} - \frac{\Phi_0}{2\pi} I_b \phi - E_J \cos\phi \tag{2-56}$$

The momentum term, denoted as p, is determined by the charge Q on the capacitance of the Josephson junction, given by $Q = 2ep/\hbar$. The quantization process is then carried out, treating ϕ as the corresponding coordinate conjugate to this momentum. The tilt is chosen such that only three to ten states remain in each of the local minima of the well, but the computational basis can be formed by the lowest two states at any minimum. In a simplified two-level approximation,

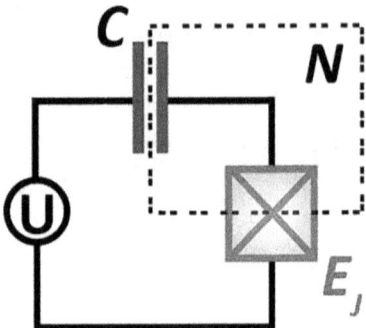

Figure 2-9 Schematic circuit diagram of a charge qubit

the phase qubit has two primary current energy states: $|0\rangle$ and $|1\rangle$. These states correspond to different phase differences across the junction.

2.4.1.2 Charge Qubit

It is a type of superconducting qubit that encodes quantum information in the charge states of Cooper pairs. Charge qubits are one of the earliest and simplest designs for superconducting qubits, as displayed in Figure 2-9. The first temporal coherence in a superconducting circuit was observed in a variant of the charge qubit known as the Cooper pair box (Bouchiat et al., 1998) (Nakamura et al., 1999). The fundamental principle behind charge qubits is the quantization of charge in a superconducting island, which is typically connected to a reservoir by one or more Josephson junctions. Charge qubits rely on the manipulation of the charge states on the island. The charge on the island can take on discrete values, such as 0, 1, 2, etc., corresponding to the number of excess Cooper pairs. These charge states are analogous to the binary 0 and 1 states of classical bits.

The Josephson inductance in the Cooper pair box is defined as

$$L_J(\Phi) = \left(\frac{\partial I}{\partial \Phi}\right)^{-1} = \frac{\Phi_0}{2\pi I_c} \frac{1}{\cos(2\pi \Phi/\Phi_0)} \qquad (2\text{-}57)$$

The energy of the nonlinear inductance takes the form of

$$E = I_c \int dt \left(\frac{d\Phi}{dt}\right) \sin\left(2\pi \frac{\Phi}{\Phi_0}\right) = -E_J \cos\left(2\pi \frac{\Phi}{\Phi_0}\right) \qquad (2\text{-}58)$$

where $E_J = \Phi_0 I_c / 2\pi$. This quantity is known as the Josephson energy which depends upon the rate of tunneling of Cooper pairs across the junction.

We need to take into account the contribution of this energy in the construction of the Hamiltonian of capacitively shunted Josephson junction. The quantized Hamiltonian of the circuit is therefore given by

$$\hat{H} = 4E_C(\hat{N} - n_g)^2 - E_J \cos\hat{\Phi} \qquad (2\text{-}59)$$

2.4 Superconducting Qubits

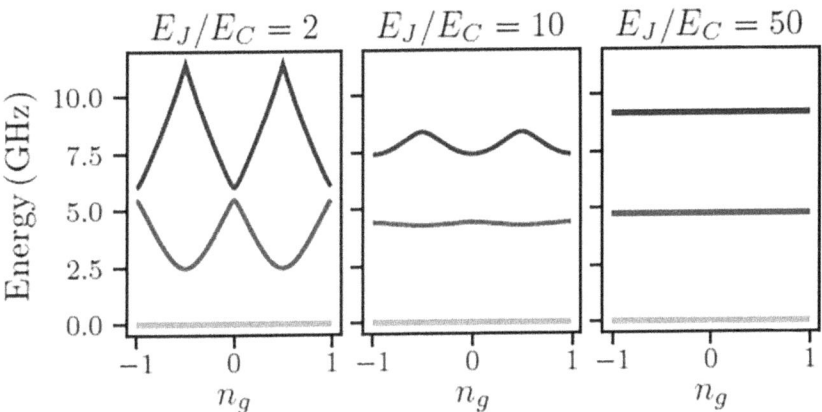

Figure 2-10 The frequency difference $\Delta\omega$ for the first three energy levels of the transmon Hamiltonian, obtained through numerical diagonalization of Equation 2-59 in the charge basis $\{|n\rangle\}$, is shown across various E_J/E_C ratios. The energy levels become insensitive to the offset charge for large values of E_J/E_C

where the charge number operator $\hat{N} = \hat{Q}/2e$ denotes the number of excess Cooper pairs on the island, $\hat{\phi}$ is the 2π-periodic operator of the phase difference across the Josephson junction, and the operators satisfy the commutation relation $[\hat{\phi}, \hat{N}] = i$. A capacitively coupled gate voltage is used to control the deviations in charge $n_g = Q_g/2e$ from the preferred charge state which is known as an offset charge. Selecting appropriate values for E_J and E_C is crucial in defining the system's sensitivity to the offset charge.

The Hamiltonian spectrum depends upon the E_J/E_c ratio. Different values of this ratio determine different types of qubits. Figure 2-10 illustrates the energy difference $\Delta\omega$ for the three lowest energy levels at various E_J/E_C ratios, as obtained through numerical diagonalization of Equation 2-59.

Charge qubits are designed in the regime $E_C \geq E_J$, such that the island charge is a good quantum number. The eigenstates of the Hamiltonian are approximately given by the eigenstates of the charge operator. The bare qubit states are $|N\rangle$ and $|N+1\rangle$, corresponding to the absence and presence of an additional Cooper pair on the island. By tuning the gate voltage, the charge state on the island can be changed, allowing for state manipulation. The readout is typically achieved by monitoring the charge or current on the island, which is sensitive to the charge state of the qubit.

The Josephson junction acts as a valve for Cooper pairs and couples these states, opening an avoided crossing of size E_J at integer multiples of offset charge $n_g = 1/2$. Although charge qubits have a large anharmonicity, $\alpha \approx \omega_{12}/2\pi - \omega_{01}/2\pi > 10\,\text{GHz}$, their lifetimes and dephasing are strongly limited by environmental charge noise. Charge noise arises from random fluctuations in the number of Cooper pairs on the island and can be a major source of decoherence. In addition, the small size of the island and Josephson junction leads to a strong susceptibility to stray capacitance, local defects, and fabrication variation, resulting in large device-to-device variability. To address these challenges, a substantial shunt capacitor has been incorporated into the charge qubit, commonly referred to as the transmon qubit, which we will be discussing extensively in the next section.

2.4.1.3 Flux Qubit

This type of superconducting qubit encodes quantum information in the magnetic flux threading a superconducting loop. This loop is interrupted by a small Josephson junction, which serves as a nonlinear inductive element, in series with either a linear inductor or several larger-area Josephson junctions acting as effective inductors. The small junction acts as a valve for magnetic flux quanta (fluxons), allowing controlled entry or exit of flux into the superconducting loop, thereby enabling precise manipulation of the qubit states. The schematic of a flux qubit is displayed in Figure 2-11.

The small Josephson junction effectively serves as a gate for magnetic fluxons. The presence or absence of these fluxons corresponds to two distinct quantum states, represented by clockwise or counterclockwise circulating supercurrents in the loop. These circulating currents satisfy the flux quantization condition, which states that the total magnetic flux threading the loop, including contributions from external fields and currents, must be quantized in units of the magnetic flux quantum $\Phi_0 = h/2e$. This condition arises due to the single-valuedness of the superconducting wave function. The interplay between the Josephson junctions, the linear inductances, and the externally applied magnetic field determines the dynamics of the system and the accessible quantum states.

The operation of a flux qubit fundamentally relies on the phenomenon of quantum superposition and interference. When the magnetic flux through the loop is close to half-integer multiples of Φ_0 (e.g., $\Phi \approx \Phi_0/2$), the two states corresponding to clockwise and counterclockwise currents become nearly degenerate. In this regime, quantum tunneling between the two states occurs, leading to the formation of symmetric and antisymmetric superpositions of these states. The energy splitting between these superposition states defines the qubit's transition frequency. The

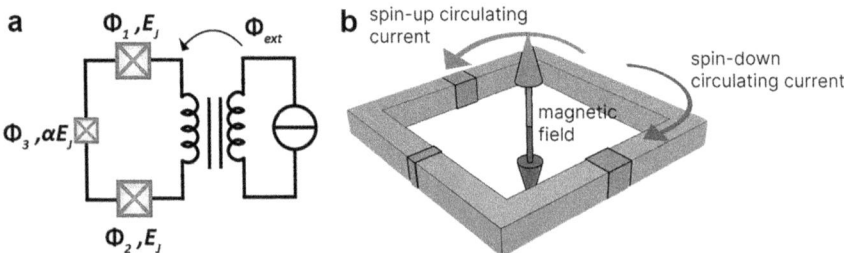

Figure 2-11 Three-junction flux qubit. (**a**) Circuit schematic of a three-junction flux qubit. The third junction is referred to as the alpha junction and has α times lower critical current than the other junctions. (**b**) Equivalent superconducting loop current flowing in the clockwise and counterclockwise directions

2.4 Superconducting Qubits

strength of the coupling is determined by factors such as E_J (Josephson energy), E_C (charging energy), and E_L (inductive energy).

A flux qubit consists of a superconducting loop interrupted by one Josephson junction (Friedman et al., 2000) or three Josephson junctions (van der Wal et al., 2000). In practice, the single-junction flux qubit suffers from strong dephasing due to the relatively large loop inductance, which generates strong magnetic fields coupling the qubit to the environment. This coupling introduces noise, degrading coherence. The three-junction flux qubit addresses this issue by effectively using the additional junctions to replace the loop inductance, reducing environmental coupling and enhancing qubit performance.

In the three-junction design, two of the junctions are identical, with Josephson energy E_J and capacitance C_J, while the third junction is smaller by a factor $\alpha < 1$. This results in reduced Josephson energy $\alpha \cdot E_J$ and capacitance $\alpha \cdot C_J$. The system operates in a regime where the ratio of Josephson energy to charging energy (E_J/E_C) is typically large, around 50, ensuring that the phase difference across the junctions, δ, is the primary quantum variable. This phase difference is directly related to the magnetic flux Φ threading the loop. The two quantum states of the flux qubit correspond to clockwise ($|\downarrow\rangle$) and counterclockwise ($|\uparrow\rangle$) circulating supercurrents in the loop, which can also be interpreted as the magnetic flux Φ pointing "up" or "down."

The potential energy landscape of the flux qubit is a double-well potential, as shown in Figure 2-12. The left well represents the zero-fluxoid state, while the right well corresponds to the one-fluxoid state, associated with clockwise and counterclockwise circulating currents, respectively. When the externally applied magnetic flux Φ_e satisfies

$$\Phi_e = \left(n + \frac{1}{2}\right)\Phi_0, \tag{2-60}$$

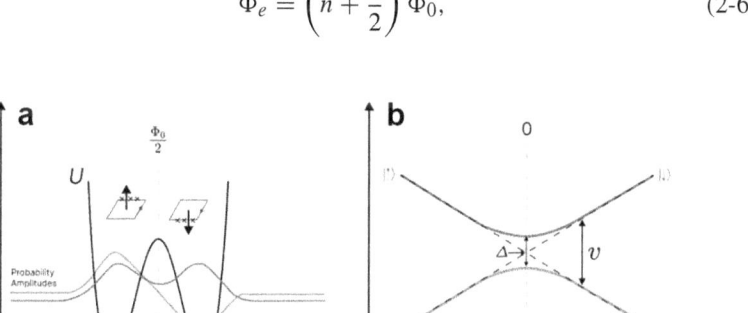

Figure 2-12 (a) The two well potential (black) versus the total flux Φ enclosed within the flux qubit. The eigenfunctions, represented by the colored curves, depict the probability amplitudes for the ground state (symmetrical, red) and the first excited state (antisymmetrical, blue). (b) The energy E of the two superposition states versus the energy bias ϵ

where n is an integer and $\Phi_0 = h/2e$ is the magnetic flux quantum, the potential becomes symmetric. In this condition, the two lowest-energy eigenstates are quantum superpositions of the basis states, formed by symmetric and antisymmetric combinations.

The potential energy difference between the wells defines the energy bias ϵ, while the tunneling energy Δ between the wells quantifies the coupling between the states. This system is effectively modeled as a two-level Hamiltonian:

$$\hat{H}_{\mathrm{TL}} = \epsilon(\Phi_z)\hat{\sigma}_z + \Delta\hat{\sigma}_x, \tag{2-61}$$

where $\epsilon = 2I_q(\Phi_e - \Phi_0/2)$, I_q is the circulating current, and Δ is the tunneling energy at $\Phi_e = \Phi_0/2$. The qubit transition frequency is given by

$$\omega_q = \sqrt{\epsilon^2 + \Delta^2}, \tag{2-62}$$

and the system behaves like a spin-1/2 particle in an effective magnetic field.

To enhance tunability, the smaller Josephson junction can be replaced by a secondary dc-SQUID loop. This modification allows Δ and ϵ to be tuned by external magnetic fluxes Φ_x and Φ_z, respectively, leading to a modified Hamiltonian:

$$\hat{H}'_{\mathrm{TL}} = \epsilon(\Phi_z, \Phi_x)\hat{\sigma}_z + \Delta(\Phi_x)\hat{\sigma}_x. \tag{2-63}$$

This flexibility transforms the flux qubit into a highly versatile spin-1/2 system with independently tunable effective fields along the z and x directions. Such tunability is critical for applications in quantum annealing, where the qubit is used to implement the transverse Ising Hamiltonian for solving optimization problems (Hauke et al., 2020).

Operating in the regime of $E_J \gg E_C$, flux qubits are largely insensitive to charge noise, a significant advantage over charge-based qubits. Additionally, the strong anharmonicity of their energy levels enables clear state discrimination, while their coherence times have been significantly improved over the years. Early flux qubits achieved coherence times exceeding $10\,\mu s$, and subsequent advancements pushed this boundary to over $23\,\mu s$, demonstrating their viability for scalable quantum computation.

To summarize, Table 2-1 provides a comprehensive comparison of three fundamental types of superconducting qubits, highlighting key parameters and characteristics that are essential for understanding their distinct properties.

2.5 Transmon Qubit

Transmon qubits are a specific type of charge qubits, distinguished by the inclusion of a large shunt capacitor in the circuit. This shunt capacitor significantly reduces the qubit's charging energy E_C relative to its Josephson energy E_J, with typical

2.5 Transmon Qubit

Table 2-1 Comparison of three fundamental superconducting qubit types and key parameters

Qubit types/parameters	Phase qubit	Charge qubit	Flux qubit
Operational principle	Based on the phase difference of the superconducting wave function across Josephson junctions	Based on the charge states of Cooper pairs on a superconducting Josephson junction	Based on the magnetic flux through a super conducting loop interrupted by Josephson junctions
Qubit states	States correspond to two levels of current energy in a Josephson junction	States correspond to two levels of charge of Cooper pairs of the Josephson junction	States correspond to two directions of superconducting current flow in its loop
Relation between EJ and EC	EJ >> EC	EJ < EC	EJ > EC
Qubit readout	Dispersion or resonant readout using microwave pulses	Charge sensing or transduction using RF pulses	Readout using a magnetometer (SQUID)
Coherence time	Relatively short coherence times (μs to ms)	Moderately short coherence time (μs to ms)	Relatively long coherence times (tens of μs to ms)
Anharmonicity	Moderate to high	Moderate	High
Noise sensitivity	Sensitive to charge noise and flux noise	Sensitive to charge noise and flux noise	Sensitive to magnetic flux noise
Decoherence mechanics	Flux noise, charge noise, and geometrical effects	Charge fluctuations, charge tunneling	Flux noise, environmental interference
Complexity	Relatively complex, requires multiple control lines and complex wirings	Relatively simple, requires fewer control lines and simpler wirings	Relatively complex, requires multiple control lines and complex wirings
Notable features	Sensitive to geometric and charge effects	Well-established, widely used in quantum devices	Unique flux-based properties
Notable examples	—	Transmon, Xmon, Gmon	Fluxonium

ratios E_J/E_C ranging from 20 to 80. By making E_C small, the energy levels become less dependent on the number of Cooper pairs (charge states), thereby delocalizing the charge degree of freedom. This delocalization reduces the qubit's sensitivity to charge noise, a common source of decoherence in traditional charge qubits. Consequently, transmon qubits exhibit improved coherence properties and high anharmonicity, enabling reliable qubit state manipulation and readout.

In a transmon qubit, the energy function of the Josephson junction is expressed as

$$\mathcal{E}_J(\Phi) = -E_J \cos\left(\frac{\Phi}{\Phi_0}\right), \tag{2-64}$$

where Φ is the phase difference across the junction, and $\Phi_0 = h/2e$ is the flux quantum. Expanding the cosine term into a Taylor series around $\Phi = 0$ gives

$$\mathcal{E}_J(\Phi) = \frac{E_J}{2}\left(\frac{\Phi}{\Phi_0}\right)^2 - \frac{E_J}{4!}\left(\frac{\Phi}{\Phi_0}\right)^4 + O\left(\Phi_j^6\right). \qquad (2\text{-}65)$$

This expansion separates the energy into two parts:

1. **Linear Part**: The quadratic term, $\mathcal{E}_J^{\text{lin}}(\Phi) = \frac{E_J}{2}\left(\frac{\Phi}{\Phi_0}\right)^2$, corresponds to the harmonic energy of a linear LC oscillator.
2. **Nonlinear Part**: The higher-order terms, such as $\mathcal{E}_J^{\text{nl}}(\Phi) = -\frac{E_J}{4!}\left(\frac{\Phi}{\Phi_0}\right)^4$, introduce nonlinearity into the system. These terms are critical for defining the transmon qubit's anharmonicity, as they break the harmonicity of the energy levels.

To simplify the analysis, we typically ignore terms of order Φ_j^6 and higher, as these introduce nonlinearity that is both negligible and difficult to control in practical systems.

Nonlinear Inductance Representation
The Josephson junction, as a nonlinear inductive element, can be conceptually split into two components:

- **Linear Inductive Element**: Represented by the quadratic term, shown in red in Figure 2-13, this part is analogous to the inductor in a linear LC quantum oscillator.

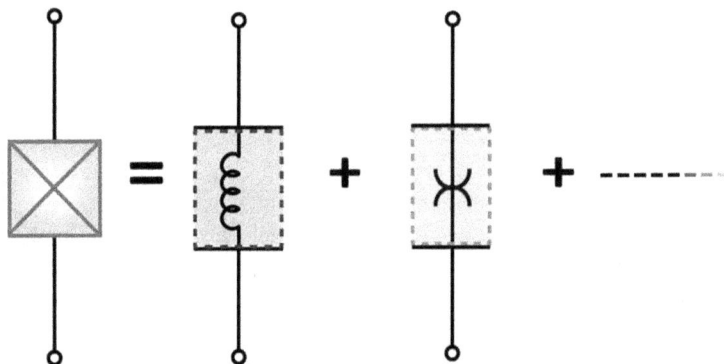

Figure 2-13 Nonlinear inductor split into linear part (marked in red color) and nonlinear part (marked in orange color)

2.5 Transmon Qubit

- **Nonlinear Inductive Element**: Represented by the higher-order terms, shown in orange in Figure 2-13, this part is responsible for the anharmonicity of the transmon's energy levels.

2.5.1 Classical Hamiltonian of Transmon Qubit

The energy stored in the Josephson junction is described as a cosine potential, while the capacitive energy remains quadratic, as in a linear LC oscillator:

$$\mathcal{E}_J(\Phi) = -E_J \cos\left(\frac{\Phi}{\Phi_0}\right),$$

$$\mathcal{E}_{\text{cap}}(\dot{\Phi}) = \frac{1}{2}C\dot{\Phi}^2, \tag{2-66}$$

Figure 2-14 illustrates the energy landscape of the Josephson junction. The cosine curve represents the actual potential energy landscape, oscillating between $+E_J$ and $-E_J$. The shaded region indicates the classically forbidden region, where a particle cannot exist at the given energy due to energy constraints.

For small phase differences ($\Phi \ll \Phi_0$), the cosine potential can be approximated to first order as a quadratic function. The dashed parabola in Figure 2-14 shows this approximation. The potential energy of the Josephson junction is nearly equal to this quadratic function in the regime of low excitation, where the system is close

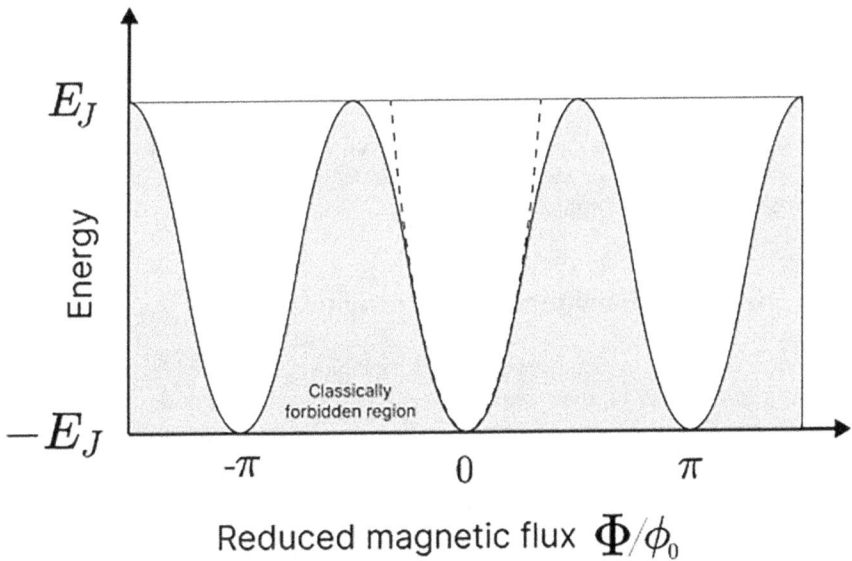

Figure 2-14 Actual and approximated energy of the Josephson junction as a function of the reduced magnetic flux

to the zero flux point. This approximation aligns with the behavior of a harmonic oscillator.

2.5.1.1 Classical Hamiltonian
The classical Hamiltonian of the Josephson junction is given by

$$\mathcal{H}(\Phi, Q) = \frac{Q^2}{2C} - E_J \cos\left(\frac{\Phi}{\Phi_0}\right), \tag{2-67}$$

This Hamiltonian describes the total energy of the system, accounting for both capacitive and inductive contributions.

Using semi-classical intuition, the energy levels of the system can be quantized. The quantized energy levels are

$$E_n = \left(n + \frac{1}{2}\right)\hbar\omega_0 = \frac{Q^2}{2C} - E_J \cos\left(\frac{\Phi}{\Phi_0}\right) \tag{2-68}$$

where n is the quantum number and ω_0 is the fundamental frequency of the oscillator. These quantized energy levels are modified by the nonlinearity introduced by the Josephson junction.

2.5.1.2 Energy Landscape in a 2D Plane
The energy function can also be visualized in a 2D plane of Q and Φ as shown in Figure 2-15.

In Figure 2-15

- The contours of constant energy represent the classical trajectories of the particle.
- At low quantum numbers, these trajectories are nearly circular, corresponding to harmonic behavior.
- As the quantum numbers increase, the trajectories become elliptical, reflecting the nonlinear nature of the system. This transition leads to the anharmonicity that characterizes the transmon qubit and enables selective qubit control.

2.5.2 Quantum Hamiltonian of Transmon Qubit

In the quantum picture, the charge and flux variables are replaced by operators. As shown in Equation 2-44, the same linear term observed earlier in the LC oscillator appears, along with quadratic terms involving the charge operator $\hat{Q}$ and the flux operator $\hat{\Phi}$. Additionally, a fourth-order term of the flux operator $\hat{\Phi}$ introduces nonlinearity.

$$\hat{H} = \frac{\hat{Q}^2}{2C} + \frac{\hat{\Phi}^2}{2L} - \frac{E_j}{4!}\left(\frac{\hat{\Phi}}{\phi_0}\right)^4 \tag{2-69}$$

2.5 Transmon Qubit

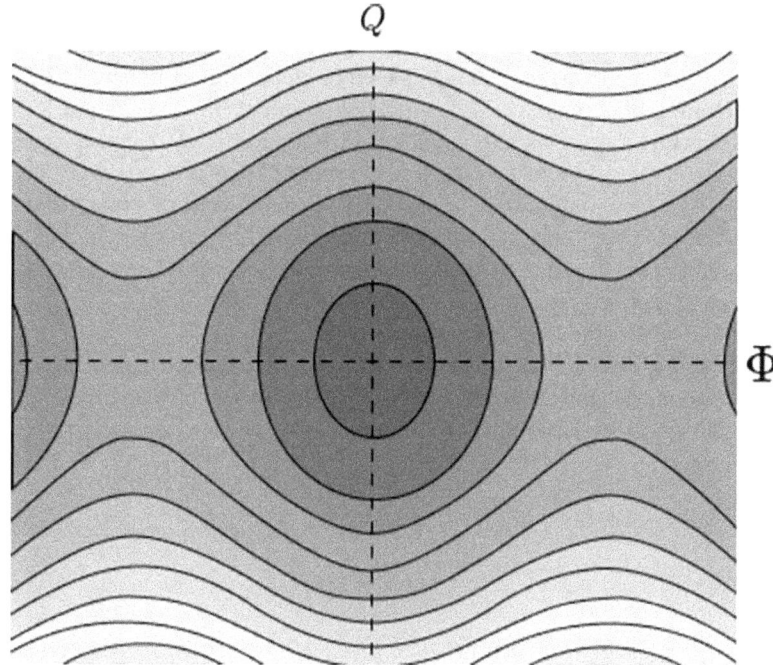

Figure 2-15 Josephson junction energy function in a 2D plane

We can simplify this Hamiltonian by leveraging the solutions from simple harmonic motion, substituting the operators $\hat{a}$ and $\hat{a}^\dagger$ for the charge $\hat{Q}$ and flux $\hat{\Phi}$. After substituting the expression for the operator $\hat{\Phi}$ as given in the equation, the Hamiltonian can be reformulated as follows:

$$\hat{H} = \hbar\omega_0 \hat{a}^\dagger \hat{a} - \frac{E_j \phi_{ZPF}^4}{4!}(\hat{a} + \hat{a}^\dagger)^4 \tag{2-70}$$

The Hamiltonian can be decomposed into two parts: the first term represents the linear Hamiltonian, H_{lin}, while the second term represents the nonlinear Hamiltonian, H_{nl}. Expanding $(\hat{a} + \hat{a}^\dagger)^4$ in H_{nl} yields several terms. For example, consider the term $\hat{a}\hat{a}\hat{a}^\dagger\hat{a}$. By leveraging the non-commutativity of $\hat{a}$ and $\hat{a}^\dagger$, this term can be rewritten as a combination of $\hat{a}^\dagger \hat{a}^3$ and $\hat{a}^2$. These components correspond to four-wave and two-wave interactions, respectively.

These interactions are described using the phase space representation of the operators. The operator $\hat{a}$ represents a wave that evolves in time as $\hat{a}(t) = \hat{a}(0)e^{-i\omega_0 t}$, corresponding to a clockwise rotation in phase space with angular frequency ω_0. Conversely, $\hat{a}^\dagger(t) = \hat{a}^\dagger(0)e^{i\omega_0 t}$ evolves as a counterclockwise rotation. When $\hat{a}$ and $\hat{a}^\dagger$ interact, their respective rotations in phase space interfere. The resulting dynamics depend on the sum of their frequencies, with clockwise and counterclockwise rotations contributing constructively or destructively. These interference effects underlie the two-wave and four-wave interactions.

In a two-wave interaction, the terms represent processes where two waves interact to modify the system's energy. For example, $\hat{a}^2$ indicates a scenario where two identical wave-like excitations in phase space interfere constructively or destructively, influencing the evolution of the system. This interaction is relatively simpler, as it involves only the creation or annihilation of pairs of wave-like quanta. The four-wave interaction, represented by terms like $\hat{a}^\dagger \hat{a}^3$, is more complex. Here, three quanta (waves) interact to generate or annihilate a fourth wave. This process is crucial in nonlinear systems, as it introduces higher-order effects, such as energy redistribution among the interacting waves.

By expanding the Hamiltonian in terms of these wave interactions, we capture the nonlinear phenomena that govern the system's behavior. After the rotating wave approximation (RWA), Equation 2-70 becomes

$$\hat{H}_4^{RWA} = \hbar\left(\omega_0 - \Delta_q\right)\hat{a}^\dagger \hat{a} - \frac{\hbar\alpha}{2}\hat{a}^{\dagger 2}\hat{a}^2 \qquad (2\text{-}71)$$

where

$$\hbar\Delta_q = \hbar\alpha \equiv \frac{1}{2}E_J\phi_{ZPF}^4 \qquad (2\text{-}72)$$

In the first term of Equation 2-71, Δ_q arises from the commutation relation, which is a direct consequence of the system's nonlinearity. The linear frequency of the oscillator undergoes renormalization due to zero-point quantum fluctuations. By substituting $\hat{a}^\dagger \hat{a}$ with the number operator $\hat{N}$, the Hamiltonian can be expressed under the rotating wave approximation as

$$\hat{H}_4^{RWA} \approx \hbar\omega_q \hat{N} - \frac{\hbar\alpha}{2}\hat{N}(\hat{N} - 1) \qquad (2\text{-}73)$$

Here, ω_q denotes the qubit frequency, defined as $\omega_q = \omega_0 - \Delta_q$, where ω_0 is the frequency of the linear part of the qubit. In this Hamiltonian, the eigenstates of the linear part are already known from the harmonic oscillator solution. The nonlinear term can be treated as a perturbation to the linear Hamiltonian.

Using first-order perturbation theory, we can determine the corrections to the eigenenergy and eigenstates. In first-order perturbation theory in quantum mechanics, we approximate the true energy and eigenstates of a system by treating the Hamiltonian as a sum of two parts: the unperturbed Hamiltonian, which has known eigenstates and eigenvalues, and a small perturbing Hamiltonian that introduces corrections to the system. The goal is to find the first-order corrections to both the energy and the wave function due to this perturbation.

The first-order corrections to the energy and eigenstate are given by

$$E_n^{(1)} = \langle n^{(0)}|\hat{H}_{nl}|n^{(0)}\rangle \qquad (2\text{-}74)$$

2.5 Transmon Qubit

$$|n^{(1)}\rangle = \sum_{k \neq n} \frac{\langle k^{(0)}|\hat{H}_{nl}|n^{(0)}\rangle}{E_n^{(0)} - E_k^{(0)}} |k^{(0)}\rangle \quad (2\text{-}75)$$

Equation 2-74 provides the first-order correction to the energy of the n-th state, denoted by $E_n^{(1)}$. This correction is simply the expectation value of the perturbing Hamiltonian $\hat{H}_{nl}$ in the unperturbed state $|n^{(0)}\rangle$. In other words, we calculate the matrix element $\langle n^{(0)}|\hat{H}_{nl}|n^{(0)}\rangle$, which represents how the perturbation affects the energy of the system when the system is in the unperturbed state. The result gives the first-order energy correction due to the perturbation. The energy of the unperturbed state is $E_n^{(0)}$, and the correction $E_n^{(1)}$ is added to it.

The first-order correction to the wave function, denoted by $|n^{(1)}\rangle$, is provided by Equation 2-75. The corrected wave function is expressed as a sum over all other unperturbed states $|k^{(0)}\rangle$ with $k \neq n$. The coefficients of this sum are determined by the matrix elements $\langle k^{(0)}|\hat{H}_{nl}|n^{(0)}\rangle$ of the perturbing Hamiltonian between the states $|n^{(0)}\rangle$ and $|k^{(0)}\rangle$, divided by the energy difference $E_n^{(0)} - E_k^{(0)}$. This term describes how the perturbation causes the unperturbed state $|n^{(0)}\rangle$ to mix with other states $|k^{(0)}\rangle$, leading to a correction in the wave function. The first-order correction to the wave function takes into account all such interactions with other states, and it is a linear combination of all unperturbed states, weighted by the strength of the perturbation and the energy differences between the states.

We can use the above equation from the first-order perturbation theory to find the energy eigenvalue and eigenstates of the Hamiltonian. We see that the eigenstate doesn't change due to perturbation. This behavior can be understood from Figure 2-14 as well. For the first-order perturbation, the solid and dashed curves are nearly the same.

To understand the theory from an experimental perspective, let us consider some typical parameters of a transmon qubit. Suppose the capacitance between the two metal pads is $C_J = 65$ fF, and the inductance associated with the nonlinear inductor is $L_J = 14$ nH. These parameters correspond to a Josephson junction energy of $E_J = 12$ GHz, a charging energy of $E_C = 0.3$ GHz, a qubit frequency of $\omega_q = 5$ GHz, and an anharmonicity of $\alpha = 0.3$ GHz.

The quantized wave functions of the transmon qubit corresponding to these parameters are plotted in Figure 2-16. The ground state exhibits the same characteristics as previously discussed in Figure 2-5. It has a mean value of zero and a standard deviation of Φ_{ZPF}. Examining the quantized wave functions of the oscillator, we observe that the first-order approximation works well for the low-lying excited states. However, as we move to higher excited states, the approximation becomes less accurate. Nevertheless, for qubit operations, our primary focus is on the two lowest energy levels, which adhere well to the approximation.

Using the specified experimental parameters, the energy difference between the second and the first excited states is $\omega_q - \alpha = 4.7$ GHz, while the energy difference between the first excited state and the ground state is $\omega_q = 5$ GHz. By employing

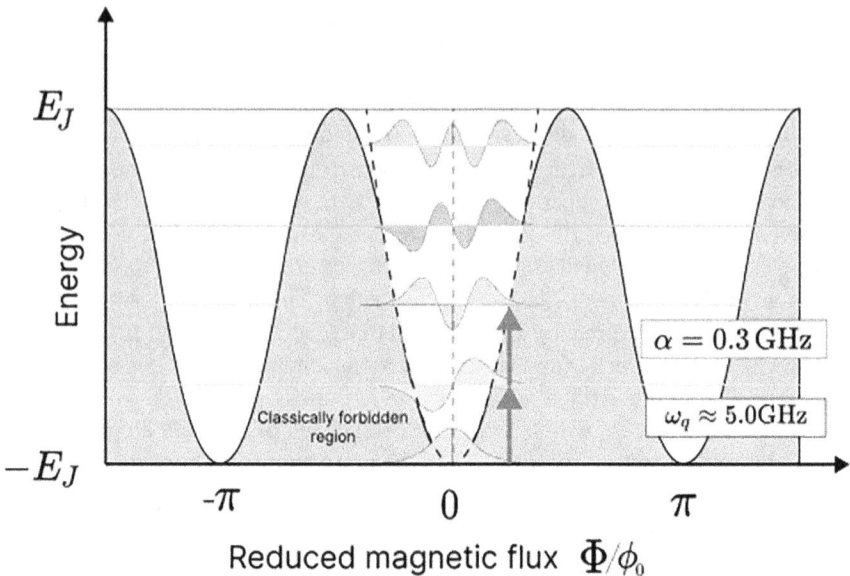

Figure 2-16 Wave function of a quantum oscillator with nonlinear inductor

the Josephson junction as a nonlinear inductor, we achieve an anharmonic energy level diagram where the levels are no longer uniformly spaced.

The actual parameters for zero-point fluctuations of charge and flux are $\Phi_{ZPF}/\Phi_0 = 0.5$ and $Q_{ZPF}/2e = 1.0$. These values suggest that in the ground state, approximately one Cooper pair fluctuates back and forth between the metal pads. Compared to the presence of 10^{12} electrons in each metal pad, a single Cooper pair represents an extremely small fraction of the charge. This is why it is essential to operate the qubit at extremely low temperatures.

To drive a qubit, a photon with a frequency equal to the energy difference between the relevant levels is required. For example, exciting a qubit from the ground state to the first excited level requires a photon with a frequency of ω_q. This transition results in a peak in the transition spectrum at ω_q. Similarly, frequency peaks corresponding to transitions between other energy levels can be observed in the spectrum. By applying or controlling a pulse within a narrow frequency range centered around $\omega_{01} = \omega_q$, we can isolate the transition from the ground state to the first excited level. This isolation is crucial for qubit operation, as it effectively confines the system's dynamics to the qubit's Hilbert space.

This concept can also be interpreted through the operators $\hat{a}$, $\hat{a}^\dagger$, and $\hat{a}^\dagger \hat{a}$. When focusing on these operators, we consider only the initial 2×2 matrix corresponding to the Fock states $|0\rangle$ and $|1\rangle$. Restricting the Hilbert space allows us to establish a connection between the annihilation and creation operators and the Pauli operators. By subtracting the identity matrix from the number operator $\hat{a}^\dagger \hat{a}$, we obtain the Pauli-Z operator. Additionally, the two-state annihilation operator $\hat{a}$ is linked to the

Pauli lowering operator σ_-, which is a combination of the Pauli-X and Pauli-Y operators. This mapping creates an analogy between an oscillator and a spin system.

2.6 Other Refinements of Superconducting Qubit

2.6.1 Xmon Qubit

The Xmon qubit, introduced by R. Barends in 2013 (Barends et al., 2013), is a variation of the transmon qubit. The name "Xmon" is derived from the distinctive X-shaped layout of its electrical circuit, which forms the qubit capacitor. Like the transmon, the Xmon operates in the $E_J \gg E_C$ regime, benefiting from an exponential suppression of charge noise. The schematic of the Xmon Qubit is displayed in Figure 2-17.

2.6.1.1 Circuit Design and Functionality

The Xmon circuit consists of a pair of Josephson junctions connected in parallel, forming a tunable superconducting quantum interference device (SQUID). The four arms of the X-shaped capacitor connect to different functional elements:

- **Top Arm**: Connects to a coplanar waveguide resonator for readout
- **Right Arm**: Interfaces with a quantum bus resonator for coupling to other qubits
- **Left Arm**: Provides XY control for qubit state excitation
- **Bottom Arm**: Enables Z control for qubit frequency tuning

The resulting circuit is equivalent to that of a grounded transmon, with the capacitor in parallel with the tunable Josephson junction.

2.6.1.2 Advantages and Applications

Xmon qubits are specifically designed to enhance coherence times compared to earlier transmon-based designs. This improvement arises from a combination of optimizations in the qubit's geometry and material properties. The tunability of Xmon qubits allows for fast two-qubit gate operations, facilitating high-performance quantum computation.

Key features of Xmon qubits include

- **Frequency Tunability**: Supports precise control over qubit states and gate operations
- **Improved Coherence**: Combines design refinements to achieve longer coherence times critical for reliable quantum computations
- **Connectivity**: Facilitates coupling between multiple qubits and other circuit elements on the same chip, enabling scalable quantum systems

These properties make Xmon qubits well suited for multi-qubit quantum computing architectures.

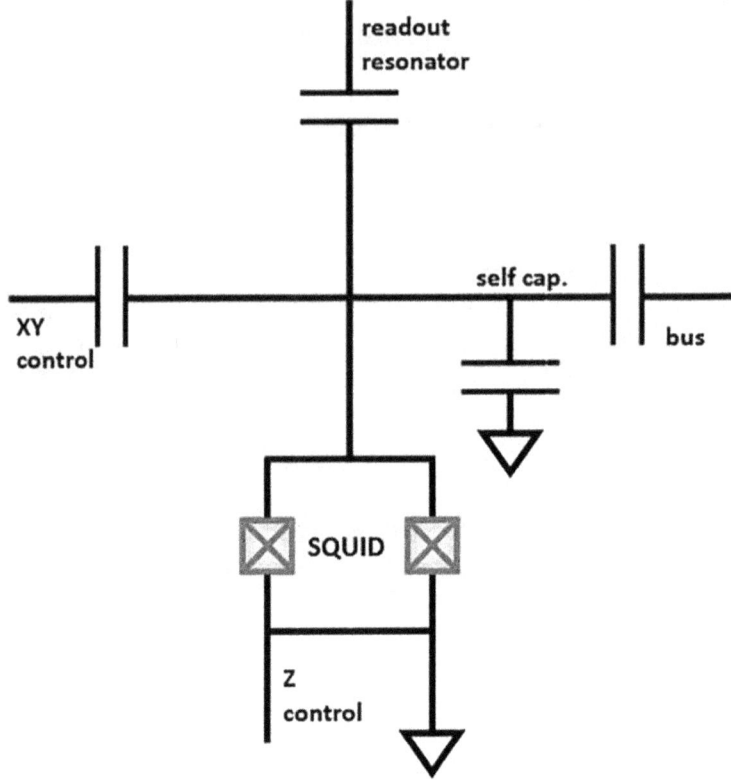

Figure 2-17 Schematic circuit diagram of an Xmon qubit

2.6.2 Quantronium Qubit

The first implementations of charge and flux qubits suffered from coherence times limited to a few nanoseconds. An early improvement addressing this limitation was the development of the quantronium qubit (Vion et al., 2002), which combines features of both charge and flux qubits. The schematic of the quantronium qubit is displayed in Figure 2-18.

2.6.2.1 Design Features

The primary innovation in the quantronium qubit lies in the separation of write and readout ports, which enables enhanced manipulation and readout of the quantum state. Additionally, the single Josephson junction of a basic Cooper pair box is replaced by two nominally identical junctions forming a superconducting loop. This configuration introduces an additional degree of freedom: the superconducting phase difference across the loop.

Figure 2-18 Schematic circuit diagram of a quantronium qubit

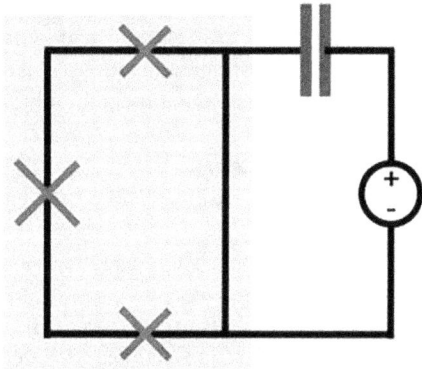

2.6.2.2 Operational Principles

In the quantronium qubit, quantum states are distinguished not by charge but by the supercurrent circulating in the loop. The quantum state is entangled with the phase of a large Josephson junction, allowing for state discrimination through the application of a readout pulse. This novel readout mechanism enables measurement of the quantum states $|0\rangle$ and $|1\rangle$.

The quantronium operates in an intermediate regime where the ratio of Josephson energy to charging energy is approximately $E_J/E_C \approx 1$. This balance improves the coherence properties of the circuit.

2.6.3 Fluxonium Qubit

A further development of the flux-qubit design to address inductance and offset charge noise issues is the fluxonium qubit (Manucharyan et al., 2009). The fluxonium circuit comprises a superconducting loop interrupted by a small Josephson junction, which is shunted by a series array of larger tunnel junctions.

2.6.3.1 Design Features

The fluxonium qubit is designed to be completely insensitive to offset charges. This is achieved by ensuring that all islands in the circuit are connected to the rest of the circuit through at least one large junction. These connections effectively screen quasistatic offset charges on all islands.

The larger junctions in the circuit provide capacitance that gives the array inductive behavior. This inductive behavior is critical for creating an inductance that exceeds that of the small Josephson junction, enabling the desired operational characteristics of the fluxonium qubit.

2.6.3.2 Operational Characteristics
Fluxonium qubits are distinguished by their unique energy spectrum, characterized by strongly anharmonic transitions. This strong anharmonicity makes them particularly well suited for quantum computing applications.

2.6.3.3 Advantages
Fluxonium qubits offer several advantages:

- **Noise Resilience**: Their design inherently reduces sensitivity to charge noise and flux noise.
- **Extended Coherence Times**: The circuit's inductive properties and noise resilience contribute to longer coherence times.
- **Tunable Energy Levels**: The energy spectrum can be engineered to fit specific applications.
- **Custom Gate Implementation**: They allow for versatile quantum gate designs.
- **Reduced Charge Sensitivity**: The effective screening of offset charges improves stability.

Fluxonium qubits represent a significant advancement in superconducting qubit technologies, combining noise resilience and enhanced coherence with a flexible, tunable design.

2.6.4 Gmon Qubit

The Gmon qubit architecture combines high-coherence qubits with tunable qubit-qubit coupling (Chen et al., 2014). This design builds upon the Xmon qubit architecture while introducing nanosecond control of the coupling strength between qubits.

2.6.4.1 Circuit Design
The Gmon qubit circuit is structured as a two-qubit unit cell with tunable coupling. At its core, the design is based on the Xmon qubit, featuring a cross-shaped capacitor resonating with a nonlinear inductor created from a superconducting quantum interference device (SQUID). To enable tunable coupling between qubits, a linear inductor is added from the junction to the ground. This linear inductor introduces a critical node in the circuit, allowing for controlled current flow between qubits. The schematic of Gmon qubit is displayed in Figure 2-19.

The coupling strength is dynamically adjusted by manipulating a junction that connects the two nodes, enabling precise control of the interaction between neighboring qubits in the Gmon circuit. Importantly, this modification does not significantly affect the qubit's nonlinearity.

2.6 Other Refinements of Superconducting Qubit

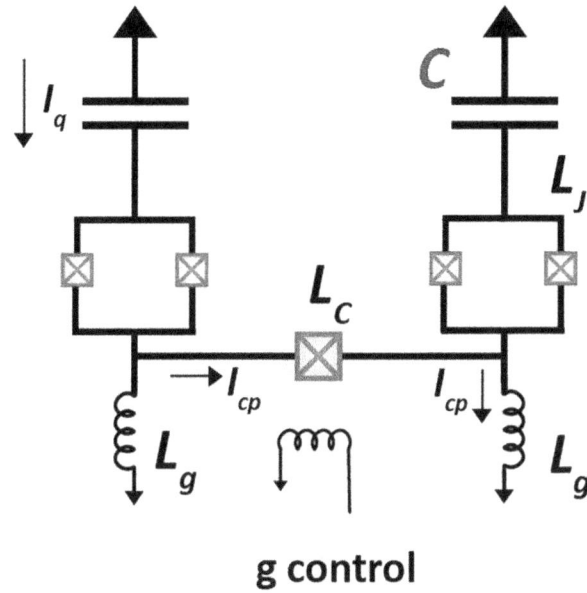

Figure 2-19 Schematic circuit diagram of Gmon qubit

2.6.4.2 Advantages and Features
The Gmon qubit architecture offers several key features:

- **Tunable Coupling**: The coupling strength between qubits can be dynamically adjusted with nanosecond resolution, providing high precision and flexibility.
- **Frequency Crowd Management**: The ability to set the qubit coupling to zero addresses the issue of frequency crowding present in fixed-coupling architectures.
- **Versatility**: The dynamic coupling feature enables a wide range of applications, including quantum logic gates and quantum simulations.
- **Scalability**: The combination of high coherence and tunable control makes the Gmon qubit a strong candidate for large-scale quantum simulation.

By integrating coherence properties with scalable and precise control, the Gmon qubit represents an important advancement in quantum computing architectures, offering a robust platform for diverse quantum applications.

2.6.5 Coaxmon Qubit

Scaling quantum circuits in a single 2D plane poses challenges, as control and readout connections scale linearly with qubit numbers, while edge connections scale

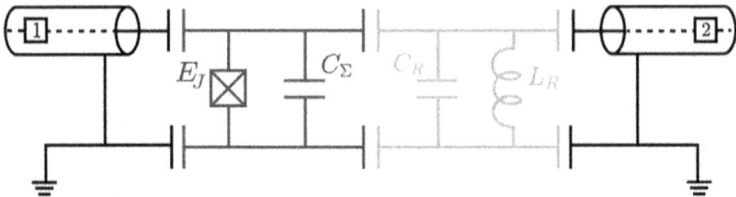

Figure 2-20 Schematic circuit diagram of the coaxmon qubit (Rahamim et al., 2017)

as $\sqrt{N}$ (where N is the total number of qubits). The coaxmon architecture addresses these issues by adopting a unique design where the qubit and resonator are placed on opposite sides of a single chip, with coaxial wiring provided perpendicularly to the chip plane for control and readout (Rahamim et al., 2017). The schematic of coaxmon qubit is displayed in Figure 2-20.

2.6.5.1 Circuit Design
The device consists of a superconducting charge qubit operating in the transmon regime with coaxial electrodes, coupled to a lumped-element LC microwave resonator fabricated on the opposite side of the chip, as depicted in Figure 2-20.

The device is controlled and measured via coaxial ports perpendicular to the chip's plane. The distance of these ports from the chip can be adjusted to modify the external quality factor of the circuits. These ports allow independent control of the qubit and measurement of the resonator in either reflection or transmission modes.

2.6.5.2 Advantages
The coaxmon qubit offers several advantages:

- **Scalability**: This design facilitates scalability to large arrays of individually controlled and measured qubits.
- **Simplified Architecture**: All wiring is located outside the qubit plane, simplifying the overall architecture and reducing spatial constraints.
- **Efficient Control and Readout**: The coaxial ports ensure efficient qubit control and resonator readout while minimizing potential sources of crosstalk.

The coaxmon architecture provides an innovative solution for scaling up quantum circuits while maintaining robust control and readout mechanisms.

2.7 Conclusion

This chapter provided a comprehensive overview of the theoretical foundations of superconducting qubits, beginning with the classical and quantum descriptions of harmonic oscillators and their limitations as qubits. The analysis then extended to LC oscillator circuits, establishing their Hamiltonians in both classical and quantum

2.7 Conclusion

frameworks. Building on this foundation, various types of superconducting qubits, including phase, charge, flux, and the widely adopted transmon qubit, were explored in detail, highlighting their design principles and operational characteristics. Further refinements, such as Xmon, quantronium, fluxonium, Gmon, and coaxmon qubits, were discussed to demonstrate advancements addressing decoherence and control limitations. Collectively, these discussions underscored the evolution of superconducting qubit architectures and their pivotal role in scalable quantum computing systems. This theoretical groundwork sets the stage for a deeper understanding of qubit design, control, and implementation in practical quantum technologies.

3

Qiskit and Introduction to Qiskit Metal

One of the fundamental steps for realizing a quantum computing circuit is the coding aspect of it. Quantum computing simulations and the realization of quantum circuits require coding and that too as expected a pretty complex method of coding. In this segment, we will understand coding in Python by developing simple circuits and code for understanding the basics of circuit building using basic quantum gates such as CNOT gates, Hadamard gates, Pauli gates, and more. This chapter will provide a slight insight into all the gates the Qiskit framework offers. So, let's start with a short description followed by an intro to quantum gates present in the *Qiskit* module that will help us in coding the circuits.

3.1 Writing Basic Code

Qiskit is a Python library that helps build, develop, and run quantum circuits, even providing a backend mode to stimulate the quantum connections locally. Generating a quantum circuit is essential as each circuit is designed specifically to cater to the needs of specific algorithms. Building these circuits marks the initial step in solving any quantum problem. In order to download the Qiskit package on your device, we can use the pip command in the Python terminal/command prompt (Python supported)/Jupyter Notebook/Anaconda prompt:

```
pip install qiskit
```

Once the mentioned pip command is executed on the local Python-supported terminal or prompt, it will download all the associated Qiskit packages into the local system, and we will be good to proceed with running Qiskit code for building quantum circuits. It's important to note that Qiskit is an evolving library, with each version introducing new functionalities while deprecating some existing ones. Therefore, it is recommended to refer to the official Qiskit documentation for up-to-date information on available functions and their usage:

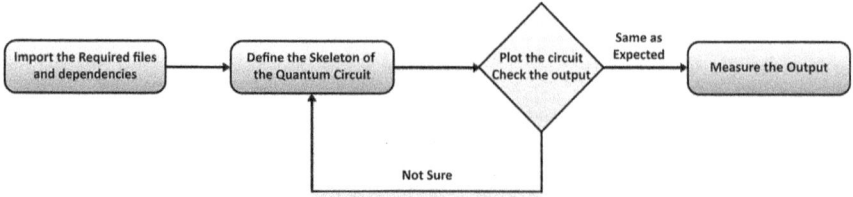

Figure 3-1 End-to-end flowchart for executing Python code for quantum circuit building

Qiskit Documentation: https://docs.quantum.ibm.com/api/qiskit/qiskit.circuit.QuantumCircuit

Let us create a basic flowchart to help us understand and write our quantum computing code. We will follow this flowchart displayed in Figure 3-1 as our guide for writing and executing the quantum computing code.

The first step is to import functions and dependencies that we will be using for our generation of code. Qiskit provides all the quantum gates and their measurement outputs with them, so let's start from basic importing functions that we will be using for designing the circuits.

```
from qiskit import QuantumCircuit
from qiskit.visualization import *
import matplotlib.pyplot as plt
```

QuantumCircuit is a class, which means it is an object that can be instantiated to create a quantum circuit. It is defined within the qiskit.circuit module. This makes the QuantumCircuit class in Qiskit a fundamental component of the Quantum Computing framework, which allows you to create and manipulate quantum circuits. When you want to test and run a quantum algorithm, you create an instance of the QuantumCircuit class, which means you create a quantum circuit object. This object is used to define the quantum gates, operations, and measurements that make up your quantum algorithm. Researchers and quantum programmers use QuantumCircuit to construct and test various quantum algorithms, such as Grover's algorithm, Shor's algorithm, and quantum machine learning algorithms. The other library `Qiskit.visualization` provides multiple functions and classes in it, such as

- `plot_histogram()`: Creates a graphical output of the analysis performed
- `plot_bloch_multivector()`: Displays the state of a qubit on the Bloch sphere, providing a visual representation of its quantum state
- `plot_state_city()`: Shows the real and imaginary components of a quantum state in a cityscape-like format, offering insight into the qubit's amplitude and phase
- `plot_state_qsphere()`: Visualizes the quantum state on a Q-sphere, helping to understand the global phase and amplitude of the qubits

- `plot_circuit_layout()`: Provides a visual of the mapping between virtual and physical qubits, which is crucial when dealing with hardware-specific optimizations

After importing the dependencies and libraries required, we move on to the next step, defining the number of qubits and the gates required. For this purpose, we use the class QuantumCircuit imported from qiskit:

```
qc = QuantumCircuit(m,n)
```

The line "qc = QuantumCircuit(m,n)" defines the primary number of qubits and classical bits that we will use for measurement and analysis purposes. The m in QuantumCircuit(m, n) indicates that you are creating a quantum circuit with m quantum bits or qubits ranging from q[0] to q[m−1]. The n in QuantumCircuit(m, n) indicates that you are also allocating n classical bits. Classical bits are used to store the measurement results from qubits after a measurement operation is performed. When you perform measurements on qubits, the outcomes are recorded as classical bits, which can take values of 0 or 1. For example, if $n = 2$, the classical bit outcome measures are 00, 01, 10, 11, and if n=3, 000, 001, 010, 011, 100, 101, 110, 111. Qiskit also supports the method where we can define the quantum and classical registers separately, and it is shown in code 3.1:

```
from qiskit import QuantumCircuit, QuantumRegister,
ClassicalRegister
n = 3
qr = QuantumRegister(n)
cr = ClassicalRegister(n)
circuit = QuantumCircuit(qr, cr)
```

In this example, we import QuantumRegister and ClassicalRegister from Qiskit, and their usage remains consistent with standard definitions. We define the number of qubits using QuantumRegister(n) and the number of classical bits used for measurement using ClassicalRegister(n), where n represents the number of qubits and classical bits we want to use, respectively. In this case, we set $n = 3$, so our system has three qubits and three classical bits.

This method, as shown in code 3.1, requires an unnecessary number of lines and code, so mostly you will witness code mentioning qc = QuantumCircuit(m,n) as it is time efficient and code space conserving, that is, the time complexity and space complexity of the code is minimum, making it extremely reliable for heavy processing applications. Whenever you see **qc = QuantumCircuit(m)**, it means that we will be using m qubits for performing the analysis and won't be using any classical bits. While defining the quantum circuit skeleton, it is important to note that mentioning the number of qubits is mandatory, whereas mentioning the number of classical bits is optional.

Now the next step of defining the skeleton of the circuit is adding basic quantum gates to the circuit. So, let us go with a simple two-qubit entangled circuit:

```
qc = QuantumCircuit(2)
qc.h(0)
qc.cx(0, 1)
```

So, for this example, we will be using a simple Hadamard gate and a CNOT gate after defining the number of qubits. Simple logic gates such as the H gate [qc.h(0)] specify the application of the Hadamard gate on the first qubit q[0], and then the CNOT gate [qc.cx(0, 1)] is applied, where 0 signifies that q[0] is the control qubit and q[1] is the target qubit for performing this simulation. More details regarding these individual gates will be provided in Section 4.2 where we will be looking into all the different gates provided by Qiskit and their corresponding code. If you run this particular snippet or any other quantum circuit code where you have just mentioned the skeleton, the compiler prompts and outputs

⟨Qiskit.circuit.instructionset.InstructionSet at 0x7f160fcd8ee0⟩

This signifies that your code has been compiled successfully and the stack location of the compiled code is set at $0 \times 7f160fcd8ee0$. The stack location varies every time you run the code as it occupies different levels in the instruction set architecture of the code. Once we obtained this output, the next step is the visualization of the circuit. For visualizing the circuit, Qiskit provides a specific library, Qiskit.visualization, which contains a specific class, circuit_drawer. This helps in visualizing the circuit that we have coded. The snippet is just a one-liner:

```
from qiskit.visualization import circuit_drawer
circuit_drawer(qc, output='mpl')
```

After running this particular snippet, it will provide an output diagram of the particular circuit qc that we just coded. The output='mpl' argument specifies that the output should be in a Matplotlib-based format, which allows you to display the quantum circuit within a Jupyter Notebook or as a stand-alone image. The output takes other values and accordingly gives corresponding plots too. Let's see what we get once we run this code snippet with all the supported values for the same quantum circuit qc compiled.

These are the four supported values for circuit_drawer in the Qiskit library and their corresponding output, and they are represented in Figure 3-2. Do not be alarmed by the output of output="latex_source", as this generates a LaTeX code output. When this code is entered into a LaTeX compiler, it will produce a graphical representation using dots and dashes. For aesthetic purposes, we prefer output="mpl"; however, it's up to the user to choose their preferred format for visualizing the image. Once we know how to develop a circuit, let's understand how to measure the outputs of this circuit. In this example, we will develop a circuit that incorporates both quantum bits and classical bits, analyze the generated output, and

3.1 Writing Basic Code

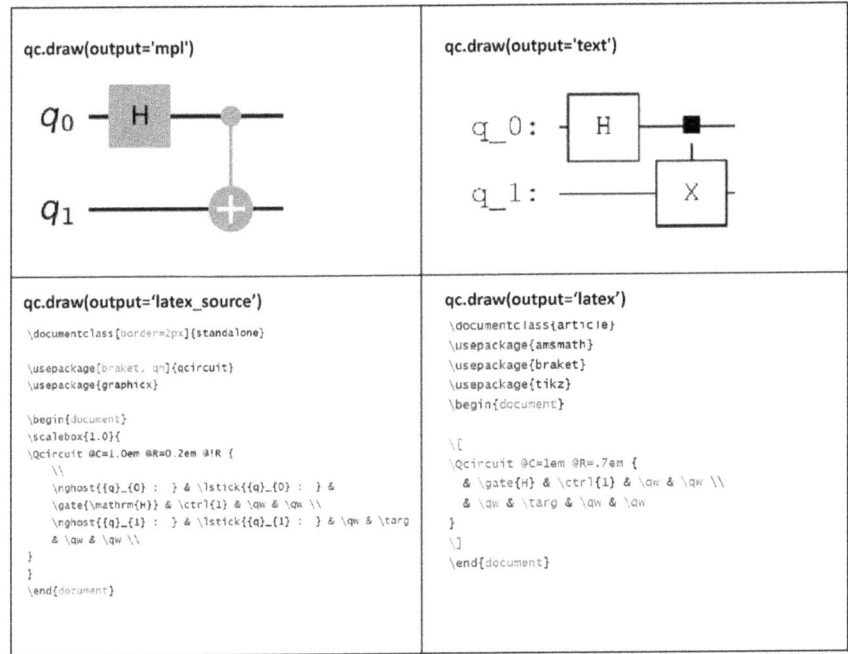

Figure 3-2 Representation of four different modes of output provided by the function draw(output)

visualize the results using a Q-sphere representation and a histogram plot, as shown in code 3.1.

```
qc = QuantumCircuit(2,2)
qc.h(0)
qc.cx(0, 1)
qc.measure([0,1], [0,1])
circuit_drawer(qc, output='mpl')
```

Now let's redefine the circuit and measure the outputs for the same. We have added two classical bits; hence, four classical bit outcomes are possible, namely, 00, 01, 10, 11. For $n = 2$, the command qc.measure([0, 1], [0, 1]) measures both qubits 0 and 1, so the first array element [0,1] specifies which qubits we want to measure, and the next [0,1] signifies which measurement output to be connected to. So, the line of code qc.measure([0, 1], [0, 1]) tells the quantum circuit to measure the state of qubits 0 and 1 and store the measurement results in classical bits 0 and 1, respectively. These measurement results will be in the form of classical bits, either 0 or 1, depending on the measurement outcomes. While drawing the circuit, the transpiled circuit looks like the one shown in Figure 3-3.

In Figure 3-3, we can see how the measurement device appears in the quantum computing circuit and which corresponding qubit is linked to each measurement operator. Now, let's look into plotting the histogram output for the measured and

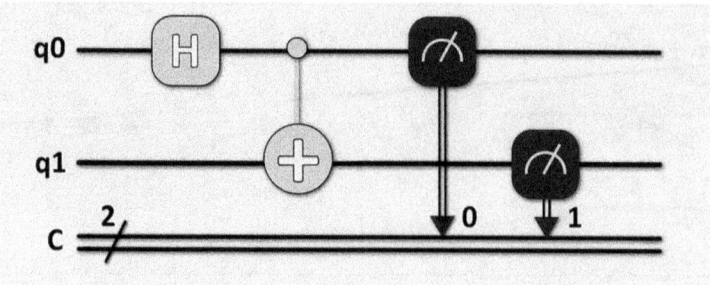

Figure 3-3 Transpiled circuit output for code 3.1

compiled circuit. We use the `plot_histogram()` function for plotting the outputs from Qiskit.visualization, and we simulate it accordingly. The code snippet looks like this:

```
from qiskit import QuantumCircuit, transpile, assemble
from qiskit_aer import Aer
from qiskit.visualization import plot\_histogram

simulator = Aer.get_backend('qasm_simulator')
compiled_circuit = transpile(qc, simulator)
result = simulator.run(compiled_circuit).result()
counts = result.get_counts()
plot_histogram(counts)
```

In this case, Aer is a module in Qiskit (supported from Qiskit version 0.7 and above) that provides access to various quantum simulators, but from Qiskit version 1.0.0 the `Aer` module has been shifted to `qiskit_aer`, so you could import the `Aer` module from the respective module based on the version you are using. If you are using a version of Qiskit greater than 1.0.0, then you could separately install it by using the pip command:

`pip install qiskit_aer`

Post running this command, you can run the simulation and figure out the counts of the circuit. Let's look at the functionalities of the code and how to extract the counts:

- `get_backend('qasm_simulator')` is used to get an instance of the quantum simulator known as the `'qasm_simulator'`. This simulator is suitable for simulating quantum circuits and obtaining measurement results.
- `compiled_circuit = transpile(qc, simulator)`: qc is assumed to be a quantum circuit that you want to simulate. The `transpile` function is used to compile and optimize the circuit for the chosen simulator. `simulator` is the backend (`'qasm_simulator'`) to which the quantum circuit is being compiled.

3.1 Writing Basic Code

- `result = simulator.run(compiled_circuit).result()`: `simulator.run(compiled_circuit)` runs the compiled quantum circuit on the specified simulator, and the results are stored in the `result` object. `result()` is used to retrieve the results of the simulation.
- `counts = result.get_counts()`: This line retrieves the measurement results from the `result` object. The `get_counts()` method returns a dictionary representing the number of times each measurement outcome occurred.
- `plot_histogram(counts)`: This line uses the `plot_histogram` function to generate and display a histogram of the measurement outcomes. The `counts` dictionary is used as input to create the histogram, which shows the frequency of each possible measurement result as bars in the plot.

In quantum computing, the term *counts* refers to the number of times a quantum circuit is executed, or *shots*, to gather measurement results and estimate the probability of each possible quantum state. By default, 1024 shots are used, meaning the circuit is executed 1024 times. This default value provides a statistically significant sample size, allowing us to approximate the probability distribution of different measurement outcomes. Each shot produces one possible outcome of the quantum system when measured. Repeating the process over 1024 shots provides a distribution of results that lets us estimate the likelihood, or probability, of each possible state. This statistical approach is crucial because quantum measurements are inherently probabilistic; we don't get a single definitive answer but rather a range of possible outcomes with different probabilities. The default of 1024 shots is a commonly used setting in Qiskit, providing a reasonable trade-off between accuracy and computational efficiency in many scenarios. However, the optimal number of shots depends on the specific use case, as higher shot counts can improve result accuracy at the cost of increased computation time.

The output from these counts typically looks like a dictionary where each key represents a quantum state (in binary format), and the associated value represents the frequency (or count) of that state occurring across the 1024 shots. This information is essential for analyzing and understanding the behavior of quantum circuits. For the quantum circuit created above and generating the histogram plot for the output counts, the visualization can be represented as shown in Figure 3-4.

The output shown in Figure 3-4 states that out of 1024 shots that were fired to the circuit, 512 shots were calculated in 00 and 512 of them in 11 states, and the remaining states have 0 shots received. This indicates that the probability of the circuit existing in states 00 and 11 is 50% each.

Well, that is exactly how you write a quantum circuit code, execute it and map out to the solutions. This is the very first stage of designing and beginning with quantum algorithms and designing superconducting qubits using the Qiskit Metal. Now we should dive into the fundamentals of quantum gates. Qiskit provides more

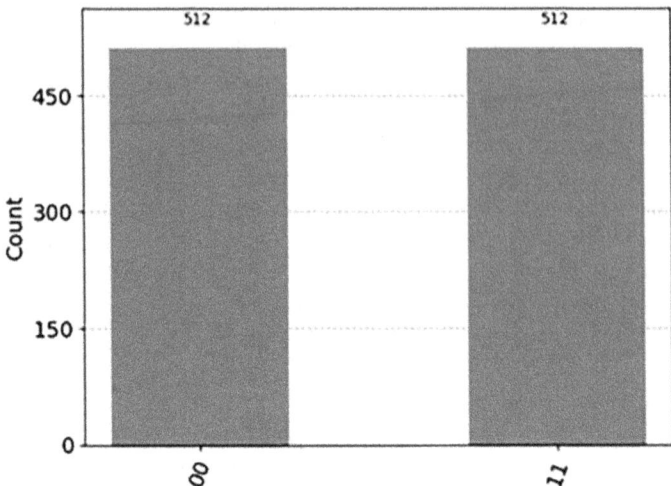

Figure 3-4 The histogram represents the results of 1024 executions of the quantum circuit shown in Figure 3-3

than 20 standard quantum gates that help in circuit building and analyzing, so let's dive into them and explore these gates with their basic fundamental code.

3.2 Logic Gates

Logic gates are the basic building blocks for building a circuit. In this section, we will be talking about the important logical gates that are used for generating and building quantum circuits. All the following gates are provided in the Qiskit library. Let's have a look at all the quantum logical gates and understand their functionalities:

- **Hadamard Gate**
  The Hadamard gate is a fundamental single-qubit gate and is responsible for converting the computational basis state $|0\rangle$ and $|1\rangle$ to superposition state $|+\rangle$ and $|-\rangle$, respectively, thus creating a superposition of the two basis states. The Hadamard matrix is represented as

$$H = \frac{1}{\sqrt{2}}\begin{bmatrix} 1 & 1 \\ 1 & -1 \end{bmatrix} \quad (3\text{-}1)$$

Hadamard when originally applied to $|0\rangle$ and $|1\rangle$ gives equal superposition. But, if the probability amplitudes are equal, then that superposition state is said to be in equal superposition. The equation for the states to be in equal superposition requires that the corresponding amplitudes of both states are $\frac{1}{\sqrt{2}}$, that is, 50%

probability, and the equation is represented as

$$|\psi\rangle = \frac{1}{\sqrt{2}}|0\rangle + \frac{1}{\sqrt{2}}|1\rangle \tag{3-2}$$

The system of equation is said to be in an unequal superposition if the corresponding amplitude of either one of the states is more than the other state; an example of states present in an unequal superposition can be represented as

$$|\psi\rangle = 0.6|0\rangle + 0.8|1\rangle \tag{3-3}$$

As we can see, the amplitudes of both states are different; hence, we can conclude that this system of equation has unequal superposition. Unequal superpositions are indeed possible in quantum systems, but they are not created by the Hadamard gate alone. They require different gates or preexisting states. As we have learned, the Hadamard gate helps in creating superpositional states from computational states; let's look at how this is achieved:

$$H|0\rangle = \frac{1}{\sqrt{2}}\begin{bmatrix} 1 & 1 \\ 1 & -1 \end{bmatrix} \times \begin{bmatrix} 1 \\ 0 \end{bmatrix} = \frac{1}{\sqrt{2}}\begin{bmatrix} 1 \\ 1 \end{bmatrix} = \frac{1}{\sqrt{2}}\begin{bmatrix} 1 \\ 0 \end{bmatrix} + \frac{1}{\sqrt{2}}\begin{bmatrix} 0 \\ 1 \end{bmatrix}$$

$$= \frac{|0\rangle + |1\rangle}{\sqrt{2}} = |+\rangle \tag{3-4}$$

$$H|1\rangle = \frac{1}{\sqrt{2}}\begin{bmatrix} 1 & 1 \\ 1 & -1 \end{bmatrix} \times \begin{bmatrix} 0 \\ 1 \end{bmatrix} = \frac{1}{\sqrt{2}}\begin{bmatrix} 1 \\ -1 \end{bmatrix} = \frac{1}{\sqrt{2}}\begin{bmatrix} 1 \\ 0 \end{bmatrix} - \frac{1}{\sqrt{2}}\begin{bmatrix} 0 \\ 1 \end{bmatrix}$$

$$= \frac{|0\rangle - |1\rangle}{\sqrt{2}} = |-\rangle \tag{3-5}$$

The Hadamard gate is responsible for converting the superpositional state to computational state basis $H|+\rangle = |0\rangle$ and $H|-\rangle = |1\rangle$. The Hadamard gate performs a rotation of π about the axis $(\hat{x} + \hat{z})/\sqrt{2}$ at the Bloch sphere and is therefore involutory.

The code to add the Hadamard gate to the circuit is

qc.h(n)

where n denotes the qubit you want to apply superposition to, that is, the Hadamard gate.

- **Identity Gate**
  The Identity gate is a fundamental single-qubit gate, represented as

$$I = \begin{bmatrix} 1 & 0 \\ 0 & 1 \end{bmatrix} \tag{3-6}$$

This gate performs an identity operation, which does not change the quantum state of the qubit to which it is applied following the relation $I \cdot |\psi\rangle = |\psi\rangle$ where $|\psi\rangle$ is the quantum state of the equation. The Identity gate is especially useful when mathematically describing the outcome of various gate operations or when analyzing multi-qubit circuits. For understanding the use of Identity gates in multi-qubit circuits, let's try and understand with an example:

Suppose there is a two-qubit system where we apply a gate U only to the first qubit. To mathematically represent this in the full two-qubit system, we apply the Identity gate to the unaffected qubit: $U \otimes I$. This notation keeps other qubits unchanged, simplifying the analysis of selective operations in multi-qubit circuits, enabling cleaner analyses in scenarios where one or more qubits are not directly affected by certain gates in the circuit. The code to add an Identity gate to the circuit is

```
qc.i(n)
```

where n denotes the qubit to which you want to apply the Identity gate.

- **Pauli-X, Pauli-Y, and Pauli-Z Gates**
  Pauli gates are fundamental single-qubit gates with matrices ($\sigma_x, \sigma_y, \sigma_z$). They apply specific transformations to individual qubits and are commonly used within both single- and multi-qubit circuits. Each Pauli gate corresponds to a rotation by 180° around one of the principal axes on the Bloch sphere. Pauli-X, Pauli-Y, and Pauli-Z gates equate, respectively, to a rotation around the x-, y-, and z-axes of the Bloch sphere by π radians. The Pauli-X gate is the quantum equivalent of the NOT gate for classical computers with respect to the standard basis $|0\rangle, |1\rangle$, which distinguishes the z-axis on the Bloch sphere. Pauli-Z leaves the basis state $|0\rangle$ unchanged and maps $|1\rangle$ to $-|1\rangle$. The gates are represented as

$$X = \sigma_x = \begin{bmatrix} 0 & 1 \\ 1 & 0 \end{bmatrix} \tag{3-7}$$

$$Y = \sigma_y = \begin{bmatrix} 0 & -i \\ i & 0 \end{bmatrix} \tag{3-8}$$

$$Z = \sigma_z = \begin{bmatrix} 1 & 0 \\ 0 & -1 \end{bmatrix} \tag{3-9}$$

The square of all the Pauli matrices is the identity matrix $I^2 = X^2 = Z^2 = Y^2$. The code to add Pauli gates to the circuit is

```
qc.x(n)
qc.y(n)
qc.z(n)
```

3.2 Logic Gates

where *n* denotes to which qubit you want to apply the Pauli gate. The qc.x(n) represents the Pauli-X gate, qc.y(n) represents the Pauli-Y gate, and qc.z(n) represents the Pauli-Z gate.

- **NOT Gate**

  The Pauli-X gate, also known as the quantum gate analogous to classical NOT gate, is used to flip the state of a qubit from $|0\rangle$ to $|1\rangle$ and vice versa. In quantum circuits, qubits are typically initialized in the $|0\rangle$ state. By applying the NOT gate, we can change the state of a qubit to $|1\rangle$. The code to add a NOT gate to a circuit is

  qc.x(n)

  where *n* denotes the qubit to which you want to apply the NOT gate.

- **Reset Gate**

  As the name suggests, the Reset gate resets the state of a qubit back to $|0\rangle$. Regardless of the input state, the Reset gate ensures that the output state of the qubit is $|0\rangle$. This operation is not reversible. The code to add a Reset gate to the circuit is

  qc.reset(n)

  where *n* denotes the qubit to which you want to apply the Reset gate.

- **SWAP Gate**

  The SWAP gate is a two-qubit operation. It exchanges the states of the two qubits involved. The SWAP gate is represented by the matrix:

  $$\text{SWAP} = \begin{bmatrix} 1 & 0 & 0 & 0 \\ 0 & 0 & 1 & 0 \\ 0 & 1 & 0 & 0 \\ 0 & 0 & 0 & 1 \end{bmatrix}. \quad (3\text{-}10)$$

  The SWAP gate is also useful in procedures like the swap test, a quantum computational method used to evaluate the similarity between two quantum states. The code to add a SWAP gate to a circuit is

  qc.swap(n, m)

  where *n* denotes the first qubit, and *m* denotes the qubit with which you want to swap states.

- **CNOT Gate**

  The CNOT (or controlled Pauli-X) gate is a multi-qubit gate that consists of two qubits. The first qubit is known as the control qubit, while the second is known as the target qubit. If the control qubit is in the state $|1\rangle$, it flips the target qubit's state from $|0\rangle$ to $|1\rangle$ or vice versa; the truth table for the CNOT gate is provided in Table 3-1. Conversely, if the control qubit is in the state $|0\rangle$, the state of the target qubit remains unchanged. The CNOT gate can be described by the mapping of

Table 3-1 Truth table of the CNOT gate

Control (A)	Target (B) (Input)	Control (A) (Output)	Target (B) (Output)
0	0	0	0
0	1	0	1
1	0	1	1
1	1	1	0

basis states:

$$|a, b\rangle \mapsto |a, a \oplus b\rangle,$$

where $\oplus$ denotes the XOR operation. The CNOT gate can also be expressed in the Pauli basis as

$$CNOT = \exp\left(i\frac{\pi}{4}(I - Z_1)(I - X_2)\right). \quad (3\text{-}11)$$

Here, I is the identity operator, which acts on the control qubit, indicating that the state of the control qubit does not change. Z_1 represents the Pauli-Z gate operation on the first qubit (the control qubit), indicating the control action on that qubit. X_2 represents the Pauli-X gate operation on the second qubit (the target qubit), which is used for flipping the state of the qubit. The code to add a CNOT gate to the circuit is

```
qc.cx(n, m)
```

where n denotes the control qubit and m denotes the target qubit.

- **RZ Gate**

  The RZ gate is one of the rotation operators. It represents a single-qubit rotation through an angle θ (in radians) around the z-axis. The action of the $R_z(\alpha)$ gate on $|\psi\rangle$ rotates the state about the z-axis of the Bloch sphere through the angle α and can be expressed as $\exp\left(-i\frac{\theta}{2}\alpha\right)$. The RZ gate is denoted as

$$R_z = \begin{bmatrix} \exp\left(-i\frac{\theta}{2}\right) & 0 \\ 0 & \exp\left(i\frac{\theta}{2}\right) \end{bmatrix}. \quad (3\text{-}12)$$

There is a relation between the RZ gate and the Pauli-Z gate, given by

$$R_z(\theta) = \exp\left(-i\frac{\theta}{2}Z\right) = \cos\left(\frac{\theta}{2}\right)I - i\sin\left(\frac{\theta}{2}\right)Z. \quad (3\text{-}13)$$

Here, I represents the part of the rotation that remains unchanged due to the operation, while Z indicates the rotation taking place due to the Pauli-Z gate with a magnitude of θ. The code to add the rotation Z gate to the circuit is

```
qc.rz(θ, n)
```

where θ represents the angle of rotation and n denotes the qubit to which you want to apply the rotation Z gate.

- **RX Gate**

  The RX gate is one of the rotation operators. It represents a single-qubit rotation through an angle θ (in radians) around the x-axis. The RX gate can be expressed as

  $$R_x(\theta) = \begin{bmatrix} \cos\left(\frac{\theta}{2}\right) & -i\sin\left(\frac{\theta}{2}\right) \\ -i\sin\left(\frac{\theta}{2}\right) & \cos\left(\frac{\theta}{2}\right) \end{bmatrix}. \qquad (3\text{-}14)$$

  There is a relation between the RX gate and the Pauli-X gate, which can be expressed as

  $$R_x(\theta) = \exp\left(-i\frac{\theta}{2}X\right) = \cos\left(\frac{\theta}{2}\right)I - i\sin\left(\frac{\theta}{2}\right)X. \qquad (3\text{-}15)$$

  Here, I indicates the part of the rotation that remains unchanged during the operation, while X indicates the rotation taking place due to the Pauli-X gate with a magnitude of θ. The code to add the rotation X gate to the circuit is

  qc.rx(θ, n)

  where θ represents the angle of rotation and n denotes the qubit to which you want to apply the rotation X gate.

- **RY Gate**

  The RY gate is one of the rotation operators. It represents a single-qubit rotation through an angle θ (in radians) around the y-axis. The RY gate can be expressed as

  $$R_y(\theta) = \begin{bmatrix} \cos\left(\frac{\theta}{2}\right) & -\sin\left(\frac{\theta}{2}\right) \\ \sin\left(\frac{\theta}{2}\right) & \cos\left(\frac{\theta}{2}\right) \end{bmatrix}. \qquad (3\text{-}16)$$

  There is a relation between the RY gate and the Pauli-Y gate, given by

  $$R_y(\theta) = \exp\left(-i\frac{\theta}{2}Y\right) = \cos\left(\frac{\theta}{2}\right)I - i\sin\left(\frac{\theta}{2}\right)Y. \qquad (3\text{-}17)$$

  Here, I indicates the part of the rotation that remains unchanged during the operation, while Y indicates the rotation taking place due to the Pauli-Y gate with a magnitude of θ. The code to add the rotation Y gate to the circuit is

  qc.ry(θ, n)

  where θ represents the angle of rotation and n denotes the qubit to which you want to apply the rotation Y gate.

- **S Gate**
  The S gate, also known as the $\sqrt{Z}$ gate, performs a rotation of $\frac{\pi}{2}$ around the Z-axis. It is represented by the following matrix:

$$S = \begin{bmatrix} 1 & 0 \\ 0 & i \end{bmatrix}. \tag{3-18}$$

  This gate does not change the state of $|0\rangle$, resulting in $S|0\rangle = |0\rangle$, while it shifts the state of $|1\rangle$ by an angle of $\frac{\pi}{2}$ on the Bloch sphere, giving $S|1\rangle = i|1\rangle$. If two S gates are applied consecutively, the result is equivalent to applying a Z gate: $S^2 = Z$. The code to add the S gate to the circuit is

  qc.s(n)

  where n denotes the qubit to which you want to apply the S gate.

- **T Gate**
  The T gate is a single-qubit operation represented by the matrix:

$$T = \begin{bmatrix} 1 & 0 \\ 0 & \exp\left(i\frac{\pi}{4}\right) \end{bmatrix} \tag{3-19}$$

  The T gate is used to apply a phase shift of 45° to the state $|1\rangle$ while leaving the state $|0\rangle$ unchanged. There is a relation between the T gate and the S gate, expressed as $S = T^2$. The code to add the T gate to the circuit is

  qc.t(n)

  where n denotes the qubit to which you want to apply the T gate.

- **$S^\dagger$ Gate**
  The S dagger gate ($S^\dagger$ gate), or conjugate transpose of the S gate, is a single-qubit operation given by

$$S^\dagger = \begin{bmatrix} 1 & 0 \\ 0 & \exp\left(-i\frac{\pi}{2}\right) \end{bmatrix}. \tag{3-20}$$

  This is a **Clifford gate** and is the square root of the Pauli-Z gate, equivalent to a $-\frac{\pi}{2}$ radian rotation about the Z-axis. The code to add the S dagger gate to the circuit is

  qc.sdg(n)

  where n denotes the qubit to which you want to apply the S dagger gate.

- **$T^\dagger$ Gate**
  The T dagger gate ($T^\dagger$), or conjugate transpose of the T gate, is a single-qubit operation given by

$$T^\dagger = \begin{bmatrix} 1 & 0 \\ 0 & \exp\left(-i\frac{\pi}{4}\right) \end{bmatrix} \tag{3-21}$$

3.2 Logic Gates

This is a **non-Clifford gate** and is the fourth root of the Pauli-Z gate. It induces a $-\frac{\pi}{4}$ phase shift. The code to add the T dagger gate to the circuit is

qc.tdg(n)

where n denotes the qubit to which you want to apply the T dagger gate.

- **CPhase** The CPhase gate, also known as the controlled-phase gate, will provide a controlled-phase shift on the target qubit if the input control qubit phase is $|1\rangle$; otherwise, it won't perform any operation. This gate functions similarly to the CNOT gate; the only difference is that instead of changing the state of the target qubit, CPhase acts on the phase of the gate. The CPhase gate operation is done on two qubits; the first is the control, and the second is the target qubit of action. The matrix of the CPhase gate is represented by

$$CPhase = \begin{bmatrix} 1 & 0 & 0 & 0 \\ 0 & 1 & 0 & 0 \\ 0 & 0 & e^{i\theta} & 0 \\ 0 & 0 & 0 & e^{i\theta} \end{bmatrix}. \quad (3\text{-}22)$$

The controlled-phase gate plays an integral part in creating important quantum computing circuits, such as the Quantum Fourier Transform algorithm. The code to add the CPhase gate to the circuit is

qc.cp(θ, n, m)

where "θ" denotes the angle of rotation, n is the first qubit (control), and m is the second qubit (target).

- **Toffoli Gate**

The quantum Toffoli gate is a three-qubit gate. If we restrict the input qubits to the states $|0\rangle$ and $|1\rangle$, the Toffoli gate applies a Pauli-X (or NOT) operation on the third qubit if the first two qubits are both in the state $|1\rangle$; otherwise, it does nothing. It is an example of a CC-U (controlled-controlled unitary) gate. As the quantum analog of a classical gate, the Toffoli gate is completely specified by its truth table. When combined with single-qubit gates such as the Hadamard gate, the Toffoli gate is universal for quantum computation.

The Toffoli gate can be represented in the Pauli basis as

$$\text{Toffoli} = \exp\left(i\frac{\pi}{8}(I - Z_1)(I - Z_2)(I - X_3)\right). \quad (3\text{-}23)$$

Here, I is the identity operator, which acts on the control qubits, indicating that their states do not change. Z_1 and Z_2 represent the Pauli-Z gate operations on the first and second qubits (the control qubits), respectively, indicating the control action on those qubits. X_3 represents the Pauli-X gate operation on the third qubit (the target qubit), which is used for flipping the state of the qubit.

The code to add a Toffoli gate to the circuit is

qc.ccx(n, m, w)

where n denotes the first control qubit, m denotes the second control qubit, and w denotes the target qubit.

From this general representation of a multi-qubit control gate with one target gate, we have

$$\text{CC}\ldots X = \exp\left(i\frac{\pi}{2^n}(I - Z_1)(I - Z_2)\ldots(I - Z_{n-1})(I - X_n)\right) \quad (3\text{-}24)$$

where n represents the number of control qubits, and Z_1 to Z_{n-1} represent the operations on the control qubits, while X_n represents the final target qubit.

- $\sqrt{X}$ **Gate**

The $\sqrt{X}$ gate, also known as the square root of the X gate, is a single-qubit operation that represents a rotation of $\frac{\pi}{2}$ around the X-axis. It is defined by the following matrix:

$$\sqrt{X} = \frac{1}{\sqrt{2}}\begin{bmatrix} 1+i & 1-i \\ 1-i & 1+i \end{bmatrix} \quad (3\text{-}25)$$

This gate transforms the computational basis states into superposition states as

$$\sqrt{X}|0\rangle = |+\rangle = \frac{1}{\sqrt{2}}(|0\rangle + |1\rangle) \quad (3\text{-}26)$$

$$\sqrt{X}|1\rangle = |-\rangle = \frac{1}{\sqrt{2}}(|0\rangle - |1\rangle) \quad (3\text{-}27)$$

Although the $\sqrt{X}$ gate appears to provide similar output to that of the Hadamard gate, it serves a different purpose. The $\sqrt{X}$ gate is a rotation of $\frac{\pi}{2}$ around the X-axis on the Bloch sphere and is often used to create specific superposition states. In contrast, the Hadamard gate transforms basis states into equal superpositions. The code to add the $\sqrt{X}$ gate to the circuit is

qc.sx(n)

where n denotes the qubit to which you want to apply the $\sqrt{X}$ gate.

- $\sqrt{X}^\dagger$ **Gate**

The $\sqrt{X}^\dagger$ gate, also known as the conjugate transpose of the $\sqrt{X}$ gate, is a single-qubit operation that represents a rotation of $-\frac{\pi}{2}$ around the X-axis. It is defined by the following matrix:

$$\sqrt{X}^\dagger = \frac{1}{\sqrt{2}}\begin{bmatrix} 1-i & 1+i \\ 1+i & 1-i \end{bmatrix}. \quad (3\text{-}28)$$

3.2 Logic Gates

The code to add the $\sqrt{X}^\dagger$ gate to the circuit is

`qc.sxdg(n)`

where n denotes the qubit to which you want to apply the $\sqrt{X}^\dagger$ gate.

- **R_{XX} Gate**
  The R_{XX} gate is a two-qubit gate that represents a rotation around the axis defined by the X basis. It is parameterized by an angle θ and is defined as

  $$R_{XX}(\theta) = \cos\left(\frac{\theta}{2}\right) I \otimes I - i \sin\left(\frac{\theta}{2}\right) X \otimes X, \quad (3\text{-}29)$$

  where I is the identity operator and X is the Pauli-X gate applied on each qubit. The code to add the R_{XX} gate to the circuit is

  `qc.rxx(θ, n, m)`

  where "θ" denotes the angle of rotation, n is the first qubit, and m is the second qubit.

- **R_{ZZ} Gate**
  The R_{ZZ} gate is a two-qubit gate that represents a rotation around the Z basis. It is parameterized by an angle θ and is defined as

  $$R_{ZZ}(\theta) = \cos\left(\frac{\theta}{2}\right) I \otimes I - i \sin\left(\frac{\theta}{2}\right) Z \otimes Z, \quad (3\text{-}30)$$

  where I is the identity operator and Z is the Pauli-Z gate applied on each qubit. The code to add the R_{ZZ} gate to the circuit is

  `qc.rzz(θ, n, m)`

  where "θ" denotes the angle of rotation, n is the first qubit, and m is the second qubit.

- **Control Gate**
  Qiskit provides a variety of control gates; these control gates are conditional blocks that help in designing and performing conditional operations to manipulate the quantum state based on the target gate operation. These control gates have a specific pattern that it will have a control qubit and a target qubit; if the state of the control qubit is $|0\rangle$, then it will not perform any gate operation on the target qubit, whereas if the state of the control qubit is $|1\rangle$, then it will perform the gate operation on the target qubit. We have talked about a few of these types of gates earlier in this section, to recollect firstly the CNOT (CX) gate, which applies a NOT operation on the target qubit only when the control qubit is in the state $|1\rangle$, and secondly the controlled-phase (CP) gate, which applies a phase shift to the target qubit when the control qubit is in the state $|1\rangle$.

  Similar to them, Qiskit also supports Controlled-Y (CY) and Controlled-Z (CZ) gates, which apply the respective Pauli-Y and Pauli-Z operations on the target qubit under the same condition, that is, to perform the gate operation of the control gate state at $|1\rangle$. These gates provide essential building blocks for constructing complex quantum circuits and provide a critical role while performing the tasks like quantum error correction, quantum teleportation, and quantum cryptography. All the control gates have one thing in common: they perform the qubit gate operation on the target qubit if the control qubit is in state $|1\rangle$, and the code for any control gate has a common structure:

```
C-(Gate) = qc.c{gate}({gate\_parameters})
```

where Gate refers to the particular gate and the gate parameters are the parameters for the gates being referred to, such as the Pauli-Y gate (`qc.cy(n,m)` where n refers to the control qubit and m refers to the target qubit where the Pauli-Y gate operation is) or RZ (`qc.crz(`θ`, n, m)` where θ refers to the angle of rotation for the target qubit, n refers to the control qubit, and m refers to the target qubit on which the RZ gate operation is to be performed). Similarly, all the control gate operations can be performed.

Qiskit provides a wide variety of gates that simplify the process of quantum computation. Among these, several advanced gates have been introduced to enhance functionalities such as the R_{XX} and R_{ZZ} gates that entangle as well as rotate two qubits with a certain angle. These newly added gates result from advancements and optimizations in quantum algorithms. They may not always reduce execution time on quantum hardware, as they are often decomposed into native gates for implementation. All complex, operation-specific gates that are developed utilize the concepts and principles of these fundamental gates in specific combinations. For example, the SWAP gate, which swaps the states of two qubits, can be decomposed into a combination of three CNOT gates, represented as

$$\text{SWAP}(0, 1) = \text{CNOT}(0, 1) \cdot \text{CNOT}(1, 0) \cdot \text{CNOT}(0, 1) \tag{3-31}$$

The creation of the SWAP gate is just one example of how new quantum gates are developed based on use case scenarios, with the aim of optimizing code efficiency and performance. Moving forward, we will explore some of the fundamental and most commonly used quantum circuits and understand how these quantum gates are used in them. This foundational knowledge will serve to clarify the basics as we delve into more advanced circuits.

3.3 Important Quantum Circuits

An important aspect of realizing any quantum algorithm is quantum circuits. In this section, we will be looking into an in-depth explanation of the important quantum circuits and the quantum algorithms they help in solving using the Qiskit code and the quantum gates that are associated in solving them.

- **Two-Qubit State Preparation: Bell States**
  Bell entanglement, also known as Bell states or EPR pairs, is a phenomenon in quantum mechanics where two qubits become intrinsically correlated, regardless of the physical distance between them. Bell states are specific types of entangled states with unique properties, and they are created by applying a Hadamard gate to q_0, followed by a CNOT gate with q_0 as the control and q_1 as the target. Bell states are typically used to describe the entanglement of two qubits, though the concept can be extended to larger systems. Each Bell state represents a specific combination of the basis states $|00\rangle, |01\rangle, |10\rangle, |11\rangle$, existing in a superposition of these configurations. Bell states exhibit non-local correlations, where measurement outcomes of one qubit are instantly correlated with the other, regardless of physical separation. When two qubits are in a Bell state, measuring one qubit determines the measurement outcome of the other, even at a distance. Though probabilistic, the outcomes are correlated in a specific way, depending on the Bell state chosen.
  There are four Bell states, defined as follows:

  $$|\phi^+\rangle = \frac{|00\rangle + |11\rangle}{\sqrt{2}}, \quad |\phi^-\rangle = \frac{|00\rangle - |11\rangle}{\sqrt{2}} \tag{3-32}$$

  $$|\psi^+\rangle = \frac{|01\rangle + |10\rangle}{\sqrt{2}}, \quad |\psi^-\rangle = \frac{|01\rangle - |10\rangle}{\sqrt{2}} \tag{3-33}$$

  In this example, we generate the Bell state $|\phi^+\rangle$. Starting with qubits initialized to the state $|00\rangle$, a Hadamard gate on q_0 creates a superposition in the computational basis. Applying a CNOT gate then produces an equal superposition of $|00\rangle$ and $|11\rangle$, with amplitudes of $\frac{1}{\sqrt{2}}$.
  Initializing the qubits to different starting states can produce other Bell states. These states have distinct properties and are widely used in quantum information processing tasks such as quantum teleportation, quantum cryptography, and various quantum computing algorithms. Bell entanglement highlights the powerful and counterintuitive nature of quantum mechanics, showcasing the intricate, non-local correlations possible between quantum systems.

  ```
  from qiskit import QuantumCircuit, QuantumRegister
  from qiskit import ClassicalRegister
  from qiskit.visualization import *

  qc = QuantumCircuit(2, 2)
  qc.h(0)
  qc.cx(0, 1)
  qc.measure([0, 1], [0, 1])

  qc.draw(output='mpl')
  ```

  The resulting output shown in Figure 3-5 for the code in 3.3 displays the output circuit and the measured output states.

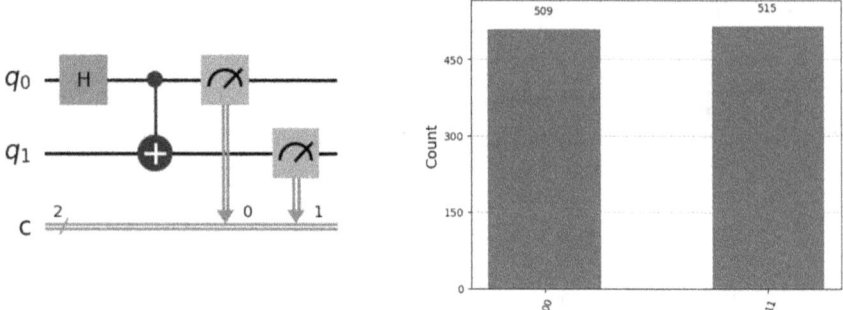

Figure 3-5 Two-qubit state preparation—Bell states for code 3.3

- **Multi-qubit State Preparation: GHZ State**

  The GHZ state, also known as the Greenberger-Horne-Zeilinger state, is a type of entangled state involving multiple qubits. In the GHZ state, all qubits are entangled so that their measurement outcomes are perfectly correlated. To create a GHZ state, a Hadamard gate (H) is applied to qubit q_0, followed by CNOT gates where q_0 is used as the control qubit, and q_1 and q_2 are the target qubits. The resulting GHZ state is

  $$|\text{GHZ}\rangle = \frac{|000\rangle + |111\rangle}{\sqrt{2}} \qquad (3\text{-}34)$$

  In other words, all three qubits are entangled in a superposition of states where they are either all in the state $|0\rangle$ or all in the state $|1\rangle$. When the qubits are measured, their outcomes will be perfectly correlated: if one qubit is measured as $|0\rangle$, the others will also be $|0\rangle$; similarly, if one is measured as $|1\rangle$, the others will be $|1\rangle$.

  The GHZ state is a valuable resource in quantum information processing, particularly in quantum error correction, quantum secret sharing, and testing fundamental aspects of quantum mechanics. It exemplifies quantum non-locality, showing that measurements on one qubit can instantaneously affect the outcomes of measurements on other entangled qubits, even when physically separated. This property has been experimentally verified, providing evidence of the non-local nature of quantum systems.

  The GHZ state has practical applications, such as

  - **Quantum Error Correction**: By creating and manipulating GHZ states, it becomes possible to detect and correct errors during quantum computations or quantum communication. The correlations within the GHZ state help identify and rectify errors, enhancing the reliability of quantum information processing.
  - **Quantum Metrology**: The entanglement within the GHZ state enables measurements with sensitivity beyond what is achievable with classical systems.

3.3 Important Quantum Circuits

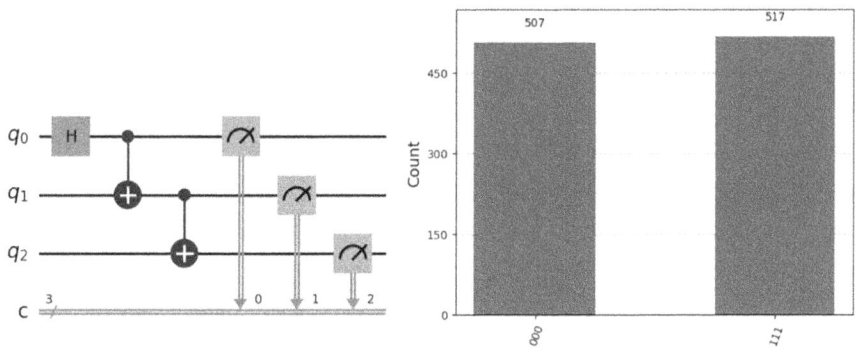

Figure 3-6 Multi-qubit state preparation—GHZ state 3.3

This property makes GHZ states useful in fields such as quantum sensing, gravitational wave detection, and magnetic field measurement.

Overall, the GHZ state plays a crucial role in understanding and utilizing entanglement and non-local correlations in quantum systems. Its significance lies in both practical applications, like error correction and metrology, and in expanding our understanding of the fundamental principles of quantum mechanics.

```
from qiskit import QuantumCircuit, QuantumRegister,
ClassicalRegister
qc = QuantumCircuit(3,3)
qc.h(0)
qc.cx(0,1)
qc.cx(1,2)
qc.measure([0,1,2], [0,1,2])
circuit_drawer(qc, output='mpl')
```

This code creates a functioning GHZ state by generating an equal superposition of states $|000\rangle$ and $|111\rangle$:

$$|GHZ\rangle = \frac{|000\rangle + |111\rangle}{\sqrt{2}} \qquad (3\text{-}35)$$

This code efficiently creates a three-qubit GHZ state as displayed in Figure 3-6, where all qubits are in a fully entangled state. Measuring any qubit collapses the state, meaning that if you measure one qubit and get 0, all others will also be 0; if you get 1, all others will be 1.

- **Quantum Teleportation Circuit**
  Quantum teleportation is a fundamental protocol in quantum information theory that enables the transfer of quantum information from one qubit to another without physically moving the qubit itself. It relies on the entanglement and classical communication between the sender, receiver, and an intermediary,

often referred to as Bob. Let's walk through the basic circuit and mathematics of quantum teleportation. The circuit for quantum teleportation involves three qubits: the sender's qubit (Alice's qubit), the receiver's qubit (Bob's qubit), and an entangled qubit shared between Alice and Bob.

Here's how the quantum teleportation protocol works step by step:

Initialization: Alice and Bob share an entangled pair of qubits, q_1 and q_2, which are in an entangled state such as a Bell state:

$$|\phi^+\rangle = \frac{|00\rangle + |11\rangle}{\sqrt{2}}. \tag{3-36}$$

Preparation: Alice possesses the qubit q_0 that she wants to teleport to Bob. Alice applies a Hadamard gate (H) to q_0 to create a superposition:

$$|\psi\rangle = \frac{|0\rangle + |1\rangle}{\sqrt{2}} \otimes |\phi^+\rangle. \tag{3-37}$$

Alice then performs a controlled-NOT (CNOT) gate with q_0 as the control and q_1 as the target, followed by a Hadamard gate on q_0.

Measurement and Classical Communication: Alice measures both q_0 and q_1 and sends the measurement outcomes to Bob via classical communication channels (typically represented as classical bits 0 or 1).

Bob's Operations: Bob applies gates to his qubit q_2 based on the measurement results received from Alice:

- If the measurement outcome for q_1 was 1, Bob applies a Pauli-X gate (X) to q_2.
- If the measurement outcome for q_0 was 1, Bob applies a Pauli-Z gate (Z) to q_2.

At the end of this protocol, Bob's qubit q_2 will be in the state $|\psi\rangle$, which is the original state of Alice's qubit q_0 that was teleported. The actual state of q_0 has been "teleported" to q_2.

The mathematics behind quantum teleportation relies on the principles of quantum gates, entanglement, and measurement outcomes to achieve the desired teleportation. The specific gates applied and the entanglement between qubits ensure that the information carried by the initial qubit is transferred to the final qubit while preserving the quantum state integrity. Successful teleportation depends on the availability of an entangled pair of qubits between Alice and Bob, along with classical communication.

Quantum teleportation has profound implications for our understanding of quantum mechanics. It demonstrates the non-local nature of entanglement and verifies the principles of quantum superposition and quantum measurement. The successful implementation of quantum teleportation provides experimental evidence supporting the validity of quantum mechanics.

3.3 Important Quantum Circuits

Overall, quantum teleportation is a critical concept in quantum information science. It enables secure communication, facilitates error correction, supports the development of quantum networks, and advances quantum computing algorithms. Quantum teleportation is fundamental in developing quantum networks, where multiple quantum devices can exchange quantum information, facilitating distributed quantum computing and collaborative quantum protocols. Quantum teleportation also serves as a core operation in many quantum algorithms and protocols, allowing the transfer of qubits and quantum states across different parts of a quantum circuit to enable complex computations and information processing tasks.

```
from qiskit import QuantumRegister, ClassicalRegister,
QuantumCircuit
from numpy import pi

qreg_q = QuantumRegister(3, 'q')
creg_c = ClassicalRegister(3, 'c')
circuit = QuantumCircuit(qreg_q, creg_c)

circuit.h(qreg_q[0])
circuit.h(qreg_q[1])
circuit.cx(qreg_q[1], qreg_q[2])
circuit.cx(qreg_q[0], qreg_q[1])
circuit.barrier(qreg_q[0], qreg_q[1], qreg_q[2])
circuit.measure(qreg_q[0], creg_c[0])
circuit.measure(qreg_q[1], creg_c[1])
circuit.barrier(qreg_q[0], qreg_q[1], qreg_q[2])
circuit.x(qreg_q[2]).c_if(creg_c, 1)
circuit.z(qreg_q[2]).c_if(creg_c, 1)
circuit.barrier(qreg_q[0], qreg_q[1], qreg_q[2])
circuit.measure(qreg_q[2], creg_c[0])
```

This code implements a **quantum teleportation** circuit using Qiskit where qubit 0 is the original state of Alice which we want to transport, qubit 1 is used for transporting the data, and qubit 2 is the state of Bob where Alice's qubit data is transferred to. It starts by creating a three-qubit register and entangles qubits 1 and 2 using a Hadamard gate followed by a CNOT gate, forming an entangled pair. Qubit 0, which holds the state to be teleported, is entangled with qubit 1 through additional CNOT and Hadamard gates. Alice measures qubits 0 and 1, and the results are stored in classical bits. Depending on Alice's measurement results, Bob applies conditional X and Z gates on qubit 2 to correct its state. After this correction, qubit 2 now holds the original state that was on qubit 0, successfully completing the teleportation. The output counts you see in Figure 3-7 represent the successful teleportation events, with an equal superposition of 0 and 1 on the classical bits. Since the measurements of the Bell pair and the adjustments (X, Z operations) are probabilistic, you will see some variation in the counts, but ideally the teleported qubit should end up in the same state as the input state.

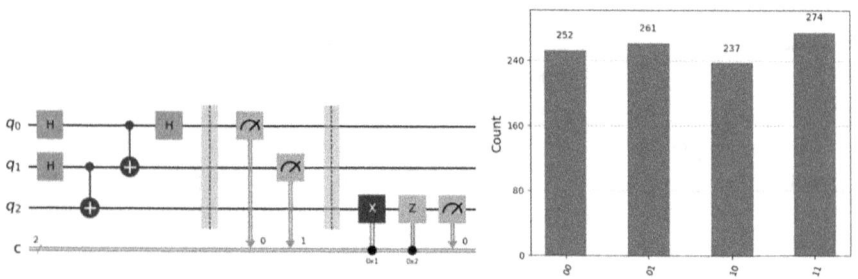

Figure 3-7 Quantum teleportation circuit example for 3.3

- **Quantum Fourier Transform (QFT)**
  The Quantum Fourier Transform (QFT) is a fundamental operation in quantum computing that plays a crucial role in many quantum algorithms, such as Shor's algorithm for factoring large numbers. The Quantum Fourier Transform is applied to an n-qubit input state $q[0], q[1], \ldots, q[n-1]$. The circuit consists of a series of Hadamard gates (H) and phase rotation gates (R) with varying rotation angles.
  Hadamard Gates (H): The Hadamard gate is applied to each qubit in the input state. It transforms the qubits from the computational basis ($|0\rangle$ and $|1\rangle$) to a superposition of both basis states.
  Phase Rotation Gates (R): Phase rotation gates are applied to each qubit, with the rotation angles dependent on the position of the qubit. The rotation angles are given by the formula $\frac{2\pi}{2^k}$, where k is the position of the qubit in the input state. For example, the first qubit ($q[0]$) undergoes no phase rotation. The second qubit ($q[1]$) undergoes a rotation of $\frac{2\pi}{2^2}$, the third qubit ($q[2]$) undergoes a rotation of $\frac{2\pi}{2^3}$, and so on. This pattern continues until the n-th qubit ($q[n-1]$), which undergoes a rotation of $\frac{2\pi}{2^{n-1}}$. The phase rotation gates introduce relative phase shifts between the basis states, which are essential for the QFT operation.
  The resulting state after applying the Quantum Fourier Transform is a transformed state in the frequency domain. It represents the amplitudes of different frequency components present in the input state. It's important to note that the circuit representation provided here is a high-level depiction of the Quantum Fourier Transform and may not show the specific control and target qubit connections required for efficient implementation. The actual implementation of the QFT may involve additional optimizations and circuit arrangements depending on the specific quantum computing platform or algorithm being used.

```
from qiskit import QuantumRegister, ClassicalRegister,
QuantumCircuit
from numpy import pi

qreg_q = QuantumRegister(3, 'q')
creg_c = ClassicalRegister(3, 'c')
```

3.3 Important Quantum Circuits

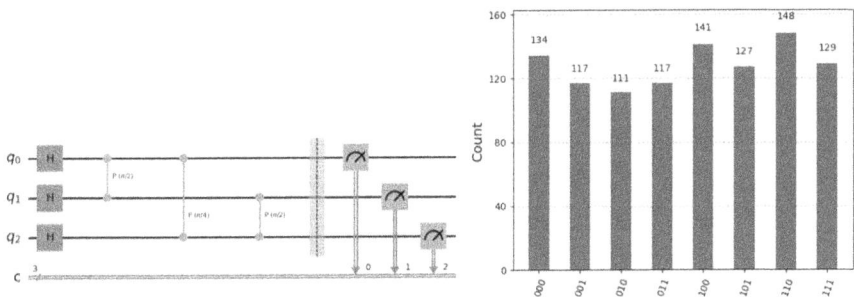

Figure 3-8 Quantum Fourier Transform circuit example for 3.3

```
circuit = QuantumCircuit(qreg_q, creg_c)

circuit.h(qreg_q[0])
circuit.h(qreg_q[1])
circuit.h(qreg_q[2])
circuit.cp(pi / 2, qreg_q[1], qreg_q[0])
circuit.cp(pi / 4, qreg_q[2], qreg_q[0])
circuit.cp(pi / 2, qreg_q[2], qreg_q[1])
circuit.barrier(qreg_q[0], qreg_q[1], qreg_q[2])
circuit.measure(qreg_q[0], creg_c[0])
circuit.measure(qreg_q[1], creg_c[1])
circuit.measure(qreg_q[2], creg_c[2])
```

The example of circuit for QFT is provided in 3.3. The code begins by applying Hadamard gates to all three qubits to put them into a superposition state. It then applies controlled-phase shift (cp) gates between pairs of qubits, which are key components of the QFT. The phase shifts are done with angles of $\frac{\pi}{2}$ and $\frac{\pi}{4}$ radians, introducing relative phases between qubits based on their states. Finally, the qubits are measured, and the results are stored in classical bits. In a QFT on a three-qubit register, as we can see in Figure 3-8, you would expect all eight possible states ("000," "001," "010," "011," "100," "101," "110," and "111") to have approximately equal probability if there were no imperfections in the circuit. Since you're using 1024 shots, each outcome should ideally have about 128 counts (1024/8 = 128). The output is now reasonably well distributed, showing that the QFT is correctly implemented and that quantum measurement is producing outcomes close to what would be expected from a proper Quantum Fourier Transform.

- **Steane Code**
  The Steane code is a quantum error correction code that protects against single-qubit errors, phase-flip errors, and some types of two-qubit errors. It encodes one logical qubit into seven physical qubits, providing error detection and correction capabilities. The circuit for the Steane code involves encoding, error detection, and error correction operations. In the circuit diagram above, $q[0]$ to $q[6]$ represent the seven physical qubits used in the Steane code. The H

gates represent the Hadamard gates, and the X gates represent the controlled-X (CNOT) gates. The ancilla qubits are used for error detection and correction. The circuit performs the encoding, error detection, and error correction operations for the Steane code. The specific gates and measurements on ancilla qubits are used to detect and correct errors in the encoded qubit.

The Steane code encodes one logical qubit into seven physical qubits, expanding the information over multiple qubits. These seven qubits are arranged in a specific pattern that allows for error detection and correction. The encoding process involves applying a series of gates to the physical qubits to create an entangled state. This entanglement spreads the information of the logical qubit across the seven physical qubits. By doing so, errors that occur on individual qubits can be detected and corrected. During error detection, ancilla qubits (extra qubits used for error detection) are entangled with the data qubits. By analyzing the state of the ancilla qubits, it is possible to determine if any errors have occurred on the data qubits. If errors are detected, the error correction process takes place. Gates are applied to the appropriate qubits to correct the errors based on the measurement outcomes of the ancilla qubits. The Steane code provides a means to protect quantum information from errors and increase the reliability of quantum computations. It is an important component in building fault-tolerant quantum computers by mitigating the impact of errors inherent in quantum systems.

```
from qiskit import QuantumRegister, ClassicalRegister, QuantumCircuit
from numpy import pi

qreg_q = QuantumRegister(7, 'q')
creg_c = ClassicalRegister(7, 'c')
circuit = QuantumCircuit(qreg_q, creg_c)

circuit.h(qreg_q[0])
circuit.h(qreg_q[2])
circuit.h(qreg_q[1])
circuit.cx(qreg_q[0], qreg_q[3])
circuit.cx(qreg_q[1], qreg_q[4])
circuit.cx(qreg_q[2], qreg_q[5])
circuit.ccx(qreg_q[0], qreg_q[1], qreg_q[6])
circuit.cx(qreg_q[2], qreg_q[6])
circuit.ccx(qreg_q[0], qreg_q[2], qreg_q[6])
circuit.cx(qreg_q[2], qreg_q[6])
circuit.cx(qreg_q[3], qreg_q[6])
circuit.cx(qreg_q[4], qreg_q[6])
circuit.cx(qreg_q[5], qreg_q[6])
circuit.ccx(qreg_q[6], qreg_q[3], qreg_q[0])
circuit.measure(qreg_q[0], creg_c[0])
circuit.ccx(qreg_q[6], qreg_q[4], qreg_q[1])
circuit.measure(qreg_q[3], creg_c[3])
circuit.measure(qreg_q[1], creg_c[1])
circuit.ccx(qreg_q[6], qreg_q[5], qreg_q[2])
```

3.3 Important Quantum Circuits

```
circuit.measure(qreg_q[4], creg_c[4])
circuit.measure(qreg_q[2], creg_c[2])
circuit.measure(qreg_q[5], creg_c[5])
circuit.measure(qreg_q[6], creg_c[6])
```

The provided code in 3.3 is implementing a quantum circuit for Steane's seven-qubit code for quantum error correction and is displayed in Figure 3-9; it is achieved by

- Hadamard gates are applied to the first three qubits to create superposition, while controlled-X (CNOT) and controlled-controlled-X (Toffoli) gates are used to entangle the qubits in a way that encodes quantum information across multiple qubits.
- The sequence of operations creates logical qubits and their entanglements, and measurements are made at the end to extract the classical outcome.
- This circuit is useful in the context of fault-tolerant quantum computing, where error correction plays a critical role in maintaining the integrity of quantum states during computations.
- The use of Toffoli and CNOT gates in conjunction with entanglement and measurement helps ensure that the encoded information can be read out and corrected if any qubits are subjected to noise or errors.
- The output counts for the same are '0110110': 128, '1101000': 135, '1111000': 109, '1100000': 114, '1011000': 128, '1001000': 123, '0000000': 152, '1010000': 135. The most frequent state is $|0000000\rangle$, which is expected for a correct encoding. The other outcomes are typical of quantum error correction code, where error syndromes can result in different measurement outcomes. The slight fluctuations in the counts across different states are normal in quantum computing due to noise and imperfect gates, and they show that the quantum error correction procedure is functioning as expected.

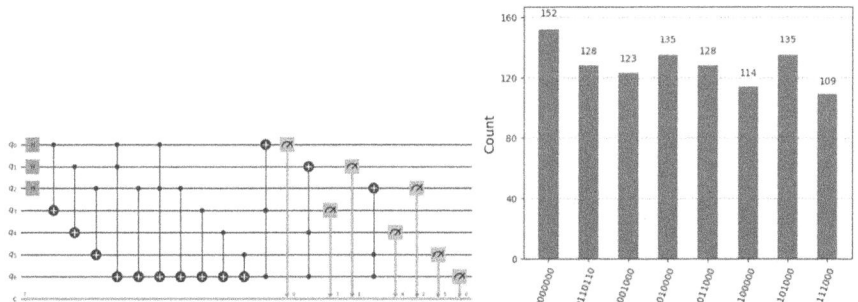

Figure 3-9 Steane error correcting circuit example for 3.3

- **Grover's Algorithm**
  Grover's algorithm is a quantum algorithm that allows searching an unsorted database with a quadratic speedup over classical algorithms. The algorithm follows these steps:

  1. **Initialization**: Apply Hadamard gates (H) to all qubits to create a superposition of all possible states.
  2. **Oracle Operation**: The oracle is implemented using controlled operations to mark the desired solution. Here, an X gate (X) is applied to the first qubit, $q[0]$, followed by a controlled-controlled-X (CCX) gate on qubits $q[1]$ and $q[2]$ with $q[0]$ as the control qubit.
  3. **Diffusion Operator**: This step amplifies the amplitude of the desired solution by applying a sequence of gates: Hadamard (H), Pauli-X (X), and controlled-controlled-X (CCX) gates. This process is often referred to as the "inversion about the mean."
  4. **Measurement**: Finally, measure all qubits, storing the results in the classical register, c.

  Grover's algorithm provides a quadratic speedup for searching unsorted databases. This efficiency can be applied to

  – **Cryptanalysis**: Grover's algorithm is useful in breaking symmetric encryption, as it significantly reduces the time required for key searches.
  – **Optimization Problems**: It can help solve combinatorial optimization problems like the Traveling Salesman Problem (TSP) or graph coloring by quickly finding optimal solutions.
  – **Quantum Simulations**: Grover's algorithm aids in locating specific states or properties within quantum systems, accelerating the exploration of quantum states.

  ```
  from qiskit import QuantumRegister, ClassicalRegister,
  QuantumCircuit
  from numpy import pi
  qreg_q = QuantumRegister(7, 'q')
  creg_c = ClassicalRegister(7, 'c')
  circuit = QuantumCircuit(qreg_q, creg_c)
  circuit.h(qreg_q)
  circuit.x(qreg_q[0])
  circuit.ccx(qreg_q[1], qreg_q[2], qreg_q[0])
  circuit.x(qreg_q[0])
  circuit.h(qreg_q)
  circuit.x(qreg_q)
  circuit.h(qreg_q[6])
  circuit.ccx(qreg_q[0], qreg_q[1], qreg_q[6])
  circuit.h(qreg_q[6])
  circuit.x(qreg_q)
  circuit.h(qreg_q)
  circuit.measure(qreg_q, creg_c)
  ```

3.4 Qiskit Metal

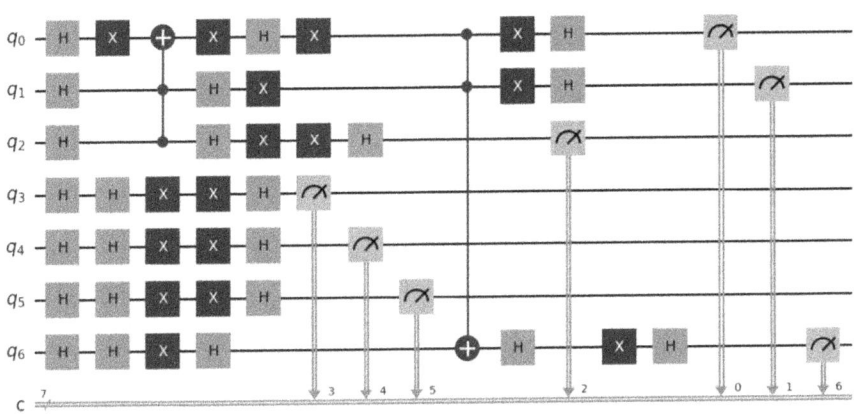

Figure 3-10 Grover's algorithm circuit example for 3.3

The provided code in 3.3 is an example of the implementation of Grover's algorithm, and the output of the code is provided in Figure 3-10; all qubits are placed into a superposition of all possible states using Hadamard gates. The algorithm then applies the oracle function, represented by a combination of X and Toffoli gates, which flips the sign of the solution state. After the oracle, the Grover diffusion operator amplifies the amplitude of the marked state, again using Hadamard and X gates along with a Toffoli gate. This process is repeated for a certain number of iterations to increase the probability of measuring the correct solution. Finally, all qubits are measured to extract the result. The algorithm operates in $O(\sqrt{N})$ time, offering a significant advantage in searching an unsorted database compared to classical algorithms.

These are some of the fundamental and essential quantum circuits widely used in the field of quantum computing. However, when working with superconducting qubits, specialized tools and packages are required to design and simulate these systems effectively. To realize and create superconducting qubits, one such tool is **Qiskit Metal**. In the following section, we will guide you through the process of installing the Qiskit Metal package on your local device. Additionally, we will explore how to develop and optimize quantum computing chips using this powerful framework.

3.4 Qiskit Metal

Qiskit Metal, developed by IBM Research and introduced by Zlatko Minev in 2020, has emerged as a game-changing tool in the field of quantum computing. It offers an open source platform for designing quantum components, especially for superconducting processors, which are central to the realization of quantum computers. The design process of quantum processors involves a complex integration of physics, engineering, and software, and Qiskit Metal simplifies this multi-step workflow.

It is primarily aimed at designing qubits, such as transmon qubits, and other essential components like resonators and couplers, which are the building blocks of quantum systems. By automating design, analysis, and optimization tasks, Qiskit Metal streamlines the process, allowing researchers and engineers to quickly iterate and refine their designs. This makes it an invaluable tool for advancing quantum technology, enabling efficient and precise development of quantum components that meet desired specifications.

Qiskit Metal benefits from robust resources and an active community of contributors. Here are some links to explore further:

- **Home**: https://qiskit.org/metal
- **Docs**: https://qiskit.org/documentation/metal
- **Code**: https://github.com/Qiskit/Qiskit-metal
- **Slack**: *#metal* (in the Qiskit workspace)

3.4.1 Designing Quantum Chips

Designing quantum processors is somewhat similar to classical chip design, as both include resonators and specific configurations. However, quantum processors differ significantly in that they require nonlinear resonators with quantum properties. To analyze these components, quantum designers must calculate Hamiltonians, wave functions, and energy levels. Qiskit Metal provides tools to facilitate these calculations and streamline the design process. In Qiskit Metal, designing and analyzing quantum parts typically involve iterative adjustments. While a single design layout and analysis may not yield the desired quantum behavior, the library's tools allow researchers to fine-tune their designs. Parameters, geometries, and layouts can be refined over multiple iterations to achieve optimal results. In essence, Qiskit Metal simplifies the task of obtaining quantum characteristics for processors that resemble classical ones structurally but require quantum-specific analysis and design; some of the benefits of Qiskit Metal software are shown in Figure 3-11.

3.4.2 Typical Quantum Processor Structure

A quantum processor may have a structure similar to Figure 3-12, comprising metals, junctions, dielectrics, and qubits. Qiskit Metal supports the detailed design and optimization of these components, enhancing the efficiency and accuracy of quantum chip development. Qiskit Metal is a key advancement for quantum research, providing the tools necessary to design and analyze quantum chips accurately and efficiently. Its role in the quantum ecosystem extends to supporting fault-tolerant quantum computing and facilitating the development of quantum processors with high fidelity, making it an indispensable resource for quantum engineers and researchers alike.

3.4 Qiskit Metal

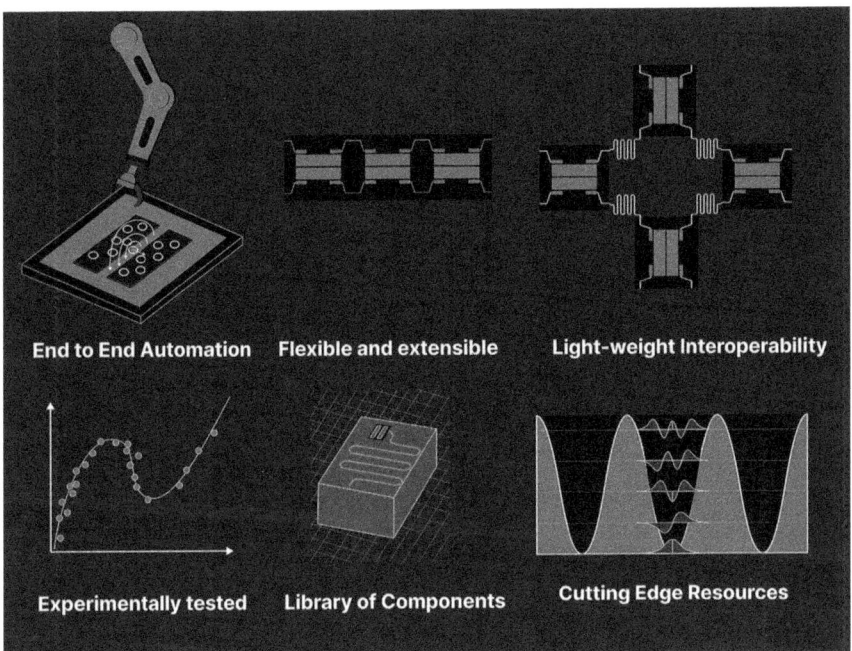

Figure 3-11 Benefits of Qiskit Metal

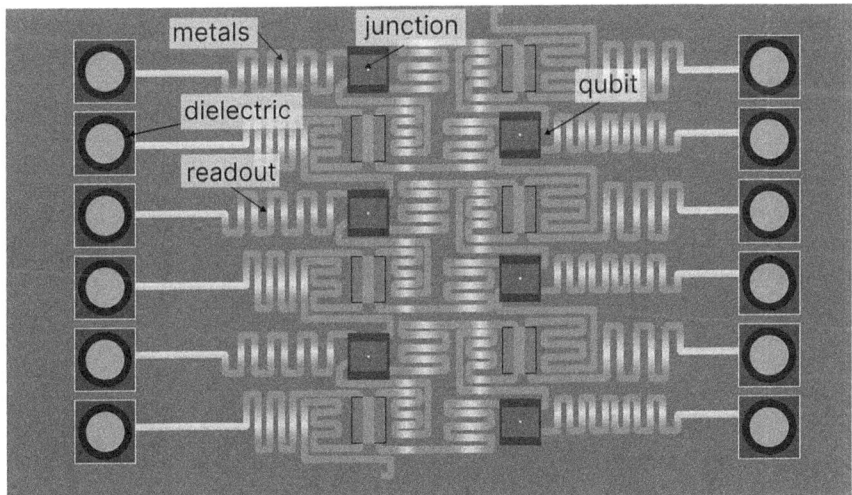

Figure 3-12 Hardware view of a superconducting qubit chip

But many things must be designed for this processor, including geometry and topology, frequency, mismatch, and qubit-to-qubit connections. All design cases for a quantum processor can be seen in Figure 3-12. The details of how to design these attributes are provided in Chapter 4.

3.5 Qiskit Metal Installation Steps

Before we begin coding with Qiskit Metal, there are a few preliminary steps to follow to install the software on your local device. This installation will enable you to render circuits and design quantum chips. To start, you'll need to download Anaconda Navigator, which is extremely helpful in running Qiskit Metal smoothly in Jupyter Notebook, making it easier to compile code.

After installing Anaconda Navigator, open the Anaconda Prompt if you are a Windows user; for macOS and Ubuntu, the following steps can be performed directly inside the home terminal. Once you open the terminal or prompt, enter this command:

`conda create -n Qiskitmetal`

As demonstrated in Figure 3-13, this command will create a virtual environment on your local system specifically for running Qiskit Metal without errors. The "Qiskitmetal" at the end of the command is the name of the environment being created, though you're free to name it as you like. Before launching Qiskit Metal, keep in mind that you'll need to retype this name, so choose something memorable and easy to recall. Additionally, ensure that no other environment with the same name exists, as this could lead to an error.

After entering the command and pressing enter, the process of creating an environment will begin. Let it run for a while until it prompts you with *proceed [y/n]* to confirm the installation. Type *y* to proceed. This will complete the creation of a virtual environment for Qiskit Metal in your local repository. Once the environment is set up, we'll need to install a few additional packages to ensure Qiskit Metal runs smoothly on your system.

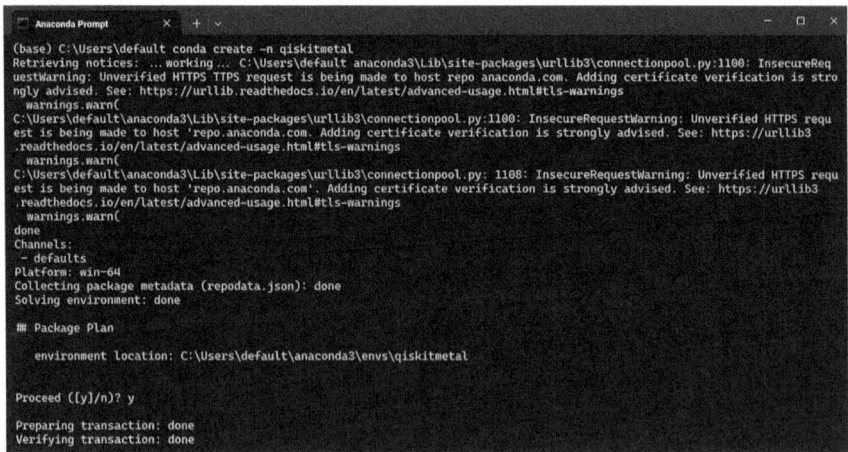

Figure 3-13 Qiskit Metal installation—creating a virtual environment using the command *"conda create -n"*

3.5 Qiskit Metal Installation Steps

First, switch from the default (base) environment to the newly created (Qiskitmetal) environment. To do this, enter the command `conda activate Qiskitmetal`, which will switch your environment from *(base)* to *(Qiskitmetal)*. This environment is empty by default, and you can confirm this by running the command `conda list`. This command will return an empty table with columns labeled "Name," "Version," and "Build Channel."

Next, install the "pip" package in this environment by running

`conda install pip`

This will allow you to install any additional packages required for Qiskit Metal. You'll see another prompt asking "***proceed [y/n]***"; type "***y***" to confirm. Ensure you have an active Internet connection, as the installation process will download all necessary pip-associated packages, as demonstrated in Figure 3-14.

Once the installation of pip packages is complete, you can verify it by entering

`conda list`

again. This will display all the installed files and packages, with "pip" included in the list. Next, let's focus on the Python version required for Qiskit Metal. The recommended stable version for Qiskit Metal is Python 3.8, but make sure to use the latest stable version available if there are updates.

To specify your Python version, use the command

`conda install python=3.8`

You can change the version of installation by replacing "3.8" with the version you prefer. When prompted with

proceed [y/n]

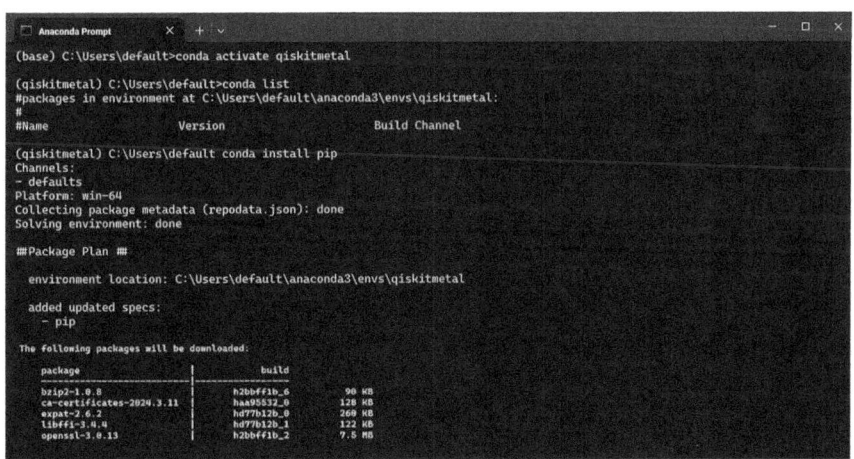

Figure 3-14 Qiskit Metal installation—installing PIP packages in the created environment for Qiskit Metal

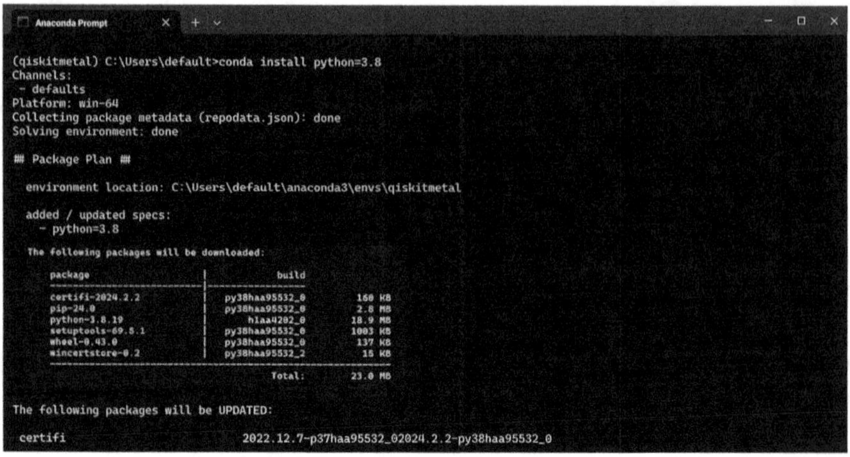

Figure 3-15 Qiskit Metal installation—installing Python in the environment

type "y" to confirm and continue the installation, as demonstrated in Figure 3-15. After the installation completes, you can verify that Python 3.8 (or your chosen version) is installed by running `conda list`
This will display all packages, including the specified Python version.

For macOS users, the installation from here will require a few additional steps. Firstly, as mentioned, you would need to install Homebrew in your created environment; it will provide the necessary wheels that will help and support the entire process of installation. In order to do that, follow these steps. This is only required for macOS users. Windows and Ubuntu should proceed directly with further installations. For installing Homebrew into your environment, run the following command:

    /bin/bash -c "\$(curl -fsSL https://raw.githubusercontent.com/Homebrew/install/HEAD/install.sh)"

This will install Homebrew into the environment. Post the installation, run the following command which is essential to activate the `brew` commands:

    echo >> /Users/subhojithalder/.zprofile

    echo 'eval "\$(/opt/homebrew/bin/brew shellenv)"' >> /Users/subhojithalder/.zprofile

    eval "\$(/opt/homebrew/bin/brew shellenv)"

These three commands will help in completing the installation process of the remaining wheels and dependencies for macOS to support Homebrew. After the installation is completed, you can now use the `brew` commands in your environment and terminal. Next, it is important to install the other dependencies for Qiskit Metal,

3.5 Qiskit Metal Installation Steps

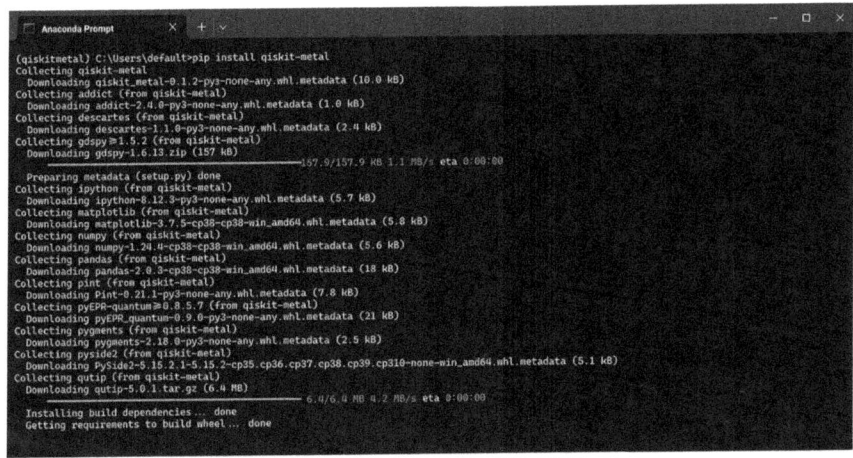

Figure 3-16 Qiskit Metal installation—installing Qiskit Metal packages

such as cmake and qt. You can proceed with the installation with brew commands in your terminal as

brew install cmake

brew install qt

Post this, all your prior dependencies and wheels required will be completed, and you can proceed with the installation of the Qiskit Metal. Unlike Windows and Ubuntu, for Qiskit Metal to be installed macOS needs a package PySide2 to be already installed as Qiskit Metal will be looking for this dependency. Instead of installing using the pip command, it is highly recommended to install it using the conda command, and it can be done by

conda install -c conda-forge pyside2

After these steps are completed, one can start with the installation of Qiskit Metal. For the final and most crucial installation step, enter the command

pip install qiskit-metal

This is demonstrated in Figure 3-16. This command will now execute smoothly, thanks to the dedicated environment you've set up and the necessary packages like "*pip*" and the compatible "*python*" version that you've installed. When running this command, ensure you have an active Internet connection, as it will download and install the Qiskit Metal package along with any dependencies required for it to function effectively in your environment.

This will install all the commands and files related to Qiskit Metal in your repository. Post the installation of Qiskit Metal, it is important to install other dependencies to ensure that the environment is supporting the chip building and generating and executing analysis on it. A few important packages to note are

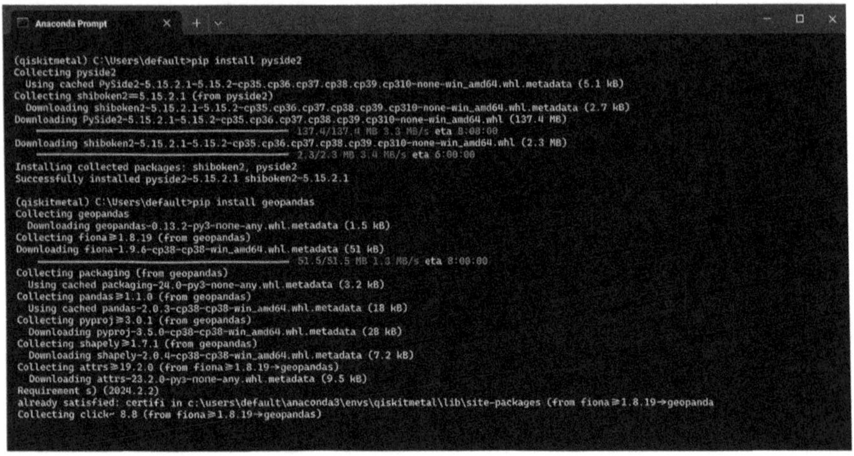

Figure 3-17 Qiskit Metal installation—installing other Qiskit Metal dependencies like pyside2 and geopandas

"*pyside*" and "*geopandas*"; also, note that during the installation process, Qiskit Metal will install the supported and stable versions of packages "numpy," "matplotlib," and "scipy." If the installations are not completed for these packages somehow, then you can complete them by running them with the pip command. To install them, run the commands

`pip install pyside2` and `pip install geopandas`

The installation commands are demonstrated in Figure 3-17.

Now once an environment is set and the packages are ready, the user can run the code, but let us also install the Jupyter Notebook in this repository so that the user can launch the Jupyter Notebook with Qiskit Metal packages in it. In order to install the Jupyter Notebook in your current environment, run the command

`pip install jupyter`

This command prompt is demonstrated in Figure 3-18.

Now that all the dependencies are installed in your local repository, you can start coding with Qiskit Metal in your Jupyter Notebook; just launch the Jupyter Notebook using the command

`jupyter notebook`

With this, it will launch the Jupyter Notebook with Qiskitmetal environment, and you can start coding freely in it.

3.5 Qiskit Metal Installation Steps

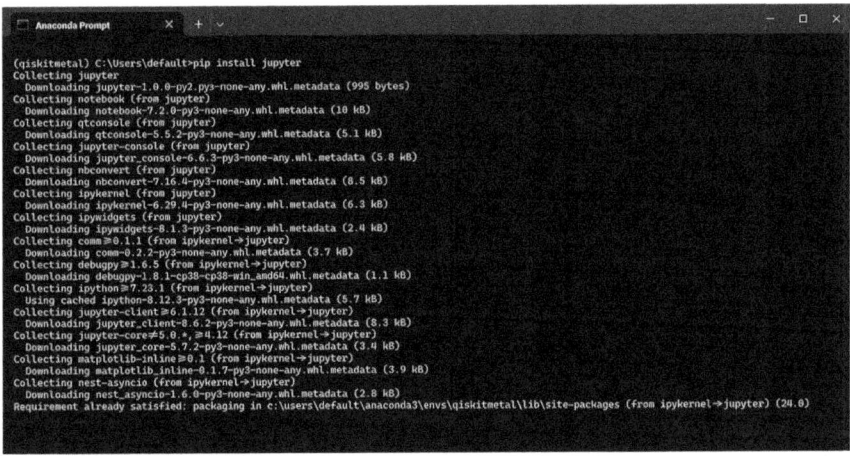

Figure 3-18 Qiskit Metal installation—installing Jupyter Notebook for coding using Qiskit Metal

If you are wondering how many times you have to do this long process, the answer is just one time during installation; post that, anytime you want to open the environment, just hit

`conda activate Qiskitmetal`

This will activate your environment with the Qiskit Metal package in it, and then hit

`jupyter notebook`

This command will launch a localhost server from your corresponding conda environment and launch Jupyter Notebook on your default browser. Once it is launched, you can import the `qiskit_metal` function and start coding in your notebook. Some of the functionalities of Qiskit Metal require the support of qiskit too; it is recommended that post launching the Jupyter Notebook, the user should proceed with the installation of Qiskit using the pip command mentioned in the beginning of the chapter, then proceed with the import of `qiskit_metal`.

To conclude, this chapter has provided a thorough introduction to coding with Qiskit, including key quantum gates, important quantum circuits, and algorithms, alongside setting up the essential tools and environment for working with Qiskit Metal. By following these steps, you have built a strong foundation for developing quantum circuits and designing quantum chips. This setup process—particularly the creation of a virtual environment, installation of necessary packages, and selection of the optimal Python version—ensures you are ready to utilize Qiskit Metal efficiently within your local system. With your environment now fully configured, you are well prepared to dive deeper into the coding aspects of Qiskit Metal.

In the next chapter, we will explore the process of coding with Qiskit Metal in greater depth, examining its various functionalities and delving into the development of quantum circuits. We'll take a step-by-step approach to essential coding techniques, from initializing components to simulating quantum chips, allowing you to fully harness Qiskit Metal's capabilities for your quantum computing projects. With your setup complete, you are poised to embark on the hands-on coding phase—an exciting step forward in your journey into quantum design.

3.6 Conclusion

In this chapter, we explored the fundamentals of coding with the Qiskit library, covering how to generate quantum circuits and simulate them to obtain measurement counts. We examined the key parameters for coding that allow customization of circuits to meet specific requirements. Additionally, we introduced the essential quantum gates available in Qiskit's library, along with important quantum algorithms, their circuit representations, and their outputs. Furthermore, we provided an overview of the benefits and applications of Qiskit Metal in designing and simulating superconducting qubits. Lastly, we presented a step-by-step guide for installing Qiskit Metal across different operating systems, including Windows, macOS, and Ubuntu.

Qiskit Metal and Introduction to Chip Design 4

As discussed in previous chapters, the **Qiskit Metal** framework plays a crucial role in designing superconducting qubits. Moving forward, we will use this framework extensively for simulations, where we'll need to code specific parameters to generate simulations, matrices, and desired outputs. The framework is built using the Python programming language, and Qiskit Metal supports a Python IDE, which facilitates efficient coding. In this chapter, we will explore how to write Python code to develop superconducting circuits. However, before diving directly into the code for superconducting qubits, it is essential to understand some basic concepts.

4.1 Qiskit Metal and Python

It's been a while since we explored coding in quantum computing using **Qiskit**, so let's quickly revisit the coding pattern. The standard approach involves starting with importing the necessary libraries, followed by creating a skeleton architecture of the circuit, and finally plotting the output. When it comes to **Qiskit Metal**, the coding process is slightly more complex compared to standard Qiskit. However, once you get accustomed to it, you'll find it quite intuitive. We will adopt a similar learning pattern as we did for Qiskit: starting with a simple flowchart, then gradually diving deeper. By the end of this chapter, you should feel confident enough to design a **Transmon qubit** on your own. Coding in **Qiskit Metal** involves using Python to create and simulate quantum circuits at the hardware level. This framework is specifically designed for the design and analysis of superconducting quantum devices.

The first step of writing a successful Qiskit Metal code is to import the libraries as we can see it from Figure 4-1. Well after the successful integration of Qiskit Metal with the local device, all dependencies will be available, so generally no need to add additional dependencies.

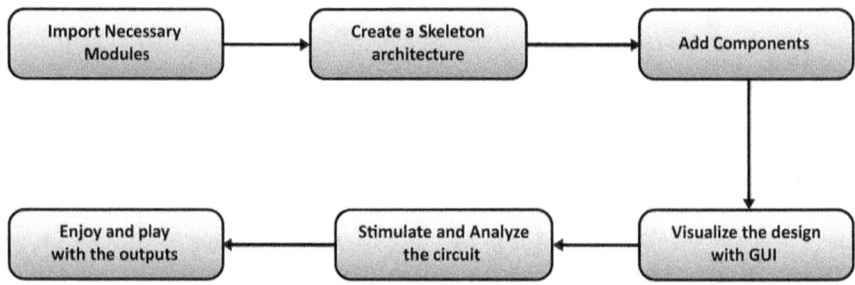

Figure 4-1 End-to-end flowchart for executing Python code for building superconducting qubits

```
from qiskit_metal import designs, draw, MetalGUI
from qiskit_metal import Dict, open_docs, metal
from qiskit_metal.qlibrary.qubits.transmon_pocket import TransmonPocket
```

Importing these two lines from qiskit_metal import designs, draw, MetalGUI, Dict, open_docs, metal and from qiskit_metal.qlibrary.qubits.transmon_pocket import TransmonPocket will sum up the entire process of importing all the libraries required for **Qiskit Metal**. Let's dive deeper into the purpose of each library:

- qiskit_metal.designs: This module provides classes for creating and manipulating quantum designs. A quantum design in Qiskit Metal represents the physical layout of qubits, resonators, and other components on a chip.
- qiskit_metal.draw: The draw module contains functions for visualizing quantum designs created using Qiskit Metal. It allows you to generate plots and drawings of your quantum circuits and components.
- qiskit_metal.MetalGUI: MetalGUI is a class that creates a graphical user interface (GUI) for working with Qiskit Metal interactively. It provides a visual representation of your quantum design and allows you to interact with and manipulate components using a graphical interface.
- qiskit_metal.Dict: The Dict class is a dictionary implementation provided by Qiskit Metal. It is designed to be used as a configuration dictionary for quantum components, allowing easy access to component parameters and settings.
- qiskit_metal.open_docs: The open_docs module provides functions for opening the Qiskit Metal documentation. This is a convenient way to access the documentation directly from within your Python environment.
- qiskit_metal.metal: The metal module provides the core functionality of Qiskit Metal. It includes classes and functions for creating quantum designs, adding components, running simulations, and performing various analyses.
- qiskit_metal.qlibrary.qubits.transmon_pocket: This module contains the TransmonPocket class, which represents a transmon qubit implemented as a pocket cavity. This pocket cavity and chip refers to a Transmon Qubit, also known as a Transmon Pocket or a Transmon component. Qiskit Metal's qubit

4.1 Qiskit Metal and Python

library includes different qubit types, and `TransmonPocket` is one example. Qubits are fundamental building blocks in quantum circuits.

These are some of the important and most commonly used libraries for building basic circuits and creating simulations. However, there are several other essential libraries that we will explore. We aim to cover as many of them as possible, along with their functions and specific use cases. Let's dive into some additional libraries:

- `qiskit_metal.analysis`: These modules provide simulation and analysis tools. For example, you might use `qiskit_metal.analysis.simulation` for setting up simulations.
- `qiskit_metal.qlibrary.terminations`: This library contains various types of terminations used to define how signals are connected or terminated in a quantum design.
- `qiskit_metal.qlibrary.qubits`: The qubits library includes different types of qubits, such as `TransmonPocket` and `Qubit_4Q_Box`, allowing you to choose different qubit implementations for your designs.
- `qiskit_metal.qlibrary.passives`: This library provides passive components like capacitors and inductors that can be used in your quantum design.
- `qiskit_metal.qlibrary.tlines`: The `tlines` library includes transmission lines, which are used to connect various components in a quantum circuit.
- `qiskit_metal.qlibrary.couplers`: The couplers library contains different types of couplers that allow for coupling of resonators or qubits in a quantum design.
- `qiskit_metal.qlibrary.hangers`: Hangers are used to connect components in a quantum circuit, and the hangers library provides various types of hangers for this purpose.
- `qiskit_metal.qlibrary.splitters`: The splitters library includes different types of power splitters used in quantum circuits.
- `qiskit_metal.qlibrary.qubits.transmon_pocket`: In addition to `TransmonPocket`, this library may contain other qubit implementations and variations.
- `qiskit_metal.qlibrary.connectors`: Connectors are used to link various elements in a quantum design. The connectors library offers different types of connectors.
- `qiskit_metal.qlibrary.qubits.transmons`: This library specifically focuses on transmon qubit implementations, providing options for different configurations.
- `qiskit_metal.renderers.renderer_ansys`: This module provides functionality for rendering Qiskit Metal designs in Ansys HFSS (High-Frequency Structure Simulator) for electromagnetic simulations.
- `qiskit_metal.renderers.renderer_blender`: The `renderer_blender` module allows rendering Qiskit Metal designs using Blender, a 3D computer

graphics software. This can be useful for creating visualizations of quantum circuits.
- `qiskit_metal.renderers.renderer_gds`: The `renderer_gds` module is used for exporting Qiskit Metal designs to GDSII (Graphic Design System II) format, which is a standard file format used in semiconductor and integrated circuit design.
- `qiskit_metal.analysis.solvers`: This module contains classes for different solvers used in Qiskit Metal, such as eigenmode solvers and other simulation techniques.
- `qiskit_metal.qlibrary.templates`: The templates module includes pre-defined templates that can be used as building blocks for designing quantum circuits. Templates provide a way to quickly create common structures.
- `qiskit_metal.toolbox_metal`: The `toolbox_metal` module includes various utility functions and tools for working with Qiskit Metal, such as file operations and analysis tools.
- `qiskit_metal.toolbox_python`: The `toolbox_python` module contains additional Python tools and utilities for working with Qiskit Metal.
- `qiskit_metal.toolbox_python.attr_dict`: The `attr_dict` module provides an `AttrDict` class, which is a dictionary with attribute-style access, allowing for cleaner and more readable code.
- `qiskit_metal.toolbox_python.transmon`: The transmon module includes functions related to Transmon qubits, providing tools for designing and analyzing circuits involving Transmons.

These are some of the libraries that we use in general, and we may encounter them in the future chapters while coding. We will explore other unused libraries that haven't been mentioned yet, along with their use cases, as we proceed with coding. Moving on to the next step, once we have successfully imported the libraries, the next step is to design the basic component structure and the skeleton architecture that we will be using while coding.

```
design = designs.DesignPlanar()
```

This line of code creates a new instance of the `DesignPlanar` class, which is part of the Qiskit Metal library that we discussed earlier. `DesignPlanar` is a class within the `designs` module. Instances of this class represent a planar quantum design. The design serves as a container for organizing and storing information about the layout of qubits, resonators, connectors, and other quantum elements on the chip. Before starting to add the components to our chip, we need to create a basic skeleton, and that's why we use this line of code to create an interface where we can add the components.

```
design = designs.DesignPlanar()
print(design)
```

If we execute the command `print(design)`, then it will return the stack location of where it is being run is stored and from which location, we can retrieve the information.

4.1 Qiskit Metal and Python

```
<qiskit_metal.designs.design_planar.DesignPlanar
object at 0x000002464A3B8648>
design.overwrite_enabled = True
design.chips.main
design.chips.main.size.size_x = '11mm'
design.chips.main.size.size_y = '9mm'
```

Let's break down the entire snippet and understand each line of the code:

- `design.overwrite_enabled = True`: This line sets the `overwrite_enabled` property of the `design` object to `True`. In Qiskit Metal, this property determines whether existing components in the design can be overwritten. Setting it to `True` allows you to overwrite existing components when adding new ones.
- `design.chips.main`: This line accesses the main chip in the design. In Qiskit Metal, a "chip" represents the physical area where quantum components are placed. By specifying `main`, you are likely indicating the main chip on the design canvas.
- `design.chips.main.size.size_x = '11mm'`: This line sets the size of the main chip along the x-axis to 11 millimeters. You can customize this value as needed. This line positions the entire circuit to extend 11 millimeters from the origin along the x-axis.
- `design.chips.main.size.size_y = '9mm'`: This line sets the size of the main chip along the y-axis to 9 millimeters. Together with the previous line, these define the dimensions of the main chip. You can customize this value as well. This line positions the entire circuit to extend 9 millimeters from the origin along the y-axis.

After designing the skeleton of the circuit, we visualize everything on the GUI. There is a simple code for that, which is

```
gui = MetalGUI(design)
gui.screenshot()
```

- `gui = MetalGUI(design)`: This line creates an instance of the `MetalGUI` class, which provides a graphical user interface (GUI) for visualizing and interacting with the quantum design. The `design` object is passed to the `MetalGUI` constructor, allowing you to view and manipulate the components on the design canvas using the GUI.
- `gui.screenshot()`: This line triggers the GUI and captures a screenshot of the current state of the design, displaying it as an image.

After running this segment, the `MetalGUI` interface is triggered, where you can add components, run code segments, and visualize the design. The GUI looks like Figure 4-2. Here, we visualize all the components that we will be adding to

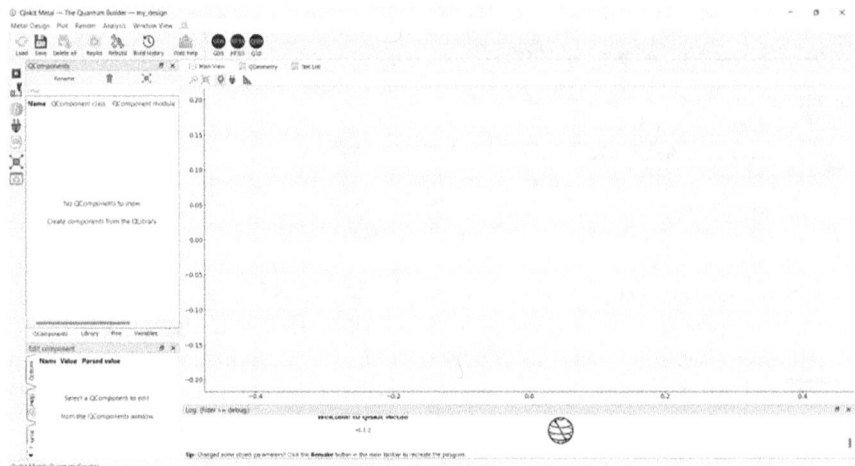

Figure 4-2 The graphical user interface for Qiskit Metal

the circuit. After we have done and built the skeleton of the circuit and made a visualization platform, we now add components to the circuit:

```
q1 = TransmonPocket(design, 'Q1',
options=dict(connection_pads=dict(a=dict())))
gui.rebuild()
gui.edit_component('Q1')
gui.autoscale()
q1.options.pos_x = '0.5 mm'
q1.options.pos_y = '0.25 mm'
q1.options.pad_height = '90um'
q1.options.pad_width  = '455um'
q1.options.pad_gap    = '30 um'
```

- `q1 = TransmonPocket(design, 'Q1', options=dict(connection_pads=dict(a=dict())))`: This line creates an instance of the `TransmonPocket` qubit and assigns it to the variable q1. It is added to the `design` object with the name 'Q1'. The `options` parameter is used to specify options for the qubit, including the connection pads.
- `gui.rebuild()`: This line rebuilds the GUI to reflect the changes made to the design. It ensures that the graphical representation is updated with the addition of the new qubit.
- `gui.edit_component('Q1')`: This line opens the GUI editor for the component named 'Q1', allowing you to interactively edit its properties and visualize it in the GUI.
- `gui.autoscale()`: This line adjusts the scaling of the GUI canvas to fit the entire design, ensuring that all components are visible within the viewport.

4.1 Qiskit Metal and Python

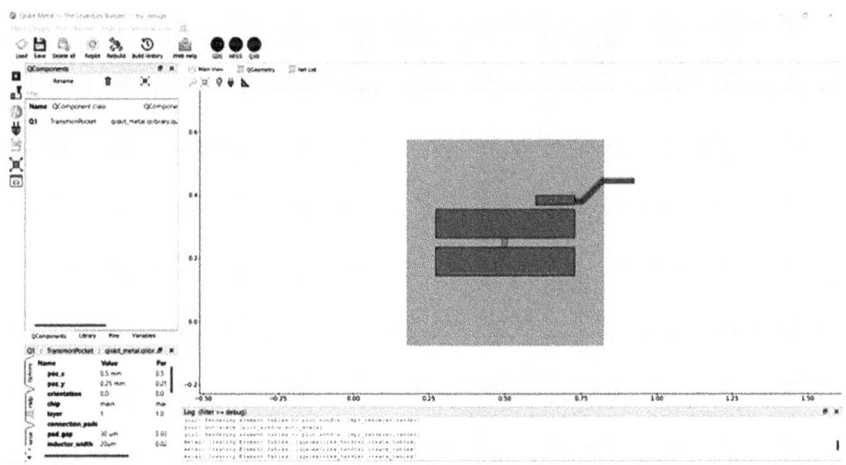

Figure 4-3 The representation of a single Transmon chip in Qiskit Meta GUI

- q1.options.pos_x, q1.options.pos_y: These lines set the x and y coordinates of the qubit q1.
- q1.options.pad_height, q1.options.pad_width: These lines set the height and width of the qubit's connection pad.
- q1.options.pad_gap: This line sets the gap length between the pads of the qubit.

After you have executed all the lines of the code, it is advised to run gui.rebuild() so that the Metal GUI interface will load the value. Once you open the Metal GUI interface again, you can see a figure representing a transmon qubit with two-qubit interface, and from this interface you can export the circuit for Q3D simulations or Ansys HFSS for further simulations and works.

Let's see the output value of the q1 Transmon qubit that we have formed and displayed in Figure 4-3. This is the corresponding value for the Transmon Pocket that we have just coded:

```
name: Q1
class: Transmon Pocket
options:
'pos_x' : '0.5 mm',
'pos_y' : '0.25 mm',
'orientation' : '0.0',
'chip' : 'main',
'layer' : '1',
'connection_pads' : {
'a' : {
    'pad_gap' : '15um',
    'pad_width' : '125um',
    'pad_height' : '30um',
    'pad_cpw_shift': '5um',
```

```
            'pad_cpw_extent': '25um',
            'cpw_width' : 'cpw_width',
            'cpw_gap' : 'cpw_gap',
            'cpw_extend' : '100um',
            'pocket_extent': '5um',
            'pocket_rise' : '65um',
            'loc_W' : '+1',
            'loc_H' : '+1', },
    },
    'pad_gap' : '30 um',
    'inductor_width': '20um',
    'pad_width' : '455um',
    'pad_height' : '90um',
    'pocket_width' : '650um',
    'pocket_height': '650um',
    'hfss_wire_bonds': False,
    'q3d_wire_bonds': False,
    'hfss_inductance': '10nH',
    'hfss_capacitance': 0,
    'hfss_resistance': 0,
    'hfss_mesh_kw_jj': 7e-06,
    'q3d_inductance': '10nH',
    'q3d_capacitance' : 0,
    'q3d_resistance' : 0,
    'q3d_mesh_kw_jj': 7e-06,
    'gds_cell_name': 'my_other_junction',
    module: qiskit_metal.qlibrary.qubits.transmon_pocket
    id: 1
```

With this, we create the quantum components that we will be using for several purposes; these quantum components are called "Qcomponents," where Q stands for quantum. Now that we are familiar with creating Qcomponents, let's dive in and look after the UI of the Qiskit Metal interface, and let's understand some other basic functionalities.

Qiskit Metal provides a lot of functionalities; let us start with some of the basic functionalities and try to understand what they say. As seen in the above example when we print the values of "Q1," we get some big array of output values; these are the functional values that we see in the Qiskit Metal. While coding, there exists a backend empty default value list of data so when we code a qubit value over it the Qiskit Metal interface what it does is that, it fetches the value from backend the default value and overwrites on that value and provides us the output that we see. So how to visualize these default values? There is a simple command that when run provides these default values:

TransmonPocket.get_template_options(design)

```
{
    'pos_x': '0.0um',
    'pos_y': '0.0um',
    'orientation': '0.0',
    'chip': 'main',
    'layer': '1',
    'connection_pads': {},
```

4.1 Qiskit Metal and Python

```
    '_default_connection_pads': {
      'pad_gap': '15um',
      'pad_width': '125um',
      'pad_height': '30um',
      'pad_cpw_shift': '5um',
      'pad_cpw_extent': '25um',
      'cpw_width': 'cpw_width',
      'cpw_gap': 'cpw_gap',
      'cpw_extend': '100um',
      'pocket_extent': '5um',
      'pocket_rise': '65um',
      'loc_W': '+1',
      'loc_H': '+1'
    },
    'pad_gap': '30um',
    'inductor_width': '20um',
    'pad_width': '455um',
    'pad_height': '90um',
    'pocket_width': '650um',
    'pocket_height': '650um',
    'hfss_wire_bonds': False,
    'q3d_wire_bonds': False,
    'hfss_inductance': '10nH',
    'hfss_capacitance': 0,
    'hfss_resistance': 0,
    'hfss_mesh_kw_jj': 7e-06,
    'q3d_inductance': '10nH',
    'q3d_capacitance': 0,
    'q3d_resistance': 0,
    'q3d_mesh_kw_jj': 7e-06,
    'gds_cell_name': 'my_other_junction'
}
```

- pos_x and pos_y: These parameters represent the position of the quantum component (Qcomponent) design in the 2D Cartesian plane. If you set pos_x=3mm and pos_y=5mm, Qiskit Metal will place the center of the Qcomponent at the coordinates (3, 5). The values for pos_x and pos_y determine the center point from which the component will be created. It is essential to specify units such as "um" for micrometers, "m" for millimeters, etc., when assigning these values.
- orientation: This parameter specifies the angle at which the Qcomponent is oriented. The default orientation is 0°. The orientation is measured in a clockwise direction. For example, setting orientation=90 rotates the Qcomponent 90° clockwise. You can assign values like 90, 180, 270, etc. If no orientation is specified, the Qcomponent will have a default orientation of 0°. Orientation plays an important role when you are trying to arrange multiple qubit chips in a layout, so to ensure proper routing between the components, for example, you want to create a chip with 10 qubits in it, now how each and every chip is placed with

which orientation will matter because how routing will take place. We will be looking at this in more depth in the upcoming sections.
- chip: This defines the chip on which the qubit is located. If not specified, the default chip is "main," meaning the primary circuit you are working on. While it is acceptable to leave this value as default when working with a single-chip architecture, specifying it becomes crucial when dealing with multiple chips to ensure the correct placement of the Qcomponent.
- layer: The layer parameter indicates the layer on which the qubit is situated. Layers are used for separating signal routing, ground planes, or specific components. If not explicitly set, the default layer is 1. Properly defining the layer is essential when working with a multilayered architecture.
- connection_pads: This parameter defines the default properties of the connection pads (connection pads enable electrical coupling between qubits and control/readout lines, facilitating signal delivery and qubit manipulation), such as their gap, width, and height. There are several fields under connection_pads related to coplanar waveguides (CPWs):
  - cpw_shift: Shift of the center conductor of the CPW pads
  - pad_cpw_extent: Extent of the CPW pads
  - cpw_width: Width of the CPW (coplanar waveguide)
  - cpw_gap: Gap between the center conductor and the ground plane in the CPW
  - cpw_extend: Extension length of the CPW beyond the qubit
  - pocket_extent: Width of the component (cavity) around the qubit
  - pocket_rise: Height of the component (cavity) surrounding the qubit
- loc_W and loc_H: These parameters determine the location of the qubit along the width (loc_W) and height (loc_H) of the chip. Typically, loc_W and loc_H values are set to +1, 0, or -1. The input values form a tuple (loc_W, loc_H). For instance:
  - Setting loc_W=+1 and loc_H=+1 places the qubit pin in the first quadrant (Cartesian coordinates (1,1)).
  - Setting loc_W=-1 and loc_H=+1 places the qubit pin in the second quadrant (Cartesian coordinates (-1,1)).

  Acceptable values for loc_W and loc_H are restricted to $(-1, 0, +1)$. Providing values outside this range may result in an incorrect or unexpected Qcomponent design. The graphical representation of the loc_W and loc_H is shown in Figure 4-4.

- hfss: These options relate to HFSS (High-Frequency Structure Simulator) simulations, including the specific material properties used in Ansys simulations and whether to include HFSS wire bonds. The parameters like hfss_inductance, hfss_capacitance, and hfss_resistance specify the inductance, capacitance, and resistance properties for the simulation. These attributes are crucial when exporting Qcomponents to run simulations in Ansys HFSS, as they define the electrical characteristics of the components. HFSS is preferred for simulations where precise 3D analysis is required where we are dealing with

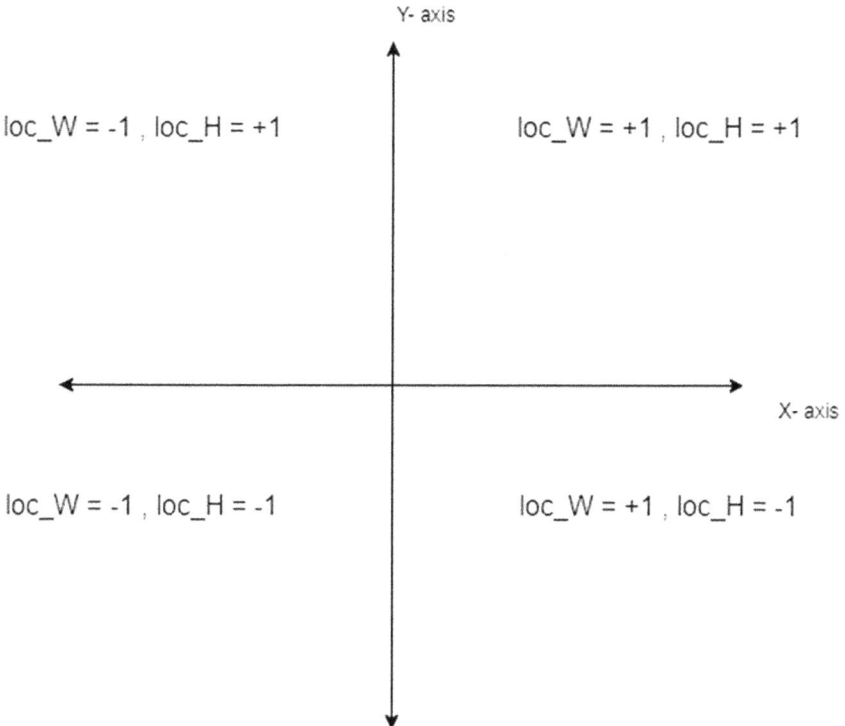

Figure 4-4 Graphical representation of loc_W and loc_H values in each quadrant

microwave frequencies such as microwave resonators, antenna analysis, and RF component analysis for signal processing component analysis.
- q3d: Similar to the HFSS parameters, these options correspond to the settings for Q3D (Quasi-3D Extractor) Extractor simulations. Q3D is another simulation tool by Ansys that focuses on extracting parasitic inductance, capacitance, and resistance values. The attributes under q3d are specifically tailored for exporting the design for Q3D simulations. Q3D is preferred for simulations where high-speed electrical transmission and power distribution come into the picture, such as finding parasitic capacitance or inductance in PCB (Printed Circuit Board) chips.

These default values facilitate the creation of simulations and Qcomponents. Now that we have examined the default options provided by Qiskit Metal, let's explore how to modify them for custom usage. Typically, we would not rely solely on the default values when creating simulations, as we often need to customize these parameters to fit specific design requirements.

It's important to note that the default design values mentioned here are specifically for a transmon qubit. These values may differ when using other types of qubits.

To change a default value, you can simply assign a new value to the corresponding attribute. For example:

```
q1.options.pos_x = '0.5 mm'
q1.options.pos_y = '250 um'
```

So, after updating, the values of pos_x and pos_y for q1 would be set to 0.5 mm and 250 um, respectively, instead of their initial default values of 0.0.

The biggest problem that occurs while dealing with multiple qubit chips is that down the line, when finalizing the routing or placement of chips or resonators, some old values need to get changed or modified. Changing a Qcomponent would mean deleting the existing Qcomponent and re-declaring the entire structure for that particular Qcomponent, and this causes a lot of issues. But, Qiskit Metal provides a unique and strong solution for this issue where it lets you overwrite the data of an existing Qcomponent without needing to re-declare it at all. This proves to be especially useful when we need quick modifications like this in your device.

Here are some common scenarios where overwriting Qcomponents might be beneficial:

- **Dynamic Design Changes**: Adjust the position, size, or orientation of qubits or other components in response to simulation results or other dynamic factors.
- **Iterative Design**: Make incremental adjustments to the design during an iterative process without creating multiple redundant instances of the same component.
- **Optimization**: Tune the parameters of qubits or other components to meet specific design objectives or optimize performance.

The ability to overwrite Qcomponents is controlled by a property called overwrite_enabled in the Qiskit Metal design object. When overwrite_enabled is set to True, you can modify existing components freely. If it is set to False, attempting to alter an existing component may lead to an error, necessitating the creation of a new component instance instead.

4.2 Quantum Pins: QPins

In the context of designing quantum circuits or quantum chips in quantum computing, "quantum pins" refer to the connection points or channels on a quantum component (such as a qubit) that are used to transmit data, connecting various quantum components to one another, and transmission and measurement of the quantum information among different components.

Let's look into some key features regarding quantum pins:

- Compared to classical circuits, quantum pins can be understood similar to that of classical electrical pins that we use in integrated circuits, but instead of classical information such as high and low pulses transmitted in classical systems, they

4.2 Quantum Pins: QPins

deal with quantum information. They act as the input and output ports (I/O ports) for quantum data transmission.

- Quantum pins play a crucial role in the process of entanglement or performing any other gate operations in the circuits. The functions of the quantum circuit are established and controlled by quantum pins.
- These quantum pins act as I/O channels for transmitting quantum information from one qubit chip to another, ensuring full connectivity in the quantum chip. Furthermore, these Qpins help in transmitting the state of qubits and handling the interactions of complex states among them.
- Qpins provide easier channels for measuring the behavior of the state the qubit is in. They allow to pass control pulses, which helps in the measurement of the quantum information that qubit is holding.
- They are easy to customize by altering the shape, width, and height as per the designer requirements without much restriction. This freedom in design also helps in managing losses for any inductance or capacitance in the chip in a real-life fabrication scenario where there might be some losses to these values. Adjusting the design parameters and values for these pins helps in overcoming these losses during the fabrication process.

Let's take an example and create a simple Qcomponent, defining its pins:

- *With Single Input Pin*

```
from qiskit_metal.qlibrary.qubits.transmon_pocket import
TransmonPocket
design.delete_all_components()
options = dict(
    pad_width = '425 um',
    pocket_height = '650um',
    connection_pads=dict(  # pin connecotrs
        a = dict(loc_W=+1,loc_H=+1)
    )
)
q1 = TransmonPocket(design, 'Q1', options = dict
 (pos_x='+0.5mm',
pos_y='+0.5mm', **options))
# Take a screenshot with the component highlighted and
 the pins shown
gui.rebuild()
gui.autoscale()
gui.edit_component('Q1')
gui.zoom_on_components(['Q1'])
gui.highlight_components(['Q1'])
gui.screenshot()
```

As we can see in Figure 4-5, we have a transmon pocket Q1 with a single Qpin that we have labeled as "a." When working with a single-qubit pin, we generally

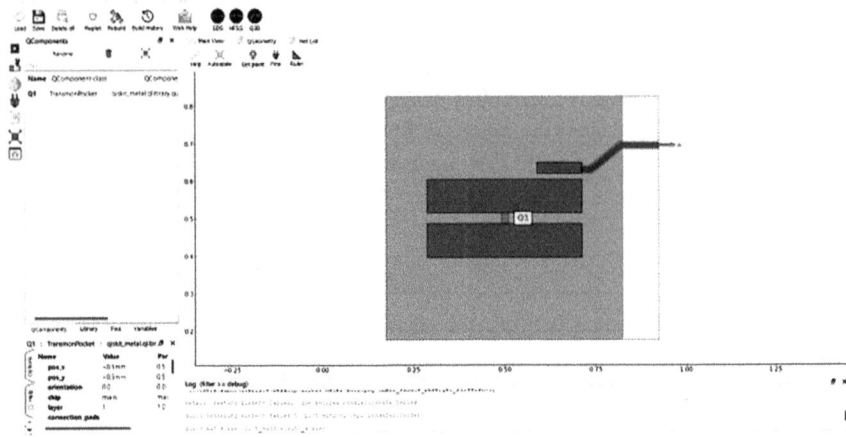

Figure 4-5 A single Transmon qubit chip with a single Qpin

just mention the position loc width and height as (+1, +1) which specifies the pin location in the first quadrant.

- **With Multiple Input Pins**

```
from qiskit_metal.qlibrary.qubits.transmon_pocket
import TransmonPocket
design.delete_all_components()
options = dict(
    pad_width = '425 um',
    pocket_height = '650um',
    connection_pads=dict(  # pin connecotrs
        a = dict(loc_W=+1,loc_H=+1),
        b = dict(loc_W=-1,loc_H=+1, pad_height='30um'),
        c = dict(loc_W=+1,loc_H=-1, pad_width='200um'),
        d = dict(loc_W=-1,loc_H=-1, pad_height='50um')
    )
)
q1 = TransmonPocket(design, 'Q1', options = dict
 (pos_x='+0.5mm',
pos_y='+0.5mm', **options))
# Take a screenshot with the component highlighted and
  the pins shown
gui.rebuild()
gui.autoscale()
gui.edit_component('Q1')
gui.zoom_on_components(['Q1'])
gui.highlight_components(['Q1'])
gui.screenshot()
```

4.2 Quantum Pins: QPins

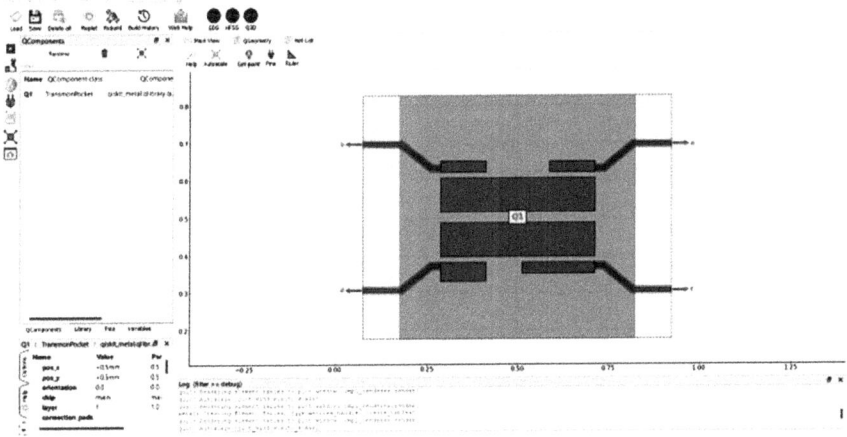

Figure 4-6 A single Transmon Qubit with multiple Qpins

We have written a code for a transmon component with four Qpins ("a," "b," "c," "d") and provided each with location and pad heights as shown in Figure 4-6.

Now that we have created Qcomponents with single as well as multiple Qpins, then we should be able to access them too. So we can access the data in these pins by running a simple command .pins; this will return all the values stored in the pin. Let us understand how we can do it for a single pin and how we can fetch the value for the qpins and what each and every value means.

q1.pins.a or q1.pins['a']

```
{
  'points': [array([0.925, 0.7]), array([0.925, 0.69])],
  'middle': array([0.925, 0.695]),
  'normal': array([1., 0.]),
  'tangent': array([0., 1.]),
  'width': 0.01,
  'gap': 0.006,
  'chip': 'main',
  'parent_name': 9,
  'net_id': 0,
  'length': 0
}
```

- **points**: Represents a list of two 2D points that define the start and end positions of the qubit pin. These coordinates specify where the pin begins and ends on the design plane. The output visible is in an array format where the first element represents the start point and the next represents the end point of the pin.

- `middle`: Indicates the midpoint between the start and end points of the qubit pin. This is essentially the geometric center of the pin. The output is in array format providing the `x` and `y` coordinates.
- `normal`: Refers to the normal vector of the qubit pin, which is perpendicular to the pin's surface. That is, the line that is perpendicular to the surface of the pin will provide the magnitude of x and y coefficients in an array format. This vector is important for defining the orientation of the pin in the quantum circuit layout.
- `tangent`: The tangent vector along the qubit pin. It describes the direction in which the pin extends, aligning with its longitudinal axis. That is, the line that is tangential to the surface of the pin will provide the magnitude of x and y coefficients in an array format.
- `width`: Specifies the width of the qubit pin. This parameter is crucial for defining the physical dimensions of the pin, especially in designs involving coplanar waveguides or transmission lines.
- `length`: Indicates the physical length of the qubit pin, measured along its tangent vector. The length is important for determining the impedance, capacitance, and other electrical properties of the pin.
- `gap`: Represents the distance between the qubit pin and the adjacent component. This spacing is vital for maintaining proper isolation and preventing electromagnetic interference between components.
- `chip`: Identifies the specific chip where the qubit pin is located. This is useful when designing circuits with multiple chips or layers.
- `parent_name`: The name or identifier of the parent component to which the qubit pin belongs. For instance, this could be the name of the transmon qubit that hosts the pin.
- `net_id`: Refers to the network identifier (net ID) associated with the qubit pin. This ID is used to group pins that are electrically connected, forming a network.

4.3 Routing Between the Qcomponents

Routes are strips of metal (or cuts in the bulk metal) that electrically connect two input-specified pins. A **pin** is a point on the perimeter of a Qcomponent, with a specific orientation, indicating an allowed point for electrical contact. The core class QRoute is designed to support different route types, currently limited to single or double coplanar waveguide (CPW) wiring.

QRoute inherits from the generic Qcomponent. It also has two attributes of type QRouteLead, which enable precise control of the start and end points of a route. In this notebook, we will describe how to utilize the QRouteLead. The QRoutePoint is a convenient format for representing directed points. QRoute is an abstract class without a make() method, and, thus, it cannot be instantiated directly as a design component. Instead, QRoute is inherited by classes that can be instantiated (i.e., those with a make() method, highlighted in blue in the image below). By further subclassing, you can implement more comprehensive routing algorithms, such as RouteMixed. A coplanar waveguide (CPW) is a type of transmission line used in microwave and radiofrequency engineering. In the context of quantum computing, CPWs are commonly employed to connect and transmit signals between superconducting qubits and other quantum components. A CPW consists of a central conductor, typically a thin strip of metal, positioned between two ground planes. The central conductor is separated from the ground planes by gaps on either side. The term "coplanar" indicates that all elements (the central conductor and ground planes) lie in the same plane.

The central conductor carries the RF (radiofrequency) signal, with its width and thickness influencing the characteristic impedance and performance of the CPW. The ground planes on either side of the central conductor act as the return path for the RF signal. The separation between the central conductor and the ground planes is crucial, as it impacts the CPW's performance. The gap between the central conductor and the ground planes is a critical parameter, influencing the capacitance of the CPW and affecting its impedance and signal propagation characteristics. The characteristic impedance of a CPW is determined by the dimensions of the central conductor, the gap, and the dielectric properties of the substrate. It is a key parameter for impedance matching in RF circuits.

CPWs support a variety of signal propagation modes, including the TEM (transverse electromagnetic) mode. The absence of higher-order modes simplifies the analysis of CPWs. They are known for low RF losses compared to other transmission line types, making them suitable for applications where signal integrity is crucial, such as in quantum computing. There are several applications of this type of transmission line. For instance, CPWs are often used to connect superconducting qubits and other quantum components on a chip, facilitating the transmission of microwave signals between qubits and other circuit elements. CPWs are also employed in the design of resonators for quantum information processing and readout lines for measuring qubit states. In the context of flux qubits, CPWs can be used to create controlled-phase gates and perform quantum operations.

Let's look into different types of routes available in Qiskit Metal. We will be understanding the concept of routing used while programming with a standard code and structure so that we can relate the final products and identify the difference between the different types of routes; for this, we will be using Transmon pockets with two QPins.

4.3.1 Straight Routing

We use straight routing when we need to connect a straight wire from one Qcomponent pin to another. Straight routing provides a direct and simple connection between two components. The straight path represents the shortest distance between two points, thereby minimizing signal propagation delay. Straight paths typically have lower losses compared to meandered paths, as there are fewer bends and transitions. Additionally, straight paths may help reduce crosstalk between adjacent lines since there are fewer opportunities for signals to couple. While there are several advantages to using straight routing, it also has some disadvantages. For instance, straight paths may not take advantage of intentional inductive coupling, which can be crucial in certain qubit coupling schemes. Furthermore, straight paths with connectors might introduce reflections, especially if the connectors are not impedance matched. The simplicity of straight paths may limit the degree of control over impedance matching, which is essential for optimizing signal integrity. Now, let us dive into how we can code a simple straight route.

```python
from qiskit_metal import designs, MetalGUI, Dict
from qiskit_metal.qlibrary.qubits.transmon_pocket import TransmonPocket
from qiskit_metal.qlibrary.tlines.straight_path import RouteStraight

# Create a new design
design = designs.DesignPlanar()

# Define some common options for transmon pockets
options = dict(
    pad_width='425um',
    pocket_height='650um',
    connection_pads=dict(
        a=dict(loc_W=+1, loc_H=+1),
        b=dict(loc_W=+1, loc_H=-1, pad_width='200um'),
    )
)

# Create two transmon pockets (Q1 and Q2)
q1 = TransmonPocket(design, 'Q1', options=dict(pos_x='+5.5mm', pos_y='+1mm', orientation=180, **options))
q2 = TransmonPocket(design, 'Q2', options=dict(pos_x='1.5mm', pos_y='+1mm', orientation=0, **options))

# Function to connect two pins with a straight path
def connect_straight(component_name: str, component1: str, pin1: str, component2: str, pin2: str, length='5mm', flip=False):
    """Connect two pins with a straight path."""
    myoptions = Dict(
        pin_inputs=Dict(
            start_pin=Dict(
                component=component1,
                pin=pin1),
            end_pin=Dict(
                component=component2,
                pin=pin2)),
        lead=Dict(
            start_straight='0.13mm'
        ),
        total_length=length,
        fillet='90um'
    )
    return RouteStraight(design, component_name, options=myoptions)
```

4.3 Routing Between the Qcomponents

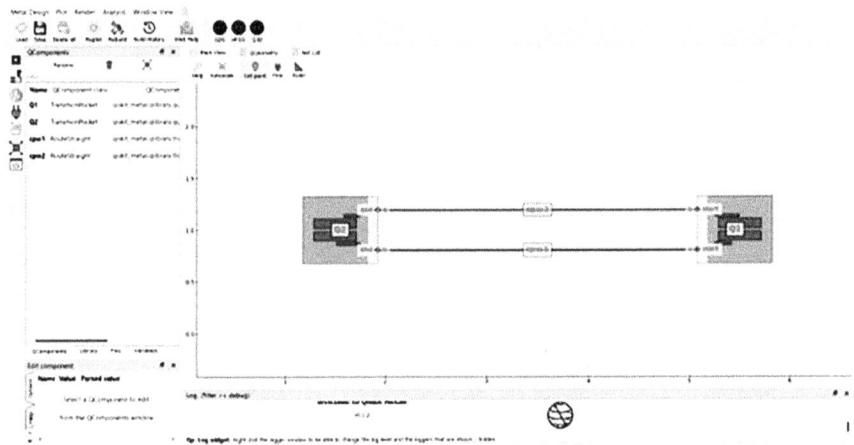

Figure 4-7 Straight routing between two Transmon Qubit chips

```
# Connect Q1 and Q2 with straight paths
cpw1 = connect_straight('cpw1', 'Q1', 'a', 'Q2', 'b')
cpw2 = connect_straight('cpw2', 'Q1', 'a', 'Q2', 'b',
length='3mm', flip=True)

# Build the GUI and visualize the components
gui = MetalGUI(design)
gui.rebuild()
gui.autoscale()
gui.highlight_components(['Q1', 'Q2', 'cpw1', 'cpw2'])
gui.screenshot()
```

In this example, we have used two transmon pockets with two pins placed 4 mm apart from each other, and we will code on it. We make a simple, straight connection between the QPin 'a' of Q1 and the QPin 'b' of Q2. We define a function called `connect_straight` in which we pass all the required arguments, such as which pin we want to connect to which, the start node, the end node, the total length, the asymmetry we want to introduce, and whether we want to flip the connection or not. We then pass all these arguments and values to the `RouteStraight()` function. These values need to be predefined because `RouteStraight()` only accepts between two and five arguments, and we need to pass several values through it. This is how we can create a straight route as can be seen in Figure 4-7.

4.3.2 Any Direction Routing

Any directional routing is essentially a fancier way of saying straight routing at a different angle. For example, in the previous case, if you change the location

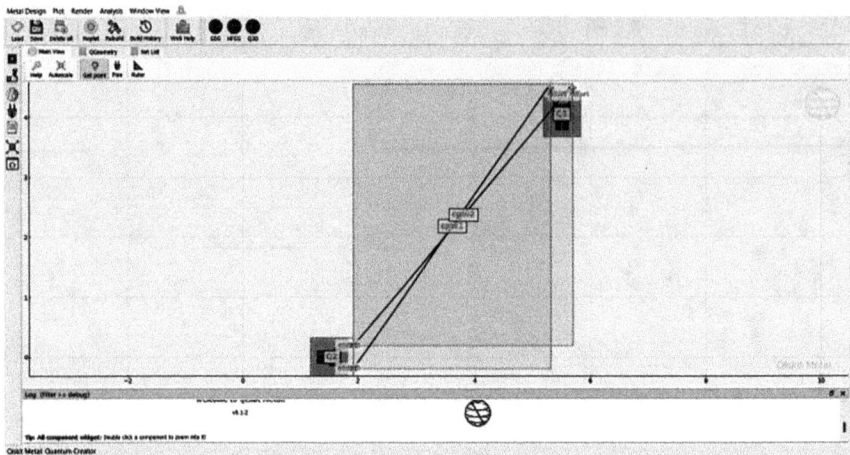

Figure 4-8 Any-direction routing between two Transmon Qubit chips

of one of the two transmon pockets, it will connect the two QPins at an inclined angle, and this is called directional routing. Let us see an example as displayed in Figure 4-8: we will take the exact same code but change the position of one of the two pockets. Let's see how the routing looks in this case. By simply changing the orientation of Q2 from 180° to 90° and adjusting the pos_y of Q1 relative to Q2 so that there is a vertical separation of 4 mm, we get a straight-line routing. Here, the two routes, CPW1 and CPW2, intersect. This type of routing, where a straight route is used but at a certain angle (rather than a flat zero-degree line), is known as directional routing. Directional routing can be done in any direction, irrespective of the location and orientation of the two or more Qcomponents. When implementing this type of routing, handling intersections becomes a crucial step to ensure the practical feasibility of the design, that is, whether the designed layout can be fabricated or not. As we can see in Figure 4-8, the two routes intersect at one point in between; this intersection can cause multiple issues, while fabrication of the chip, such as this type of intersection, leads to qubit crosstalk and electromagnetic signal interference, which can lead to decoherence in the qubit. Intersecting routes can be mitigated through techniques such as layer stacking, where overlapping paths are assigned to different metal layers, or by simply rerouting paths to avoid physical overlap. These methods ensure that the final layout maintains electrical and physical integrity, preventing shorts or unintended coupling between routes. The following is a code for any-direction routing:

```
from qiskit_metal import designs, MetalGUI, Dict
from qiskit_metal.qlibrary.qubits.transmon_pocket import
 TransmonPocket
from qiskit_metal.qlibrary.tlines.straight_path import
 RouteStraight

# Create a new design
```

4.3 Routing Between the Qcomponents

```python
design = designs.DesignPlanar()

# Define some common options for transmon pockets
options = dict(
    pad_width='425um',
    pocket_height='650um',
    connection_pads=dict(
        a=dict(loc_W=+1, loc_H=+1),
        b=dict(loc_W=+1, loc_H=-1, pad_width='200um'),
    )
)

# Create two transmon pockets (Q1 and Q2)
q1 = TransmonPocket(design, 'Q1', options=dict(pos_x='+5.5mm',
pos_y='+5mm', orientation=90, **options))
q2 = TransmonPocket(design, 'Q2', options=dict(pos_x='1.5mm',
pos_y='+1mm', orientation=0, **options))

# Function to connect two pins with a straight path
def connect_any_direction(component_name: str, component1: str,
pin1: str, component2: str, pin2: str, length='5mm',
 flip=False):
    """Connect two pins with a straight path."""
    myoptions = Dict(
        pin_inputs=Dict(
            start_pin=Dict(
                component=component1,
                pin=pin1),
            end_pin=Dict(
                component=component2,
                pin=pin2)),
        lead=Dict(
            start_straight='0.13mm'
        ),
        total_length=length,
        fillet='90um'
    )
    return RouteStraight(design, component_name,
      options=myoptions)

# Connect Q1 and Q2 with straight paths
cpw1 = connect_any_direction('cpw1', 'Q1', 'a', 'Q2', 'b')
cpw2 = connect_any_direction('cpw2', 'Q1', 'a', 'Q2', 'b',
 length='3mm',
flip=True)

# Build the GUI and visualize the components
gui = MetalGUI(design)
gui.rebuild()
gui.autoscale()
gui.highlight_components(['Q1', 'Q2', 'cpw1', 'cpw2'])
gui.screenshot()
```

The code provided shows any-direction routing where both the transmon components are in the same plane, which means the structure is planar, and this will cause the two lines to intersect at a point. Due to this intersection, unnecessary coupling takes place along with electromagnetic interference at this point of intersection, leading to the decoherence in the qubit. To avoid this, we can modify the above code by stacking layers, that is, by keeping the first chip in the first layer and changing the layer for the second chip by replacing the defined `connect_any_direction` function with

```
def connect_any_direction(component_name: str, component1: str,
 pin1: str, component2: str, pin2: str, length='5mm',
  flip=False):
    """Connect two pins with a straight path."""
    myoptions = Dict(
        pin_inputs=Dict(
            start_pin=Dict(
                component=component1,
                pin=pin1),
            end_pin=Dict(
                component=component2,
                pin=pin2)),
        lead=Dict(
            start_straight='0.13mm'
        ),
        total_length=length,
        fillet='90um',
        layer=2  # changing the layer of the qubit by stacking it
    )
    return RouteStraight(design, component_name,
     options=myoptions)
```

By adding the parameter `layer=2`, we stack the layers of the qubit, avoiding the problem with intersection between the two routes. But as expected, this type of design is not feasible or practical when handling complex superconducting circuit designs. Furthermore, stacking layers possesses fabrication challenges and is costlier. So, let's look into the other solution by changing the routes in between the components by bending the angle of the routes to avoid intersection. This method helps in keeping the design planar as well as avoids all the challenges faced in any-direction routing. In the next section, we will be talking about routing at bent angles to avoid this intersection process.

4.3.3 Routing at Bent Angles

When dealing with circuits, we encounter several types of configurations. Some orientations may not be straightforward or aligned in a straight line; instead, they may be at specific angles such as 90°, 30°, or others. To tackle such complexities, Qiskit Metal provides a library called `RoutePathfinder`. It finds the most appropriate and suitable route to the specified pin while allowing us to specify parameters like

4.3 Routing Between the Qcomponents

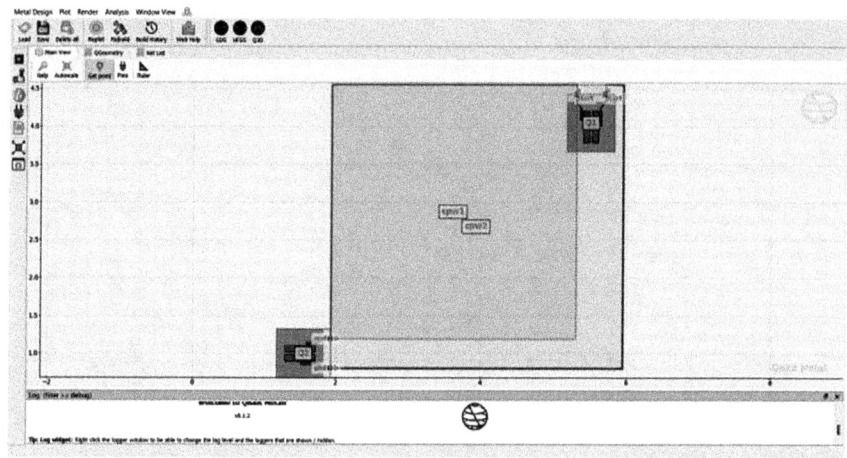

Figure 4-9 Routing at bent angles between two Transmon Qubit chips

the bend radius. For instance, in this case, we have set the bend radius to be 90 μm; the resulting output is shown in Figure 4-9.

```
from qiskit_metal import designs, MetalGUI, Dict
from qiskit_metal.qlibrary.qubits.transmon_pocket
import TransmonPocket
from qiskit_metal.qlibrary.tlines.pathfinder import
 RoutePathfinder

# Create a new design
design.delete_all_components()
design = designs.DesignPlanar()

# Define some common options for transmon pockets
options = dict(
    pad_width='425um',
    pocket_height='650um',
    connection_pads=dict(
        a=dict(loc_W=+1, loc_H=+1),
        b=dict(loc_W=+1, loc_H=-1, pad_width='200um'),
    )
)

# Create two transmon pockets (Q1 and Q2)
q1 = TransmonPocket(design, 'Q1', options=dict(pos_x='+5.5mm',
pos_y='+4mm', orientation=90, **options))
q2 = TransmonPocket(design, 'Q2', options=dict(pos_x='1.5mm',
pos_y='+1mm', orientation=0, **options))

# Function to connect two pins with a 90-degree path
def connect_90deg(component_name: str, component1: str,
pin1: str, component2: str, pin2: str):
    """Connect two pins with a 90-degree path."""
```

```
    myoptions = Dict(
        pin_inputs=Dict(
            start_pin=Dict(
                component=component1,
                pin=pin1),
            end_pin=Dict(
                component=component2,
                pin=pin2)),
        lead=Dict(
            start_straight='0.13mm'
        ),
        bend_radius='90um'
    )
    return RoutePathfinder(design, component_name,
     options=myoptions)

# Connect Q1 and Q2 with 90-degree paths
cpw1 = connect_90deg('cpw1', 'Q1', 'a', 'Q2', 'a')
cpw2 = connect_90deg('cpw2', 'Q1', 'b', 'Q2', 'b')

# Build the GUI and visualize the components
gui = MetalGUI(design)
gui.rebuild()
gui.autoscale()
gui.highlight_components(['Q1', 'Q2', 'cpw1', 'cpw2'])
gui.screenshot()
```

Furthermore, `RoutePathfinder` allows other parameters that can help in the customization of the routes beyond the bend radius (e.g., route width, layer specification) where instead of just changing the angle one can change the width of the route; also, if your chips are stacked up in multiple layers and routing is to be done between two components in different layers, we can achieve it by running the function

```
RoutePathfinder(design, 'route1', options='start_pin':
('Qubit1', 'pin'), 'end\_pin': ('Qubit2', 'pin'),
'layer_start': 1,'layer_end': 2})
```

This command will make sure to route two different components in two layers by defining the direction of routing between the two components that we need to connect from layer 1 to layer 2, from Qubit 1 to Qubit 2. Similar to this, it has another option named that can be used to find the route by avoiding to route close to the chip edges:

`avoid_edges=True`

This function takes boolean input `True` or `False`. The default value for it is set to `False`, and one can change it as per requirement. Similarly, `RoutePathfinder` provides another parameter where it can make the route to take the longer path instead of the smaller path between two pins, and the function to achieve it is

`meander=True`

4.3 Routing Between the Qcomponents 139

This function takes boolean input `True` or `False`. The default value for it is set to `False`, and one can change it as per requirement.

4.3.4 CPW Route Meander

Using CPW (coplanar waveguide) and creating a route meander is one of the most popular and widely regarded techniques in circuit design. The primary feature of `RouteMeander` is its ability to create transmission line structures with a meandered or serpentine geometry. Meandered or serpentine geometry refers to a transmission line design where the path is intentionally zigzagged or folded back and forth, increasing its effective length in a compact physical area to achieve a desired electrical length or delay.

Let's dive into some of the parameters of route meander that make it unique:

- `asymmetry`: The `asymmetry` parameter allows for adjusting the asymmetry in the meandered structure, providing control over the electrical characteristics such as the impedance, reducing crosstalk (crosstalk is a phenomenon where there is an induced interference and noise due to signal in one transmission line on to the other), and improving signal speed. These factors help in the tuning of the performance of the signal being transmitted and reduce the noise errors.
- `total_length`: The `total_length` parameter enables control over the total length of the meandered transmission line. Total length in a meandered structure helps in providing a compact layout with longer transmission lines, which can help in improving the impedance matching in transmission, which results in reduced loss of data and reduced noise formation. Increasing the total length also ensures keeping the electrical length in check by improving the phase of the signal. Electrical length is the effective length of a transmission line or component expressed in terms of the phase shift it causes to a signal, typically measured in degrees or radians, relative to the signal's wavelength.
- `fillet`: The `fillet` parameter introduces rounded corners in the meandered structure. This bend in structure helps in smooth transmission of electromagnetic waves. As for sharp corners, when transmission of electromagnetic waves is done in the wire with sharp angles, it runs into the risk of getting accumulated in the corner and starts getting concentrated at that singular point; in simpler terms, imagine driving through a lane where an accident took place at the corner because of which all the vehicles get halted at that turn. Similar to this, the electromagnetic wave transmission also works. This congestion leads to loss in data and power losses and can even lead to interference with other electromagnetic waves. This problem is reduced by bending the corners at an angle and not keeping it a sharp corner.
- `snap` and `prevent_short_edges`: `RouteMeander` includes options for snapping vertices to the grid (`snap`) and preventing the generation of short edges (`prevent_short_edges`), contributing to a well-defined and manufacturable layout. Short edges, as the name suggests, refer to the shorter side of the

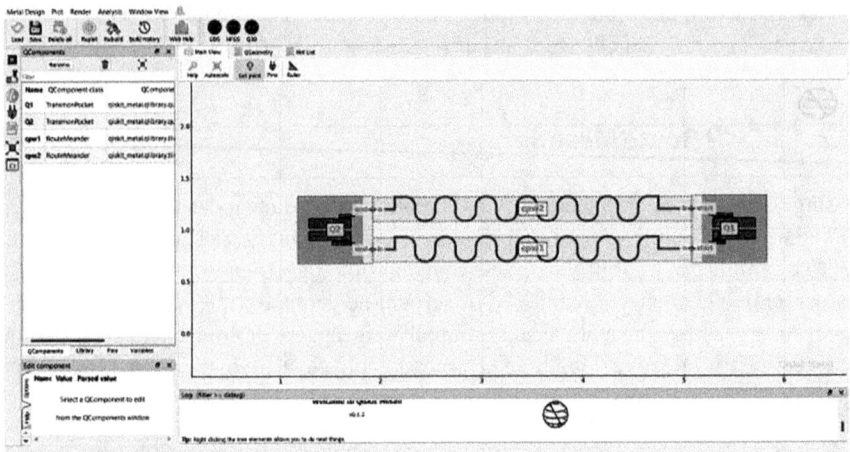

Figure 4-10 Route meander routing between two Transmon Qubit chips

component in a design. Avoiding short edges is ideal, as close proximity of the component due to the shorter edge leads to electromagnetic interference between the two signals and can lead to crosstalk between them.

Having these parameters makes `RouteMeander` a very popular style of transmission line. With all that said, let's look into how the structure of a `RouteMeander` looks like in Qiskit Metal.

As we can see in Figure 4-10, the Zig-Zag line pattern is known as the meandered structure that the `Route.Meander` function generates between two qubits. We can also see that in comparison to any other routing method discussed earlier, such as "straight routing," the length of the transmission line is much longer than it but is still present and confined between the two structures in a compact format.

Let us look into how this type of meandered structure can be obtained between two Transmon qubits:

```
# Create a new design
design = designs.DesignPlanar()

# Define some common options for transmon pockets
options = dict(
    pad_width='425um',
    pocket_height='650um',
    connection_pads=dict(
        a=dict(loc_W=+1, loc_H=+1),
        b=dict(loc_W=+1, loc_H=-1, pad_width='200um'),
    )
)

# Create two transmon pockets (Q1 and Q2)
q1 = TransmonPocket(design, 'Q1', options=dict(pos_x='+5.5mm',
```

4.3 Routing Between the Qcomponents

```python
                pos_y='+1mm', orientation=180, **options))
q2 = TransmonPocket(design, 'Q2', options=dict(pos_x='1.5mm',
                pos_y='+1mm', orientation=0, **options))

# Function to connect two pins with a straight path
def connect(component_name: str, component1: str,
pin1: str, component2: str, pin2: str,
            length: str,
            asymmetry='0 um', flip=False):
    """Connect two pins with a CPW."""
    myoptions = Dict(
        pin_inputs=Dict(
            start_pin=Dict(
                component=component1,
                pin=pin1),
            end_pin=Dict(
                component=component2,
                pin=pin2)),
        lead=Dict(
            start_straight='0.13mm'
        ),
        total_length=length,
    fillet = '90um')
    myoptions.update(options)
    myoptions.meander.asymmetry = asymmetry
    myoptions.meander.lead_direction_inverted = 'true' if flip
    else 'false'
    return RouteMeander(design, component_name, myoptions)
asym=100
# Connect Q1 and Q2 with straight paths
cpw1 = connect('cpw1', 'Q1', 'a', 'Q2', 'b', f'+{asym}um')
cpw2 = connect('cpw2', 'Q1', 'b', 'Q2', 'a', f'+{asym}um',
 flip=True)

# Build the GUI and visualize the components
gui = MetalGUI(design)
gui.rebuild()
gui.autoscale()
gui.highlight_components(['Q1', 'Q2', 'cpw1', 'cpw2'])
gui.screenshot()
```

Let us talk about the advantages that the meandered routing method provides:

- Meandered structures can be designed to achieve specific impedance matching, ensuring efficient signal transmission along the transmission line.
- Meandered traces are also employed to reduce crosstalk between neighboring transmission lines by introducing additional distance and geometric structures.
- Meandered structures allow for longer transmission lines within limited physical spaces, facilitating the compact layout of quantum circuits.
- Meandering helps extend the effective path length of the transmission line, providing more room for tuning and matching.

- This structure enables designers to control the effective electrical length of the transmission line, thereby reducing signal distortion in high-frequency applications.

Even though the meandered geometry of routing provides significant advantages, it poses a few significant challenges too, such as

- The added bends in the meandered structure can cause additional signal attenuation (attenuation is a process in which the signal loses its signal strength and gradually the signal strength reduces overtime), especially at high frequencies.
- The longer path in the meandered structure leads to a longer electrical path, which can lead to a delay in signal propagation between two qubits.
- Manufacturing issues pose a significant challenge when designing complex chips with the meandered structure, as fabricating these designs with bent angles can lead to unwanted electromagnetic interference between two channels.

These are the different types of routing we use in Qiskit Metal that make the job easier while developing the Qcomponents of the circuit.

4.4 Types of Qubit

As the name suggests, when working with superconducting qubits, we encounter many types, with the transmon qubit being one of the most popular. Transmon qubits are highly versatile and can perform a wide range of functions. However, there are various types of transmon qubits, each suited to different applications. In this section, we will explore the different types of transmon qubits, as each has its unique characteristics and use cases. Understanding these differences is crucial for selecting the appropriate qubit type when developing specific quantum systems.

4.4.1 Xmon Qubit

The Single Grounded Transmon Qubit, commonly known as the Xmon Qubit or Transmon Cross, is a widely used qubit design, particularly used in the creation of various couplers and resonators. The Xmon qubit is an extremely popular type of qubit that is used in the construction of all large quantum systems, making it the basic building block in quantum computing subsystems. Another reason that makes the Xmon qubit a special and widely used and recognized qubit is the fact that it is very easy to access, and this qubit is compatible with various quantum gates; for example, for a single-qubit gate operation, it is compatible with the Hadamard gate; Pauli-X, Pauli-Y, and Pauli-Z gates; and rotation gates ($R_X(\theta)$, $R_Y(\theta)$, $R_Z(\theta)$). For a double-qubit gate operation, it is compatible with the controlled Pauli-Z gate and controlled-phase gate. This compatibility with basic logic gates makes the Xmon

4.4 Types of Qubit

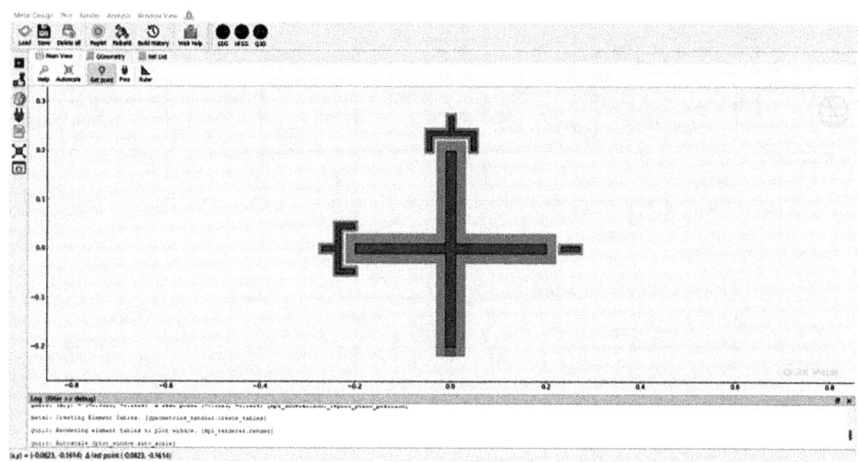

Figure 4-11 Xmon qubit structure

qubit versatile and easy to access compared to a Transmon Qubit. Figure 4-11 represents the structure of the Xmon Qubit.

To conveniently incorporate this qubit into a quantum circuit, a prebuilt `Transmon Cross` qubit is available in the Qcomponent Library. The corresponding module to import is `transmon_cross`, and the class representing the qubit is `TransmonCross`. As with all quantum components, `TransmonCross` inherits from the `Qcomponent` class.

```
from qiskit_metal.qlibrary.qubits.transmon_cross
import TransmonCross
```

For added flexibility, connector lines can be introduced using the `connection_pads` dictionary, where each connector pad is assigned a name and comes with a set of default properties. This feature allows for seamless integration and customization within quantum circuits. Connection pads play an important role in the Xmon qubit as they provide an easy way to facilitate precise control and read out the qubit by enabling efficient coupling of microwave signals to the qubit.

We get the default values of a transmon cross (Xmon qubit) if we run the command

```
TransmonCross.get_template_options(design)
```

Let us look into the output and try to decipher what each and every default option means:

```
{
  'pos_x': '0um',
  'pos_y': '0um',
  'connection_pads': {},
  '_default_connection_pads': {
    'connector_type': '0',
```

```
        'claw_length': '30um',
        'ground_spacing': '5um',
        'claw_width': '10um',
        'claw_gap': '6um',
        'connector_location': '0'
    },
    'cross_width': '20um',
    'cross_length': '200um',
    'cross_gap': '20um',
    'orientation': '0',
    'hfss_inductance': '10nH',
    'hfss_capacitance': 0,
    'hfss_resistance': 0,
    'hfss_mesh_kw_jj': 7e-06,
    'q3d_inductance': '10nH',
    'q3d_capacitance': 0,
    'q3d_resistance': 0,
    'q3d_mesh_kw_jj': 7e-06,
    'gds_cell_name': 'my_other_junction'
}
```

- pos_x and pos_y: These parameters specify the x and y coordinates of the center position of the Transmon Cross qubit. In this case, it is positioned at the origin (0, 0).
- connection_pads: This dictionary is used to specify connection pads for the qubit. Currently, there are no specific connection pads defined.
- _default_connection_pads: connector_type: 0, claw_length: 30um, ground_spacing: 5um, claw_width: 10um, claw_gap: 6um, connector_location: 0. These are the default properties for connection pads. If no specific connection pads are defined, these default properties will be used.
- cross_width, cross_length, and cross_gap: These parameters define the width, length, and gap of the Transmon Cross qubit.
- orientation: The orientation of the qubit. In this case, it is set to 0, indicating the default orientation.
- hfss_inductance, hfss_capacitance, hfss_resistance, and hfss_mesh_kw_jj: These parameters are related to electromagnetic simulation settings for the High-Frequency Structural Simulator (HFSS), specifying inductance, capacitance, resistance, and mesh-related properties.
- q3d_inductance, q3d_capacitance, q3d_resistance, and q3d_mesh_kw_jj: Similar to HFSS settings, these parameters are related to electromagnetic simulation settings for Q3D simulations.
- gds_cell_name: This parameter specifies the GDS cell name for the Transmon Cross qubit in the layout.

Let us look into how to code this type of qubit as we can see in Figure 4-11.

```
xmon_options = dict(
    connection_pads=dict(
        a = dict( connector_location = '0', connector_type = '0'),
```

```
            b = dict(connector_location = '90', connector_type = '0'),
            c = dict(connector_location = '180', connector_type = '1'),
        ),
    )
    q1 = TransmonCross(design, 'Q1', options=xmon_options)
    gui.rebuild()
    gui.autoscale()
    gui.zoom_on_components(['Q1'])
    gui.screenshot()
```

Let us talk about the advantages that the Xmon Qubit provides:

- Xmon qubits are compatible with wide varieties of single-qubit and multi-qubit gates as discussed earlier, which makes it a component that can be used widely in multiple situations.
- Xmon qubits allow for tunable coupling between qubits, providing flexibility in implementing various quantum gates and enabling efficient qubit connectivity.
- Xmon qubits have planar architecture which makes it easier for integration with existing semiconductor fabrication processes, facilitating scalability for larger quantum processors.
- Xmon qubits have high fidelity with the controlled-phase and controlled-Z gates which makes these qubits effective in error-prone quantum algorithms.

Even though the Xmon qubit has significant advantages, it poses a few significant challenges too, such as

- Xmon qubits are prone to qubit crosstalk and electromagnetic interference.
- Xmon qubits support some frequency tunability, but they are not as tunable as other qubit types like flux qubits, which limits dynamic control during operation.
- Xmon qubits are sensitive to temperature fluctuations, which can lead to noise and instability, thus requiring stringent cryogenic cooling conditions.

4.4.2 Concentric Transmon

A concentric transmon represents a unique design of superconducting qubits, sharing similarities with the conventional transmon qubit but distinguished by its geometric arrangement. In this configuration, Josephson junctions (composed of superconducting material separated by a thin insulating barrier) are arranged in a circular pattern, differing from the linear arrangement typical of standard transmons. The circular arrangement forms a superconducting ring, with the manipulation of the qubit's quantum states accomplished by controlling the phase of this superconducting structure. Much like the standard transmon, the concentric transmon possesses capacitance and inductance associated with its Josephson junctions. These parameters play a pivotal role in determining the qubit's energy levels and its coupling strength to other qubits or external resonators. Notably, the energy levels of the concentric transmon exhibit anharmonicity, meaning that the

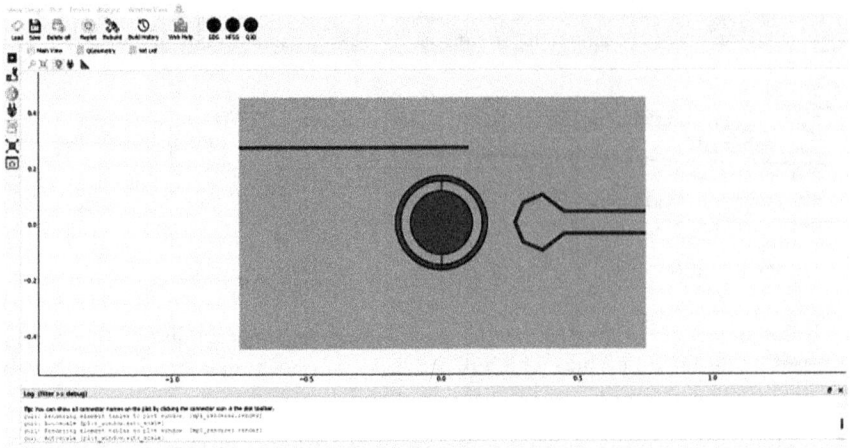

Figure 4-12 Concentric Transmon qubit structure

frequency separation between adjacent energy levels is not constant, which is an advantageous characteristic for quantum computing applications. Anharmonicity plays an extremely crucial role in quantum computing applications as it ensures that energy levels are unevenly spaced, making sure that the qubit operates between two desired states ($|0\rangle$ and $|1\rangle$) without accidentally transitioning to higher energy levels, which reduces the noise and increases the gate fidelity in the system. Figure 4-12 represents the structure of the Xmon Qubit.

For ease of implementation, a prebuilt concentric transmon qubit is available in the Qcomponent Library. To incorporate this qubit into a quantum circuit, the module to import is `transmon_concentric.py`, and the corresponding class is `TransmonConcentric`. As with all quantum components, `TransmonConcentric` inherits from the `Qcomponent` class, offering flexibility in quantum circuit design by allowing the tuning of properties such as energy levels and qubit-qubit coupling strength through adjustments to specific design parameters.

```
from qiskit_metal.qlibrary.qubits.transmon_concentric import
TransmonConcentric
TransmonConcentric.get_template_options(design)
```

We get the default values of a concentric transmon qubit if we run the command

`TransmonConcentric.get_template_options(design)`

Let us look into the output and try to decipher what each and every default option means:

```
{
  'pos_x': '0.0um',
  'pos_y': '0.0um',
  'orientation': '0.0',
  'chip': 'main',
```

4.4 Types of Qubit

```
    'layer': '1',
    'connection_pads': {},
    '_default_connection_pads': {},
    'width': '1000um',
    'height': '1000um',
    'rad_o': '170um',
    'rad_i': '115um',
    'gap': '35um',
    'jj_w': '10um',
    'res_s': '100um',
    'res_ext': '100um',
    'fbl_rad': '100um',
    'fbl_sp': '100um',
    'fbl_gap': '80um',
    'fbl_ext': '300um',
    'pocket_w': '1500um',
    'pocket_h': '1000um',
    'cpw_width': '10.0um',
    'inductor_width': '5.0um'
}
```

- pos_x and pos_y: These parameters specify the x and y coordinates of the center position of the concentric transmon qubit. In this case, it is positioned at the origin (0, 0).
- orientation: The orientation of the qubit. Here, it is set to 0.0, indicating the default orientation.
- chip: Specifies the chip on which the concentric transmon qubit is located. In this case, it is on the main chip.
- layer: Indicates the metal layer on which the concentric transmon qubit is placed. It is set to layer 1.
- connection_pads and _default_connection_pads: These dictionaries are used to specify connection pads for the qubit. Currently, no specific connection pads are defined.
- width and height: These parameters define the overall width and height of the concentric transmon qubit.
- rad_o and rad_i: Define the outer radius (rad_o) and inner radius (rad_i) of the concentric structure.
- gap: Specifies the gap between different parts of the concentric transmon qubit, such as between the outer and inner rings.
- jj_w: Represents the width of the Josephson junction in the qubit.
- res_s and res_ext: Define the size (res_s) and extension (res_ext) of the resistor in the qubit.
- fbl_rad, fbl_sp, fbl_gap, and fbl_ext: Specify parameters related to the flux bias line, including its radius (fbl_rad), spacing (fbl_sp), gap (fbl_gap), and extension (fbl_ext).
- pocket_w and pocket_h: Define the width (pocket_w) and height (pocket_h) of the component in the concentric transmon qubit.

- `cpw_width` and `inductor_width`: Specify the widths of the coplanar waveguide (`cpw_width`) and the inductor (`inductor_width`).

Let us look into how this type of qubit is coded and how the output of the transmon looks like as shown in Figure 4-12.

```
concentric_options = dict(
    pos_x = '1um',
    pos_y = '2um',
    layer = '5',
    pocket_w='1500um',
    pocket_h='900um',
)

q1 = TransmonConcentric(design, 'qubit1',
 options=concentric_options)

gui.rebuild()
gui.autoscale()
gui.zoom_on_components(['qubit1'])
gui.screenshot()
```

Let us talk about the advantages that the Concentric Transmon Qubit provides:

- Concentric Transmon qubits have a circular disk shape which enhances the design for isolation from parasitic modes and environmental noises.
- Concentric Transmon qubits exhibit the notion of anharmonicity with its energy level which proves to be an advantageous characteristic in quantum computing.
- Concentric Transmon qubits have planar-symmetric architecture which makes it beneficial when dealing with qubits with dense and stacked chip architecture.
- Concentric Transmon qubits have a symmetric circular geometry which helps in minimizing the stray unwanted electric fields.

Even though the concentric Transmon qubit has significant advantages, it poses a few significant challenges too, such as

- The concentric Transmon qubit's structure, despite having better isolation, can still introduce unwanted parasitic modes due to improper grounding, crosstalk, improper spacing, and creation of imperfect non-circular edges caused during the fabrication process.
- The concentric Transmon qubit's concentric structure may limit tuning and coupling adjustments due to its fixed geometry.
- Concentric Transmon qubits have a circular geometry which is more challenging to fabricate precisely compared to simpler shapes like rectangular transmons.

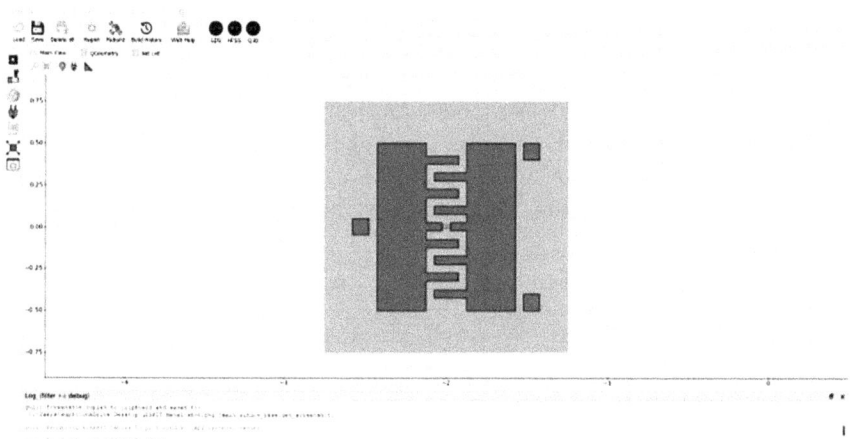

Figure 4-13 Interdigitated Transmon qubit structure

4.4.3 Interdigitated Transmon Qubit

An interdigitated transmon qubit is a type of superconducting qubit design that features interdigitated, finger-like structures in its Josephson junction. This design introduces additional degrees of freedom for qubit control and manipulation. The key features of an interdigitated transmon qubit include

- The architectural design of the interdigitated transmon, as shown in Figure 4-13, features interdigitated fingers on each electrode, creating multiple areas that contribute to the Josephson junctions. Furthermore, this increase in area for the interdigitated transmon qubit creates overlapping regions between the electrodes in the Josephson junction, resulting in more capacitance between them. This increase in capacitance leads to an increase in coupling and better control over the qubit.
- The interdigitated transmon qubit has one special characteristic: it shows the property of anharmonicity in its energy levels. While anharmonicity is an important parameter to consider, the higher capacitance places a crucial role for this qubit as it not only improves anharmonicity but also makes the qubit less sensitive to charge noise, which is a critical factor in achieving long coherence times.
- Interdigitated transmon has tunable parameters similar to those of other transmon qubits, such as external magnetic flux and gate voltages. These parameters result in precise control and manipulation of the qubit's quantum states.
- The interdigitated design provides flexibility in adjusting the physical characteristics of the qubit, allowing for optimization based on specific requirements or constraints in a quantum processor.

For ease of implementation, a prebuilt interdigitated transmon qubit is available in the Qcomponent Library. To incorporate this qubit into a quantum circuit, the module to import is `Transmon_Interdigitated`, and the corresponding class is `TransmonInterdigitated`. As with all quantum components, `TransmonInterdigitated` inherits from the `Qcomponent` class, offering flexibility in quantum circuit design by allowing the tuning of properties such as energy levels and qubit-qubit coupling strength through adjustments to specific design parameters.

```
from qiskit_metal.qlibrary.qubits.Transmon_Interdigitated
import TransmonInterdigitated
    TransmonInterdigitated.default_options
```

Let us look into the output and try to decipher what each and every default option means:

```
{
    'pad_width': '1000um',
    'pad_height': '300um',
    'finger_width': '50um',
    'finger_height': '100um',
    'finger_space': '50um',
    'pad_pos_x': '0um',
    'pad_pos_y': '0um',
    'comb_width': '50um',
    'comb_space_vert': '50um',
    'comb_space_hor': '50um',
    'jj_width': '20um',
    'cc_space': '50um',
    'cc_width': '100um',
    'cc_height': '100um',
    'cc_topleft_space': '50um',
    'cc_topleft_width': '100um',
    'cc_topleft_height': '100um',
    'cc_topright_space': '50um',
    'cc_topright_width': '100um',
    'cc_topright_height': '100um',
    'rotation_top_pad': '180',
    'inductor_width': '20um'
}
```

- `pad_width` and `pad_height`: Dimensions of the main pad that forms part of the qubit structure
- `finger_width`, `finger_height`, and `finger_space`: Parameters related to the interdigitated fingers in the Josephson junction, including the width, height, and spacing of the fingers
- `pad_pos_x` and `pad_pos_y`: Coordinates specifying the position of the main pad on the x- and y-axes
- `comb_width`, `comb_space_vert`, and `comb_space_hor`: Parameters related to the interdigitated comb-like structure, defining the width and vertical/horizontal spacing between the comb elements

4.4 Types of Qubit

- `jj_width`: Width of the Josephson junction
- `cc_space`, `cc_width`, and `cc_height`: Parameters for the coupling capacitor, including spacing, width, and height
- `cc_topleft_space`, `cc_topleft_width`, and `cc_topleft_height`: Specific parameters for the top-left coupling capacitor, including spacing and dimensions
- `cc_topright_space`, `cc_topright_width`, and `cc_topright_height`: Specific parameters for the top-right coupling capacitor, including spacing and dimensions
- `pos_x` and `pos_y`: Overall coordinates of the interdigitated transmon qubit, defining its center position
- `orientation` and `rotation_top_pad`: The orientation angle and rotation of the top pad of the qubit
- `layer`: Specifies the metal layer on which the interdigitated transmon qubit is placed

Let us look into how this type of qubit is coded and how the output of the transmon looks like as shown in Figure 4-13.

```
from qiskit_metal.qlibrary.qubits.Transmon_Interdigitated import
TransmonInterdigitated
design.overwrite_enabled = True
q1 = TransmonInterdigitated(design, 'qubit1',
options=dict(pos_x='-2.0mm',orientation='-90'))
gui.rebuild()
gui.autoscale()
gui.zoom_on_components(['qubit1'])
gui.screenshot()
```

Let us talk about the advantages that the Concentric Transmon Qubit provides:

- Interdigitated Transmon has a higher surface area, which leads to more capacitance between the electrodes, and this higher capacitance results in an increase in anharmonicity. The increased capacitance also makes the qubit less sensitive to charge noise, which is critical for achieving long coherence times.
- Interdigitated transmon has the interdigitated structure which allows for fine-tuning and flexibility in optimizing the qubit's physical parameters based on specific use case requirements. This provides multiple options to the user and can be used in a variety of situations.
- Interdigitated Transmon qubit improves noise resilience compared to other qubit designs. Noise resilience refers to a system's ability to maintain stable and accurate operation despite the presence of external disturbances, errors, or fluctuations. The interdigitated geometry with finger-like nodes in the electrodes and more surface area leads to a better coupling mechanism in the qubit, increasing its stability and allowing for better isolation and improved control, which helps mitigate the impact of noise.

Even though the interdigitated transmon qubit has significant advantages, it poses a few significant challenges too, such as

- Interdigitated Transmon qubits pose significant fabrication issues; the interdigitated structure with nodes between the electrodes poses a significant fabrication challenges, as well as creating this type of qubit being very costly.
- Interdigitated Transmon qubits are less sensitive to charge noises, but they are very susceptible to thermal temperature changes and flux noise affecting the coherence time significantly.
- Interdigitated Transmon qubits have very high capacitance, which limits the tunability of the qubit for high-frequency applications.

Having discussed about the different qubits, let's summarize the contents of all the qubits discussed so far in a tabular format for a quick comparison which will help in identifying easily which qubit to use at which instance. The comparison between all the qubits is listed in Table 4-1.

Table 4-1 Comparison between the four different types of qubits

Feature	Transmon pocket	Transmon cross	Concentric transmon	Interdigitated transmon
Geometry	Rectangular shape with pocket	Cross shaped	Circular shape	Variable, interdigitated fingers
Josephson junction	Typically has a single Josephson junction	Typically has a single Josephson junction	Circular arrangement of Josephson junctions	Interdigitated fingers in the junction
Capacitance	Moderate	Moderate	Higher due to circular geometry	Higher due to interdigitated structure
Anharmonicity	Moderate	Moderate	Higher due to circular geometry	Higher due to interdigitated structure
Tuning Parameters	External magnetic flux, gate voltages	External magnetic flux, gate voltages	External magnetic flux, gate voltages	External magnetic flux, gate voltages
Design flexibility	Rectangular pocket design allows some flexibility	Cross-shaped design allows some flexibility	Circular design may limit some aspects of design	Flexible design, allows for tuning parameters

4.5 Designing a Full-Fledged Chip in Qiskit Metal

Now that we have covered the basics and have designed Qcomponents with multiple QPins and understood the fundamentals of the values stored in each component while designing the pins, we should dive into how we can develop a full-fledged quantum chip with multiple Qcomponents and CPWs to connect these components. With a complete understanding of how to design Qcomponents such as Transmon pockets with both single and multiple QPins, as well as how to connect them using CPWs, let us begin by creating the first chip.

To create the chip, we will use multiple Transmon pockets. For this design, let us choose four Transmon pockets, each with three QPins. We will connect each of these using CPW connectors. Now, let us begin by coding these four Qcomponents:

```
design.delete_all_components()
options = dict(
    pad_width = '425 um',
    pocket_height = '650um',
    connection_pads=dict(  # pin connecotrs
        a = dict(loc_W=+1,loc_H=+1),
        b = dict(loc_W=-1,loc_H=+1, pad_height='30um'),
        c = dict(loc_W= +1,loc_H=-1, pad_width='200um'),
    )
)
q1 = TransmonPocket(design, 'Q1', options = dict(pos_x='+3.5mm',
pos_y='+1.0mm', orientation=90, **options))
q2 = TransmonPocket(design, 'Q2', options = dict(pos_x='+5.5mm',
pos_y='+2.5mm', orientation=180, **options))
q3 = TransmonPocket(design, 'Q3', options = dict(pos_x='+3.5mm',
pos_y='+3.5mm', orientation=270, **options))
q4 = TransmonPocket(design, 'Q4', options = dict(pos_x='1.5mm',
pos_y='+2.5mm', orientation=0, **options))
# Take a screenshot with the component highlighted and the pins shown
gui.rebuild()
gui.autoscale()
gui.highlight_components(['Q1', 'Q2', 'Q3', 'Q4'])
gui.screenshot()
```

In this segment, we have created four transmon pockets, each with three qpins named "a," "b," "c," and they have been highlighted. Now we have used and specified the position of all the four Qcomponents that we will be using with pos_x and pos_y and then mentioned orientation so that we can fit the four chips and keep the diagram clean and make the connections easily.

The resulting output looks like the one shown in Figure 4-14 when we run the code snippet. Now that we have created the basic architecture and skeleton of the circuit, let us proceed to create the connectors so that we can complete the chip and finalize the circuit. We will use CPW connectors between each Qcomponent and connect them so that we can share and transmit information.

Before writing the code for the CPW connectors, we need to understand a few things. In order to design a connector, we need to import a library. Let us first look into the library that needs to be imported and the explanation of each and every return statement it provides:

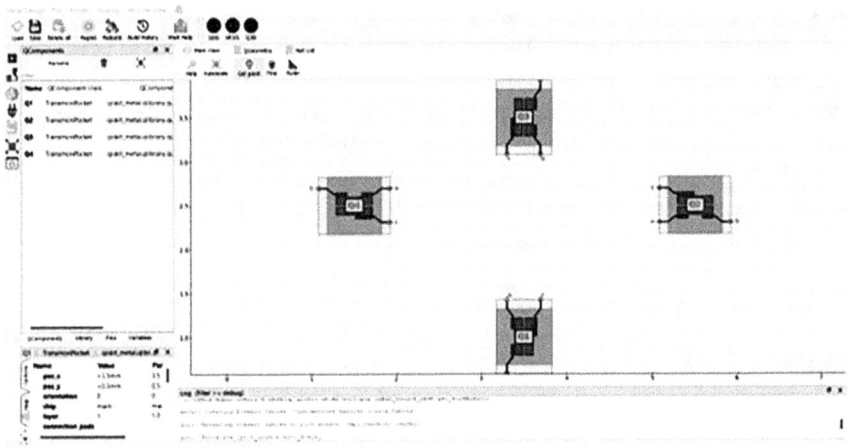

Figure 4-14 Full quantum chip: placement of four Transmon Qubits with three Qpins in four locations for generating a quantum chip

```
from qiskit_metal.qlibrary.tlines.meandered import
  RouteMeander
RouteMeander.get_template_options(design)


{
  'chip': 'main',
  'layer': '1',
  'pin_inputs': {
    'start_pin': {'component': "", 'pin': ""},
    'end_pin': {'component': "", 'pin': ""}
  },
  'fillet': '0',
  'lead': {
    'start_straight': '0mm',
    'end_straight': '0mm',
    'start_jogged_extension': "",
    'end_jogged_extension': ""
  },
  'total_length': '7mm',
  'trace_width': 'cpw_width',
  'meander': {
    'spacing': '200um',
    'asymmetry': '0um'
  },
  'snap': 'true',
  'prevent_short_edges': 'true',
  'hfss_wire_bonds': False,
  'q3d_wire_bonds': False
}
```

4.5 Designing a Full-Fledged Chip in Qiskit Metal

When we run the code, this is the return value we get, and we have to take a look at what these return values mean:

- `chip`: Specifies the chip or component on which the meandered trace will be created.
- `layer`: Specifies the layer on which the meandered trace will be created. When working with a multilayer structure, we should mention the layer, as each layer will have a different meander.
- `pin_inputs`: Defines the pins at the start and end of the meandered trace.
- `fillet`: Specifies the fillet radius at the corners of the meandered trace.
- `lead`: Defines the lead (straight segments) at the start and end of the meandered trace.
- `total_length`: Specifies the total length of the meandered trace.
- `trace_width`: Specifies the width of the meandered trace.
- `meander`: Defines parameters related to the meander structure, such as spacing between meanders and asymmetry.
- `snap`: Specifies whether to enable snapping of vertices to the grid.
- `prevent_short_edges`: Specifies whether to prevent the generation of short edges in the meandered trace.
- `hfss_wire_bonds`: Specifies whether to include wire bonds in HFSS simulations.
- `q3d_wire_bonds`: Specifies whether to include wire bonds in Q3D simulations.

Now that we have understood the basics, let us proceed with the coding to complete the CPW connections in our chip:

```python
options = Dict(
    meander=Dict(
        lead_start='0.1mm',
        lead_end='0.1mm',
        asymmetry='0 um')
)

def connect(component_name: str, component1: str, pin1: str,
component2: str, pin2: str,
            length: str,
            asymmetry='0 um', flip=False):
    """Connect two pins with a CPW."""
    myoptions = Dict(
        pin_inputs=Dict(
            start_pin=Dict(
                component=component1,
                pin=pin1),
            end_pin=Dict(
                component=component2,
                pin=pin2)),
        lead=Dict(
            start_straight='0.13mm'
        ),
```

```
            total_length=length,
        fillet = '90um')
        myoptions.update(options)
        myoptions.meander.asymmetry = asymmetry
        myoptions.meander.lead_direction_inverted = 'true' if flip
        else 'false'
        return RouteMeander(design, component_name, myoptions)

asym = 10
cpw1 = connect('cpw1', 'Q1', 'c', 'Q2', 'a', f'+{asym}um')
cpw2 = connect('cpw2', 'Q3', 'a', 'Q2', 'c', f'-{asym}um',
 flip=True)
cpw3 = connect('cpw3', 'Q3', 'c', 'Q4', 'a',  f'+{asym}um')
cpw4 = connect('cpw4', 'Q1', 'a', 'Q4', 'c', f'-{asym}um',
 flip=True)

gui.rebuild()
gui.autoscale()
gui.toggle_docks(True)
gui.highlight_components(['Q1', 'Q2', 'Q3', 'Q4','cpw1', 'cpw2',
'cpw3', 'cpw4'])
```

To make the connections, we use CPWs and employ four CPW registers. We create connections using CPW1, connecting the Qpin with the start node as Q1 pin "c" and the end node as Q2 pin "a" and so on. The parameter "asym" represents the amount of asymmetry in the meandered traces. The expression "f'+asymum" is an f-string formatting used to dynamically insert the value of "asym" into the string. It results in a string with an output "f'+10 m," where 10 is the value of "asym," and μm indicates micrometers. The purpose of this is to incorporate the asymmetry value into the total length of the meandered trace.

The "flip" parameter is used to control the direction of the meandered trace. When "flip = True," it means the direction of the meandered trace is inverted. In the code, it is applied to the connect function when connecting Q2 and Q3. By setting "flip = True," it flips the direction of the meandered trace, impacting the arrangement of the CPW; the following is shown in Figure 4-15. Well, you can also figure out the characteristics of each CPW connector by running this command:

```
design.components.cpw2

name: cpw2
class: Route Meander
options:
  'chip': 'main',
  'layer': '1',
  'pin_inputs': {
    'start_pin': {
      'component': 'Q3',
      'pin': 'a'
    },
    'end_pin': {
      'component': 'Q2',
      'pin': 'c'
```

4.5 Designing a Full-Fledged Chip in Qiskit Metal

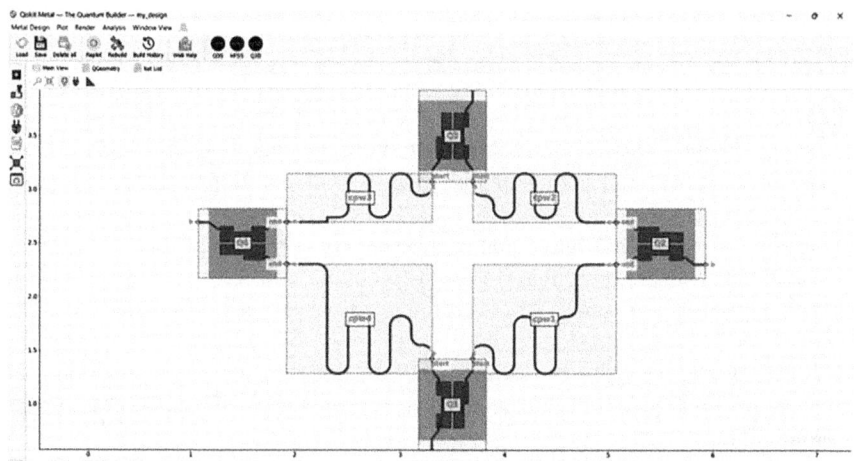

Figure 4-15 Full quantum chip: connecting the four Transmon chips using the CPW route meander

```
      }
    },
    'fillet': '90um',
    'lead': {
      'start_straight': '0.13mm',
      'end_straight': '0mm',
      'start_jogged_extension': "",
      'end_jogged_extension': ""
    },
    'total_length': '-10um',
    'trace_width': 'cpw_width',
    'meander': {
      'spacing': '200um',
      'asymmetry': '0um',
      'lead_start': '0.1mm',
      'lead_end': '0.1mm',
      'lead_direction_inverted': 'true'
    },
    'snap': 'true',
    'prevent_short_edges': 'true',
    'hfss_wire_bonds': False,
    'q3d_wire_bonds': False,
    'trace_gap': 'cpw_gap',
    '_actual_length': '2.989203371761571mm',
  module: qiskit_metal.qlibrary.tlines.meandered

  id: 88
```

Following these steps mentioned and using these basic parameters and chip placement, one can design their own quantum chip; we can summarize the steps of creating your own chip as follows:

- Decide on the basic qubits that you want to use for your quantum chip.
- Decide on the rough layout of placement of all the chips inside the layout, keeping routing in mind.
- Decide on the type of routing you want to use for connecting.
- Additionally, decide whether you want to couple your designed quantum chip with resonators or couplers or Josephson junctions as per requirements.

Moving forward, we will discuss how to create and add Josephson junctions and couplers to your quantum chip to achieve some special functionalities to your quantum chip.

4.6 Josephson Junction

The basic structure of a Josephson junction consists of two superconducting electrodes separated by a thin insulating barrier. When a voltage is applied across this barrier, a supercurrent can tunnel through it, creating a phase difference across the junction. These special junctions, which form the basis of superconducting qubits, can be created using the commands available in Qiskit Metal. There are two styles in which we can design the Josephson junction in Qiskit Metal, the "Dolan" style and the "Manhattan" style:

- **Manhattan Style**: In this type, the junctions are fabricated using perpendicular layers of superconducting materials, often in a square or rectangular shape.
- **Dolan Style**: In this type, the junctions are fabricated by creating overlapping superconducting layers with a thin insulating barrier for the junction.

Both formats of the junctions have their own applications. The Dolan style is typically used for high-precision junctions, often in lab-scale experiments, whereas the Manhattan style is typically used to solve the potential scalability issue in large-scale fabrication.

Before moving into the coding aspects of both the styles, let us first revisit the Josephson energy (E_J) and charging energy (E_C) and explore their relation to anharmonicity and their impact on qubit states and parameters.

As we have discussed about the Hamiltonian in Chapter 2, for a transmon qubit a Hamiltonian has two parts—the charging energy part and the Josephson energy part:

- **Charging Energy** (E_C): Represents the energy stored inside the capacitor formed by the qubit electrode and the ground plane

4.6 Josephson Junction

- **Josephson Energy** (E_J): Represents the energy stored inside the Josephson junction created between the two electrodes

Considering these terms, we get the value of the Hamiltonian for the transmon qubit to be

$$H = 4E_C(n_c - n_g)^2 - E_J \cos(\phi) \quad (4\text{-}1)$$

where n_c represents the number of Cooper pairs and n_g represents the offset charge number responsible for external gate operations and external flux. Solving for the eigenstates for this Hamiltonian provides us the distinct energy level for the transmon qubit. In order to do so, we need the eigenvalues of the system, and we obtain them by solving the Schrödinger equation for the Hamiltonian. But this is a very tediously long process.

For a transmon qubit, the value of transition frequency can be determined with the formula

$$E_n \propto \sqrt{8E_J \cdot E_C}\left(n + \frac{1}{2}\right) - \frac{E_C}{12}\left(6n^2 + 6n + 3\right) \quad (4\text{-}2)$$

where n represents the energy level of the state. Calculating the energy states from the qubit Hamiltonian is a very long and time-consuming process, so there is another parameter that helps us in providing a more in-depth and detailed analysis for the working of the qubit. We use the E_J/E_C ratio to describe the functioning of the qubit. Let's look into the properties that the E_J/E_C ratio helps with:

- Large value of the E_J/E_C ratio
  - Qubit behaves more like a harmonic oscillator.
  - Reduced sensitivity to charge noise.
  - Reduced qubit stability.
  - Lower value of anharmonicity.
- Small value of the E_J/E_C ratio
  - Qubit behaves less like a harmonic oscillator.
  - Increased sensitivity to charge noise.
  - Increased qubit stability.
  - Higher value of anharmonicity.

Having said the important concept regarding Josephson junctions and how they affect anharmonicity, let us now look into how we can create these junctions with simple code.

4.6.1 Manhattan Style

The term "Manhattan-style Josephson junction" refers to a specific geometric configuration of a Josephson junction, where the junctions are fabricated using perpendicular layers of superconducting materials. It is characterized by a rectangular or "Manhattan" geometry, resembling the layout of streets in Manhattan, New York City. This design is chosen to match fabrication constraints, making it easier for making the deposition process on the chip and creating the pattern for this style during the manufacturing process. The Manhattan-style layout aims to reduce parasitic capacitance by minimizing unwanted environmental interactions and creating isolation, thereby preserving qubit coherence and improving stability. The geometry of the junction directly influences its Josephson energy which facilitates tuning for specific quantum operations.

The rectangular shape and right-angle turns in the design facilitate the integration of Manhattan-style Josephson junctions into complex quantum circuits. This is particularly important for precise positioning and connectivity within the quantum processor. Figure 4-16 represents the architectural diagram of the Manhattan-style Josephson junction.

The jj_manhattan module in the Qcomponent Library, specifically in the qiskit_metal.qlibrary.qubits package, contains the class jj_manhattan, which represents this Manhattan-style Josephson junction. Like all quantum components, jj_manhattan inherits from the Qcomponent class:

```
from qiskit_metal.qlibrary.qubits.JJ_Manhattan import
jj_manhattan
design.overwrite_enabled = True
jj2 = jj_manhattan(design, 'JJ2', options=dict(pos_x="0.1",
pos_y="0.0"))
```

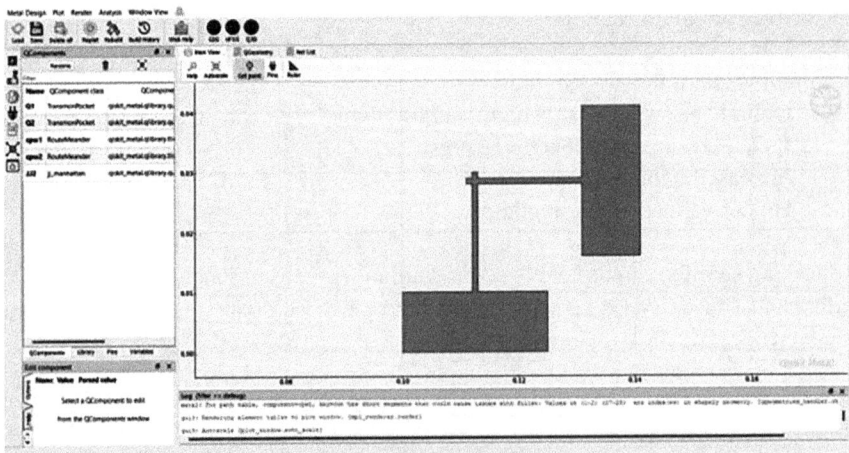

Figure 4-16 Chip structure of the Manhattan-style Josephson junction

```
gui.rebuild()
gui.autoscale()
gui.zoom_on_components(['JJ2'])
gui.screenshot()
```

Having discussed how to code a Manhattan-style Josephson junction, let's talk about the advantages it has:

- The Manhattan-style Josephson junction has a straight, orthogonal layout of junctions which helps in minimizing unwanted electromagnetic coupling to adjacent components, improving isolation and reducing noise.
- The Manhattan style has a rectangular, grid-like layout of the junction, inspired by Manhattan-style streets, which allows for compact designs that fit into smaller spaces; this helps optimize the chip's area utilization and makes it easier to integrate into a chip with heavy traffic.
- The Manhattan style provides a clear, well-defined path for tuning elements like flux and gate voltages, facilitating better control of the qubit's energy levels and coherence properties. Due to this simple and compact structure, scalable quantum circuit designs can be created, enabling large circuits with precise control over energy levels.

Even though the Manhattan-style Josephson junction provides good energy levels with a simple structure process and compact design, it still possesses a few disadvantages:

- The Manhattan-style Josephson junction provides isolation from environmental noise but is prone to qubit crosstalk, making it harder to isolate from qubit interactions.
- The Manhattan-style Josephson junction's structure has sharp bends and intersections which can introduce parasitic inductances and capacitances. These unwanted effects may lead to increased resistance or loss in signal transmission, potentially degrading qubit performance.
- The Manhattan-style Josephson junction has a fixed layout design which makes it harder to achieve proper qubit-qubit coupling, which can lead to restrictions in creating a chip with multiple components.

4.6.2 Dolan Style

The term "Dolan-style Josephson junction" refers to a specific Josephson junction design, crucial in superconducting qubits for quantum computing. Named after its inventor, John Dolan, who played a significant role in the development of superconducting qubits, this design typically employs a single Josephson junction. This junction comprises two superconducting electrodes separated by a thin insulating barrier. Similar to other Josephson junctions, the Dolan-style design allows control over the Josephson energy, a vital parameter influencing qubit behavior. Considerations for the fabrication process are inherent in the Dolan-style design, accounting for lithographic patterning and deposition techniques employed in superconducting qubit fabrication. We will be discussing in depth the unique fabrication process that is required in creating this unique style of Josephson junction later in Chapter 8.

To create a Dolan-style Josephson junction, you can utilize the Qcomponent Library, specifically the jj_dolan module, which contains the jj_dolan class. As with all quantum components, jj_dolan inherits from the Qcomponent class. The Dolan-style Josephson junction is displayed in Figure 4-17.

```
from qiskit_metal.qlibrary.qubits.JJ_Dolan import jj_dolan
design.overwrite_enabled = True
jj2 = jj_dolan(design, 'JJ2', options=dict(pos_x="0.1",
pos_y="0.0"))
gui.rebuild()
gui.autoscale()
gui.zoom_on_components(['JJ2'])
gui.screenshot()
```

Having discussed how to code a Dolan-style Josephson junction, let's talk about the advantages it has:

- The Dolan-style Josephson junction uses the Dolan bridge technique that allows for the creation of narrow, well-defined gaps in the junction, which minimizes parasitic capacitance and reduces unwanted coupling, which helps in improving the qubit's performance in high-frequency operations.
- The Dolan-style Josephson junction tends to exhibit more uniformity across different qubits in a chip. This consistency is key in scaling up quantum circuits and maintaining coherence between qubits.

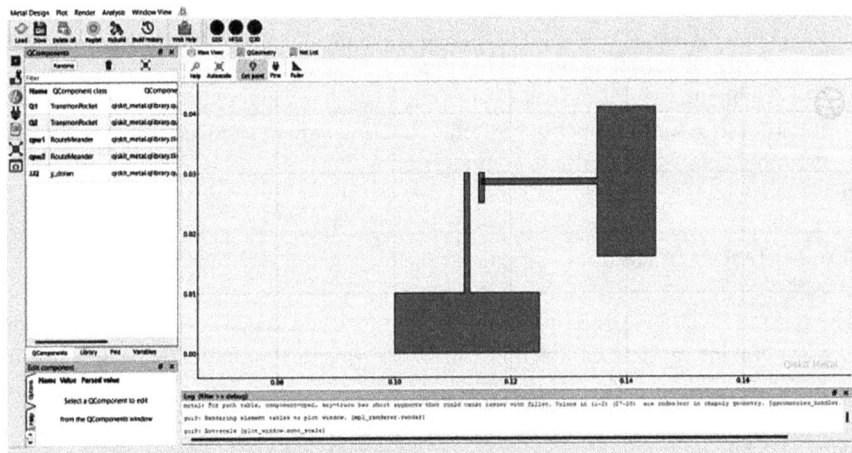

Figure 4-17 Chip structure of the Dolan-style Josephson junction

- The Dolan-style Josephson junction is compatible with the planar fabrication process, which is crucial in modern superconducting qubit designs. This integration is essential for building large-scale quantum processors and simplifies the overall design by allowing for a flat, integrated layout of various components.

Even though the Dolan-style Josephson junction provides good resistance to parasitic capacitance with planar structure and compatible with high-frequency operations, it still possesses a few disadvantages:

- The Dolan-style Josephson junction requires advanced techniques like shadow evaporation, etching, and accurate alignment of multiple layers. These complex fabrication steps make the creation of this junction expensive, time-consuming, and extremely tedious.
- The Dolan-style Josephson junction, like other thin-film junctions, is sensitive toward thermal effects and thermal fluctuations, which leads to the introduction of noise and causes decoherence in qubits, making it extremely difficult to operate in those scenarios where longer coherence time is required.
- The Dolan-style Josephson junction allows for tuning, which is limited by factors like quantum capacitance, critical current variations, and sensitivity to environmental factors such as temperature or flux. This means that perfect tuning across large arrays may be difficult and require additional calibration and optimization.

Having explored the design principles of two distinct formats for creating simple Josephson junctions, it's essential to compare their efficiency for their intended purposes. Let's analyze and contrast the two formats to understand their respective strengths and applications. The tabular comparison between the two types of Josephson junction is provided in Table 4-2.

4.7 Qubit Coupler

Qubit couplers are components in quantum computing circuits that facilitate interactions between qubits. Their primary purpose is to enable the controlled exchange of quantum information between neighboring qubits. Qubit coupling is crucial for implementing two-qubit gates, which are fundamental building blocks in quantum algorithms and quantum error correction. There are many types of couplers that we use when designing superconducting qubits. Let's dive into it and look at some of these qubit couplers.

Before moving into an in-depth analysis of how couplers work, let us look into the different types of coupling methods and how they are used for a better understanding of the coupling process:

- **Inductive Coupling**: Inductive coupling arises from the mutual inductance between current-carrying loops or elements, such as the superconducting loops

Table 4-2 Comparison between Manhattan-style and Dolan-style junctions

Feature	Dolan-style Josephson junction	Manhattan-style Josephson junction
Geometry	Typically has a triangular shape	Characterized by a rectangular or "Manhattan" geometry with right-angle turns
Inventor	Named after its inventor, John Dolan	–
Junction structure	Typically uses a single Josephson junction	–
Control over energy	Provides control over the Josephson energy	Provides control over the Josephson energy
Considerations	Fabrication considerations for lithographic patterning and deposition techniques	Chosen to comply with fabrication constraints, simplifying processes
Advantages	May offer specific advantages related to its triangular geometry	Geometric layout aims to reduce parasitic capacitance and integrates well into complex circuits
Qubit integration	–	Easier integration into complex quantum circuits due to the rectangular shape and right-angle turns

of qubits. This type of coupling is governed by a shared magnetic flux. Mutual inductance is the process where, due to the flow of time-varying current in one superconducting loop, it will induce a magnetic flux in the nearby loop. Mutual inductance couples the two superconducting loops as the variation or change in the flow of current through one loop will have an effect on the induced magnetic field on the other loop. In inductive coupling, the energy exchange between qubits is proportional to the shared flux. The Hamiltonian of the inductive coupling is represented as

$$H_{ind} = \frac{M}{L_1 L_2} \cdot I_1 I_2 \qquad (4\text{-}3)$$

where M represents the mutual inductance between the two coils, L_1 and L_2 represent the inductance of the two qubits or resonators being coupled, and I_1 and I_2 represent the current flowing through the two loops. The properties for this type of coupling are as follows:

- This makes two systems coupled without the need for any direct connections.
- This type of coupling is recommended for flux-sensitive systems and applications.
- This type of coupling is generally used in tunable couplers as the effect of the coupling can be dynamically adjusted.

- The issue with inductive coupling is that since it works on the logic of mutual inductance it makes the coupling sensitive to stray external magnetic fields which can induce noise and decoherence.
- **Capacitive Coupling**: Capacitive coupling arises from a shared electric field between the capacitors of the layout component or qubit. Unlike inductive coupling, capacitive coupling relies on charge interactions rather than magnetic flux. When two systems share a capacitor, it leads to the charge between the two components being coupled due to the electric field, which results in capacitive coupling. The Hamiltonian of capacitive coupling is represented as

$$H_{cap} = \frac{C_{shared}}{C_1 C_2} \cdot Q_1 Q_2 \qquad (4\text{-}4)$$

where C_{shared} represents the shared capacitance between the two components. C_1 and C_2 represent the self-capacitance of the coupled components, and Q_1 and Q_2 represent the self-charges of the two components. The properties for this type of coupling are as follows:

- Capacitive coupling is relatively easy to design and control during fabrication compared to other coupling methods.
- Another advantage of capacitive coupling is that it is less sensitive to magnetic noise compared to inductive coupling because capacitive coupling does not rely on magnetic inductance to couple with.
- Capacitive coupling is typically used in transmon qubits where the coupling strength is controlled by the overlap of electrode geometries. It is also used for entangling quantum gates by coupling two transmons using a capacitor.
- Capacitive coupling has limited strength compared to inductive coupling, and it is prone to the generation of parasitic capacitance, which can lead to decoherence in the qubit.

- **Resonator Coupling**: Resonator coupling arises when two qubits or resonators have overlapping frequencies, allowing efficient energy transfer. When two qubits or a qubit and a resonator have the same or nearly the same frequencies, they exchange energy through photon-mediated interactions. Photon-mediated interactions occur when qubits or resonators exchange energy through photons in a shared electromagnetic field, enabling coupling between their quantum states. Resonator coupling's strength depends on how close the frequencies of the two components are to each other. The Hamiltonian of resonator coupling is represented as

$$H_{res} = g(ab^\dagger + a^\dagger b) \qquad (4\text{-}5)$$

where g represents the coupling strength, a and $a^\dagger$ represent the annihilation and creation operators for the first system, and b and $b^\dagger$ represent the annihilation and creation operators for the second system. The properties for this type of coupling are as follows:

Table 4-3 Comparison of inductive, capacitive, and resonant coupling

Feature	Inductive	Capacitive	Resonant
Mechanism	Magnetic field interaction	Electric field (charge-based) interaction	Frequency overlap
Hamiltonian of the coupler	$H_{ind} = \frac{M}{L_1 L_2} \cdot I_1 I_2$	$H_{cap} = \frac{C_{shared}}{C_1 C_2} \cdot Q_1 Q_2$	$H_{res} = g(ab^\dagger + a^\dagger b)$
Use case	Flux qubit	Transmon qubit coupling	Transmon-resonator interaction
Advantages	Strong tunable coupling	Simple design	High fidelity
Challenges	Sensitive to flux noise	Limited strength and prone to parasitic capacitance	Requires precise frequency tuning

- Resonator coupling provides high-fidelity interaction when tuned properly and increases the stability of the qubit and resonator interaction.
- Resonator coupling is used for coherent information transfer in quantum circuits.
- The coupling parameter g is determined by the shared frequency between the qubit and the resonator, which makes tuning the resonator coupling much easier compared to other methods.
- The biggest challenge that resonator coupling faces is that it requires extremely precise frequency alignment to get coupled. In resonance, resonator coupling acts the best, but off resonance the frequencies can lead to significant detuning issues and can put the qubits out of coherence.

These are the most important types of coupling used for creating superconducting circuits. Having discussed all the parameters and in-depth ideas of each type of coupling, let's tabulate a comparison between the three types of coupling methods in Table 4-3.

Having explored the different types of coupling, let us now look at how to code three of the most popular types of couplers that Qiskit Metal provides us with in the following section.

4.7.1 Direct Coupler (Transmon-Transmon)

In the realm of quantum computing frameworks like Qiskit Metal, a direct coupler connecting two transmon qubits is represented using specialized components or connectors that model the physical coupling elements, such as capacitors or inductors, facilitating interaction between the qubits. Transmon qubits, integral to quantum operations and gate implementations, are superconducting circuits featuring Josephson junctions. The term "direct coupler" implies a direct and con-

4.7 Qubit Coupler

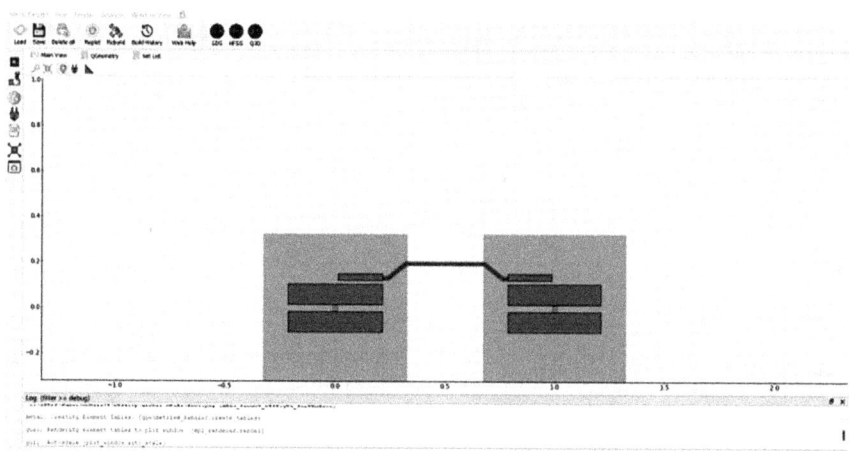

Figure 4-18 Chip structure of the direct coupler between two transmon chips with single Qpins

trolled interaction between transmon qubits, eliminating the need for intermediary components. This coupling is pivotal for achieving entanglement and implementing two-qubit quantum gates. Capacitive coupling involves the sharing of electric charge between qubits, ensuring a controlled interaction. Inductive coupling, on the other hand, utilizes shared magnetic flux or magnetic fields between qubits, achievable by placing them in close proximity. Additionally, resonant energy transfer, wherein qubits with matching resonant frequencies transfer energy between them, is another mechanism enabling effective coupling.

One of the fundamental components when designing a direct coupler is the straight routing between two components. The direct coupler uses this special type of routing to facilitate the transmission and coupling between two corresponding Qcomponents. Traditionally, we use transmon pockets when developing a direct coupler, but there are some other types of Qcomponents that we can use as well when developing these quantum chips. To create two transmon pockets, each with one qpin, coupled together with straight routing to form a direct coupler, we use the following code, and the output is shown in Figure 4-18:

```
from qiskit_metal.qlibrary.qubits.transmon_pocket import TransmonPocket
from qiskit_metal.qlibrary.tlines.straight_path import RouteStraight
design.delete_all_components()
q1 = TransmonPocket(design, 'Q1', options = dict(pad_width = '425
um', pocket_height = '650um', connection_pads=dict(readout = dict(loc_W=+1,loc_H=+1, pad_width='200um'))))
q2 = TransmonPocket(design, 'Q2', options = dict(pos_x = '1.0 mm',
pad_width = '425 um', pocket_height = '650um',
connection_pads=dict(readout = dict(loc_W=-1,loc_H=+1,
```

```
pad_width='200um'))))
bus = RouteStraight(design, 'coupler',
Dict(pin_inputs=Dict(start_pin=Dict(component='Q1',
pin='readout'),end_pin=Dict(component='Q2', pin='readout')), ))
gui.rebuild()
gui.autoscale()
gui.screenshot()
```

Having discussed how to code a direct coupler, let's talk about the advantages it has:

- Direct couplers have an extremely simple and straightforward design, making them easy to fabricate and implement. This simplicity of the design of direct couplers allows for easy integration with multi-qubit systems.
- Direct couplers have extremely strong interactions between qubits because they are coupled without any intermediate components, which results in fast gate operations. Due to this direct interaction without any intermediate components, it also minimizes the loss of energy.
- Direct coupling uses very few components, which reduces the risk of component failure and unnecessary errors induced due to it.

Even though the direct coupler provides several advantages that can help in making simple and large scalable operations, it still possesses a few disadvantages:

- Direct couplers, compared to tunable couplers, lack the ability to fine-tune dynamically to adjust the coupling strength.
- Direct couplers are prone to qubit crosstalk and unwanted interactions when components are present in its proximity.
- Direct couplers lack the intermediate components that can lead to reduced isolation between coupled qubits.

4.7.2 Tunable Couplers

A tunable coupler, in the context of quantum computing, refers to a qubit coupler whose coupling strength can be dynamically adjusted or tuned. The ability to control the coupling strength between qubits is crucial in quantum computing architectures, as it enables the implementation of controlled gates and the creation of entangled states. In tunable couplers, this control is typically achieved by introducing an intermediate coupling element, such as a tunable superconducting inductor, a flux-tunable Josephson junction, or a capacitively coupled resonator. By varying an external control parameter—such as the magnetic flux through a superconducting loop—the effective inductance or capacitance of the coupler is modified. This, in turn, shifts the resonance frequency of the coupler, thereby dynamically adjusting the interaction strength between the qubits. As a result, the coupling can be turned on or off, or continuously tuned, allowing precise control over multi-qubit

4.7 Qubit Coupler

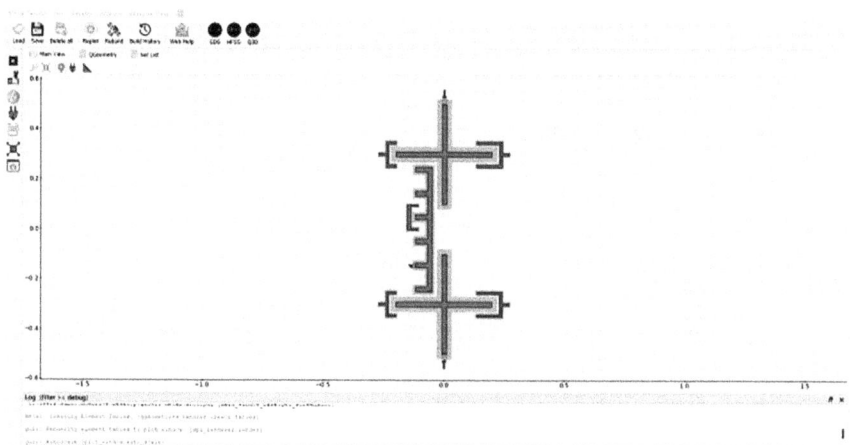

Figure 4-19 Chip structure of a tunable coupler with two Xmons and an integrated Transmon Qubit

gate operations and entanglement generation while mitigating unwanted crosstalk. Tunable couplers provide dynamic control over qubit-qubit interactions during the quantum computation process. This dynamic control is essential for executing specific quantum algorithms and optimizing the performance of quantum circuits.

Tunable couplers play a crucial role in generating entanglement between qubits. Tunable couplers are often used to implement two-qubit gate operations, such as CNOT gates. These gates are fundamental for performing quantum computations and building quantum algorithms. The tunability of couplers provides flexibility in designing quantum circuits. It allows researchers and engineers to adapt the coupling strength based on the specific requirements of a quantum algorithm or application.

One of the fundamental components when designing a tunable coupler is the Transmon Cross. Tunable couplers use this special type of qubit to implement the gates. Traditionally, we use transmon pockets when developing quantum chips, but there are some other types of qubits that we use as well when developing these quantum chips. To create two crossmon coupled together with an interdigitated tunable coupler, we use the following code, and the output circuit is shown in Figure 4-19:

```
from qiskit_metal.qlibrary.qubits.transmon_cross_fl import
TransmonCrossFL
from qiskit_metal.qlibrary.couplers.tunable_coupler_01 import
TunableCoupler01
design.delete_all_components()
Q1 = TransmonCrossFL(design, 'Q1', options = dict(pos_x = '0',
pos_y='-0.3mm', connection_pads = dict(bus_01 =
dict(connector_location = '180',claw_length ='95um'), readout =
dict(connector_location = '0')), fl_options = dict()))
```

```
Q2 = TransmonCrossFL(design, 'Q2', options = dict(pos_x = '0',
pos_y='0.3mm', orientation = '180', connection_pads = dict(bus_02 =
dict(connector_location = '0',claw_length ='95um'), readout =
dict(connector_location = '180')), fl_options = dict()))
tune_c_Q12 = TunableCoupler01(design,'Tune_C_Q12', options =
dict(pos_x = '-0.06mm', pos_y = '0', orientation=90, c_width='500um'))
gui.rebuild()
gui.autoscale()
all_component_names = design.components.keys()
gui.zoom_on_components(all_component_names)
gui.screenshot()
```

Having discussed how to code a tunable coupler, let's talk about the advantages it has:

- The biggest advantage of tunable couplers is that they enable real-time adjustments of qubit coupling strength, allowing flexible operations for different quantum gate requirements, providing a dynamic control over the entire circuit.
- Tunable couplers can significantly reduce qubit crosstalk, interference due to other signals, and unwanted interactions by turning the coupling off when not in use.
- Tunable couplers can adjust and increase the fidelity of the system by tuning the coupling to the desired strength as per the requirement to match the system requirements.

Even though the tunable coupler provides significant advantages that can help in making a stable system by dynamically tuning the coupler as per the system requirements, it still possesses a few disadvantages:

- Tunable couplers are easy to tune by external parameters, which can lead to induced noise from control signals, potentially affecting qubit coherence and stability.
- Tunable couplers are prone to heating and warm up faster compared to other couplers, which can disrupt the superconducting system that works at very low temperatures; in other words, this issue can disrupt the cryogenic process of the superconducting system (Miyanaga et al., 2021; Campbell et al., 2022).
- Tunable couplers require precise calibrations, which makes it harder to tune as per requirements during complex superconducting qubit applications.

4.7.3 Bus Resonator Coupler (Transmon-Transmon)

A bus resonator coupler is a specific type of coupling mechanism used in quantum computing between two transmon qubits. It involves the utilization of a resonator, often referred to as a "bus resonator," to mediate the interaction between transmon qubits. This approach is designed to enhance the control and flexibility of the qubit-qubit coupling in quantum circuits. The bus resonator is an additional

4.7 Qubit Coupler

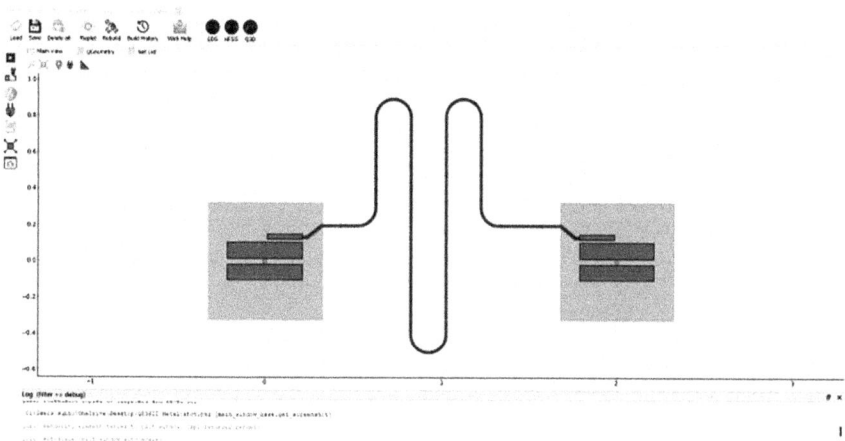

Figure 4-20 Chip structure of a bus resonator coupler between two transmon chips with single Qpins

superconducting resonator, often implemented as a transmission line or a cavity resonator. The bus resonator acts as an intermediary or a "bus" that facilitates the coupling between the two transmon qubits, providing a pathway for quantum information transfer. The bus resonator is capacitively coupled to each transmon qubit. Capacitive coupling involves the sharing of electric charge, enabling a controlled interaction between the resonator and the qubits. The capacitance and frequency of the bus resonator can be tuned to control the strength and frequency of the coupling. When one of the transmon qubits is excited, it induces a change in the charge distribution in the bus resonator due to capacitive coupling. This change in charge distribution in the bus resonator affects the other transmon qubits, leading to a controlled interaction or coupling between the two qubits. The use of a bus resonator allows for tunable and adjustable coupling strengths between qubits. The bus resonator can be detuned or turned off to decouple the qubits, providing control over the quantum circuit. Bus resonator couplers are employed in quantum circuits for implementing controlled-phase (CZ) gates and other multi-qubit operations. They are particularly useful in the design of quantum processors for scalable quantum computing.

One of the fundamental components when designing a bus resonator coupler is the meander routing between two components. The bus resonator coupler uses this special type of routing to facilitate the transmission and coupling between two corresponding Qcomponents. Traditionally, we use transmon pockets when developing a bus resonator coupler, but there are other types of Qcomponents that we can use as well when developing these quantum chips. To create two transmon pockets, each with one qpin, coupled together with a meander route to form a bus resonator coupler, we use the following code, and the output is displayed in Figure 4-20:

```
from qiskit_metal.qlibrary.qubits.transmon_pocket import TransmonPocket
from qiskit_metal.qlibrary.tlines.meandered import RouteMeander
q1 = TransmonPocket(design, 'Q1', options = dict(pad_width = '425 
um',pocket_height = '650um',connection_pads=dict(readout = 
dict(loc_W=+1,loc_H=+1, pad_width='200um'))))
q2 = TransmonPocket(design, 'Q2', options = dict(pos_x = '2.0 
mm',pad_width = '425 um',pocket_height = 
'650um',connection_pads=dict(readout = dict(loc_W=-1,loc_H=+1, 
pad_width='200um'))))
coupler_options = Dict(pin_inputs=Dict(start_pin=Dict(component='Q1', 
pin='readout'),end_pin=Dict(component='Q2', 
pin='readout')),fillet='99.9um',total_length = '5mm',lead = 
Dict(start_straight = '200um'))
bus = RouteMeander(design, 'coupler', options= coupler_options)
gui.rebuild()
gui.autoscale()
all_component_names = design.components.keys()
gui.zoom_on_components(all_component_names)
gui.screenshot()
```

Having discussed how to code a bus resonator coupler, let's talk about the advantages it has:

- Bus resonator couplers allow for adjustable coupling strength by varying the qubit-resonator detuning. They also provide better isolation between qubits compared to direct coupling, resulting in reduced crosstalk.
- Bus resonator couplers can mediate and govern the interactions between multiple qubits simultaneously, which enables it to perform complex and multiple gate operations at once.
- Bus resonator couplers are best used for connecting distant qubits in a layout in larger quantum processors, making it easier to integrate with complex superconducting circuit designs.

Even though the bus resonator coupler provides several advantages that can help in reducing issues with crosstalk and providing better isolation, it still possesses a few disadvantages:

- Bus resonator couplers, as the name suggests, require an additional piece of resonator to its structure, which makes the design more complex that results in a complicated and expensive fabrication and manufacturing process.
- Bus resonator couplers have additional resonators, which create an additional dependency on an intermediate component to work for this type of coupler, causing the potential for energy dissipation in the resonator, impacting system performance. Furthermore, the resonator can introduce additional thermal noise, affecting qubit coherence.
- Making the bus resonator coupler to work on perfect resonance frequency requires detailed calibrations and tuning, which makes it difficult to integrate with complex existing designs.

Table 4-4 Comparison between tunable, direct, and bus couplers

Feature	Tunable coupler	Direct coupler	Bus resonator coupler
Coupling mechanism	Capacitive coupling with tunable parameters	Direct interaction between qubits	Capacitive coupling through a resonator
Tunable parameters	Capacitance, frequency, and other parameters	None	Capacitance, frequency, and other parameters
Control over coupling	Highly tunable and adjustable coupling strength	Limited control, fixed coupling strength	Tunable and adjustable coupling strength
Decoupling possibility	Can be detuned or turned off to decouple qubits	Decoupling may be challenging	Can be detuned or turned off to decouple qubits
Qubit interaction	Allows for controlled-phase (CZ) gates and multi-qubit operations	Direct interaction, suitable for specific quantum operations	Enables controlled interaction through a resonator
Applications	Quantum processors, scalable quantum computing	Limited applications, specific quantum operations	Quantum circuits with enhanced tunability
Flexibility	Highly flexible and dynamic in quantum circuit design	Limited flexibility, more specific use cases	Enhances control and tunability in quantum circuits

Now that we have seen the three most commonly used and popular types of coupling with their basic code structure and how they should look like, let us differentiate between the three so that we can have better understanding of which one to use when the time comes. Table 4-4 provides a detailed comparison between the three different couplers we have discussed.

4.8 Electromagnetic Analysis and Quantization and Qiskit Metal

After designing the layout of the structure and checking it, it is time to analyze the created layout. In the previous section of the layout, we created a quantum structure. At this point, we want to assess how well this created structure works. What are its quantum properties? What is the Hamiltonian, what is its dissipated energy, and does it follow anharmonicity? At this stage, a connection must be made between the quantum and classical worlds. There are different analysis methods, each with its own complexities. Two of the most popular types of analysis are the full-wave method and the quasi-static method. Let's understand what these methods say:

- **Full-Wave Method**: Full-wave methods account for the entire electromagnetic field distribution, including the slight variations in the field to provide an accurate

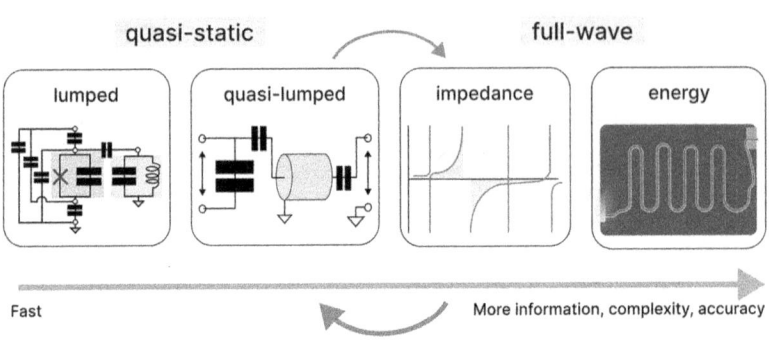

Figure 4-21 Visual representation and understanding of each analysis model under each analysis method

simulation and analysis of the complex quantum circuits. These methods are especially useful for high-frequency designs where the wavelength of signals is comparable to device dimensions, making quasi-static approximations insufficient.

- **Quasi-static Method**: Quasi-static methods approximate the behavior of electromagnetic fields by assuming that variations in the fields are slow or negligible compared to the speed of light. These methods are particularly effective for low-frequency designs or when the physical dimensions of the device are much smaller than the wavelength of the signals. By ignoring wave propagation effects, quasi-static methods provide computationally efficient solutions for initial parameter optimization and early-stage design analysis. Static

A summary of the different techniques for structure analysis is shown in Figure 4-21, which is divided into two main groups: quasi-stationary and full-wave. As displayed in Figure 4-21, the techniques provided for analysis in the quasi-static method include lumped oscillator models and quasi-lumped models. Full-wave analysis methods include the impedance model and the energy-participation ratio model. Here are some brief ideas and understanding of each of the four analysis models:

- **Lumped Oscillator Model**: The lumped oscillator model simplifies the representation of quantum components by treating them as discrete basic classical elements like inductors, capacitors, and resistors. This approach is ideal for devices where the physical dimensions are much smaller than the wavelength of operation, allowing circuit behavior to be analyzed using Kirchhoff's laws

ideally transforming a quantum circuit into classical. It provides an intuitive understanding of the interactions between quantum components in a circuit.
- **Quasi-lumped Oscillator Model**: The quasi-lumped oscillator model extends the lumped oscillator model approach by taking into consideration some distributed effects that account for components where dimensions are approaching the wavelength but are not fully distributed. This model bridges the gap between lumped oscillator model and full-wave analyses, enabling a more accurate representation of intermediate-scale systems without the computational complexity of full-wave methods.
- **Impedance Model**: The impedance model focuses on the analysis of resonant circuits by examining their input and transfer impedance characteristics. The transfer impedance characteristics are an important parameter in understanding the signal propagation and interaction within complex networks. This works by describing the relationship between the voltage and current at different points in a system, which provides a detailed report on the power and signal integrity that is being transmitted in the components. It helps in determining resonance frequencies, quality factors, and coupling strengths. This approach is particularly useful for optimizing microwave and RF components in quantum systems to ensure efficient energy transfer and minimal loss.
- **Energy-Participation Ratio Model**: The energy-participation ratio (EPR) model quantifies the proportion of energy stored in different circuit components or modes relative to the total system energy. This model is extremely crucial in identifying the dominant contributors to system dynamics, such as losses or anharmonicity, and plays a critical role in designing superconducting qubits by balancing trade-offs between coherence and coupling.

We will be talking in depth regarding the theoretical and fundamental concepts for each of the four models discussed and understand how to perform the corresponding analysis with examples and code in the next chapters.

Currently, Ansys HFSS software is used for full-wave analysis, but the group of Qiskit software developers is trying to make these analyses possible with the help of other software such as COMSOL, Keysight, and ADS. The way of working is that the design of the part is done in Qiskit Metal. This design is then rendered and transferred to HFSS. We simulate in Qiskit Metal, and the results show us what the electric field of the qubit is like. Let us talk about these software and their advantages and why they can be preferred over Ansys HFSS:

- **COMSOL Multiphysics**: COMSOL is a versatile software that is extremely helpful in providing analysis by taking the physical phenomena into consideration along with electromagnetic simulations. COMSOL is capable of handling external physical interactions such as thermal properties or mechanical properties of the system into considerations while providing the simulated output. This makes it particularly useful when designing quantum devices that require understanding of multi-physics interactions, such as the effects of temperature gradients on superconducting materials.

- **Keysight ADS**: Keysight ADS (Advanced Design System) is widely used for RF (radiofrequency) or microwave circuit design and analysis. It excels in designing and optimizing lumped and distributed components (quasi-lumped) models, including transmission lines, couplers, and mixers. ADS excels in the quasi-static method of analysis compared to the full-wave method of analysis. ADS is capable of time-domain simulations, which provide a quick analysis of transient responses, which can complement Ansys HFSS's frequency-domain focus.

While performing analysis, it is important to know which software will achieve the given task; from a broader perspective, we can say that ADS can provide better understanding if we want to perform the quasi-static analysis compared to HFSS, which can provide a fine-tuned and accurate output while performing the full-wave analysis method. Let's compare the software to use for the analysis between ADS and HFSS. While ADS focuses on circuit-level and RF simulations, making it great for designing signal chains and integrated circuits, HFSS provides detailed accuracy for complex shapes and complex electromagnetic behavior, acting as a full-wave solver. ADS works better for simpler circuit designs, while HFSS is ideal for fine-tuning the electromagnetic performance of specific components. The choice depends on whether you need a broader circuit overview (ADS) or detailed field analysis (HFSS).

If we want to make the simulation more accurate, it is better to use the special mode method. This method solves Maxwell's equations. In this way, we design the layout, and Qiskit Metal renders it automatically in the simulation software. In this method, the software divides the quantum chip into parts and performs the analysis for each part separately, as it is very heavy to do it all at once. In this simulation, chip segmentation is very important, but the simulation results in this method are excellent.

Chip segmentation is the process where the chip design is broken down into smaller, clearly defined regions based on its physical and functional components, such as resonators, qubits, couplers, and interconnecting components. This approach allows for the use of localized meshes and boundary conditions tailored to each specific region, enhancing simulation efficiency. For instance, a high-resolution mesh might be applied to the Josephson junction of a qubit, while coarser meshes are sufficient for the surrounding ground planes. By simulating each segment independently and coupling their interactions later, segmentation simplifies the computational process. It reduces the overall system load by breaking down complex equations into component-specific models and then linking them. This method ensures high accuracy by thoroughly analyzing each component while significantly easing the computational burden.

After the simulation is done by the chip segmentation method, the Hamiltonian is extracted, and the characteristics of the transformer are obtained. With the help of Qiskit Metal, you can get an output report of the results. Figure 4-22 shows the results provided by the full-wave analysis method. According to these results,

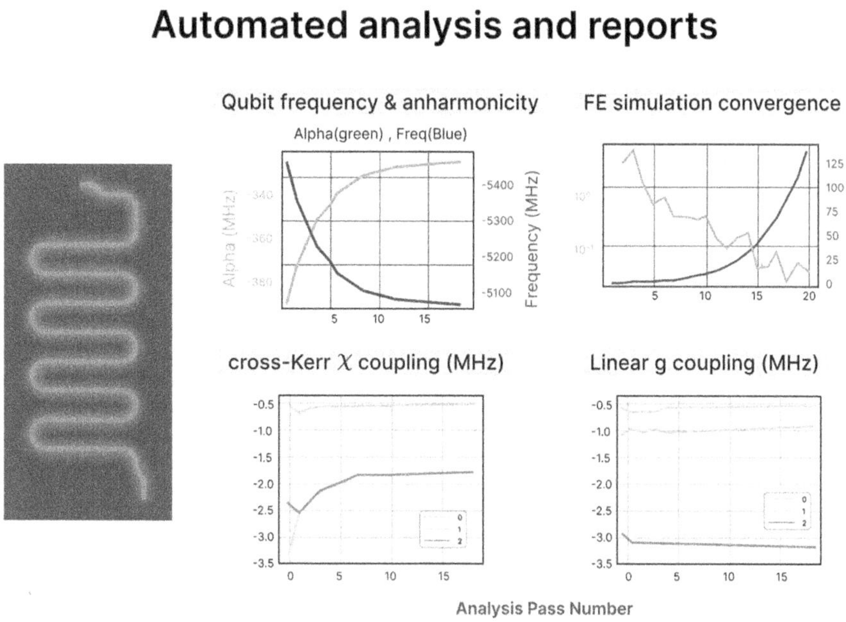

Automated analysis and reports

Figure 4-22 Automated analysis and convergence plot for the full-wave analysis method

the convergence can be checked; an example of the analysis report is shown in Figure 4-22.

The analysis report has a few important parameters that help in providing a broader perspective on the designed superconducting chip's stability and functionalities:

- **Convergence Plot**: A convergence plot is a critical tool that helps in providing a detailed assessment of the reliability and accuracy of simulation results. It runs the simulations over multiple iterations by increasing the mesh density of the chip components till it starts converging to a singular point as the mesh refines. This plot helps showcase how key parameters, such as energy, resonant frequencies, or field distributions, stabilize over multiple iterations by increasing the mesh density. Convergence helps in ensuring that the results are not dependent on arbitrary simulation settings, providing confidence in the physical validity of the model. A lack of convergence might indicate insufficient meshing, poor boundary conditions, or numerical instability.
- **Frequency Response**: Frequency response analysis evaluates the interactions of a quantum component or circuit when exposed to signals over a spectrum of frequencies. It helps in obtaining the resonant peaks, bandwidth, and performance under varying conditions. This analysis provides a detailed understanding of the frequency range that is ideal for the operation of the superconducting system.

Furthermore, it even provides a range of frequency that should be avoided to ensure no parasitic capacitance is introduced.
- **Quality Factors and Loss Mechanisms**: Quality factors (Q-factors) measure the energy retention capability of resonators or qubits by comparing the stored energy to energy lost per cycle. High Q-factors indicate minimal dissipation and longer coherence times, essential for reliable quantum operations. Loss mechanisms, such as dielectric losses, surface roughness, or radiation losses, directly affect Q-factors. By identifying and mitigating these losses, designers can optimize the performance and coherence of quantum systems.

After the design is finalized, we click the Export to GDS option in the Qiskit Metal software. Transferring the circuit to the GDS is very fast, indicating that this step is easy. For this, we click the GDS render option from the top menu. This section has different options. For example, we can specify what we want to transfer or whether we want to use a positive or negative mask (to make a part by semiconductor technology). Exporting the output to GDS proves to be particularly helpful during photolithography, where exposed areas define the features to be fabricated on the chip. On the contrary, exporting to GDS proves to be particularly challenging when applied in lift-off processes, where unexposed areas define the features by protecting them during material removal.

Qiskit Metal is a new innovation that has been designed to make the creation, visualization, and analysis of superconducting quantum chips easy. This software focuses on designing and analyzing quantum chips using Python, which enables users to visually layout superconducting circuits and export these designs seamlessly for detailed analysis in external software like HFSS or ADS. Focused on automating both classical as well as quantum analyses, Qiskit Metal allows for a highly flexible plug-in interface where the user can choose the desired tools, generate construction designs, and streamline the workflow with a single click. Its versatility lies in its interaction with a graphical user interface, comprehensive code integration via Jupyter Notebook, simulator view, and physical output view, which help in customizing and making it highly user-friendly. Qiskit Metal provides an extensive library of quantum components that can be customized based on the use cases and requirements. All these characteristics help Qiskit Metal become an essential resource for designing, simulating, and analyzing precise quantum circuits with ease.

Next, we will explore additional concepts crucial for coding with Qiskit Metal and observe the advancements made since the inception of the first quantum computer. The fundamental principles learned in this chapter are the building blocks for designing any superconducting circuit. As we progress, we will delve into advanced topics in superconducting qubit design, including the lumped oscillator model (LOM), quasi-LOM modeling, and EPR modeling. By applying the knowledge gained in this chapter, we will gain insights into these advanced topics, further enhancing our understanding of quantum circuit design.

4.9 Conclusion

This chapter provided a foundational understanding of designing quantum chips using Qiskit Metal. It explored the essential components, including Josephson junctions and couplers, required for creating quantum circuits. We examined how to position and configure various types of qubits, customize inputs and orientations, and implement different routing formats between components. A step-by-step example guided the process of designing a quantum chip, offering practical insights. Additionally, we explored simulation techniques to evaluate the performance and stability of quantum chips, ensuring they meet the desired specifications.

Lumped Oscillator Model Analysis

The Lumped Oscillator Model, also known as the LOM model, is one of the methods for analyzing superconducting circuits. The Lumped Oscillator Model is based on the quantization of the classical lumped model from classical electronics. The concept of a lumped-element model can be distilled as a fundamental portrayal of a physical system or circuit. This model simplifies the complexity by assuming that all components such as the LCR (Inductor-Capacitor-Resistor) components are localized to a single point, with their behaviors captured through an idealized mathematical framework.

The lumped-element model offers a pragmatic approach for understanding and analyzing intricate systems or circuits. It operates on the assumption that the components within the system are concentrated at a specific point rather than being distributed throughout space. This simplification allows for the use of mathematical models that describe idealized behavior, facilitating analysis without delving into intricate spatial relationships.

In this model, complex interactions among components are abstracted into mathematical equations that consider interactions as occurring instantaneously at the single point. This approach is particularly effective when the size of the components is significantly smaller compared to the wavelengths of the signals involved, leading to minimal variation in properties over the extent of the component. It is useful in electrical systems (including electronics), mechanical multibody systems, heat transfer, acoustics, and more. The lumped-element model used in electronic circuits simplifies things by imagining that the key characteristics of the circuit, such as resistance, capacitance, inductance, and gain, are all packed into idealized electrical components like resistors, capacitors, and inductors. These components are connected by perfect conducting wires.

To put it simply, the lumped-element model is like pretending that all the important features in an electronic circuit are located in specific parts like resistors, capacitors, and inductors. It's as if these parts are concentrated in one spot and connected by perfect conducting wires. This makes it easier to work with and understand how the circuit behaves, even though in real circuits, components are spread out.

The Lumped Oscillator Model is a simplified representation of classical electronic oscillators, commonly used in the field of electronics and circuit theory. It describes the behavior of an oscillator circuit that generates a periodic waveform without the need for an external input signal. The model assumes that the oscillator's behavior can be effectively captured by a few lumped circuit elements, such as an LC tank circuit and an amplifier. It is primarily used in the analysis and design of oscillators for lower-frequency electronic applications. In the context of superconducting and quantum computing, the model is applied to systems at very high frequencies and often at cryogenic temperatures. Classical lumped models might be used for lower-frequency applications, but the Lumped Oscillator Model in quantum circuits deals with much higher frequency ranges.

We will now begin with the fundamentals of the lumped-element model in classical computing and electronic circuits, highlighting its role in advancing superconducting circuits for quantum computing. Among the four primary approaches (lumped oscillator model, quasi-lumped model, inductance model, energy participation model) discussed in Chapter 4 for the analyses of superconducting circuits, the Lumped Oscillator Model stands as a significant method.

5.1 Elements in Classical Lumped Model

In the realm of classical electronics and circuitry, circuits are constructed using familiar components like resistors, inductors, and capacitors. However, when it comes to the intricate design of superconducting qubits, the process diverges significantly and becomes challenging to accomplish without a solid foundation in classical electronics principles. In this section, we will delve into the creation of LOM (Lumped Oscillator Model) circuits using conventional electronic elements.

5.1.1 LC Tank Circuit

At the heart of the Lumped Oscillator Model lies the LC tank circuit, which comprises an inductor (L) and a capacitor (C) linked together in parallel. Figure 5-1 represents the circuit diagram of a basic LC tank oscillator. In this setup, energy oscillates between the inductor and capacitor, leading to oscillations. Just a quick recap on the electronic components, a capacitor is a passive electronic component that stores energy in an electric field, defined by its capacitance as $C = Q/V$ where C represents the capacitance of the circuit, Q represents the charge stored, and V represents the potential energy across the capacitor. On the other hand, an inductor is a passive electronic component that stores energy in a magnetic field when current flows through it, defined by its inductance $L = \Phi/I$ where L represents the

5.1 Elements in Classical Lumped Model

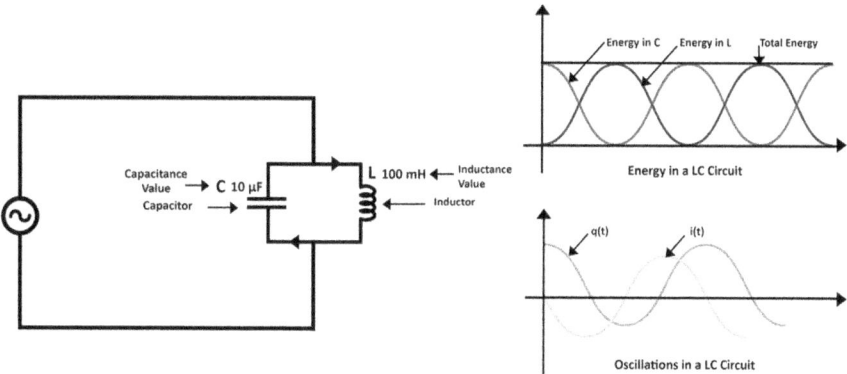

Figure 5-1 Circuit diagram of a basic LC tank oscillator

inductance, Φ represents the magnetic field, and I represents the current flowing through the wire.

During energy storage in the inductor, the capacitor discharges, and vice versa, inducing a rhythmic movement of charges within the circuit.

This utility is designed to determine the resonant frequency of a tank circuit when the values of capacitance and inductance are provided. The significance of tank circuit resonance is particularly notable in electrical engineering, especially within radio technology. For instance, radio transmitters and receivers heavily rely on tank circuits. A basic radio transmitter employs a class C amplifier integrated with a tank circuit at its load end. Upon activation, the tank circuit generates sufficient energy to connect the amplifier's signal to the antenna, thereby emitting the signal. Similarly, radio receivers utilize a tank circuit to tune in to a specific signal frequency for reception. The lumped-element model is applicable when $L_c \ll \lambda$, where L_c represents the circuit's characteristic length, and λ refers to the circuit's operational wavelength. The operational wavelength (λ) and signal frequency (f) are inversely related and is given as

$$\lambda = \frac{v}{f} \tag{5-1}$$

where λ represents the signal operational wavelength; v represents the speed of the signal propagation in the medium, which is equal to the speed of light in vacuum; and f represents the signal frequency.

However, if the circuit's length approaches the order of a wavelength, more comprehensive models like the distributed-element model, which involves transmission lines and is described by Maxwell's equations, must be considered. Since the section transits to quantum circuits, it might be helpful to note that LC tank circuits are analogous to quantum harmonic oscillators when quantized.

Figure 5-2 Circuit diagram of a basic amplifier using an LC tank oscillator

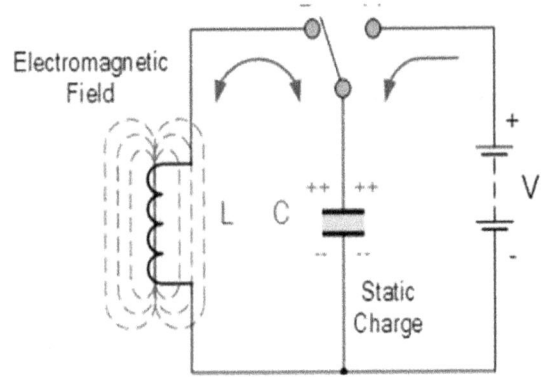

5.1.2 Amplifier

To maintain smooth vibrations in a circuit and prevent energy loss, an amplifier is often introduced into the lumped oscillator model. Amplifiers are not inherent to LC circuits; they are added to create an active oscillatory system. An LC circuit, by itself, is a passive circuit that can resonate at a particular frequency due to the interplay of inductance (L) and capacitance (C). This amplifier serves a critical purpose by enhancing the energy within the circuit to offset the energy that dissipates during circuit operation. The central component of the oscillator is the LC tank circuit, consisting of an inductor (L) and a capacitor (C). The circuit diagram of a basic amplifier is provided in Figure 5-2.

However, real-world factors like wires and components lead to energy loss as heat. This energy loss gradually slows down the circuit's vibrations, eventually causing them to cease. This is where the amplifier steps in. Comparable to adding more fuel to a moving car to sustain its motion, the amplifier injects additional energy into the circuit. This extra energy compensates for the energy loss, enabling the LC tank circuit to maintain its vigorous and steady vibrations. In essence, the amplifier acts as a superhero within the lumped oscillator model. It combats energy loss by consistently supplying supplementary energy to the circuit. This strategy maintains the strength of vibrations, preventing them from diminishing too swiftly.

The circuit comprises an inductive coil (L) and a capacitor (C). The capacitor accumulates energy as an electrostatic field, generating a potential difference (static voltage) between its plates. Conversely, the inductive coil stores energy within an electromagnetic field. When the capacitor reaches its maximum charge at the DC supply voltage (V), achieved by switching to position A and subsequently to position B, it connects in parallel with the inductive coil. Consequently, the capacitor discharges through the coil, causing the voltage across it to decline while the coil's current rises. This growing current establishes an electromagnetic field around the coil that resists the current's flow.

As the capacitor discharges fully, the energy initially stored as an electrostatic field in the capacitor transitions to an electromagnetic field within the inductive coil. With no external voltage maintaining the coil's current, the current decreases as the electromagnetic field collapses. An induced back electromotive force (back emf) sustains the current's direction according to Faraday's law ($e = -L\frac{di}{dt}$). This current, in turn, charges the capacitor with a polarity opposite to its original charge. The charging process continues until the current reaches zero, and the electromagnetic field collapses entirely. The energy initially introduced into the circuit through the switch returns to the capacitor, which now holds an electrostatic voltage potential, albeit of the opposite polarity.

Subsequently, the capacitor discharges once more through the coil, initiating the cycle anew. This repeated energy transfer between the capacitor and inductor generates an AC-like sinusoidal voltage and current pattern. This process forms the basis of an LC oscillator's tank circuit, theoretically capable of perpetual cycling. However, real-world imperfections and energy losses during these transfers gradually diminish the oscillations until they fade away entirely. The oscillatory exchange of energy between the capacitor and inductor would persist indefinitely if not for energy losses stemming from factors such as the real resistance of the inductor coil, the dielectric properties of the capacitor, and radiation from the circuit. Consequently, the oscillations gradually dampen, with each oscillation half-cycle experiencing a decrease in voltage amplitude, ultimately leading to cessation. The extent of this damping is determined by the circuit's quality factor, or Q-factor. The quality factor, or the Q-factor, is a parameter used to analyze the efficiency and stability of the electromagnetic circuit. The quality factor of the component is the ratios of the energy stored to that of the energy lost or dissipated in the system.

5.1.3 Oscillator Frequency and Stability Response

Equation 5-2 reveals that decreasing either L or C leads to an increase in frequency. The resulting frequency is commonly denoted as f_r, representing the resonant frequency. In an LC tank circuit, to sustain ongoing oscillations, we must replenish all the energy lost during each oscillation cycle and also maintain a consistent amplitude for these oscillations. The energy replenished should match the energy lost during each cycle. If the energy replacement is excessive, the amplitude could surge to a point where it hits the supply limits. Conversely, inadequate energy replacement would eventually cause the amplitude to diminish to zero, halting the oscillations.

$$f_r = \frac{1}{2\pi\sqrt{LC}} \tag{5-2}$$

The simplest approach to restoring the lost energy is to extract a portion of the LC tank circuit's output, amplify it, and then reintroduce it back into the circuit. This can be achieved using a voltage amplifier, which may employ an operational amplifier (op-amp), field-effect transistor (FET), or bipolar transistor as the active component. However, if the feedback amplifier's loop gain is too low, the desired oscillation fades away. If the loop gain is too high, the waveform distorts.

To achieve consistent oscillation, it's crucial to precisely regulate the amount of energy fed back into the LC network. Furthermore, an automatic amplitude or gain control mechanism is necessary to counteract any deviation from a reference voltage, whether the amplitude tries to increase or decrease. For stable oscillation, the overall circuit gain must be precisely one, or unity. Any gain lower than unity will prevent oscillations from initiating or cause them to fade to zero. Any gain greater than unity will result in oscillations, but with an amplitude clipped by the supply limits, leading to distortion. The unity gain formula refers to the condition in amplifier or feedback circuits where the magnitude of the gain is equal to one ($|A| = 1$). This condition ensures that the output signal is neither amplified nor attenuated, maintaining the same amplitude as the input signal. In feedback systems, unity gain is crucial for achieving stable oscillations, as it satisfies the Barkhausen criterion for sustained oscillatory behavior when combined with the correct feedback phase.

For an oscillator to sustain its oscillations, it needs to fulfill some specific criteria. Firstly, the feedback loop should introduce positive feedback, meaning that the phase shift around it should be either 0° or 360°. This type of feedback strengthens the oscillations, ensuring they grow instead of fading away. Secondly, the amplifier's role is crucial; it must offer enough amplification to counteract the losses occurring in the circuit. The amplifier's gain must be greater than the losses to sustain consistent oscillations with a steady intensity. Sometimes, the oscillator might need a gentle push or an initial input to start its oscillation process. Once initiated, the oscillator will sustain its oscillations by following the rules of feedback and gain. The key principle remains the same that is maintaining the conditions of positive feedback, adequate gain, and, if necessary, that initial nudge to keep the oscillator humming.

5.2 Lumped Oscillator Model Analysis (LOM)

The Lumped Oscillator Model (LOM) is a simplified representation used to analyze the behavior of oscillators, which are circuits that generate repetitive waveforms. The LOM assumes that the circuit components are concentrated or "lumped" at specific points rather than distributed throughout space. This simplification allows for easier analysis of oscillatory behavior and aids in the design and understanding of oscillators in a more manageable way. LOM analysis involves applying circuit theory principles to study the behavior of oscillators. It considers components like resistors, inductors, capacitors, and amplifiers as individual elements within the circuit. LOM is particularly useful in understanding the conditions required for sustained oscillation, as well as the frequency and amplitude characteristics of the generated waveform.

In LOM analysis, the focus is on achieving a balance between positive feedback (to sustain oscillation) and the appropriate gain (to overcome losses and maintain amplitude). The concept often involves understanding the phase relationships between different components in the oscillator circuit to ensure proper reinforcement of the oscillations. A fundamental concept in LOM analysis is the balance between positive feedback and the necessary gain. Positive feedback is crucial for sustaining oscillations. It refers to the phenomenon where a portion of the output signal is fed back to the input with the same phase. This reinforcement of the input signal ensures that the oscillator maintains its oscillations rather than dwindling away. However, a careful balance is needed to prevent the circuit from becoming unstable or producing distorted waveforms. The gain, on the other hand, refers to the amplification factor applied to the signal as it travels through the circuit. This gain must be sufficiently high to overcome the energy losses in the circuit due to resistance, radiation, and other factors. If the gain falls short, the oscillations will weaken and eventually die out.

5.3 Matrices

Now that we have explored the concept of the Lumped Oscillator Model (LOM) and its fundamental aspects, let's delve into the systematic procedure for constructing and analyzing it, with a focus on how matrices play a pivotal role in this process. Matrices are essential tools in circuit analysis, enabling engineers and researchers to represent relationships between components, such as inductance, capacitance, impedance, or admittance, in a concise and computationally efficient manner. This approach is particularly valuable in analyzing oscillator circuits, where matrices simplify the study of interactions between components and facilitate the examination of complex, large-scale systems.

The systematic procedure for constructing and analyzing the Lumped Oscillator Model involves several key steps:

- First, the circuit components, such as resistors, capacitors, inductors, and sources, are identified and classified.
- Next, the relationships between these components are defined using mathematical principles like Kirchhoff's current and voltage laws.
- These relationships are then translated into matrix-based representations, such as nodal or mesh equations, to form systems of linear equations.
- Finally, matrix operations, including inversion or diagonalization, are applied to solve these equations, providing insights into the circuit's behavior, resonance characteristics, and stability.

This structured methodology enables a deeper understanding of oscillator circuits and their crucial roles in signal generation, frequency synthesis, and communication systems.

5.3.1 Capacitance Matrix

In the world of electronics and circuit analysis, the capacitance matrix is a powerful tool that unveils the intricate relationships between capacitors in a circuit. It provides a comprehensive view of how these passive components interact, influence each other, and collectively shape the behavior of a circuit. Understanding the capacitance matrix is essential for grasping the dynamics of complex systems and designing circuits with desired characteristics. At its essence, the capacitance matrix captures the coupling and influence between capacitors within a circuit. It is a mathematical representation that encapsulates the mutual interactions of charges stored in different capacitors due to changes in voltage. This interaction stems from the nature of capacitors, which store and release energy in the form of electric fields between their plates.

Let us look into how to represent the capacitance matrix mathematically. The capacitance matrix C for a system of n conductors is an $n \times n$ square symmetric matrix which is defined as

$$q_i = \sum_{j=1}^{n} C_{ij} V_j \tag{5-3}$$

where q_i represents the charge on the conductor i, V_j represents the electric potential on conductor j, and C_{ij} represents the capacitance coefficients, describing how the charge on conductor i is influenced by the potential on conductor j.

The capacitance matrix is a square matrix, with each element representing the capacitance between a pair of nodes in a circuit. The diagonal elements of the matrix are negative, and these values correspond to the self-capacitance of individual capacitors, indicating how much charge a capacitor stores for a given voltage across its terminals. On the other hand, the rest of the matrix elements are symmetric in nature, that is, $C_{ij} = C_{ji}$, due to the reciprocal nature of the electrostatic interactions as derived from Maxwell's equations.

The capacitance matrix is positive semi-definite. A matrix is called positive semi-definite (PSD) if it satisfies three relations:

- The matrix has to be symmetric in nature. That is, the matrix and the matrix transpose should be the same: $A = A^T$.
- The matrix should have a nonnegative value for any nonzero vector x satisfying the condition $x^T \cdot A \cdot x \geq 0$.
- The eigenvalues of the matrix should be nonnegative, that is, either positive or zero.

Since the capacitance matrix is PSD in nature, it ensures that the potential energy stored across is nonnegative in nature. To calculate the potential energy stored across this junction, we follow the basic mathematical equation for calculating the potential

5.3 Matrices

energy stored across a capacitor, which is given by

$$U = \frac{1}{2} Q \cdot V \tag{5-4}$$

where Q and V represent the charge and potential energy stored across the capacitor. By substituting the values obtained from Equation 5-3, we get

$$U = \frac{1}{2} \sum_{j=1}^{n} C_{ij} \cdot V_j \cdot V_i \tag{5-5}$$

where U represents the potential energy stored and V_i represents the potential of the first conductor. In order to obtain the capacitance matrix for superconducting qubits, we have to solve the Poisson's equation:

$$\nabla \cdot (\epsilon \nabla \phi) = -\rho \tag{5-6}$$

Equation 5-6 is the Poisson equation for electromagnetic systems, where ϕ represents the electric potential, ρ represents the electric field density, and ϵ represents permittivity of the material. Subjecting the equation to boundary conditions on the conductor surfaces gives the potential distribution and allows for the computation of C_{ij}. Solving them, the value of the coefficients comes out to be

$$C_{ij} = \frac{\partial q_i}{\partial V_j} \tag{5-7}$$

Using the equation provided in Equation 5-7, we can figure out the coefficients for the capacitance matrix. Using this capacitance matrix, one can derive the electrostatic potential energy matrix and kinetic energy matrix. In order to do so, let us first define the charge vector matrix:

$$\mathbf{Q} = C \cdot \mathbf{V} \tag{5-8}$$

where the $\mathbf{Q}$ represents the vector of charge matrix, C represents the capacitance matrix, and $\mathbf{V}$ represents the vector of voltages, and the matrices for them are represented as

$$\mathbf{Q} = \begin{bmatrix} q_1 \\ q_2 \\ \vdots \\ q_n \end{bmatrix}, C = \begin{bmatrix} C_{11} & C_{12} & \cdots & C_{1n} \\ C_{21} & C_{22} & \cdots & C_{2n} \\ \vdots & \vdots & \ddots & \vdots \\ C_{n1} & C_{n2} & \cdots & C_{nn} \end{bmatrix}, \mathbf{V} = \begin{bmatrix} V_1 \\ V_2 \\ \vdots \\ V_n \end{bmatrix} \tag{5-9}$$

The total electrostatic potential energy U stored in matrix representation is represented as

$$U = \frac{1}{2}\sum_{i=1}^{n} q_i V_i \tag{5-10}$$

Replacing the value of Equation 5-3 into Equation 5-10, it provides us with

$$U = \frac{1}{2}\sum_{i=1}^{n}\sum_{j=1}^{n} V_i C_{ij} V_j \tag{5-11}$$

By representing the summation in vector format, we get the electrostatic potential energy matrix **U** as

$$U = \frac{1}{2}\mathbf{V}^T \cdot C \cdot \mathbf{V} \tag{5-12}$$

In superconducting circuits, the classical variables **V** (voltage matrix) and **Q** (charge matrix) are replaced by the quantum variables $\mathbf{Q_0}$ as conjugate charge matrix and $\mathbf{\Phi}$ as the node flux matrix:

$$\mathbf{Q_0} = C \cdot \frac{d\mathbf{\Phi}}{dt} \tag{5-13}$$

The kinetic energy of the system arises from the movement of charge that is stored inside the capacitors. It is analogous to the energy stored in classical mechanical systems. Solving in a similar manner that we did for finding the electrostatic potential energy matrix, we find the total kinetic energy of the system to be

$$\mathbf{T} = \frac{1}{2}\mathbf{Q_0}^T \cdot C^{-1} \cdot \mathbf{Q_0} \tag{5-14}$$

The elements of C^{-1} (referred to as the *inverse capacitance matrix*) define the coupling strengths between the nodes, influencing the qubit frequencies and interactions. After figuring out the kinetic energy of the system, let us define the Hamiltonian of the system. The Hamiltonian of the system combines the kinetic energy term from the capacitors and the potential energy term from the Josephson junction. We have seen the electrostatic potential energy stored in Josephson junction calculation in Chapter 4, as follows:

$$U = E_J \cos\phi \tag{5-15}$$

where $\phi = 2\pi\Phi/\Phi_0$ represents the phase across the junction, and $\Phi_0 = h/2e$ represents the superconducting flux quantum. If there are multiple Josephson

5.3 Matrices

junctions, the total potential energy is the sum of their each individual contribution:

$$U = \sum_j -E_{J_j} \cos\left(\frac{2\pi \Phi_j}{\Phi_0}\right) \tag{5-16}$$

Using the equations obtained from Equations 5-14 and 5-16, we obtain the Hamiltonian which is the sum of the energies for a capacitance matrix:

$$\mathcal{H} = \frac{1}{2}\mathbf{Q}_0^T \cdot C^{-1} \cdot \mathbf{Q}_0 - \sum_j E_{J_j} \cos\left(\frac{2\pi \Phi_j}{\Phi_0}\right) \tag{5-17}$$

For a capacitance matrix, the diagonal elements denote the mutual capacitance between pairs of capacitors, reflecting how changes in voltage across one capacitor influence the stored charge in another. The capacitance matrix plays an important role in transient analysis, as it helps in understanding the charge distribution across capacitors during voltage changes. Additionally, it is crucial for assessing the stability of the circuit by evaluating equilibrium and potential oscillations.

When designing circuits, understanding the capacitance matrix allows engineers to optimize the arrangement of capacitors, control signal paths, and minimize undesirable interactions. Properly managing the interactions between capacitors is crucial for achieving the desired circuit performance. The capacitance matrix is essential in LOM analysis as it models electrostatic energy storage and coupling between nodes, enabling the derivation of the circuit's Hamiltonian for analyzing dynamics, eigenfrequencies, and energy interactions.

5.3.2 Resistance Matrix

The resistance matrix is a pivotal tool that unveils the interconnections and interdependencies of resistive elements within a circuit. This matrix provides insights into how resistors influence each other's behavior, contributing to the overall electrical characteristics of the circuit. Understanding the resistance matrix is essential for comprehending the flow of currents, voltage drops, and energy dissipation within complex circuits. The resistance matrix encapsulates the relationships between resistive components within a circuit. It reveals how changes in current through one resistor affect the voltage drops across others and how energy losses propagate through the network of resistors. Similar to other matrices used in circuit analysis, the resistance matrix is also a square matrix. Each element in the matrix represents the resistance between a pair of nodes in the circuit. Diagonal elements correspond to the self-resistance of individual resistors, depicting how much a resistor impedes the flow of current through it. Off-diagonal elements denote the mutual influence between resistors, reflecting how current flow in one resistor affects the voltage drop in another.

The resistance matrix is an $n \times n$ symmetric matrix where n represents the total number of nodes connected by the resistor. Using Ohm's law, we obtain the resistance matrix as

$$\mathbf{V} = R \cdot \mathbf{I} \qquad (5\text{-}18)$$

where $\mathbf{V}$ represents the voltages at each node and $\mathbf{I}$ represents the current entering each node of the network. The matrix representation of the voltage and current is provided as

$$\mathbf{I} = \begin{bmatrix} I_1 \\ I_2 \\ \vdots \\ I_n \end{bmatrix}, R = \begin{bmatrix} R_{11} & R_{12} & \cdots & R_{1n} \\ R_{21} & R_{22} & \cdots & R_{2n} \\ \vdots & \vdots & \ddots & \vdots \\ R_{n1} & R_{n2} & \cdots & R_{nn} \end{bmatrix}, \mathbf{V} = \begin{bmatrix} V_1 \\ V_2 \\ \vdots \\ V_n \end{bmatrix} \qquad (5\text{-}19)$$

The resistance matrix is a symmetric matrix that is $R_{ij} = R_{ji}$. Similar to the capacitance matrix, the resistance matrix is also positive semi-definite (PSD), as it describes physical energy dissipation in the network. The diagonal elements R_{ii} are typically larger in magnitude than the other elements R_{ij}, representing the self-resistance of the nodes. We can calculate the energy power dissipated in a resistive network by the power current and voltage relationship governed by

$$\mathbf{P} = \mathbf{I}^T \cdot \mathbf{V} \qquad (5\text{-}20)$$

Now from Ohm's law relation obtained from Equation 5-18, by substituting for the value of $\mathbf{V}$ in the power equation, we obtain the relationship as

$$\mathbf{P} = \mathbf{I}^T \cdot R \cdot \mathbf{I} \qquad (5\text{-}21)$$

This equation provides an understanding of how the resistance matrix influences the power dissipation in a network, and this relationship helps in determining the power dissipated in comparison to the resistance matrix.

When applying Ohm's law to complex circuits, the resistance matrix aids in calculating current distributions and voltage drops across multiple resistors, enabling engineers to predict and control circuit behavior. In circuit design, the resistance matrix assists engineers in optimizing resistor arrangements to minimize voltage drop variations, optimize power distribution, and ensure balanced current flows. The resistance matrix plays a pivotal role in circuit design, influencing decisions about resistor values, configurations, and placements. Properly managing the interactions between resistors is essential for achieving balanced current paths, minimizing voltage drops, and optimizing the circuit's overall performance.

In the context of superconducting qubits, resistances typically play a minor role because superconductors ideally have zero resistance. However, real-world circuits include parasitic resistances (due to imperfections) or intentional resistive elements (e.g., for dissipation engineering or filtering). When resistive elements are present, the resistance matrix and dissipation must be incorporated into the circuit's Hamiltonian derivation.

5.3.3 Impedance Matrix

The impedance matrix is a powerful tool that unveils the intricate relationships and interactions between various circuit components, including resistors, capacitors, and inductors. This matrix provides an abstract view of how these components influence each other's behavior, aiding in the analysis and design of complex circuits. Understanding the impedance matrix is essential for grasping the dynamics of circuit responses, particularly in alternating current (AC) scenarios. The impedance matrix encapsulates the combined effects of resistance, capacitance, and inductance in a circuit. Impedance is a complex quantity that characterizes the opposition a circuit element offers to the flow of AC current. The impedance matrix reveals how changes in voltage or current across one element affect the others in a complex network.

Similar to other matrices in circuit analysis, the impedance matrix is a square matrix. Each element represents the impedance between a pair of nodes in the circuit. Diagonal elements denote the self-impedance of individual elements, accounting for their inherent opposition to AC current. Other non-diagonal elements indicate the mutual inductance between the two elements, illustrating how changes in one element's voltage or current affect the impedance of another. In a network of n inductors, the inductance matrix is represented as

$$\mathbf{\Phi} = L \cdot \mathbf{I} \tag{5-22}$$

where $\mathbf{\Phi}$ represents the total flux linkage vector, and $\mathbf{I}$ represents the total current vector. The matrices are represented for the three of them as

$$\mathbf{I} = \begin{bmatrix} I_1 \\ I_2 \\ \vdots \\ I_n \end{bmatrix}, L = \begin{bmatrix} L_{11} & M_{12} & \cdots & M_{1n} \\ M_{21} & L_{22} & \cdots & M_{2n} \\ \vdots & \vdots & \ddots & \vdots \\ M_{n1} & M_{n2} & \cdots & L_{nn} \end{bmatrix}, \mathbf{\Phi} = \begin{bmatrix} \Phi_1 \\ \Phi_2 \\ \vdots \\ \Phi_n \end{bmatrix} \tag{5-23}$$

As you can see, the matrix values of the inductance matrix as displayed has two distinct terms, L_{ii} representing the diagonal elements as self-inductance and M_{ij} representing the non-diagonal elements as mutual inductance between the i and j inductors. The values of these two are provided as

$$L_{ii} = \frac{\Phi_i}{I_i}, \quad \text{(when } I_j = 0 \text{ for } j \neq i\text{)}. \tag{5-24}$$

$$M_{ij} = \frac{\Phi_{i(\text{due to } j)}}{I_j}, \quad (\text{when } I_k = 0 \text{ for } k \neq j). \tag{5-25}$$

Equation 5-24 represents the self-inductance on the inductor that quantifies the flux linkage in the inductor caused by its own current, and Equation 5-25 represents the mutual inductance of inductor i due to j that measures the flux linkage in inductor i due to the current in inductor j.

Note that, similar to the capacitance matrix, the impedance matrix is symmetric in nature, that is, $M_{ij} = M_{ji}$ as the mutual inductance is reciprocal in nature—the mutual inductance due to i on j is the same as the mutual inductance on j due to i. The impedance matrix is also positive semi-definite (PSD), stating that energy stored in the inductive network is nonnegative. Now the equation obtained in Equation 5-22 can be decomposed to provide a linear equation, that is, the matrix representation can be split into summation format as follows:

$$\Phi_i = \sum_j L_{ij} I_j \tag{5-26}$$

$$\Phi_i = L_{ii} I_i + \sum_{i \neq j} M_{ij} I_j \tag{5-27}$$

Splitting the provided matrix representation in summation part provides us with linear values with total flux linkage at point i. Now once we have defined these basic terms, let's talk about the energy stored in the system and how we can calculate them using the impedance matrix. The formula for energy stored in an inductor is given as

$$U = \frac{1}{2} L \cdot I^2 = \frac{1}{2} \Phi \cdot I \tag{5-28}$$

Now, each inductor in a network experiences its own flux linkage as well as the flux linkage due to other inductors in the system. Equation 5-27 represents the total flux in the system, taking into account each inductor's self-inductance as well as the mutual inductance due to other inductors. Hence, the total energy stored in the system is represented as the sum of energy due to each individual conductor. So, Equation 5-28 can be rewritten as

$$U = \sum_i \frac{1}{2} \Phi_i \cdot I_i \tag{5-29}$$

5.3 Matrices

By substituting the value of flux linkage obtained from Equation 5-26 into Equation 5-29, the modified equation turns out to be

$$U = \frac{1}{2}\sum_i \left(\sum_j L_{ij} \cdot I_j\right) \cdot I_i \quad (5\text{-}30)$$

Now we can rearrange the terms of Equation 5-30 to split into its components—self-inductance and mutual inductance:

- Diagonal terms ($i = j$)
  The self-inductance terms are represented in the format

$$\sum_i L_{ii} \cdot I_i^2 \quad (5\text{-}31)$$

- Non-diagonal terms ($i \neq j$)
  The mutual inductance terms of the matrix. As the mutual inductance values are symmetric and reciprocal, that is, $M_{ij} = M_{ji}$, each pair of (i, j) is counted twice; hence, the resulting equation can be written as

$$2\sum_i \sum_{j>i} M_{ij} \cdot I_i \cdot I_j \quad (5\text{-}32)$$

Substituting these two decomposed values into Equation 5-30, we obtain the following value for the energy stored in the system:

$$U = \frac{1}{2}\sum_i L_{ii} \cdot I_i^2 + \sum_i \sum_{j>i} M_{ij} \cdot I_i \cdot I_j \quad (5\text{-}33)$$

This equation looks complex and is hard to deal with, so the generic format of the representation of this energy stored into the system in vector matrix format is as follows:

$$\mathbf{U} = \frac{1}{2}\mathbf{I}^T \cdot L \cdot \mathbf{I} \quad (5\text{-}34)$$

In superconducting qubit circuits, the impedance matrix plays a critical role in modeling the dynamics of Josephson junctions, inductive couplers, and flux qubits. Similar to the derivation that we have done for the capacitance matrix for figuring out the kinetic energy term, the same steps are used for the derivation of the potential energy term of the inductor. Following the same steps for the impedance matrix, the potential energy term for the system comes to be equal to

$$\mathbf{T} = \frac{1}{2}\boldsymbol{\Phi}^T \cdot L^{-1} \cdot \boldsymbol{\Phi} \tag{5-35}$$

Using this potential energy term, we can derive the Hamiltonian of the system by combining the kinetic energy term for the capacitance matrix and potential energy term of the inductive matrix. The Hamiltonian of the system turns out to be

$$\mathcal{H} = \frac{1}{2}\mathbf{Q}_0^T \cdot C^{-1} \cdot \mathbf{Q}_0 + \frac{1}{2}\boldsymbol{\Phi}^T \cdot L^{-1} \cdot \boldsymbol{\Phi} \tag{5-36}$$

As we can observe, the Hamiltonians for both the capacitance matrix and the impedance matrix are different. But the impedance matrix includes both the terms capacitance and inductance. This happens because a superconducting circuit contains both inductors and capacitors. Capacitors are responsible for the contribution in kinetic energy, which is associated with charge, while inductors are responsible for the contribution in potential energy, which is associated with flux linkage. Now we use capacitance matrix analysis primarily when the superconducting circuit is capacitor dominated; during that time, the potential energy stored due to the Josephson junctions trumps the potential energy stored due to flux linkage. That is why the potential due to the Josephson junction is considered during the capacitance matrix calculation. While inductor-dominated circuits have capacitors present in the circuit in some form or another (e.g., stray capacitance or explicitly added capacitance in resonant circuits), their kinetic energy is part of the total system's Hamiltonian.

In AC circuit analysis, the impedance matrix is crucial for understanding the interactions between resistive, capacitive, and inductive components. It facilitates calculations involving voltage drops, current distributions, and phase relationships in complex networks. For high-frequency and RF circuits, the impedance matrix plays a significant role in analyzing signal integrity, including impedance matching, transmission line effects, and minimizing signal distortion.

When designing AC filters, such as low-pass or high-pass filters, the impedance matrix assists in predicting how various components affect the filter's frequency response and signal attenuation characteristics. The impedance matrix also guides decisions regarding component selection, placement, and arrangement in AC circuits. It allows engineers to predict and manage impedance-related interactions, ensuring efficient signal transfer and optimized circuit performance. The impedance matrix is vital in LOM analysis as it represents the voltage-current relationship across circuit nodes, enabling the study of energy dissipation, signal transfer, and the derivation of system dynamics and resonance properties.

5.3.4 Admittance Matrix

The admittance matrix is a crucial tool that offers a comprehensive view of the interactions and behaviors of circuit components, particularly in alternating current (AC) scenarios. This matrix provides insights into how elements like resistors, capacitors, and inductors influence one another's behaviors, enabling engineers to analyze and design complex circuits with accuracy. The admittance matrix characterizes the ease with which AC current flows through different components in a circuit. It encompasses the reciprocal of impedance, allowing engineers to understand the flow of current in terms of ease or "admittance."

The admittance matrix is an inverse of the resistance matrix for a purely resistive circuit and is provided with the relations as

$$Y = \frac{1}{R} = j\omega C = \frac{1}{j\omega L} \tag{5-37}$$

where R represents the resistance value, C represents the capacitance, L represents the inductance, and ω represents the angular frequency of the AC circuit. If you notice carefully, the mapping of admittance with capacitance or inductance provides an imaginary term. Similar to the resistance matrix, the admittance matrix is also a square symmetric matrix. In matrix notation, one can represent the admittance matrix as

$$Y = Re(R^{-1}) = Z^{-1} \tag{5-38}$$

Equation 5-38 shows that the admittance matrix is represented by the real part of the resistance matrix. For a purely resistive circuit, the admittance matrix is represented as the inverse of the resistance matrix, but for AC systems where the other electrical components come into picture, the admittance matrix is represented by the inverse of the impedance matrix. So we can decompose Ohm's law discussed earlier into

$$\mathbf{I} = Y \cdot \mathbf{V} \tag{5-39}$$

Now let's look into how we can calculate the power in an AC circuit with the help of the admittance matrix. The instantaneous power in an AC circuit is represented as

$$P(t) = v(t) \cdot i(t) \tag{5-40}$$

where $P(t)$ represents the instantaneous AC power in the system and is represented by the product of the instantaneous voltage ($v(t)$) and the instantaneous current ($i(t)$), which are given as

$$v(t) = V_m \cos \omega t \quad i(t) = I_m \cos \omega t + \phi \tag{5-41}$$

Hence, the average power over a cycle of the AC system is given as

$$P = V_{rms} I_{rms} \cos \phi \tag{5-42}$$

where P represents the average real power of the AC system, V_{rms} and I_{rms} represent the root mean squared values of the voltages and current, respectively, and $\cos \phi$ represents the power factor. Now for an AC system, as we have discussed, Equation 5-38 shows that the admittance matrix is the inverse of the inductance matrix, and the value is represented as

$$Y = G + jB \tag{5-43}$$

Equation 5-43 represents the real and imaginary part of the system, where the real part of the system G represents the conductance, and the imaginary coefficient B represents the susceptance. Now substituting the value obtained for the admittance matrix in Equation 5-43 into the current voltage relation provided in Equation 5-39, we obtain the value as

$$I = (G + jB) \cdot V \tag{5-44}$$

Now we can substitute the value obtained from Equation 5-44 into the AC power relationship to get the value of the total power of the system as

$$P = V_{rms} \cdot I_{rms} \cos \phi = V_{rms} \cdot ((G + jB) \cdot V_{rms}) \cos \phi \tag{5-45}$$

$$P = G \cdot V_{rms}^2 \cos \phi + jBcdot V_{rms}^2 \cos \phi \tag{5-46}$$

As we can see, there are two coefficients present for the total power consumed, the real and the imaginary part:

- **Real Part**: The real part corresponds to the actual power dissipated into the system, and it corresponds to the fact that the power dissipated within the AC system is due to the conductance G.
- **Imaginary Part**: The imaginary part corresponds to the reactive power of the system, and this part does not play any role in the power dissipated into the system.

Like other matrices used in circuit analysis, the admittance matrix is square. Each element within the matrix represents the admittance between a pair of nodes in the circuit. Diagonal elements correspond to the self-admittance of individual components, indicating the ease with which AC current flows through them. Off-diagonal elements denote the mutual influence of components, reflecting how changes in current through one element affect the admittance of another. In network analysis, the admittance matrix aids in characterizing and predicting the flow of AC current through different elements. This understanding is vital for designing

5.3.5 Mutual Inductance Matrix

The mutual inductance matrix is a vital tool that sheds light on the intricate interactions and dependencies between inductive components. This matrix reveals how changing current through one coil influences the magnetic field and subsequently induces voltage in another coil. Understanding the mutual inductance matrix is crucial for comprehending the behavior of coupled inductors and designing circuits with precise control over magnetic interactions.

The mutual inductance matrix encapsulates the coupling between different coils in a circuit. It quantifies how changes in current through one coil induce a voltage in another coil due to the shared magnetic field. Like other matrices in circuit analysis, the mutual inductance matrix is a square matrix. Each element represents the mutual inductance between a pair of coils. Diagonal elements indicate self-inductance, reflecting the magnetic influence of each coil on itself. Off-diagonal elements denote the mutual influence of coils, representing how changes in current through one coil induce voltage in another.

The mutual inductance M_{ij} quantifies the magnetic coupling between inductors i and j. It is given by Equation 5-25:

$$M_{ij} = k_{ij}\sqrt{L_{ii}L_{jj}} \tag{5-47}$$

where k_{ij} represents the magnetic coupling coefficient between the two inductors, and it depends on

- Distance between inductors (inversely proportional)
- Relative orientation (maximum for perfectly aligned coils; zero for orthogonal coils)
- Geometry and material properties (e.g., core permeability)

The range of values of the coupling coefficient is between $k_{ij} \in [-1, 1]$ and is formulated as provided in Equation 5-48:

$$k_{ij} = \frac{\Phi_{ij}}{\sqrt{\Phi_{ii} \cdot \Phi_{jj}}} \tag{5-48}$$

Mutual inductance is used to create effective interactions between qubits, enabling entanglement. When designing transformers, the mutual inductance matrix aids in predicting how changes in current on one winding induce voltage on another winding, guiding the selection of turns ratio and core materials. In circuits where signal isolation is critical, the mutual inductance matrix assists in assessing how magnetic coupling between coils affects signal transfer, ensuring minimal interference. Understanding the mutual inductance matrix is pivotal when designing circuits involving multiple coils. It enables engineers to optimize coil arrangements, select appropriate materials, and ensure precise control over magnetic interactions.

5.3.6 Inverse Inductance Matrix

The inverse impedance matrix is a valuable tool that sheds light on the relationships and interactions among complex impedance in a circuit. This matrix provides insights into how various circuit elements influence each other's behaviors, particularly when dealing with nonlinear or complex impedance interactions. Understanding the inverse impedance matrix is crucial for analyzing circuits with intricate impedance characteristics and designing systems that incorporate nonlinear elements.

The inverse impedance matrix is fundamentally about revealing the reciprocal relationships between complex impedance in a circuit. It assists in understanding how changing the impedance of one element affects the currents and voltages across other elements in the circuit. Similar to other matrices in circuit analysis, the inverse impedance matrix is a square matrix. Each element represents the inverse of the impedance between a pair of nodes in the circuit. Diagonal elements denote the self-impedance of individual elements, reflecting their inherent opposition to current flow. Off-diagonal elements indicate the reciprocal influence of elements, illustrating how changes in one's impedance affect the response of another.

The inverse inductance matrix, also known as the elastance matrix, is represented by the inverse of the inductance matrix, similar to that of the relation between the resistance matrix and the admittance matrix. The elastance matrix is related to the current vector and magnetic flux:

$$\mathbf{I} = L^{-1} \cdot \mathbf{\Phi} \tag{5-49}$$

L^{-1}, being the inverse of a symmetric positive definite matrix, is also symmetric and positive definite. Hence, the elastance matrix is also square symmetric and a positive definite (PSD).

Looking into the physical significance of the matrix, the diagonal elements of the elastance matrix relates the current in inductor i to the flux across it, while the non-diagonal element represents the influence of flux in inductor j due to the current in inductor i. If you look closely in the matrix representation of the potential energy stored in the system that is used to calculate the Hamiltonian of the inductance matrix, it uses the L^{-1} term for the potential energy and flux calculation from Equation 5-36.

In circuits with nonlinear components, the inverse impedance matrix helps in understanding the influence of nonlinearity on overall circuit behavior. It assists in analyzing the interactions between linear and nonlinear elements. Understanding the inverse impedance matrix is essential when dealing with circuits containing nonlinear or complex impedance elements. It guides engineers in managing impedance interactions to achieve desired circuit performance.

The elastance matrix is fundamentally used by flux qubits to encode quantum information on the magnetic flux and to understand the electromagnetic environments of these qubits.

In quantum computing, flux qubits are a type of superconducting qubit that rely on magnetic flux to encode quantum information. The elastance matrix plays a critical role in understanding the electromagnetic environment of these qubits:

- **Inductive Coupling**: Flux qubits are often coupled via shared inductors or mutual magnetic fields. The elastance matrix helps model the interplay between the qubit loops, ensuring coherence and minimizing crosstalk.
- **Energy-Level Calculation**: The elastance matrix contributes to determining the qubit's energy levels, which are governed by capacitance, inductance, and external flux. Accurate modeling ensures predictable quantum behavior.
- **Error Reduction**: By analyzing the elastance, engineers can identify and reduce decoherence sources such as stray capacitance, leading to more robust qubit designs.

5.3.7 Scattering Matrix (S-Matrix)

The scattering matrix, often denoted as the S-matrix, is a fundamental tool that unveils the interactions and behaviors of signals as they propagate through multiport networks. This matrix sheds light on how signals are reflected, transmitted, and distributed across various ports, making it essential for understanding and designing complex RF and microwave systems. The scattering matrix captures how electromagnetic waves interact at different ports within a network. It provides a comprehensive view of signal propagation, reflection, and transmission, which is crucial for analyzing signal integrity and optimizing circuit behavior. The scattering matrix is a rectangular matrix that characterizes the relationships between input and output signals at various ports in a network. Each element within the matrix corresponds to the amplitude and phase of a signal as it moves from one port to another.

The scattering matrix S relates the incident wave amplitudes **a** to the outgoing wave amplitudes **b** in a network:

$$\mathbf{b} = S \cdot \mathbf{a} \qquad (5\text{-}50)$$

where S represents the scattering wave matrix, which encodes the reflection and transmission properties, **a** represents the incident wave amplitude of the incident wave and fluxes, and **b** represents the scattered output wave amplitude.

The scattering matrix is a square symmetric matrix, that is, $S_{ij} = S_{ji}$. The diagonal elements of the scattering matrix, that is, S_{ii}, represent the reflections at port i, whereas the non-diagonal elements, S_{ij}, represent the portion of the wave transmitted from port i to port j. Taking the norm of the matrix, we can reach some very interesting conclusions, such as

- $|S| \leq 1$: The scattering matrix norm for passive components is less than or equal to 1. Passive circuit components, or simply passive components, are circuit elements that can only absorb electrical energy and release it as heat or store it in an electric or magnetic field, for example, resistors, capacitors, inductors, etc.
- $|S| > 1$: The scattering matrix norm for active components is always greater than 1. Active components or active circuit elements are those elements that can provide electric power to circuits, for example, amplifiers, transistors, photodiodes, etc.

The scattering matrix is causal in nature, which means the output response cannot precede the input. Another interesting property of the scattering matrix is that, when you multiply the scattering matrix's conjugate transpose with the scattering matrix itself, it will provide an identity matrix ($S^\dagger \cdot S = I$ where $S^\dagger$ represents the conjugate transpose of the scattering matrix) stating that the system is completely lossless.

When designing RF and microwave circuits, the scattering matrix is used to analyze signal paths, evaluate impedance matching, and optimize power distribution across different ports. In antenna arrays and systems, the scattering matrix assists in predicting signal radiation patterns, evaluating antenna efficiency, and understanding how signals couple between different elements. Understanding the scattering matrix is pivotal when dealing with high-frequency circuits and systems. It guides engineers in optimizing signal paths, minimizing losses, and ensuring efficient signal transfer. While various matrix forms play vital roles in the creation of electronic systems, the capacitance, resistance, and inductance matrices stand as central components for the development of superconducting qubits.

In our subsequent exploration, we will delve into the process of constructing a capacitance matrix using the Lumped Oscillator Model (LOM) within the Qiskit Metal framework. Furthermore, we will look into an in-depth, step-by-step examination of creating a dual-coupled Transmon Qubit through the technique of direct coupling. Let's proceed to the next phase of our journey.

5.4 Capacitance Matrix and Lumped Oscillator Model Analysis

Now that we have explored the concept of the Lumped Oscillator Model and comprehended its fundamental aspects, let's dive into the systematic procedure for constructing and analyzing the Lumped Oscillator Model. This structured approach enables engineers and researchers to decipher the intricate behaviors of oscillator circuits. Oscillators play a crucial role in electronics, producing repetitive waveforms that are indispensable for tasks such as signal creation, frequency generation, and communication systems. Below is a comprehensive guide detailing

5.4 Capacitance Matrix and Lumped Oscillator Model Analysis

the sequential stages of Lumped Oscillator Model (LOM) analysis conducted using Qiskit Metal for the capacitance matrix.

First, import the necessary files for the project, including the `qiskit_metal` library. Also, import the relevant functions required for the project, such as design, draw, and others. Next, assign the design variables; for instance, set the `cpw_width` to 15 μm and the `cpw_gap` to 9 μm.

```
%reload_ext autoreload
%autoreload 2

import qiskit_metal as metal
from qiskit_metal import designs, draw
from qiskit_metal import MetalGUI, Dict, Headings

design = designs.DesignPlanar()
gui = MetalGUI(design)

from qiskit_metal.qlibrary.qubits.transmon_pocket import
 TransmonPocket
from qiskit_metal.qlibrary.tlines.meandered import
RouteMeander

design.variables['cpw_width'] = '15 um'
design.variables['cpw_gap'] = '9 um'
```

The command `design.overwrite_enabled = True` enables overwriting of the design in case the cell is run multiple times. Next, let's create a chip with transmon qubit; the `options = dict(...)` statement defines custom options for the transmons, specifying parameters such as pad width, pocket height, and connection pads for each transmon. After defining the options, we specify the number of qubits to be developed. In this case, we are developing four transmon qubits, named q1, q2, q3, and q4, where we define their positions, orientations, and other properties using the custom options defined earlier. We will be connecting the transmon qubits using the route meander. The line `RouteMeander.get_template_options(design)` retrieves the template options for the route meanders, which will be used for connecting the components.

```
# Allow running the same cell here multiple times
to overwrite changes
design.overwrite_enabled = True

## Custom options for all the transmons
options = dict(
    # Some options we want to modify from the
    defaults
    # (see below for defaults)
    pad_width = '425 um',
    pocket_height = '650um',
    # Adding 4 connectors (see below for defaults)
    connection_pads=dict(
```

```
            readout = dict(loc_W=1, loc_H=-1,
            pad_width='200um'),
            bus1 = dict(loc_W=-1, loc_H=1,
            pad_height='30um'),
            bus2 = dict(loc_W=-1, loc_H=-1,
            pad_height='50um')
    )
)

## Create 4 transmons
q1 = TransmonPocket(design, 'Q1', options = dict(
    pos_x='+2.42251mm', pos_y='+0.0mm', **options))
q2 = TransmonPocket(design, 'Q2', options = dict(
    pos_x='+0.0mm', pos_y='-0.95mm', orientation =
    '270', **options))
q3 = TransmonPocket(design, 'Q3', options = dict(
    pos_x='-2.42251mm', pos_y='+0.0mm',
    orientation = '180', **options))
q4 = TransmonPocket(design, 'Q4', options = dict(
    pos_x='+0.0mm', pos_y='+0.95mm', orientation =
    '90', **options))

RouteMeander.get_template_options(design)

options = Dict(
    lead=Dict(
        start_straight='0.2mm',
        end_straight='0.2mm'
    ),
    trace_gap='9um',
    trace_width='15um'
)
```

Let us define a function that will handle the connections between two pads and different components using a coplanar waveguide (CPW) route, named connect. It takes parameters such as component names, pins, length, asymmetry, and fillet radius. Following this, the lines where cpw1 to cpw4 are defined describe the connections (CPWs) between the transmons using the connect function, specifying the relevant components, pins, and other connection parameters. The lines gui.rebuild() and gui.autoscale() refresh the Qiskit Metal GUI (graphical user interface) to visualize the designed components and connections.

```
def connect(component_name: str, component1: str,
pin1: str,
component2: str, pin2: str,
            length: str, asymmetry='0 um',
            flip=False, fillet='90um'):
    """Connect two pins with a CPW."""
    myoptions = Dict(
        fillet=fillet,
        hfss_wire_bonds = True,
        pin_inputs=Dict(
            start_pin=Dict(
```

5.4 Capacitance Matrix and Lumped Oscillator Model Analysis

```
                component=component1,
                pin=pin1),
            end_pin=Dict(
                component=component2,
                pin=pin2)),
        total_length=length
    )
    myoptions.update(options)
    myoptions.meander.asymmetry = asymmetry
    myoptions.meander.lead_direction_inverted =
    'true' if flip else
    'false'
    return RouteMeander(design, component_name,
    myoptions)

asym = 140
cpw1 = connect('cpw1', 'Q1', 'bus2', 'Q2', 'bus1',
'6.0 mm', f'+{asym}um')
cpw2 = connect('cpw2', 'Q3', 'bus1', 'Q2', 'bus2',
f'-{asym}um', flip=True)
cpw3 = connect('cpw3', 'Q3', 'bus2', 'Q4', 'bus1',
f'+{asym}um')
cpw4 = connect('cpw4', 'Q1', 'bus1', 'Q4', 'bus2',
'6.1 mm', f'-{asym}um', flip=True)

gui.rebuild()
gui.autoscale()
```

Recollecting the chip design that we created in Chapter 4, you can see that we will be using the same chip design for calculating the capacitance matrix. So the designed chip diagram is displayed in Figure 5-3.

Once the connection is established, we can proceed to develop the Lumped Oscillator Model (LOM) analysis for the circuit. Qiskit Metal provides a unique function in its library where you can use it to perform analysis and figure out the matrices and values from it. `qiskit_metal.analyses` provides a nice framework to provide the LOM analysis. You can import it by simply importing the LOManalysis class from the `qiskit_metal.analyses.quantization` module.

```
from qiskit_metal.analyses.quantization import LOManalysis
c1 = LOManalysis(design, "q3d")
```

The `c1 = LOManalysis(design, "q3d")` command initializes an instance of the LOManalysis class named `c1`; a user can name it anything as per convenience, but as per standard practice we will be naming it `c1`. It takes two arguments:

- design: This refers to the Qiskit Metal design object representing the quantum circuit layout that you want to analyze.
- "q3d": This string specifies the simulation tool to be used for the analysis. In this case, "q3d" refers to the Q3D simulator, which is often used for electromagnetic simulation and extraction of circuit parameters.

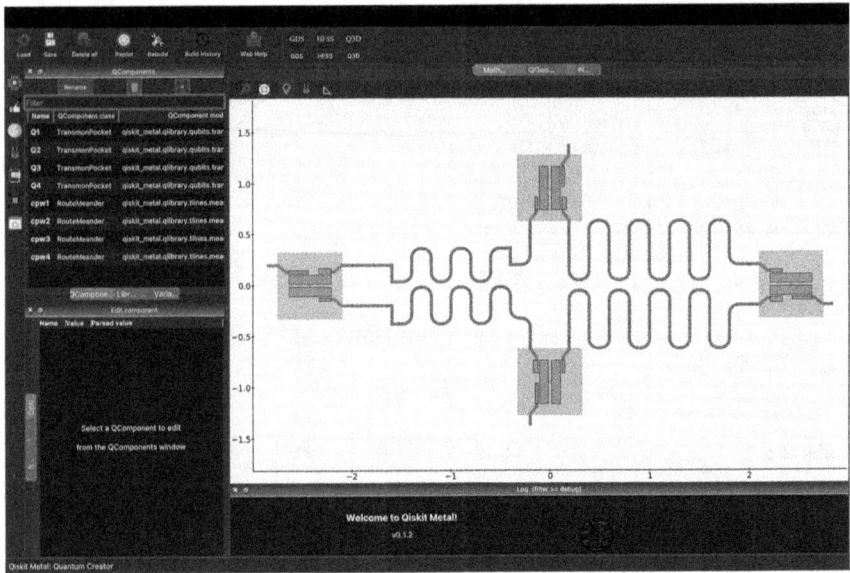

Figure 5-3 Chip design used for calculating the capacitance matrix

By creating an instance of LOManalysis, we are setting up the analysis to study the behavior of the quantum circuit using the Lumped Oscillator Model approach. This involves extracting relevant parameters, studying energy levels, and understanding how the circuit components interact.

c1.sim.setup: This command queries the current simulation setup, displaying the settings and configurations that are currently in place for the LOM analysis. The max_passes parameter controls the maximum number of passes the solver will make. By setting it to six, you're instructing the solver to make up to six passes during the simulation. Passes when talked in terms of LOM analysis mean the iterative method in which, with every pass of simulation, the mesh is refined more, which increases the accuracy of the simulation more and more. During each pass, the solver refines its mesh, numerical approximations, or parameter calculations, depending on the type of analysis. For example, in a Lumped Oscillator Model (LOM) analysis, passes might involve refining how the circuit's parameters—such as capacitances, inductances, and mutual couplings—are calculated or how the boundary conditions are modeled, improving the precision of the simulation results. By setting max_passes = 6, you are specifying that the solver should attempt up to six iterations to achieve convergence or an acceptable level of error in the results.

c1.sim.setup_update(solution_order = 'Medium', auto_increase_ solution_order = 'False'): This line updates multiple settings in the simulation setup simultaneously. It modifies the solution_order parameter to 'Medium' and turns off the automatic increase of the solution order by setting auto_increase_ solution_order to 'False'.

5.4 Capacitance Matrix and Lumped Oscillator Model Analysis

- `solution_order`: This parameter specifies the order of the solution used in the simulation. The solution order typically refers to the level of numerical accuracy or approximation used by the solver. This parameter can be set to three values: `Low`, `Medium`, and `High`. If the value of the parameter is set to `Low`, it makes the computation faster but compromises the accuracy of the system and is mostly used for faster computation. If the parameter is set to `Medium`, it balances the accuracy with the computation time but takes more time to compute with higher accuracy and is often used for standard simulation practices. If the parameter is set to `High`, it takes a very long computation time and provides an output with extremely high accuracy; though higher accuracy seems tempting, it comes with higher computation resource and time.
- `auto_increase_solution_order`: This parameter controls whether the simulation automatically increases the solution order during the analysis if convergence issues arise. A convergence issue arises when the qubit chip designed overtime does not converge to a specific value and just keeps on varying with every iteration. This parameter can be set to two values, `True` or `False`. If set to `True`, the solver dynamically adjusts the solution order to a higher value to force the system to reach a convergence by disregarding the value set for `solution_order`; it is particularly enforced for designing those systems where higher precision is required to ensure convergence. If the parameter is set to `False`, the solver maintains the specified solution order (in this case, "Medium") throughout the analysis, regardless of convergence challenges, and does not force convergence to take place.

```
c1.sim.setup

# example: update single setting
c1.sim.setup.max_passes = 6
# example: update multiple settings
c1.sim.setup_update(solution_order = 'Medium',
auto_increase_solution_order = 'False')

c1.sim.setup
```

After updating the values using `sim.setup_update`, we update all the values passed in parameters. As mentioned and discussed earlier, we have updated three parameters in total: we have set the value of `max_passes` to 6, `solution_order` to "Medium," and `auto_increase_solution_order` to "False." Now when we print the `sim.setup` values, we get the following corresponding output mentioning all the parameters and their corresponding set values. Let's understand in depth what each parameter means. One thing to note is that in Jupyter Notebook we do not need to specifically mention the print statement to print the values; just by passing the line we want to print at the end, it will provide the output without formatting any values, maintaining its structure.

```
{'name': 'Setup',
'reuse_selected_design': True,
'reuse_setup': True,
```

```
'freq_ghz': 5.0,
'save_fields': False,
'enabled': True,
'max_passes': 6,
'min_passes': 2,
'min_converged_passes': 2,
'percent_error': 0.5,
'percent_refinement': 30,
'auto_increase_solution_order': 'False',
'solution_order': 'Medium',
'solver_type': 'Iterative'}
```

- **name**: This parameter sets up the name of the simulation. The default name provided to the simulation is "Setup." One can change it as required.
- **reuse_selected_design**: This parameter mentions whether you want to run the simulations on the existing chip design on the GUI or not, that is, whether you want to reuse your design or not. This parameter takes two boolean inputs, True or False. If it is set to True as used in this case, it will be taking the design of the chip we have created in Figure 5-3. If it is set to False, then it will use the new design of the chip, that is, you have to create a new chip on which the analysis will be performed.
- **reuse_setup**: Specifies whether to reuse a previously defined setup. This parameter takes two boolean inputs, True or False. True indicates a previous setup will be reused instead of creating a new one. False indicates a new setup has to be defined and that will be used.
- **freq_ghz**: This parameter sets the target frequency for operation. The solver focuses on the specified frequency of operation and will analyze the circuit with that frequency value only. The value of operation is set to GHz. The default value that the solver considers for operation is 5 GHz.
- **save_fields**: Determines whether to save the calculated field data (e.g., electric and magnetic fields) from the simulation. The input is taken in boolean format True or False. If set to True, it will save all the calculated fields into the simulation; otherwise, if set to False, it will not save the information. The default value of the simulation is set to True.
- **enabled**: Indicates whether this setup is active and will be run during simulation. The input is taken in boolean format True or False. The default value of the simulation is set to True.
- **min_passes**: Similar to max_passes values, this value determines the minimum passes that will be used during the simulation to iterate over in order to find the convergence value. The default value of min_passes is 2.
- **min_converged_passes**: As discussed earlier, the values of passes need to converge to a certain point in order to calculate the convergence value. This parameter helps in defining the minimum number of passes required to check whether the simulation is converging to a point. For example, if the value is set to 3, then the solver will check for three consecutive iterations to check whether

5.4 Capacitance Matrix and Lumped Oscillator Model Analysis

the value is getting converged to a certain number or not. The default value of the `min_converged_passes` is set to 2.
- `percent_error`: This parameter helps in determining the percentage error between two convergence points achieved in consecutive iterations to determine convergence value. This parameter defines that error range. Here, it is set to 0.5, meaning the solver will aim for a solution with less than 0.5% error. The default value of this parameter is 0.5%.
- `percent_refinement`: This parameter defines by what percentage the mesh will be refined during consecutive iterations. The default value for this parameter is 30%. That means with each consecutive iteration, the mesh will be refined by 30% more.
- `solver_type`: This parameter determines the method used to solve the mathematical equations in simulations, and its options typically include Direct, Iterative, Hybrid, Multigrid, Adaptive, and Eigen. The Direct solver provides high accuracy and fast convergence but requires significant memory, making it suitable for small to medium problems, whereas Iterative solvers are more memory efficient and ideal for large problems but may take longer to converge. The Hybrid solver balances the strengths of Direct and Iterative methods, while Multigrid accelerates convergence by using multiple grid resolutions, particularly for large-scale problems. Adaptive solvers adjust settings dynamically to optimize performance, and eigensolvers specialize in eigenvalue problems, such as resonance or frequency analysis. The choice of solver depends on the problem's size, complexity, and the simulation tool being used.

Now that we have defined the parameters for the analysis and set them by updating the `sim.setup_update`, we need to run the analysis to check and measure the capacitance matrix of the system. In order to do that, we run the function `sim.run`.

`c1.sim.run(components=['Q1'], open_terminations=[('Q1', 'readout'), ('Q1', 'bus1'), ('Q1', 'bus2')])` initiates a simulation run for a specific component ('Q1') and specifies the open terminations for that component. Open terminations are connection points that are treated as open circuits during the simulation, allowing for more accurate analysis of the device behavior.

After the simulation run, the `c1.sim.capacitance_matrix` command computes and retrieves the capacitance matrix. The capacitance matrix represents the capacitance between different nodes or components in the circuit, helping us in obtaining the desired output.

```
c1.sim.run(components=['Q1'], open_terminations=[('Q1', 'readout'),
('Q1', 'bus1'), ('Q1', 'bus2')])
c1.sim.capacitance_matrix
```

The command `c1.sim.setup.freq_ghz=4.8` updates the simulation setup frequency to 4.8 GHz. The `freq_ghz` parameter specifies the frequency at which the simulation will be performed. Now we use the command `c1.sim.run()` to execute the simulation. Following the simulation run, the `c1.sim.capacitance_matrix` command computes and retrieves the capacitance matrix, which represents the capacitance interactions in the circuit.

```
c1.sim.setup.freq_ghz = 4.8
c1.sim.run()
c1.sim.capacitance_matrix

type(c1.sim.capacitance_matrix)
```

Using capacitance matrices obtained from each pass, save the many parameters of the Hamiltonian of the system. `get_lumped_oscillator()` operates on four setup parameters: Lj: float, Cj: float, fr: Union[list, float], fb: Union[list, float]. The line `c1.setup.junctions = Dict({'Lj': 12.31, 'Cj': 2})` sets up the junction parameters for the simulation. Here, `'Lj'` represents the Josephson inductance, and `'Cj'` represents the Josephson junction capacitance. Following that, we specify the readout and bus frequencies for the analysis. `freq_readout` is set to 7.0 GHz, and `freq_bus` is set to a range of [6.0, 6.2] GHz.

`c1.plot_convergence()`, `c1.plot_convergence_chi()`

These lines generate plots to visualize the convergence information of the LOM analysis. The `plot_convergence` method displays the convergence behavior, while `plot_convergence_chi` specifically focuses on the chi-convergence behavior.

```
c1.setup.junctions = Dict({'Lj': 12.31, 'Cj': 2})
c1.setup.freq_readout = 7.0
c1.setup.freq_bus = [6.0, 6.2]

c1.run_lom()
c1.lumped_oscillator_all

c1.plot_convergence()
c1.plot_convergence_chi()
```

`c1.lumped_oscillator_all` ... After the analysis run, this command retrieves the LOM analysis results, including properties of the lumped oscillators in the circuit. These are the steps that we can use to perform the analysis for the capacitance matrix using LOM analysis. Now, we will look into the two-transmon qubit LOM analysis.

5.5 Two Transmons Coupled by a Direct Coupler

Before moving on to developing the circuits and performing the Lumped Oscillator Model (LOM) analysis, we need to import the necessary dependencies. We import various modules, such as `scqubits`, a module for studying superconducting qubits, and the `qiskit_metal.analyses.quantization` modules, which are used for LOM analysis. The speed of light constant (`c_light`) from the `scipy.constants` module is imported. Additionally, `matplotlib.pyplot` is imported for plotting, and `matplotlib.inline` is used to display plots directly in the notebook.

5.5 Two Transmons Coupled by a Direct Coupler

```
%load_ext autoreload
%autoreload 2

import scqubits as scq

from qiskit_metal.analyses.quantization.lumped_capacitive
import load_q3d_capacitance_matrix
from qiskit_metal.analyses.quantization.lom_core_analysis
import CompositeSystem, Cell, Subsystem, QuantumSystemRegistry

from scipy.constants import speed_of_light as c_light

import matplotlib.pyplot as plt
%matplotlib inline
```

The command QuantumSystemRegistry.registry() is calling a method to retrieve and display the list of available quantum systems stored in the QuantumSystemRegistry. This registry serves as a mechanism for maintaining information about various quantum systems that have been defined and stored for analysis. These systems can include different types of quantum components, such as qubits, resonators, and other elements used for analysis and simulation within the Qiskit Metal framework. The output of this command provides insights into the types and names of quantum systems available for further exploration and analysis. For instance, the registry may display stored systems like Transmon, fluxonium, and others.

```
QuantumSystemRegistry.registry()
```

Running the command QuantumSystemRegistry.registry(), we obtain the output of the stored system in a dictionary format as

```
{
'TRANSMON':
qiskit_metal.analyses.quantization.lom_core_analysis.
TransmonBuilder,
    'FLUXONIUM':
qiskit_metal.analyses.quantization.lom_core_analysis.
FluxoniumBuilder,
    'TL_RESONATOR':
qiskit_metal.analyses.quantization.lom_core_analysis.
TLResonatorBuilder,
    'LUMPED_RESONATOR':
qiskit_metal.analyses.quantization.lom_core_analysis.
LumpedResonatorBuilder
}
```

Moving on ahead, we need to develop a q3d stimulation model of two transmons coupled by a direct coupler. A Maxwell capacitance matrix provides the relation between the voltages on a set of conductors and the charges on those conductors. For a generic conductor set, the following relation holds:

$$Q = C \cdot V \qquad (5\text{-}51)$$

where C is the Maxwell capacitance matrix, and V and Q are the voltage and charge vectors, respectively. The matrix shown below demonstrates the general condition of a Maxwell capacitance matrix.

In the setup, two transmons (named Alice and Bob) are coupled to each other through a direct coupler. Additionally, each transmon is coupled to its own readout resonator. By accessing the path to the two-transmon capacitance matrix file, we obtain the capacitance values for the two transmon qubits (Alice and Bob). The information related to both qubits is illustrated in the following snippets. We will provide the path information of both transmon capacitance matrices that we have explored in the previous example.

```
# loading alice's simulation results
path1 = './Q1_TwoTransmon_CapMatrix.txt'
ta_mat, _, _, _ = load_q3d_capacitance_matrix(path1)
```

In this snippet, we import the file by providing the capacitance matrix text file path and then opening it with the function call `load_q3d_capacitance_matrix(path1)`. This will provide an output of the capacitance matrix provided in the input in a nice tabular format. So, running for the first transmon qubit capacitance matrix, Alice's simulation provides the output shown in Table 5-1.

Similarly, we can import the path for Bob's capacitance matrix and can visualize the output similarly as

```
# loading bob's simulation results
path2 = './Q2_TwoTransmon_CapMatrix.txt'
tb_mat, _, _, _ = load_q3d_capacitance_matrix(path2)
```

Tables 5-1 and 5-2 provide the output of the capacitance matrix for their individual transmon qubits. The output of the table represents the capacitance between the two points taken in reference from the column header and row header. The matrices `coupler_connector_pad_Q1` and `coupler_connector_pad_Q2` refer to the same node corresponding to the direct coupler between the qubits, but they are listed under different names in the capacitance matrix results file. To merge the two capacitance matrices in the Lumped Oscillator Model (LOM) analysis, we

Table 5-1 Capacitance matrix for Alice's simulation, showing the capacitance between pairs of plates indicated in the row and column headers (in fF)

	coupler_connector_pad_Q1	ground_main_plane	pad_bot_Q2	pad_top_Q2	readout_connector_pad_Q2
coupler_connector_pad_Q1	64.52	−38.63	−2.18	−22.93	−0.22
ground_main_plane	−38.63	267.40	−49.28	−49.30	−38.67
pad_bot_Q2	−2.18	−49.28	121.38	−45.24	−23.06
pad_top_Q2	−22.93	−49.30	−45.24	121.24	−2.18
readout_connector_pad_Q2	−0.22	−38.67	−23.06	−2.18	64.70

5.5 Two Transmons Coupled by a Direct Coupler

Table 5-2 Capacitance matrix for Bob's simulation, showing the capacitance between pairs of plates indicated in the row and column headers (in fF)

	coupler_ connector_ pad_Q1	ground_ main_ plane	pad_ bot_ Q2	pad_ top_ Q2	readout_ connector_ pad_Q2
coupler_connector_ pad_Q1	64.52	−38.63	−2.18	−22.93	−0.22
ground_main_plane	−38.63	267.40	−49.28	−49.30	−38.67
pad_bot_Q2	−2.18	−49.28	121.38	−45.24	−23.06
pad_top_Q2	−22.93	−49.30	−45.24	121.24	−2.18
readout_connector_ pad_Q2	−0.22	−38.67	−23.06	−2.18	64.70

need to rename them to the same identifier. For clarity, we will also rename the nodes `readout_connector_pad_Q1` and `readout_connector_pad_Q2`.

The following three parameters—`ind_dict`, `jj_dict`, and `cj_dict`—share the same structure. Each of these is a dictionary where the keys are tuples representing the nodes between which a junction is placed, and the values provide the corresponding parameters associated with the junction. Specifically:

- `ind_dict`: Specifies the junction inductance in nanohenries (nH)
- `jj_dict`: Assigns a unique identifier to each Josephson junction (e.g., "j1"), which can be any name, provided it remains consistent throughout the analysis
- `cj_dict`: Defines the junction capacitance in femtofarads (fF)

Now we create a dictionary with all the information required for the analysis for both Alice and Bob. The dictionaries `opt1` and `opt2` contain various options for configuring the cell:

- `node_rename`: Renames specific nodes for clarity, such as the connector pads
- `cap_mat`: Represents the capacitance matrix of the qubit, typically derived from a previous analysis
- `ind_dict`: Defines the inductance values for specific junctions
- `jj_dict`: Maps Josephson junction identifiers to particular connections
- `cj_dict`: Specifies the capacitance values for each junction

These configurations encapsulate the parameter details for the respective transmon qubits, streamlining the management and analysis of their properties within the `QuantumSystemRegistry`.

```
# cell 1: transmon Alice cell
opt1 = dict(
    node_rename = {'coupler_connector_pad_Q1': 'coupling',
    'readout_connector_pad_Q1': 'readout_alice'},
    cap_mat = ta_mat,
    ind_dict = {('pad_top_Q1', 'pad_bot_Q1'): 10},  # junction
```

```
        inductance in nH
    jj_dict = {('pad_top_Q1', 'pad_bot_Q1'): 'j1'},
    cj_dict = {('pad_top_Q1', 'pad_bot_Q1'): 2}    # junction
        capacitance in fF
)
cell_1 = Cell(opt1)

# cell 2: transmon Bob cell
opt2 = dict(
    node_rename = {'coupler_connector_pad_Q2': 'coupling',
    'readout_connector_pad_Q2': 'readout_bob'},
    cap_mat = tb_mat,
    ind_dict = {('pad_top_Q2', 'pad_bot_Q2'): 12},   # junction
        inductance in nH
    jj_dict = {('pad_top_Q2', 'pad_bot_Q2'): 'j2'},
    cj_dict = {('pad_top_Q2', 'pad_bot_Q2'): 2}    # junction
        capacitance in fF
)
cell_2 = Cell(opt2)
```

Now, after this step, we need to create subsystems. The subsystem constructor takes three required arguments, and there are four currently supported system types: TRANSMON, FLUXONIUM, TL_RESONATOR (Transmission Line Resonator), and LUMPED_RESONATOR. The nodes parameter allows you to specify which nodes the subsystem should be assigned within the cells, ensuring consistency with the node names assigned earlier. The q_opts parameter lets you define any optional parameters, such as the scqubits parameters for qubits that are extremely important for characterizing the physical properties, defining its Hamiltonian, and enabling numerical analysis of its dynamics and energy spectra for a superconducting qubit, including ncut used for determining the truncation of the charge basis used to represent the Hamiltonian of the quantum system and truncated_dim.

The subsystem constructor is utilized to create a subsystem, and various options can be specified:

- name: Specifies the name of the subsystem
- sys_type: Specifies the type of the subsystem, such as "TRANSMON" for transmon qubits
- nodes: Lists the nodes associated with this subsystem, for example, node j1

This section also defines the subsystem for the "Alice Readout Resonator." The q_opts dictionary includes several options for configuring the resonator:

- f_res: Specifies the dressed frequency of the resonator in GHz
- Z0: Denotes the characteristic impedance of the resonator in Ohms
- vp: Represents the phase velocity of the resonator

5.5 Two Transmons Coupled by a Direct Coupler

The subsystem is created using the subsystem constructor, where you specify its name, type (e.g., TL_RESONATOR for a transmission line resonator), nodes, and additional options through the q_opts dictionary.

This code snippet demonstrates the definition of four subsystems within the QuantumSystemRegistry, each representing different components of the quantum circuit, including transmon qubits and readout resonators. These subsystems are essential for organizing and managing the elements of the circuit, facilitating effective analysis and simulation.

```
composite_sys = CompositeSystem(
    subsystems=[transmon_alice, transmon_bob, res_alice,
    res_bob],
    cells=[cell_1, cell_2],
    grd_node='ground_main_plane',
    nodes_force_keep=['readout_alice', 'readout_bob']
)
```

This composite system integrates various subsystems and cells into a unified representation for further analysis and simulation. The CompositeSystem class constructor is used to create the composite system, which takes several parameters:

- **subsystems**: A list of previously defined subsystems, including the transmon qubits and readout resonators for Alice and Bob.
- **cells**: A list of previously defined cells, each representing a qubit's layout and properties.
- **grd_node**: Specifies the node that serves as the ground connection for the composite system. In this case, it is set to ground_main_plane.
- **nodes_force_keep**: A list of nodes that should be preserved and not pruned from the composite system. Here, the readout nodes for Alice and Bob are specified to be kept.

The command cg = composite_sys.circuitGraph() generates and prints a circuit graph using the circuitGraph() method from the CompositeSystem instance. This graph visually represents the connections and relationships between different elements of the composite system. If we print the output obtained using the print statement print(cg), it will provide the inverse inductance matrix and the capacitance matrix for the combined Alice and Bob system, and the output for the code provides the L_{inv_k} (reduced inverse inductance matrix) in Table 5-3, the c_k (reduced capacitance matrix) in Table 5-4 and the Chi matrix for transmon and the readout values in Table 5-5.

Table 5-3 Reduced inverse inductance matrix (L_{inv_k}) for the system

	j1	j2	readout_alice	readout_bob
j1	0.1	0.0	0.0	0.0
j2	0.0	0.083333	0.0	0.0
readout_alice	0.0	0.0	0.0	0.0
readout_bob	0.0	0.0	0.0	0.0

Table 5-4 Reduced capacitance matrix (C_k)

	j1	j2	readout_alice	readout_bob
j1	63.185549	−0.766012	8.318893	−0.323188
j2	−0.766012	84.343548	−0.342145	10.039921
readout_alice	8.318893	−0.342145	55.591197	−0.144354
readout_bob	−0.323188	10.039921	−0.144354	60.347427

Table 5-5 Chi matrix in MHz for the Hamiltonian results

	transmon_alice	transmon_bob	readout_alice	readout_bob
transmon_alice	−353.239816	−0.542895	−4.132854	−0.003120
transmon_bob	−0.542895	−263.940908	−1.460416	−0.000017
readout_alice	−4.132854	−1.460416	55.591197	3.829744
readout_bob	−0.003120	−0.000017	3.829744	60.347427

Let's create a Hilbert space for the composite system using the create_hilbertspace() method and then print the information about the Hilbert space by

```
hilbertspace = composite_sys.create_hilbertspace()
print(hilbertspace)
```

A Hilbert space, in the context of quantum systems, represents the set of all possible quantum states that the system can occupy. The output indicates that a Hilbert space object has been successfully created for the composite system using Qiskit Metal, and the Hilbert space of the system results in

```
HilbertSpace: subsystems
-----------------------

Transmon-------------- [Transmon_1]
    EJ: 16346.15128067812
    EC: 312.756688730393
    ng: 0.001
    ncut: 22
    truncated_dim: 10
    |
    dim: 45

Transmon-------------- [Transmon_2]
    EJ: 13621.792733898432
```

5.5 Two Transmons Coupled by a Direct Coupler

```
        EC: 234.32049269967633
        ng: 0.001
        ncut: 22
        truncated_dim: 10
        |
        dim: 45

   Oscillator------------ [Oscillator_1]
        E_osc: 8000
        l_osc: None
        truncated_dim: 3
        |
        dim: 3

   Oscillator------------ [Oscillator_2]
        E_osc: 7600.0
        l_osc: None
        truncated_dim: 3
        |
        dim: 3
```

By adding interactions to the previously created Hilbert space for the composite system using the `add_interaction()` method, we can define the specific interactions within the system. Subsequently, the Hamiltonian of the system is calculated using the `hamiltonian()` method. The Hamiltonian represents the total energy operator of the quantum system, encapsulating the dynamics and energy contributions of all its components.

```
hamiltonian_results = composite_sys.hamiltonian_results (hilbertspace,
evals_count=30)

        Finished eigensystem.

system frequencies in GHz:
-------------------------
{'transmon_alice': 6.05336688886868, 'transmon_bob': 4.798983222888094,
 'readout_alice': 8.009054820710865, 'readout_bob': 7.604421010766995}

Chi matrices in MHz:
```

Hence, the final output for the system comes out to be

```
transmon_alice.h_params
----------------------
{
    'EJ': 16346.15128067812,
    'EC': 312.756688730393,
    'Q_zpf': 3.204353268e-19,
    'default_charge_op': Operator(op=array(
            [[-22,   0,   0, ...,   0,   0,   0],
             [  0, -21,   0, ...,   0,   0,   0],
             [  0,   0, -20, ...,   0,   0,   0],
             ...,
             [  0,   0,   0, ...,  20,   0,   0],
```

```
              [  0,   0,   0, ...,   0,  21,   0],
              [  0,   0,   0, ...,   0,   0,  22]]), add_hc=False)
}

transmon_bob.h_params
---------------------
{
    'EJ': 13621.792733898432,
    'EC': 234.32049269967633,
    'Q_zpf': 3.204353268e-19,
    'default_charge_op': Operator(op=array(
              [[-22,   0,   0, ...,   0,   0,   0],
              [  0, -21,   0, ...,   0,   0,   0],
              [  0,   0, -20, ...,   0,   0,   0],
              ...,
              [  0,   0,   0, ...,  20,   0,   0],
              [  0,   0,   0, ...,   0,  21,   0],
              [  0,   0,   0, ...,   0,   0,  22]]), add_hc=False)
}
```

The output suggests the following:

- EJ: Represents the Josephson junction energy which governs the nonlinear inductance of the Josephson junction and directly influences the anharmonicity of the Transmon qubits.
- EC: Represents the charging energy that is inversely proportional to the capacitance governing the energy level spacing in the transmon qubit. A higher value represents more anharmonicity.
- Q_zpf: Represents the zero-point fluctuation of the charge of the transmon that describes the quantum mechanical fluctuations of the charge operator in the zero-point state.
- $default\_charge\_op$: Represents the charge in the Hamiltonian of the Transmon. The diagonal matrix represents the eigenvalues of the charge operator in range $[-22, 22]$ indicating the number of charged states considered in the numerical representation.
- add_hc: Represents whether the hermitian conjugate is added to the operator $default\_charge\_op$ or not. False indicates that no hermitian conjugate was added to the operator as the matrix is self-adjoining.

These parameters help in understanding the harmonic parameters of the Transmon coupler between Alice and Bob. The EJ/EC ratio can be calculated using the output values obtained. As calculated, the EJ/EC ratio for Alice is 52.26475, and for Bob it is 58.133168 due to $EJ \gg EC$ stating that the Transmon operates in a weakly anharmonic regime. The parameters EJ and EC and the charge operator for each Transmon are used to calculate the coupled system's Hamiltonian. The analysis also ensures that stray couplings, such as the formation of unintended Josephson junctions or spurious modes, are minimized.

5.6 Advantages of Lumped Oscillator Model Analysis

The Lumped Oscillator Model (LOM) simplifies complex systems into lumped elements, making it easier to analyze and understand their behavior. It provides an intuitive way to study the interactions between components, allowing for quick prototyping and design iterations of electronic circuits. LOM enables engineers and researchers to predict and optimize the behavior of circuits before physically building them.

LOM analysis extracts the key parameter matrices such as the capacitance matrix and inductance matrix which provides an accurate simulation reading for the analysis of the qubit chip. LOM analysis also provides a better understanding of the circuit and its applications in the frequency domain helping in the analysis of the stability of the quantum chip generated.

With LOM, engineers can systematically explore the effects of component values and configurations on circuit behavior, aiding in the optimization of circuit performance. The LOM approach is not limited to electronics but can be extended to various fields such as quantum systems, microwave engineering, and even mechanical systems. In quantum systems, LOM analysis is instrumental in the design and study of superconducting qubits and other quantum components. Furthermore, LOM serves as a stepping stone for more advanced modeling techniques, helping engineers and researchers transition to more complex simulations.

5.7 Conclusion

In this chapter, we explored the classical approach of the lumped oscillator model (LOM) and its significance in analyzing superconducting qubit chips. We examined how understanding the classical perspective helps in understanding the fundamentals of LOM analysis for superconducting circuits. Additionally, we dived into the mathematical fundamentals, including the capacitance and inductance matrices, which are integral to this analysis. We also reviewed methods for calculating the capacitance matrix of the designed superconducting chip, incorporating Qiskit Metal for simulation and Ansys HFSS for obtaining precise output values. Furthermore, we analyzed a practical example of a two-transmon coupler system, represented by Alice and Bob's transmons. Through this example, we computed the system's Hamiltonian, determined the EJ/EC ratio, and examined its anharmonicity, providing a detailed understanding of the system's quantum behavior.

Energy-Participation Ratio Method for Quantization and Analysis

In this chapter, we explore the energy-participation ratio (EPR) method, a pivotal technique for quantizing and analyzing superconducting circuits. The EPR method enables us to systematically quantify how energy is distributed across different components and vibrational modes in a physical system, such as superconducting qubits, resonators, or coupled systems. While the method has roots in the study of mechanical and vibrational systems, its application to electromagnetic structures—like resonators, cavities, and Josephson circuits—has been transformative. By identifying and quantifying the contribution of each mode to the total energy, the EPR method serves as a critical tool for understanding system dynamics, optimizing circuit designs, and enabling accurate quantization. This chapter demonstrates how the EPR method is applied to superconducting circuits, both conceptually and practically, with an emphasis on its implementation in Qiskit Metal, a comprehensive framework for modeling and simulating superconducting qubits.

This chapter begins with an introduction to the EPR method for quantizing superconducting circuits. We first illustrate its principles using a simple coupled qubit-cavity system, followed by an extension to the quantization of general Josephson circuits. Next, we discuss how the EPR method integrates with Qiskit Metal, a comprehensive framework for designing and simulating superconducting qubits, to facilitate practical analysis and modeling. The chapter concludes with a series of illustrative examples, including a stand-alone transmon qubit, a CPW resonator, and hybrid systems combining qubits and resonators. These examples culminate in advanced applications, such as coupled transmon qubits and double-hanger resonators.

6.1 The EPR Method for Quantization of Superconducting Circuit

The quantization of a Josephson circuit revolves around a fundamental inquiry: How is energy distributed across the various components of the circuit? Specifically, a key challenge is calculating the proportion of energy stored in the Josephson junction relative to the total energy in the system. This energy ratio is a vital parameter that bridges the gap between classical and quantum circuit analysis, enabling the accurate derivation of quantum Hamiltonians.

Unlike traditional approaches, such as those relying on the impedance response matrix, the energy-participation ratio (EPR) method offers a more direct and flexible framework. By focusing on energy distribution, the EPR method eliminates the need for calculating the full network response, streamlining the process of circuit quantization while providing deeper insights into the contribution of individual circuit elements. This section introduces the EPR method and its application to superconducting circuits, beginning with simple coupled systems before extending to general Josephson circuits.

6.1.1 Simple Circuit Quantization: Coupled Qubit and Cavity System

This subsection focuses on the quantization of a fundamental coupled system comprising a transmon qubit embedded within a cavity. The transmon configuration resides in the cavity as depicted in Figure 6-1a, representing a black-box distributed structure. The horizontal blue arrows in the diagram illustrate the direction of the electric field $\mathbf{E}_m(\mathbf{r})$ associated with the fundamental cavity mode, where $\mathbf{r}$ represents the spatial position. The corresponding lumped circuit model, shown in Figure 6-1b, highlights the key components, including the Josephson junction shunted by a capacitance.

The total Hamiltonian of the system can be expressed as the sum of two components: the linear Hamiltonian, $\hat{H}_{\text{lin}}$, and the nonlinear Hamiltonian, $\hat{H}_{\text{nl}}$, as

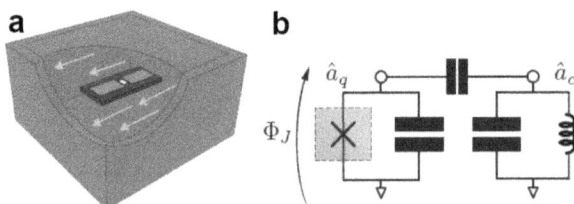

Figure 6-1 (a) Schematic of 3D cavity containing a transmon qubit. Horizontal blue arrows indicate the direction of the electric field ($\mathbf{E}_m(\mathbf{r})$) of the cavity mode. (b) Lumped model representation of the coupled circuit. The operators $\hat{a}_q$ and $\hat{a}_c$ represent the qubit and cavity mode annihilation operators, respectively

6.1 The EPR Method for Quantization of Superconducting Circuit

shown in Equation 6-1. The linear term comprises the resonator Hamiltonian and the linear response of the transmon, while the nonlinear term accounts for the nonlinearity arising from the Josephson junction:

$$H_{\text{full}} = \hat{H}_{\text{lin}} + \hat{H}_{\text{nl}}$$
$$= \hbar\omega_c \hat{a}_c^\dagger \hat{a}_c + \hbar\omega_q \hat{a}_q^\dagger \hat{a}_q - E_J \left(\cos\left(\hat{\phi}_J\right) + \frac{\hat{\phi}_J^2}{2}\right), \quad (6\text{-}1)$$

where ω_c and ω_q are the eigenfrequencies of the cavity mode and the linearized qubit mode, respectively. The operators $\hat{a}_c$ and $\hat{a}_q$ are the annihilation operators corresponding to the cavity and qubit modes.

The magnetic flux operator across the Josephson junction, $\hat{\phi}_J$, is given by

$$\hat{\phi}_J = \phi_q (\hat{a}_q^\dagger + \hat{a}_q) + \phi_c (\hat{a}_c^\dagger + \hat{a}_c), \quad (6\text{-}2)$$

where $\hat{\phi}_J$ is derived from the classical flux variable $\phi_J(t) = \int_{-\infty}^{t} v_J(\tau) \, d\tau / \Phi_0$, with $v_J(\tau)$ being the instantaneous voltage across the Josephson junction and $\Phi_0 = \hbar/2e$ the reduced flux quantum.

This expression for $\hat{\phi}_J$ is a linear, real-valued, and nonnegative combination of the qubit and cavity operators. It also incorporates the quantum zero-point fluctuations of the junction flux, represented by ϕ_q and ϕ_c, which describe the contributions from the qubit and cavity modes, respectively.

To construct the complete Hamiltonian for the quantum circuit, it is essential to determine key parameters, namely ω_c, ω_q, ϕ_q, and ϕ_c. These parameters are extracted by performing an eigenanalysis of the classical distributed circuit associated with the linear Hamiltonian. Specifically, the qubit resonance frequency (ω_q) and cavity resonance frequency (ω_c) can be computed using finite element simulations of the coupled qubit-cavity system.

This computational analysis incorporates several factors, including the geometric layout of the qubit-cavity system, material properties, electromagnetic boundary conditions, and a detailed model of the Josephson junction, which is treated as a lumped-element linear inductor. The eigensolver is then employed to analyze the system within the frequency range of interest. This process yields a set of eigenmodes, each characterized by its frequency, quality factor, and field solutions. By identifying the hybridized cavity and qubit modes from these eigenmodes, the resonance frequencies ω_c and ω_q are extracted. These frequencies fully define the linear Hamiltonian, $\hat{H}_{\text{lin}}$.

The excitation of a specific mode m allows for the computation of the energy-participation ratio (p_m), which quantifies the distribution of energy among circuit components. This ratio is determined using the eigenfield solutions for the electric field $\mathbf{E}_m(\mathbf{r})$ and magnetic field $\mathbf{H}_m(\mathbf{r})$, where $\mathbf{r}$ denotes the spatial position. These field solutions play a critical role in establishing the relationship between the classical electromagnetic behavior and the quantum properties of the system.

Further technical details regarding the electromagnetic simulations performed using the finite element method (FEM) are elaborated upon later in this section, providing a comprehensive understanding of how these computations are implemented in practice.

The participation p_m of the junction quantifies the proportion of inductive energy allocated to the Josephson junction relative to the total inductive energy stored in the circuit for a given mode $m \in \{c, q\}$. It serves as a measure of how strongly the Josephson junction interacts with a specific mode of the circuit. Mathematically, it is defined as

$$p_m = \frac{\text{Energy Stored in the Junction}}{\text{Inductive Energy Stored in Mode } m} = \frac{\mathcal{E}_{j,m}}{\mathcal{E}_{\text{ind},m}}, \qquad (6\text{-}3)$$

where $\mathcal{E}_{j,m}$ is the energy stored in the Josephson junction, and $\mathcal{E}_{\text{ind},m}$ represents the total inductive energy stored in mode m.

The value of p_m ranges between 0 and 1:

- **Minimum Participation** ($p_m = 0$): This indicates that the Josephson dipole inductor does not participate in the mode. Even in the presence of excitation, no energy is transferred to the junction.
- **Maximum Participation** ($p_m = 1$): This implies that the Josephson junction fully participates in the mode. When the mode is excited, all the inductive energy is directed to the Josephson dipole, with no energy stored in any other inductor.

By analyzing the participation factor p_m, we gain insights into the energy dynamics of the quantum circuit, which is crucial for optimizing the qubit-cavity interaction and ensuring reliable quantization of the system.

6.1.1.1 Calculation of p_m in the Classical Picture (Using FEM Simulation)

To calculate the classically defined energy-participation ratio (EPR), we perform a finite element method (FEM) eigenanalysis simulation of the linearized Josephson circuit, which corresponds to the Hamiltonian H_{lin}. Use FEM-based eigenmode analysis in electromagnetic simulation software (e.g., Ansys HFSS) to model the superconducting circuit. This will help determine the electromagnetic field distribution of the circuit's resonant modes and obtain the stored electric and magnetic energy distributions within the structure. In this simulation, we approximate the Josephson junction as a simple rectangular sheet with a lumped boundary condition characterized by the inductance L_j. This inductance L_j represents the inductive behavior of the Josephson dipole when operating at the equilibrium point.

The rectangular sheet serves as a simplified model of the physical layout of the Josephson dipole and its wiring connections. This approximation is valid because the size of the Josephson junction is in the deep sub-wavelength regime; specifically, it is five orders of magnitude smaller than the mode wavelength of interest. As a result, the lumped-element approximation captures the essential characteristics of the junction while reducing computational complexity.

6.1 The EPR Method for Quantization of Superconducting Circuit

In the FEM simulation, we model the Josephson junction as a two-dimensional sheet S, which is subject to a surface-impedance boundary condition. This boundary condition is expressed as

$$\mathbf{E}\big|_\parallel = Z_s \left(\hat{n} \times \mathbf{H}\big|_\parallel\right), \tag{6-4}$$

where $\mathbf{E}\big|_\parallel$ and $\mathbf{H}\big|_\parallel$ represent the tangential electric and magnetic fields on the surface of the sheet, respectively. Here, $\hat{n}$ is the unit vector normal to the sheet, and Z_s is the complex-valued surface impedance that corresponds to the total sheet inductance L_j. The hat symbol over $\hat{n}$ denotes a unit vector in the context of electromagnetic fields. This formulation captures the inductive effects of the Josephson junction in the simulation, enabling an accurate representation of the circuit's electromagnetic behavior.

The quantum circuit under consideration contains a single Josephson junction, allowing us to directly compute the energy-participation ratio (EPR), p_m, for the dipole in the mode using the global electric and magnetic eigenmode energies. In a resonantly excited mode, the electromagnetic energy is equally divided between inductive ($\mathcal{E}_{\text{ind}}$) and capacitive ($\mathcal{E}_{\text{cap}}$) contributions. This energy balance remains valid even in the presence of dissipation and is fundamental to defining the eigenmode condition.

For a Josephson dipole, the inductive energy is further subdivided into magnetic ($\mathcal{E}_{\text{mag}}$) and kinetic ($\mathcal{E}_{\text{kin}}$) components. The magnetic component arises from the magnetic fields and geometric inductance, while the kinetic component is associated with the Josephson dipole's kinetic inductance, electron flow, and inertia. From the perspective of finite element (FE) analysis, magnetic energy is stored in the magnetic eigenfields ($\mathbf{H}_m$), whereas kinetic energy is localized in the lumped-element boundary condition applied to S_J. In the absence of lumped-element capacitive boundary conditions in the model, the capacitive eigenmode energy is entirely stored in the electric eigenfields ($\mathbf{E}_m$), making the capacitive energy ($\mathcal{E}_{\text{cap}}$) equivalent to the electric energy ($\mathcal{E}_{\text{elec}}$).

The energies associated with the electric and magnetic fields are calculated using the eigenfield phasors as follows:

$$\mathcal{E}_{\text{elec}} = \frac{1}{4}\text{Re}\int_V \mathbf{E}^*_{\text{max}} \cdot \overleftrightarrow{\epsilon} \cdot \mathbf{E}_{\text{max}}\, dv,$$

$$\mathcal{E}_{\text{mag}} = \frac{1}{4}\text{Re}\int_V \mathbf{H}^*_{\text{max}} \cdot \overleftrightarrow{\mu} \cdot \mathbf{H}_{\text{max}}\, dv, \tag{6-5}$$

where $\mathbf{E}_{\text{max}}$ and $\mathbf{H}_{\text{max}}$ represent the eigenmode electric and magnetic phasors, respectively. The symbols $\overleftrightarrow{\epsilon}$ and $\overleftrightarrow{\mu}$ denote the electric permittivity and magnetic permeability tensors, and the spatial integrals are performed over the entire volume V of the device.

Using these global quantities and the energy balance, the EPR can be computed as

$$p_m = \frac{\mathcal{E}_{\text{kin}}}{\mathcal{E}_{\text{ind}}} = \frac{\mathcal{E}_{\text{elec}} - \mathcal{E}_{\text{mag}}}{\mathcal{E}_{\text{elec}}}. \tag{6-6}$$

The entire process, including the computations described, is automated using the open source software package pyEPR [Minev et al. (2021)], which provides a streamlined framework for analyzing quantum circuits.

6.1.1.2 Calculation of Quantum Zero-Point Fluctuations

To determine $\hat{H}_{\text{nl}}$, it is essential to compute the quantum zero-point fluctuations, ϕ_q and ϕ_c. These fluctuations are derived from the participation of the Josephson junction in the complete quantum circuit. In the quantum framework, the energy-participation ratio (EPR) introduced in Equation 6-3 provides a bridge between the EPR (p_m), the quantum zero-point fluctuations, and the state of the circuit. In this quantum context, the EPR is expressed as

$$p_m = \frac{\overline{\langle \mathcal{E}_{j.m} \rangle}}{\overline{\langle \mathcal{E}_{\text{ind}.m} \rangle}}, \tag{6-7}$$

where the overline ($\overline{x}$) indicates a time average, and the expectation value is evaluated over the state $|\psi_m\rangle$.

The state $|\psi_m\rangle$ represents either a coherent state or a Fock excitation of mode m. The numerator in Equation 6-7 corresponds to the average energy stored in the Josephson junction for mode m, while the denominator represents the average inductive energy in the same mode. These calculations form the basis for extracting the quantum zero-point fluctuations ϕ_q and ϕ_c, which are pivotal for defining the nonlinear Hamiltonian $\hat{H}_{\text{nl}}$.

In the classical domain of linear circuits, the energy of an eigenmode oscillates in time between inductive and capacitive components. The inductive energy of a mode periodically reduces to zero at intervals determined by π/ω_m. Consequently, the time-averaged energy of both the Josephson dipole and the eigenmode is used. Notably, the time-averaged energy is equivalent to half of the peak energy. This observation enables us to express the total inductive energy as half of the overall mode energy:

$$\overline{\langle \hat{\mathcal{E}}_{\text{ind}} \rangle} = \frac{1}{2}\overline{\langle \hat{H}_{\text{lin}} \rangle} = \frac{1}{2} \sum_m \hbar \omega_m \overline{\langle \hat{a}_m^\dagger \hat{a}_m \rangle}. \tag{6-8}$$

To eliminate contributions from vacuum energy, all energies in Equation 6-7 are referenced relative to their ground-state expectation values. Using Equation 6-8, we

6.1 The EPR Method for Quantization of Superconducting Circuit

can write the denominator of Equation 6-7 as

$$\mathcal{E}_{\text{ind.m}} = \frac{1}{2}\hbar\omega_m \langle \hat{a}_m^\dagger \hat{a}_m \rangle. \tag{6-9}$$

To substitute the expression for $\mathcal{E}_{\text{ind.m}}$ into Equation 6-7, we write

$$p_m = \frac{\langle \psi_m | \frac{1}{2} E_J \hat{\phi}_J^2 | \psi_m \rangle}{\langle \psi_m | \frac{1}{2} \hat{H}_{\text{lin}} | \psi_m \rangle}$$

$$= \frac{\langle \frac{1}{2} E_J \left(\Phi_{m=0}^{\text{ZPF}} \right)^2 \left(\hat{a}_m + \hat{a}_m^\dagger \right)^2 \rangle}{\langle \frac{1}{2} \hbar\omega_m \hat{a}_m^\dagger \hat{a}_m \rangle} \tag{6-10}$$

$$= \frac{\frac{1}{2} E_J \left(\phi_m^{\text{ZPF}} \right)^2}{\hbar\omega_m} \langle \hat{a}_m^\dagger \hat{a}_m + \hat{a}_m \hat{a}_m^\dagger + \hat{a}_m^2 + \hat{a}_m^{\dagger 2} \rangle$$

In the expression above, the only nonzero term is the $\hat{a}_m^\dagger \hat{a}_m$ term, corresponding to the occupation number of mode m. Thus, the energy-participation ratio (EPR) of the Josephson junction for the Fock state $|\psi_m\rangle$ simplifies to

$$p_m = \frac{E_J \left(\phi_m^{\text{ZPF}} \right)^2}{\hbar\omega_m}. \tag{6-11}$$

The classical participation p_m allows us to express the variance of quantum zero-point fluctuations. For two eigenmodes–namely, the cavity mode and the qubit mode–the participation ratios (p_c and p_q) correspond to their respective zero-point fluctuations ϕ_c and ϕ_q. These are given by

$$\phi_c^2 = p_c \frac{2E_J}{\hbar\omega_c}, \quad \text{and} \quad \phi_q^2 = p_q \frac{2E_J}{\hbar\omega_q}. \tag{6-12}$$

The values of ϕ_c and ϕ_q fully determine $\hat{H}_{\text{nl}}$, thereby completing the system Hamiltonian $\hat{H}_{\text{full}}$. In the scenario of a single Josephson junction, the values of ϕ_c and ϕ_q are taken to be positive.

From $\hat{H}_{\text{full}}$, one can extract transition frequencies and nonlinear coupling between modes. Depending on the case, this extraction can be performed approximately or exactly using numerical or analytical techniques. A straightforward method involves applying perturbation theory, where $\hat{H}_{\text{nl}}$ is treated as a perturbation to $\hat{H}_{\text{lin}}$. In such scenarios, the full Hamiltonian of the qubit-cavity system can be approximated by an effective, excitation number–conserving Hamiltonian Minev et al. (2021):

$$\hat{H}_{\text{eff}} = (\omega_q - \Delta_q)\hat{n}_q - (\omega_c - \Delta_c)\hat{n}_c + \chi_{qc}\hat{n}_q\hat{n}_c - \frac{1}{2}\alpha_q\hat{n}_q(\hat{n}_q - 1)$$
$$- \frac{1}{2}\alpha_c\hat{n}_c(\hat{n}_c - 1), \qquad (6\text{-}13)$$

where $\hat{n}_q$ and $\hat{n}_c$ are the qubit and cavity excitation number operators, defined as $\hat{n}_q = \hat{a}_q^\dagger \hat{a}_q$ and $\hat{n}_c = \hat{a}_c^\dagger \hat{a}_c$, respectively.

Here:

- Δ_q represents the "Lamb shift" of the qubit frequency, caused by the dressing of this nonlinear mode by quantum fluctuations of the fields.
- The anharmonicities of the qubit (α_q) and the cavity (α_c) are parameters that quantify the deviation of their energy levels from harmonic behavior.
- χ_{qc} denotes the qubit-cavity dispersive shift, also referred to as the cross-Kerr coupling.

These Hamiltonian parameters can be calculated directly from the energy-participation ratio (EPR).

$$\alpha_q = \frac{1}{2}\chi_{qq} = \frac{p_q^2 \hbar \omega_q^2}{8E_J}, \quad \alpha_c = \frac{1}{2}\chi_{cc} = \frac{p_c^2 \hbar \omega_c^2}{8E_J} \qquad (6\text{-}14)$$

$$\chi_{qc} = \frac{p_q p_c}{\hbar \omega_q \omega_c} \frac{1}{4E_J} \qquad (6\text{-}15)$$

The energy-participation ratios (EPRs), p_c and p_q, follow certain properties as discussed below:

- **EPR is confined within the range of 0 and 1.**
  The EPR is a fraction of energy, expressed as a real number between zero and one. This is because the Josephson dipole energy is always positive and either equal to or less than the total inductive energy of the mode:

$$0 \leq p_q, p_c \leq 1. \qquad (6\text{-}16)$$

- **The total EPR adheres to a sum rule.**
  The total EPR of a Josephson dipole is conserved and remains exactly unity across all modes, as the energy is distributed between the qubit and the cavity mode:

$$p_q + p_c = 1. \qquad (6\text{-}17)$$

6.1.2 Quantization of the General Josephson System

We now generalize the energy-participation ratio (EPR) calculation of a simple qubit-cavity circuit to a more complex configuration that consists of an arbitrary nonlinear circuit. This configuration is modeled as an enclosed distributed electromagnetic structure, represented as a black box. In the absence of the enclosed nonlinear devices, the electromagnetic circuit can be treated as a linear system. Figure 6-2 provides an understanding of the schematic representation of the Josephson circuit and its nonlinear elements. To elaborate further, these nonlinear devices can be conceptualized as inductive and lumped elements, representing distributed nonlinear components within the circuit.

The most basic form of a nonlinear device consists of just one component, such as a Josephson tunnel junction (see Figure 6-2a), an atomic-point contact, a nanobridge, a semiconductor nanowire, or a similar hybrid structure. On the other hand, a multi-element device consists of a subcircuit comprising purely inductive lumped elements. In such subcircuits, the Josephson junctions are arranged in a loop or in an array structure. Examples of these devices include a SNAIL element (Figure 6-2b), a SQUID (Figure 6-2c), a superinductance, or a junction array (Figure 6-2d). These subcircuits can also be influenced by external controls, such as voltage or flux biases, enabling tunable and dynamic behavior.

The nonlinear device under consideration is termed a **Josephson dipole** and is a lumped, purely inductive subcircuit with two terminals. A defining feature of the Josephson dipole is its characteristic energy function:

$$\mathcal{E}_j(\Phi_j, \Phi_j^{\text{ext}}) = E_J(\Phi_j^{\text{ext}}) \cos\left(\frac{\Phi_j}{\Phi_0}\right), \tag{6-18}$$

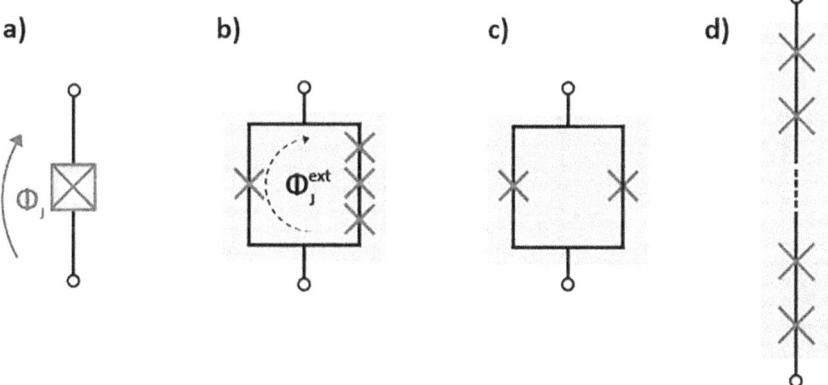

Figure 6-2 Schematic representation of the Josephson circuit and its nonlinear elements. (**a**) A simple example of a Josephson dipole—a Josephson tunnel junction. (**b**) An example of a composite junction, comprising four Josephson junctions in a ring, frustrated by an external magnetic flux Φ_j^{ext} threading the loop

which comprehensively captures all aspects of its composition. Here:

- Φ_j represents the generalized flux across the device terminals.
- E_J is the effective Josephson energy.
- Φ_j^{ext} stands for the external flux bias.

The subscript j indicates the j-th Josephson dipole in the circuit. To simplify notation, parameters such as Φ_j^{ext} will henceforth be implicit.

Figure 6-3 illustrates the general Josephson dipole. Similar to the single-junction transmon, the general Josephson dipole, designated as j, can be conceptually decomposed into its linear and nonlinear constituents as per Equation 6-19:

$$\mathcal{E}_j(\Phi_j) = \mathcal{E}_j^{\text{lin}}(\Phi_j) + \mathcal{E}_j^{\text{nl}}(\Phi_j), \tag{6-19}$$

where the linear contribution is given by

$$\mathcal{E}_j^{\text{lin}}(\Phi_j) = \frac{1}{2} E_j \left(\frac{\Phi_j}{\Phi_0}\right)^2. \tag{6-20}$$

Here, the constant E_j establishes the scale of the junction energy. This energy scale can be equivalently expressed in terms of the linear inductance L_J, given by

$$L_J = \frac{\Phi_0^2}{E_J}, \tag{6-21}$$

which characterizes the Josephson dipole's behavior when experiencing minor perturbations around its equilibrium state.

In the presence of external controls, such as voltage or flux biases, persistent currents arise in the circuit. These currents have the potential to modify the static (dc) equilibrium of the Josephson system. For example, inducing a magnetic flux in

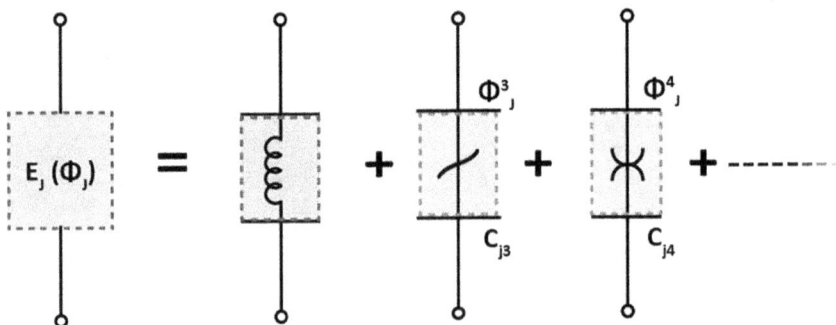

Figure 6-3 Breaking down a general Josephson dipole, symbolized as "j," into its conceptual components

6.1 The EPR Method for Quantization of Superconducting Circuit

a superconducting ring creates a persistent circulating current. In a loop containing a Josephson dipole, the definition of flux Φ_j in Equations 6-19 and 6-20 varies as a function of the equilibrium state. As a result, terms linear in Φ_j are deliberately absent from Equation 6-20.

The potential energy function $\mathcal{E}_j(\Phi_j)$ can be further expressed using a Taylor expansion, breaking it down into a series of nonlinear inductive contributions that increase in order. These contributions are represented by Φ_j^p, with each term having a relative amplitude c_{jp}, where p denotes the position in the series. This energy function can also be influenced by external bias parameters, such as flux or voltage biases.

6.1.2.1 Quantum Hamiltonian of General Josephson System

Having conceptually carved out the nonlinear contributions from the system Hamiltonian $\hat{H}^{\text{full}}$ and collected them into the set of functions $\mathcal{E}_j^{\text{nl}}$, we define the linearized Josephson circuit to correspond to the remaining components. This linear circuit consists of the electromagnetic structure external to the Josephson dipoles, combined with their linear inductances L_J.

We will now use the eigenmodes of the linearized circuit to explicitly construct the full system Hamiltonian, $\hat{H}^{\text{full}}$. The eigenmode frequencies and their corresponding field distributions can be readily obtained using a finite element solver. Linearized Hamiltonian: The Hamiltonian of the linearized Josephson circuit can be expressed as

$$\hat{H}_{\text{lin}} = \sum_{m=1}^{M} \hbar \omega_m \hat{a}_m^\dagger \hat{a}_m, \qquad (6\text{-}22)$$

where

- M is the number of modes addressed by the numerical simulation.
- ω_m is the eigenfrequency of mode m, obtained from the solver.
- $\hat{a}_m$ and $\hat{a}_m^\dagger$ are the annihilation and creation operators, respectively, associated with mode m.

It is important to emphasize that the eigenfrequencies ω_m will be perturbed by the Lamb shifts Δ_m and hence should be regarded as intermediate parameters in the calculation of the remaining nonlinear Hamiltonian. Nonlinear Hamiltonian: The nonlinear Hamiltonian of the system is constructed as

$$\hat{H}_{\text{nl}} = \sum_{j=1}^{J} \mathcal{E}_j^{\text{nl}} = \sum_{j=1}^{J} E_j \sum_{p=1}^{3} c_{jp} \hat{\phi}_p^j, \qquad (6\text{-}23)$$

where

- J is the total number of Josephson junctions.

- c_{jp} are the coefficients corresponding to the nonlinear contributions in the Taylor expansion.
- $\hat{\phi}_j$ is the normalized phase across the jth Josephson dipole.

The normalized phase $\hat{\phi}_j$ is explicitly given by

$$\hat{\phi}_j = \frac{\hat{\Phi}_j}{\phi_0} = \sum_{m=1}^{M} \phi_{mj} \left(\hat{a}_m^\dagger + \hat{a}_m\right), \quad (6\text{-}24)$$

where

- $\hat{\Phi}_j$ is the generalized flux across the j-th dipole.
- ϕ_{mj} represents the contribution of mode m to the phase of dipole j.
- ϕ_0 is the reduced flux quantum.

This formalism provides a rigorous method to quantify the interplay between the linear circuit eigenmodes and the nonlinear contributions arising from the Josephson dipoles. In Equation 6-23, we have expanded the nonlinear energy term $\mathcal{E}_j^{nl}$ using a Taylor series, where the Josephson energy E_J and the expansion coefficients c_{jp} are determined during the fabrication of the Josephson circuit. With the operators $\hat{\phi}_j$ expressed as a linear combination of the mode amplitudes, the full system Hamiltonian $\hat{H}_{\text{full}}$ is now defined. The parameters ϕ_{mj}, which represent the dimensionless quantum zero-point fluctuations of the reduced flux in junction j for mode m, are the key quantities required to complete the Hamiltonian. These parameters can be determined by generalizing the concept of the energy-participation ratio (EPR).

The EPR p_{mj} quantifies the fraction of inductive energy stored in junction j when mode m is excited:

$$p_{mj} = \frac{\text{Energy stored in junction } j}{\text{Energy stored in mode } m}, \quad (6\text{-}25)$$

which extends the definition from Equation 6-3. The EPR is calculated using the field solutions $\mathbf{E}_m(\mathbf{r})$ and $\mathbf{H}_m(\mathbf{r})$. If $p_{mj} = 0$, it indicates that junction j does not contribute to the excitation of mode m. Conversely, if $p_{mj} = 1$, junction j is the only inductive component excited in that mode.

From the EPR values p_{mj}, the variance of the quantum zero-point fluctuations ϕ_{mj} is computed as

$$\phi_{mj}^2 = p_{mj} \frac{\hbar \omega_m}{2 E_j}. \quad (6\text{-}26)$$

This relationship bridges the classical behavior of the linearized Josephson circuit with the quantum description provided by $\hat{H}_{\text{full}}$. The quantum fluctuations

6.1 The EPR Method for Quantization of Superconducting Circuit

ϕ_{mj} are not independent, as the EPRs are subject to several universal constraints that apply to all circuit topologies and types of Josephson dipoles. These constraints are crucial for assessing the performance of different circuit designs and understanding their limitations. The constraints take the form of a sum rule for each junction j and a set of inequalities for each mode m:

$$\sum_{m=1}^{M} p_{mj} = 1 \quad \text{and} \quad 0 \leq \sum_{j=1}^{J} p_{mj} \leq 1. \tag{6-27}$$

The total EPR of a Josephson dipole is independent of the number of modes, always summing to unity across all modes in which the dipole is involved. However, the total EPR for any mode cannot exceed unity. This sum rule is most useful when the total number of relevant modes M matches the total number of modes considered in the system.

Another essential property is the orthogonality of the EPRs. Rewriting equation 6-26 in terms of the fluctuation amplitude, we have

$$\phi_{mj} = s_{mj} \sqrt{\frac{p_{mj} \hbar \omega_m}{2 E_j}}, \tag{6-28}$$

where s_{mj} is the sign associated with the EPR, which can be either $+1$ or -1. The sign s_{mj} encodes the direction of the current across the junction, and only the relative signs between different junctions, s_{mj} and $s_{mj'}$ for $j \neq j'$, carry physical significance. The sign is calculated concurrently with the EPR from the field solutions $\mathbf{H}(\mathbf{r})$.

Finally, the orthogonality condition for the signs of the EPRs is expressed as

$$\sum_{m=1}^{M} s_{mj} s_{mj'} \sqrt{p_{mj} p_{mj'}} = 0, \tag{6-29}$$

which holds when the sum over modes includes all relevant modes of the system.

In summary, the knowledge of the energy-participation ratios fully specifies the nonlinear Hamiltonian $\hat{H}_{nl}$ through the Equations 6-23, 6-24, and 6-26. Once the EPRs are determined, the Hamiltonian can be diagonalized either analytically or numerically using appropriate computational methods.

In the previous sections, we established the theoretical foundation of the energy-participation ratio (EPR) method, a crucial tool for accurately modeling the interaction between linear eigenmodes and the nonlinear contributions in quantum circuits. By quantifying the inductive energy participation of Josephson junctions across various modes, the EPR formalism bridges classical circuit design with quantum Hamiltonian descriptions. In the next sections, we will explore the practical application of EPR analysis in Qiskit Metal, a versatile platform for designing and simulating quantum circuits. We will demonstrate the EPR workflow through a series of examples, including a single transmon qubit, a CPW resonator, and their combined system. Further, we will analyze more complex systems such as coupled transmon qubits and advanced resonator configurations like the double-hanger resonator. These examples will provide a comprehensive understanding of the EPR method's utility in optimizing quantum circuit designs for diverse applications.

6.2 EPR Analysis of Quantum Circuit in Qiskit Metal

In this section, we outline the process of designing, simulating, and analyzing a quantum circuit using Qiskit Metal and PyEPR software. The workflow involves computing energy-participation ratios (EPRs), which quantify the fraction of energy stored in different components of the system, to derive the system's full quantum Hamiltonian, encompassing nonlinearities and couplings. The process is divided into three key steps, as shown in Figure 6-4.

6.2.1 Step 1: Design the Circuit Layout in Qiskit Metal

The first step is to create the circuit layout in the Qiskit Metal GUI. This involves designing the chip's components, such as qubits, coupling elements, pads, and resonators. For the linearized circuit model, Josephson junctions are represented as rectangular linear inductors to simplify the simulation. Qiskit Metal provides an intuitive interface for defining and parameterizing these components, ensuring compatibility with downstream simulations.

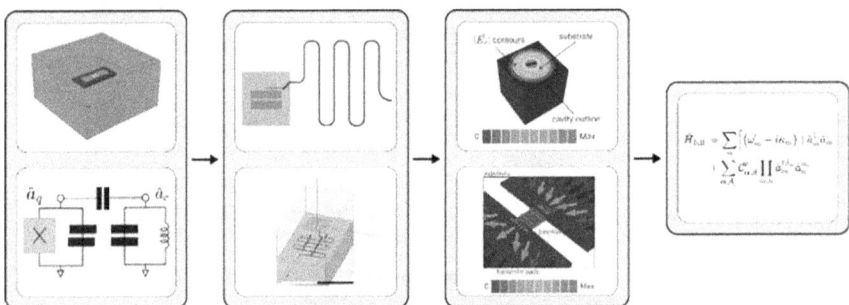

Figure 6-4 Workflow for modeling superconducting qubits in Qiskit Metal, illustrating the three key steps: (1) circuit design, (2) eigenmode analysis, and (3) EPR-based quantum Hamiltonian extraction

6.2.2 Step 2: Perform Eigenmode Analysis in Ansys HFSS

Once the circuit layout is complete, it is rendered in Ansys HFSS for finite element eigenmode analysis. This step begins by setting up boundary conditions, assigning material properties such as substrate permittivity, and defining lumped elements like linear inductors. For efficient memory usage, the circuit is often divided into smaller segments during rendering. The eigenmode analysis provides essential results, including the eigenfrequencies (ω_m) and eigenfield solutions ($E_m(\mathbf{r})$ and $H_m(\mathbf{r})$) of the system.

Using the eigenfield solutions, we extract the energy-participation ratio (p_{mj}) and the sign (s_{mj}) for each mode and nonlinear junction. Convergence plots are generated to verify the accuracy and reliability of the simulation results. Visualizing the fields can also offer valuable insights into the system's electromagnetic behavior.

6.2.3 Step 3: Run EPR Analysis and Construct the Quantum Hamiltonian

The final step involves analyzing the extracted data using the PyEPR library. The participation ratios indicate the fraction of energy stored in each nonlinear junction for the given eigenmodes. This information is used to construct the EPR junction dictionary, which serves as the input for further analysis. The PyEPR module computes the qubit frequencies, anharmonicities, and coupling strengths, ultimately providing the full quantum Hamiltonian of the circuit. The results include key metrics essential for qubit design and optimization.

By following these three steps, we can seamlessly transition from classical electromagnetic simulation to quantum analysis, enabling precise modeling of superconducting qubits and their interactions. The subsequent sections demonstrate this workflow through practical examples, showcasing its application in various quantum circuit configurations.

6.3 EPR Examples in Qiskit Metal

6.3.1 Example of Single Transmon Qubit

This section demonstrates the modeling of a single transmon qubit using Qiskit Metal, providing detailed steps and code snippets for a comprehensive understanding of the workflow. The process includes setting up the qubit design, creating the layout, and positioning components within the chip.

6.3.1.1 Import Required Libraries
Before proceeding, ensure you have the necessary libraries imported in your Jupyter Notebook. These libraries include Qiskit Metal for design and simulation and

PyEPR for energy-participation ratio (EPR) analysis:

```
import qiskit_metal as metal
from qiskit_metal import designs, draw
from qiskit_metal import MetalGUI, Dict, Headings
import pyEPR as epr
```

6.3.1.2 Create a Qubit Design in Qiskit Metal GUI

Set Chip Dimensions Define a chip with dimensions 2 mm × 2 mm, which will also be used for rendering in Ansys.

Add Components Place a single transmon qubit named q1 and a readout resonator at the center of the chip to minimize external effects.

Component Specifications Specify the qubit pad width, pocket height, and the connection pad dimensions.

The following code sets up the design:

```
# Initialize the chip design
design = designs.DesignPlanar({}, True)

# Define chip size
design.chips.main.size['size_x'] = '2mm'
design.chips.main.size['size_y'] = '2mm'

# Open the GUI
gui = MetalGUI(design)

# Import TransmonPocket class and delete previous components
from qiskit_metal.qlibrary.qubits.transmon_pocket import
TransmonPocket
design.delete_all_components()

# Create a transmon qubit
q1 = TransmonPocket(design, 'Q1', options=dict(
    pad_width='425um',
    pocket_height='650um',
    connection_pads=dict(
        readout=dict(loc_W=+1, loc_H=+1, pad_width='200um')
)))

# Rebuild the GUI and adjust view
gui.rebuild()
gui.autoscale()
```

At the end of this step, the graphical user interface (GUI) should display the transmon qubit and its associated readout resonator, as shown in Figure 6-5.

This configuration represents the foundational layout of the quantum circuit, enabling subsequent steps like rendering in Ansys and performing EPR analysis.

6.3 EPR Examples in Qiskit Metal

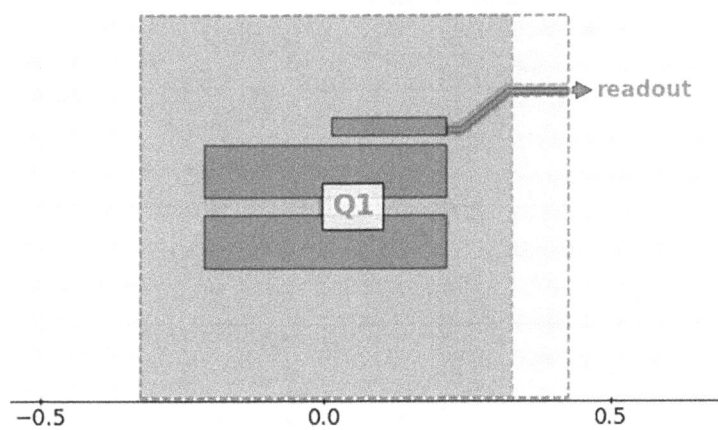

Figure 6-5 Transmon qubit with the readout resonator in the Qiskit Metal GUI

6.3.1.3 Finite Element Eigenmode Analysis

After designing the qubit in Qiskit Metal, the next step involves performing a finite element eigenmode analysis using Ansys HFSS. This process includes rendering the design in HFSS, setting up the analysis, and running simulations to extract key parameters like eigenfrequencies and convergence data.

Setup

To begin, render the Qiskit Metal design in Ansys HFSS with the following commands:

```
hfss.open_ansys()
hfss.add_eigenmode_design("TransmonQubit")
hfss.render_design(['Q1'], [])
```

Executing these commands establishes a connection with Ansys HFSS, creates an eigenmode simulation project named TransmonQubit, and renders the qubit design. Once the design is rendered, you should see a visualization in HFSS similar to Figure 6-6.

Select Analysis Tool

Qiskit Metal allows you to seamlessly interface with external simulation tools for quantum analysis. Here, we use the EPRanalysis tool for quantization. The following commands initialize the analysis:

```
from qiskit_metal.analyses.quantization import EPRanalysis

eig_qb = EPRanalysis(design, "hfss")
```

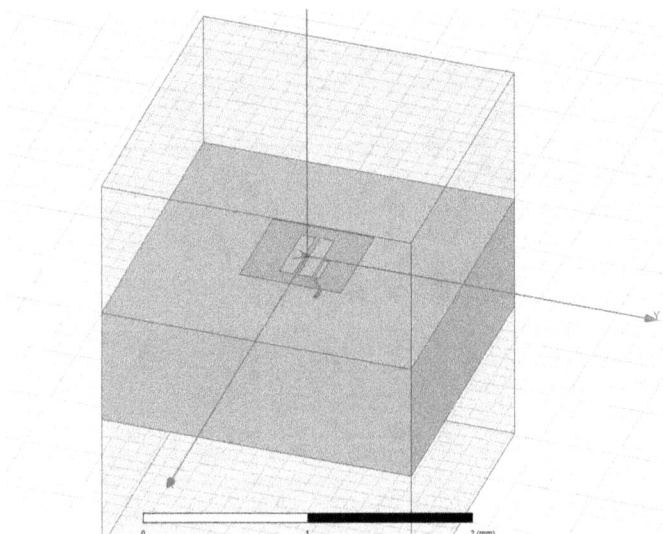

Figure 6-6 Rendered design in HFSS from Qiskit Metal

This command associates the design created in Qiskit Metal with the EPRanalysis module and selects HFSS as the external simulator.

Set Up and Update Simulation Parameters
Next, you need to review and update the simulation parameters for the eigenmode analysis. Convergence settings ensure the accuracy of the computed eigenfrequencies. Use the following code to inspect and modify these settings:

```
# Review the current setup
eig_qb.sim.setup

# Update a single setting
eig_qb.sim.setup.max_passes = 6   # Maximum number of passes
eig_qb.sim.setup.vars.Lj = '11 nH'  # Set junction inductance

# Update multiple settings at once
eig_qb.sim.setup_update(max_delta_f=0.4, min_freq_ghz=1.1)
```

Convergence Criteria

Max Passes Limits the number of simulation passes to balance accuracy and computational cost.

Max Delta f Defines the maximum acceptable difference in eigenfrequency (Δf) between successive passes. Convergence is considered achieved when Δf falls below this value.

Min Frequency Ensures the analyzed eigenfrequencies are above the defined threshold.

The converged eigenfrequency obtained after running the simulation represents the qubit's operating frequency, crucial for subsequent steps in the EPR analysis.

6.3.1.4 Execute Simulation and Verify Convergence and Electromagnetic Fields

In this step, we perform eigenmode simulations for the single transmon qubit with short terminations and examine the convergence of eigenfrequencies. A convergence plot provides insights into the accuracy of the simulation, helping us determine whether the results are reliable. If the frequency fails to converge, you can enhance the renderer's precision by increasing the value of `minpasses`.

For an efficient workflow, the `run()` method integrates both eigenmode and EPR (energy-participation ratio) analyses in a single execution. However, ensure that the EPR analysis setup is properly configured if you choose this approach. The input parameters remain consistent for both simulation methods.

Run the simulation and plot the convergence results using the following commands:

```
eig_qb.sim.run(name="Qbit", components=['Q1'],
open_terminations=[],
box_plus_buffer=False)
eig_qb.sim.plot_convergences()
```

The convergence plot generated by the above commands is shown in Figure 6-7.

Convergence Analysis

The convergence plot illustrates how the eigenfrequency stabilizes as the number of simulation passes increases, approaching an asymptotic value. Similarly, the `delta_freq` (the frequency difference between successive passes) decreases with additional passes, indicating the simulation's progression toward convergence.

The decreasing `delta_freq` signifies diminishing frequency variations between iterations, validating the reliability of the computed eigenfrequencies. Moreover, as the number of passes increases, the finite element mesh becomes finer in regions with rapid field variations, ensuring greater accuracy in the field distribution.

Visualizing the Electromagnetic Fields

The electric field distribution can be visualized using the following commands:

```
eig_qb.sim.plot_fields('main')
eig_qb.sim.save_screenshot()
```

The resulting field plot, shown in Figure 6-8, provides a detailed visualization of the electric field distribution across the qubit structure.

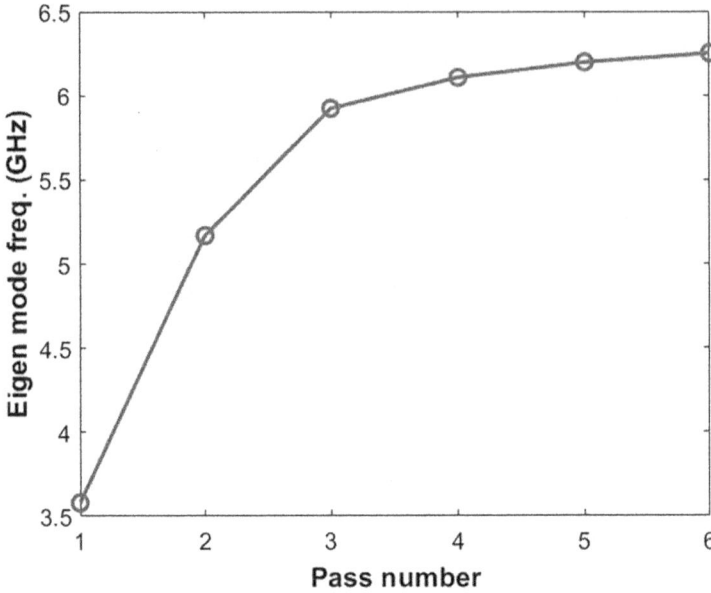

Figure 6-7 Convergence plot of eigenfrequency and delta_freq with respect to the number of passes

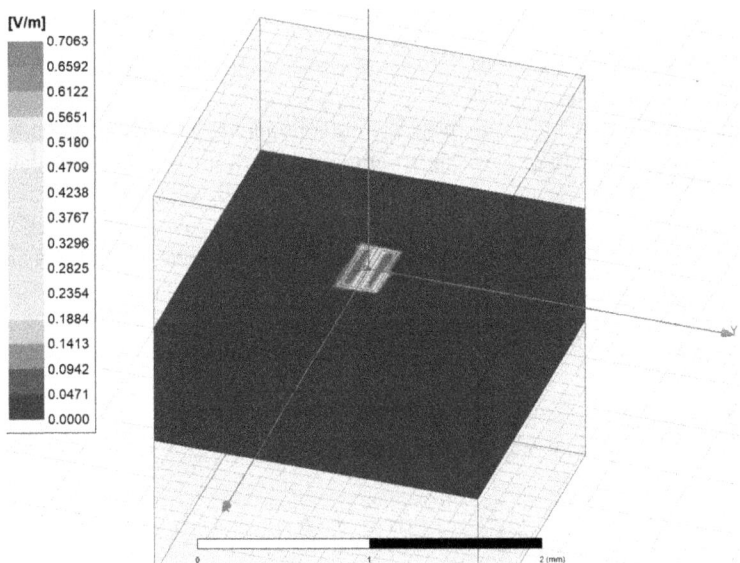

Figure 6-8 Electric field distribution (V/m) of the qubit

Electric Field Insights
In Figure 6-8, the electric field (measured in V/m) is predominantly concentrated near the edges of the metallic structures. This is consistent with the expected behavior, where charge accumulation occurs at sharp edges and corners due to the geometry of the qubit. Understanding the field distribution is essential for accurately modeling qubit performance, as it directly influences parameters such as coupling strengths and anharmonicities.

With the eigenmode analysis and field visualization complete, we now proceed to the EPR analysis of the qubit to extract its quantum properties.

6.3.1.5 EPR Analysis Setup
To perform the EPR (energy-participation ratio) analysis, we need to identify the nonlinear (Josephson) junctions in the model and list these junctions in the EPR setup. Let's begin by viewing the default setup configuration to understand the existing parameters, so we can modify them as needed.

Use the following command to retrieve the default setup:

```
eig_qb.setup
```

Default Output:

```
{'junctions': {'jj': {'Lj_variable': 'Lj',
   'Cj_variable': 'Cj',
   'rect': '',
   'line': ''}},
 'dissipatives': {'dielectrics_bulk': ['main']},
 'cos_trunc': 8,
 'fock_trunc': 7,
 'sweep_variable': 'Lj'}
```

In the output above, we can see the configuration for the Josephson junction (jj). The variables for inductance (Lj) and capacitance (Cj) are defined, but the names for the shapes corresponding to the junction (denoted as rect and line) are currently missing. These names can be identified using the renderer in Qiskit Metal. Once the shapes are located, update the dictionary with the actual names.

For example, update the dictionary as follows:

```
eig_qb.setup.junctions.jj.rect = 'JJ_rect_Lj_Q1_rect_jj'
eig_qb.setup.junctions.jj.line = 'JJ_Lj_Q1_rect_jj_'
eig_qb.setup
```

Updated Output:

```
{'junctions': {'jj': {'Lj_variable': 'Lj',
   'Cj_variable': 'Cj',
   'rect': 'JJ_rect_Lj_Q1_rect_jj',
   'line': 'JJ_Lj_Q1_rect_jj_'}},
 'dissipatives': {'dielectrics_bulk': ['main']},
 'cos_trunc': 8,
 'fock_trunc': 7,
 'sweep_variable': 'Lj'}
```

With the junctions properly defined, we now proceed to calculate the electric and magnetic energy stored in the system, including the substrate of the design. Use the following commands to compute these values:

```
e_elec = eprd.calc_energy_electric()
e_elec_substrate = eprd.calc_energy_electric(None, 'main')
e_mag = eprd.calc_energy_magnetic()

print(f"""
e_elec_all = {e_elec}
e_elec_substrate = {e_elec_substrate}
EPR of the substrate = {e_elec_substrate / e_elec * 100}%
e_mag = {e_mag}
""")
```

Output:

```
e_elec_all = 1.56 × 10^-24
e_elec_substrate = 1.44 × 10^-24
EPR of the substrate = 92.1%
e_mag = 7.94 × 10^-27
```

From the output, we observe that 92.1% of the energy is stored in the substrate. This is primarily due to the high permittivity of the substrate material, which absorbs most of the energy, contributing significantly to dissipation. The remaining energy is stored in the magnetic fields, which is minimal compared to the electric energy in the substrate.

Next, we perform the EPR analysis for all modes and variations to obtain the Hamiltonian of the system. This step helps quantify how the energy is distributed across different components of the system.

Use the following code to perform the EPR analysis and post-analysis:

```
eprd.do_EPR_analysis()
# Perform Hamiltonian spectrum post-analysis
epra = epr.QuantumAnalysis(eprd.data_filename)
epra.analyze_all_variations(cos_trunc=8, fock_trunc=7)

# Report solved results
swp_variable = 'Lj'
epra.plot_hamiltonian_results(swp_variable=swp_variable)
epra.report_results(swp_variable=swp_variable, numeric=True)
```

After executing this code, the final output will provide us with the qubit's frequency and anharmonicity. For this particular design, the dressed frequency of the qubit is calculated to be 6055.64 MHz, with an anharmonicity of 341.09 MHz.

6.3.2 Example of CPW Resonator

6.3.2.1 Create a Design in Qiskit Metal GUI

To analyze a coplanar waveguide (CPW) resonator, we extend the previously created design by connecting the CPW resonator to the transmon qubit. One end of the

CPW resonator connects to the readout pin of the transmon qubit, while the other end terminates with an open-to-ground (OTG) structure. The OTG serves as an open boundary condition, ensuring proper impedance matching and functionality of the resonator.

Below is the code to update the design in Qiskit Metal:

```
from qiskit_metal.qlibrary.terminations.open_to_ground import
OpenToGround
from qiskit_metal.qlibrary.tlines.meandered import RouteMeander

# Add open-to-ground termination
otg = OpenToGround(design, 'open_to_ground', options=dict(
    pos_x='1.75mm',
    pos_y='0um',
    orientation='0'))

# Add meandered CPW resonator
RouteMeander(design, 'readout', Dict(
    total_length='6 mm',
    hfss_wire_bonds=True,
    fillet='90 um',
    lead=dict(start_straight='100um'),
    pin_inputs=Dict(
        start_pin=Dict(component='Q1', pin='readout'),
        end_pin=Dict(component='open_to_ground', pin='open'))
))

# Rebuild and scale the design in GUI
gui.rebuild()
gui.autoscale()
```

In this code:

- RouteMeander is used to create a meandered CPW resonator with a total length of 6 mm and a fillet radius of 90 μm for smooth bends.
- The start pin connects to the transmon qubit's readout pin, and the end pin connects to the open pin of the open-to-ground termination.
- The resonator is configured with hfss_wire_bonds=True to ensure compatibility with HFSS simulation for accurate modeling.

After running the above code, the updated composite system consisting of the transmon qubit and the CPW resonator is displayed in the GUI, as shown in Figure 6-9.

6.3.2.2 Finite Element Eigenmode Analysis

To analyze the CPW resonator independently, we create a dedicated eigenmode analysis focusing on its readout functionality. This analysis includes both the readout component and the open-to-ground termination. While specifying open terminations alone may suffice, explicitly including the open-to-ground termination accelerates system convergence, thereby optimizing simulation efficiency.

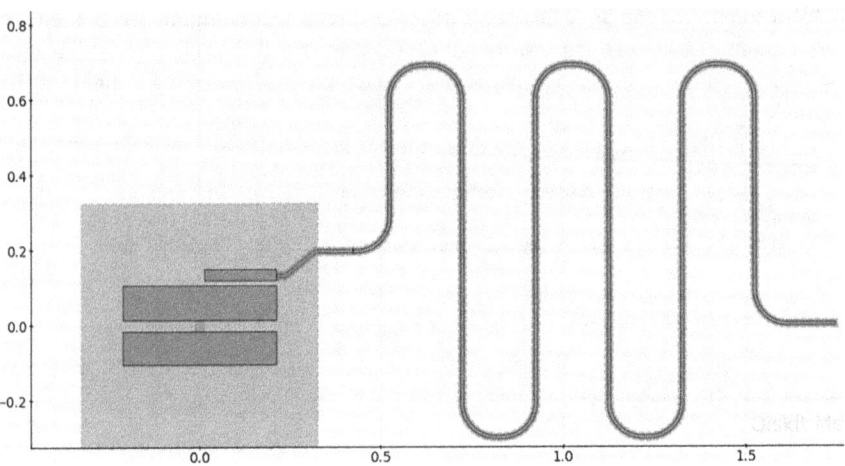

Figure 6-9 Transmon qubit connected to a CPW resonator with an open-to-ground termination

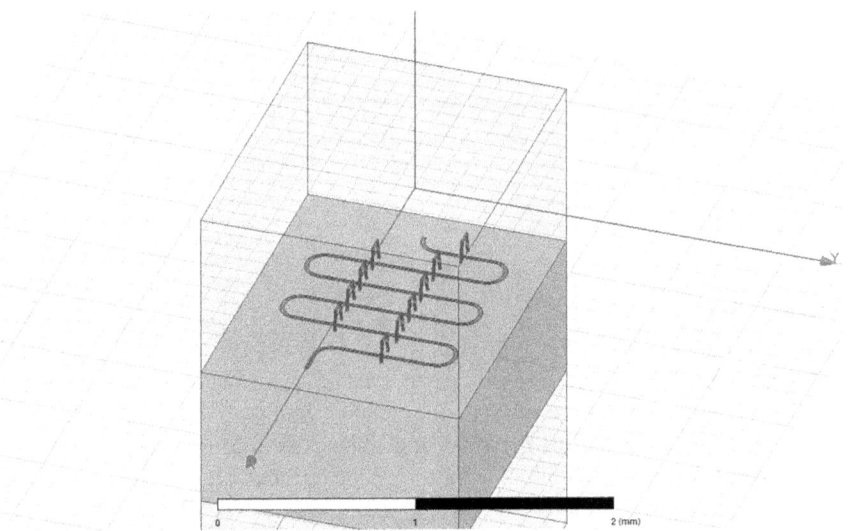

Figure 6-10 Rendered CPW resonator in HFSS with open-to-ground termination

The following code establishes the eigenmode analysis setup in HFSS:

```
hfss.connect_ansys()
hfss.add_eigenmode_design("Readout")
hfss.render_design(['readout', 'open_to_ground'],
                   [('readout', 'start'), ('readout', 'end')])
```

Running the above code renders the CPW resonator in HFSS, as shown in Figure 6-10.

6.3 EPR Examples in Qiskit Metal

The HFSS setup includes default parameters for the resonator. If adjustments are necessary, they can be modified as demonstrated below:

```
# Access and edit analysis properties
setup = hfss.pinfo.setup
setup.passes = 10  # Number of passes
print(f"""
Number of eigenmodes to find = {setup.n_modes}
Number of simulation passes = {setup.passes}
Convergence freq max delta percentage diff = {setup.deltaf}
""")

# Update design variables
pinfo.design.set_variable('Lj', '10nH')  # Josephson inductance
pinfo.design.set_variable('Cj', '0nH')   # Josephson capacitance
(if applicable)

# Run the analysis and plot convergence
setup.analyze()
hfss.plot_convergence()
```

After running the setup, HFSS generates the frequency convergence plots. Next, we extract the eigenmode frequencies and visualize the electric field distribution on the chip's surface:

```
eig_rd.get_frequencies()        # Retrieve eigenmode frequencies
eig_rd.sim.plot_fields('main')  # Plot E-field distribution
eig_rd.sim.save_screenshot()    # Save E-field plot as an image
```

For this design, the eigenmode frequency converges around 9.69 GHz, indicating successful simulation convergence. Figure 6-11 represents the electric field (E-field) plot of the resonator.

6.3.2.3 Refining Convergence and EM Field Analysis

Since the initial analysis showed suboptimal convergence and unclear electromagnetic field distributions, we increased the number of passes to improve results. The updated setup increases the number of passes by five, reruns the simulation, and plots the convergence and E-field distribution:

```
# Update number of passes
setup.passes = 15
setup.analyze()

# Plot convergence and E-field
hfss.plot_convergence()
hfss.plot_ansys_fields('main')
hfss.save.screenshot()
```

Figure 6-12 shows the updated E-field distribution. Compared to the earlier setup, the bright regions have become noticeably smoother, indicating improved convergence. This refinement ensures a more accurate representation of the field distribution in the resonator.

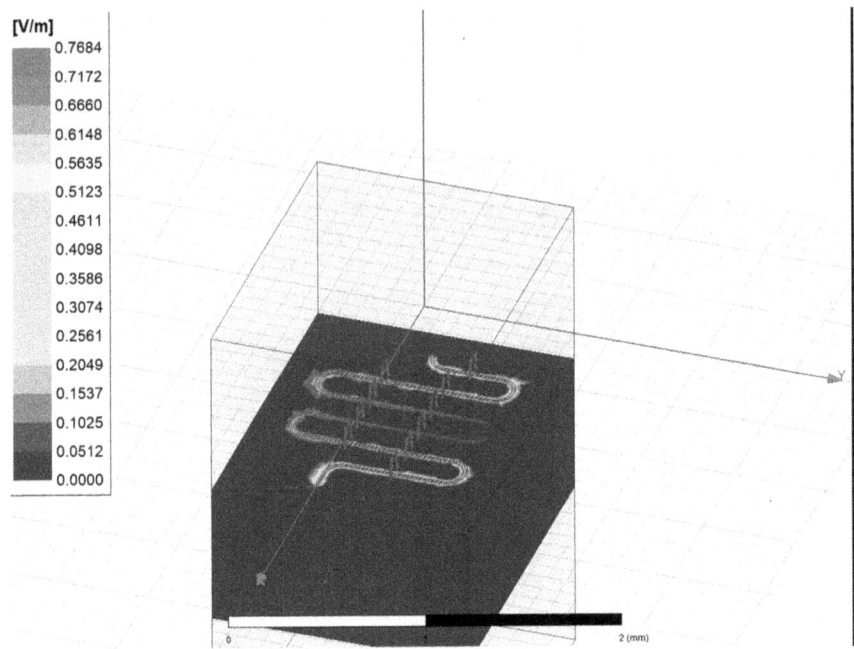

Figure 6-11 E-field plot of the resonator

6.3.2.4 EPR Analysis of the Resonator

Next, we perform EPR analysis on the resonator to determine the electric and magnetic energy distribution in the system. Since this analysis does not involve any junctions, we set the no_junctions parameter to True.

eig_rd.run_epr(no_junctions=True)

Results: The EPR analysis yields the following values.

- **Total electric energy**: $e_{\text{elec\_all}} = 3.546 \times 10^{-24}$ J
- **Electric energy in the substrate**: $e_{\text{elec\_substrate}} = 3.232 \times 10^{-24}$ J
- **Electric energy stored in the substrate**: $\text{EPR}_{\text{substrate}} = 91.2\%$
- **Total magnetic energy**: $e_{\text{mag}} = 3.546 \times 10^{-24}$ J
- **Magnetic energy as a percentage of total electric energy**: 100.0%

The high electric energy stored in the substrate (91.2%) indicates significant energy dissipation, largely due to the substrate's high permittivity.

Having thoroughly modeled and analyzed both the individual transmon qubit and the resonator, we now proceed to study the integrated system comprising the qubit and the resonator. This holistic analysis will provide insights into their coupled behavior and performance metrics.

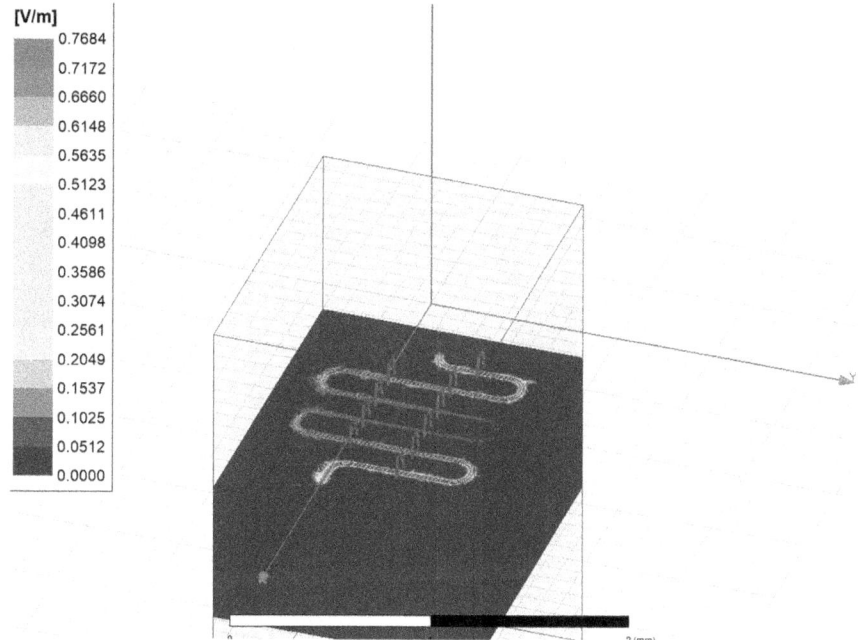

Figure 6-12 E-field plot of the resonator after increasing passes

6.3.3 Example of the Combined System of Transmon Qubit and CPW Resonator

To analyze the combined system of a transmon qubit and a CPW resonator, we first create the design in Qiskit Metal's GUI using the methodology outlined in Section 6.2.2. The combined design, as shown in Figure 6-13, connects one end of the transmon qubit to the CPW resonator, while the other end is terminated with an open-to-ground termination. We then take this design into Ansys HFSS for detailed analysis.

Run the following code to define and render the combined system in HFSS:

```
hfss.connect.ansys()
hfss.add_eigenmode_design("TransmonResonator")
hfss.render_design(['Q1', 'readout', 'open_to_ground'],
[('readout', 'end')])
hfss.save.screenshot()
```

6.3.3.1 Setting Convergence Parameters and Junction Properties

For this combined system, we analyze two eigenmodes:

1. A mode with stronger electric fields near the transmon qubit
2. A mode with stronger electric fields near the CPW resonator

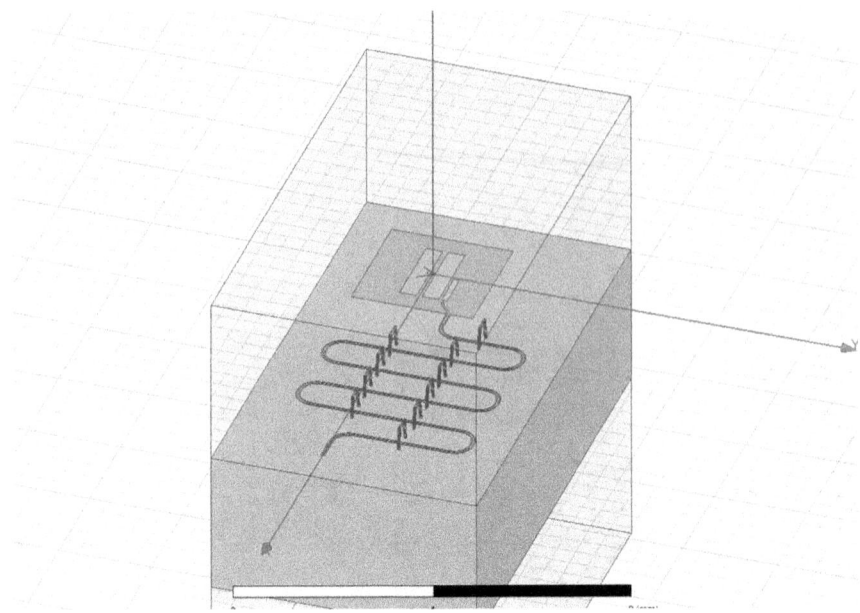

Figure 6-13 Rendered combined design in HFSS

We set up the analysis properties in Ansys HFSS, including the number of eigenmodes, simulation passes, and junction properties:

```
# Set up analysis properties
setup = eig_qres.sim.setup
setup.n_modes = 2
setup.passes = 10
print(f"""
Number of eigenmodes to find          = {setup.n_modes}
Number of simulation passes           = {setup.passes}
Convergence freq max delta percent diff = {setup.delta_f}
""")

# Define junction properties
pinfo = hfss.pinfo
pinfo.design.set_variable('Lj', '10 nH')
pinfo.design.set_variable('Cj', '0 fF')

# Run the analysis and plot convergence
setup.analyze()
eig_qres.sim.plot_convergences()
```

The convergence plot generated will show two converging lines, each corresponding to one of the two modes.

6.3 EPR Examples in Qiskit Metal

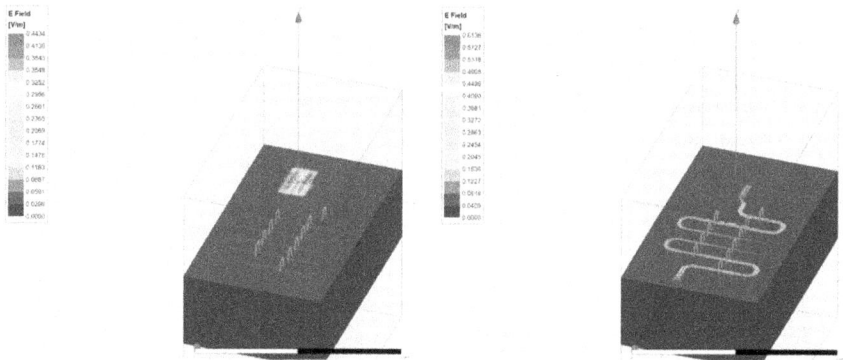

Figure 6-14 E-field plot of the combined system at two different eigenmodes

6.3.3.2 Visualizing the Electric Field Distribution

To visualize the electric field distribution for the eigenmodes on the chip surface, use the following commands:

```
eig_qres.sim.plot_fields('main', eigenmode=1)
eig_qres.sim.save_screenshot()
```

This will generate a plot of the E-field distribution for the first eigenmode as shown in Figure 6-14. The brighter regions in the plot indicate areas of stronger electric fields.

6.3.3.3 Electric Field Distribution for Combined System

The electric field distributions for the two eigenmodes are shown in Figure 6-14. In the first mode, the electric field is highly focused around the transmon, while in the second mode, the concentration shifts predominantly to the resonator. These observations align with the design expectations for the combined system.

6.3.3.4 EPR Analysis of the Combined System

To perform the energy-participation ratio (EPR) analysis, we first identify the junction in the setup. In this example, the junction is labeled as jj. The configuration is updated as follows:

```
eig_qres.setup.junctions.jj.rect = 'JJ_rect_Lj_Q1_rect_jj'
eig_qres.setup.junctions.jj.line = 'JJ_Lj_Q1_rect_jj_'
eig_qres.setup
```

The output configuration confirms the setup details:

```
{'junctions': {'jj': {'Lj_variable': 'Lj',
   'Cj_variable': 'Cj',
   'rect': 'JJ_rect_Lj_Q1_rect_jj',
   'line': 'JJ_Lj_Q1_rect_jj_'}},
 'dissipatives': {'dielectrics_bulk': ['main']},
 'cos_trunc': 8,
```

```
'fock_trunc': 7,
'sweep_variable': 'Lj'}
```

6.3.3.5 Microwave Analysis and Energy Results
Next, we execute the EPR analysis to determine the electric and magnetic energy stored in the substrate and the entire system:

```
eig_qres.run_epr()
```

The output results are as follows:

- Electric energy (total): 7.748×10^{-24} J
- Electric energy (substrate): 7.118×10^{-24} J
- EPR of substrate: 91.9%
- Magnetic energy (total): 6.719×10^{-26} J
- Magnetic energy % of total electric energy: 0.9%

The calculated EPR of the substrate is 91.9%. With a Josephson inductance (L_J) value of 10 nH, the eigenfrequencies of the first and second modes are found to be

- First eigenmode frequency: 5925.63 MHz
- Second eigenmode frequency: 9326.06 MHz

These represent the dressed frequencies of the qubit.

6.3.3.6 Kerr Nonlinear Results
The Kerr nonlinear coefficients obtained from the analysis are presented in Table 6-1.
From Table 6-1:

- Self-Kerr of mode 0 (anharmonicity): 323.51 MHz
- Cross-Kerr coupling between mode 0 and mode 1: 2.29 MHz
- Self-Kerr of the resonator (mode 1): 4.5 kHz

The anharmonicity value (323.51 MHz) characterizes the qubit's nonlinearity, while the cross-Kerr coupling quantifies the interaction strength between the qubit and resonator.

Table 6-1 Self-Kerr and cross-Kerr coefficients

	Mode 0	Mode 1
Mode 0	323.51 MHz	2.29 MHz
Mode 1	2.29 MHz	4.5×10^{-03} MHz

6.3.4 Example of a Combined System of Two Transmon Qubits

In this section, we model a more complex system consisting of two transmon qubits connected via a short coupler. The following code demonstrates how to create this setup using Qiskit Metal:

```
hfss.add_eigenmode_design("TwoTransmon")

from qiskit_metal.qlibrary.qubits.transmon_pocket import
TransmonPocket
from qiskit_metal.qlibrary.tlines.straight_path import
RouteStraight

# Create Transmon Qubit 1 (Q1)
q1 = TransmonPocket(design, 'Q1', options=dict(
    pad_width='425 um',
    pocket_height='650 um',
    connection_pads=dict(
        readout=dict(loc_W=+1, loc_H=+1, pad_width='200 um')
)))

# Create Transmon Qubit 2 (Q2)
q2 = TransmonPocket(design, 'Q2', options=dict(
    pos_x='1.0 mm',
    pad_width='425 um',
    pocket_height='650 um',
    connection_pads=dict(
        readout=dict(loc_W=-1, loc_H=+1, pad_width='200 um')
)))

# Create a coupler between Q1 and Q2 using a straight route
coupler = RouteStraight(design, 'coupler',
Dict(hfss_wire_bonds=True,
    pin_inputs=Dict(
        start_pin=Dict(component='Q1', pin='readout'),
        end_pin=Dict(component='Q2', pin='readout')
)))

# Rebuild and autoscale the GUI
gui.rebuild()
gui.autoscale()
```

This code creates two transmon qubits, Q1 and Q2. The Q1 qubit has a pad width of 425 micrometers and a pocket height of 650 micrometers, while Q2 is positioned 1.0 millimeters along the x-axis and has the same dimensions. The coupler, created using the `RouteStraight` class, connects the readout pads of Q1 and Q2 using a straight path. HFSS wire bonds are enabled for the coupler. The GUI image of the design is shown in Figure 6-15.

6.3.4.1 Defining Junction Inductance and Capacitance
In the default setup, each junction is assigned an inductance, capacitance, and resistance. However, to customize these values, we replace them with variable

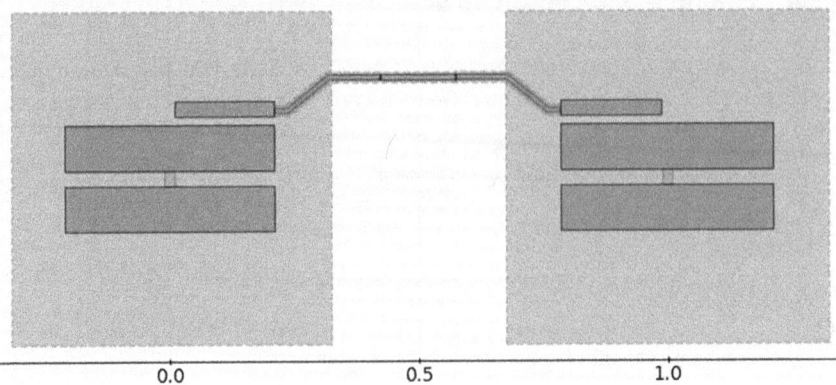

Figure 6-15 GUI design of two transmon qubits coupled by a straight route coupler

names that can be assigned in the renderer. Use the following code to specify the inductance and capacitance for the two transmon junctions:

```
qcomps = design.components   # Short handle (alias)
qcomps['Q1'].options['hfss_inductance'] = 'Lj1'
qcomps['Q1'].options['hfss_capacitance'] = 'Cj1'
qcomps['Q2'].options['hfss_inductance'] = 'Lj2'
qcomps['Q2'].options['hfss_capacitance'] = 'Cj2'
```

6.3.4.2 Eigenmode Analysis Setup

To perform eigenmode analysis, we first create an appropriate analysis object. This can be done by executing the following:

```
from qiskit_metal.analyses.quantization import EPRanalysis
eig_2qb = EPRanalysis(design, "hfss")
```

Next, we modify some of the parameters in the setup. The following code defines the variables for inductance and capacitance that were assigned earlier and increases the accuracy of convergence. We also specify that we are looking for two eigenmodes—one for each transmon qubit junction.

```
# Define setup parameters
setup = eig_2qb.sim.setup
setup.n_modes = 2   # We are looking for two eigenmodes
setup.passes = 15   # Number of simulation passes
setup.convergence_accuracy = 'high'   # Increase accuracy of
convergence

# Assign variable names to junction inductances and capacitances
setup.variables = {
    'Lj1': '10nH',   # Example inductance for Q1
    'Cj1': '0.2fF',  # Example capacitance for Q1
    'Lj2': '10nH',   # Example inductance for Q2
    'Cj2': '0.2fF'   # Example capacitance for Q2
```

```
}

# Perform the analysis
eig_2qb.run()
```

This setup will run the eigenmode analysis for two transmon qubits connected via a short coupler, and the accuracy of the simulation will be improved with more simulation passes and convergence settings.

6.3.4.3 Eigenmode Analysis Setup with Buffer Adjustment

In this section, we modify the eigenmode analysis setup to improve convergence and customize the buffer size around the qubit components.

The following code sets up the eigenmode analysis for the two transmon qubits and their coupler:

```
setup.hfss.pinfo_setupeig_2qb.sim.setup.max_passes = 15
eig_2qb.sim.setup.max_delta_f = 0.05
eig_2qb.sim.setup.n_modes = 2
eig_2qb.sim.setup.vars = Dict(Lj1= '13 nH', Cj1= '0 fF',
                              Lj2= '9 nH', Cj2= '0 fF')
eig_2qb.sim.setup
```

Output:

```
{'name': 'Setup',
 'reuse_selected_design': True,
 'min_freq_ghz': 1,
 'n_modes': 2,
 'max_delta_f': 0.05,
 'max_passes': 15,
 'min_passes': 1,
 'min_converged': 1,
 'pct_refinement': 30,
 'basis_order': 1,
 'vars': {'Lj1': '13 nH', 'Cj1': '0 fF', 'Lj2': '9 nH', 'Cj2':
 '0 fF'}}
```

By default, the analysis considers all components listed in the run_sim() method. To specify how much of the ground plane around the qubit should be considered, the bux_plus_buffer parameter can be used. When this parameter is omitted, the ground plane is assumed to be as large as the minimum enclosing rectangle plus a default buffer of 200 μm.

To modify the default buffer size, we can use the following code. In this example, we increase the default buffer value from 200 to 500 μm:

```
# TODO: fold this inside either an analysis class method or
inside the
analysis class setup

eig_2qb.sim.renderer.options['x_buffer_width_mm'] = 0.5
eig_2qb.sim.renderer.options['y_buffer_width_mm'] = 0.5
eig_2qb.sim.renderer.options
```

Output:

```
{'Lj': '10nH',
 'Cj': 0,
 '_Rj': 0,
 'max_mesh_length_jj': '7um',
 'project_path': None,
 'project_name': None,
 'design_name': None,
 'x_buffer_width_mm': 0.5,
 'y_buffer_width_mm': 0.5,
 'wb_threshold': '400um',
 'wb_offset': '0um',
 'wb_size': 5,
 'plot_ansys_fields_options': {'name': 'NAME:Mag_E1',
  'UserSpecifyName': '0',
  'UserSpecifyFolder': '0',
  'QuantityName': 'Mag_E',
  'PlotFolder': 'E Field',
  'StreamlinePlot': 'False',
  'AdjacentSidePlot': 'False',
  'FullModelPlot': 'False',
  'IntrinsicVar': "Phase='0deg'",
  'PlotGeomInfo_0': '1',
  'PlotGeomInfo_1': 'Surface',
  'PlotGeomInfo_2': 'FacesList',
  'PlotGeomInfo_3': '1'}}
```

Now that the buffer size has been adjusted, we can proceed with the simulation by running the following command to observe the convergence:

```
eig_2qb.sim.run(name="TwoTransmons",
                components=['coupler', 'Q1', 'Q2'])
```

Let's observe the E-field on the chip's surface for the HFSS rendered design displayed in Figure 6-16. Since we have analyzed two modes, we need to select the mode to visualize. The default mode is set to 1, but any integer between 1 and `setup.n_modes` can be used as the mode parameter.

```
eig_2qb.sim.plot_fields('main', eigenmode=2)
eig_2qb.sim.save_screenshot()
```

In Figure 6-17, we are not able to observe the resonance. Turn on the log scale to visualize it.

Now, we will set up the EPR analysis. First, identify the two nonlinear models in the junction. In this case, we have two junctions, which we will refer to as "jj1"

6.3 EPR Examples in Qiskit Metal

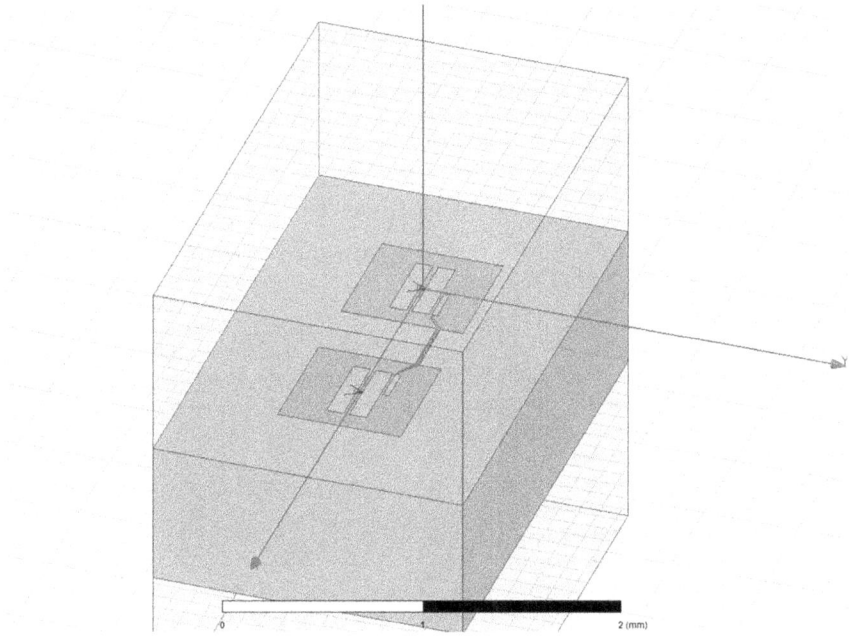

Figure 6-16 Two transmon designs rendered in HFSS

and "jj2." We are also defining the dissipative reference shapes by executing the following code:

```
eig_2qb.setup.junctions.jj1 = Dict(rect='JJ_rect_Lj_Q1_rect_jj',
line='JJ_Lj_Q1_rect_jj_',
                Lj_variable='Lj1', Cj_variable='Cj1')
eig_2qb.setup.junctions.jj2 = Dict(rect='JJ_rect_Lj_Q2_rect_jj',
line='JJ_Lj_Q2_rect_jj_',
                Lj_variable='Lj2', Cj_variable='Cj2')
eig_2qb.setup.sweep_variable = 'Lj1'
eig_2qb.setup

eig_2qb.run_epr()
```

Output:

```
{'junctions': {'jj1': {'rect': 'JJ_rect_Lj_Q1_rect_jj',
   'line': 'JJ_Lj_Q1_rect_jj_',
   'Lj_variable': 'Lj1',
   'Cj_variable': 'Cj1'},
  'jj2': {'rect': 'JJ_rect_Lj_Q2_rect_jj',
   'line': 'JJ_Lj_Q2_rect_jj_',
   'Lj_variable': 'Lj2',
   'Cj_variable': 'Cj2'}},
 'dissipatives': {'dielectrics_bulk': ['main']},
 'cos_trunc': 8,
```

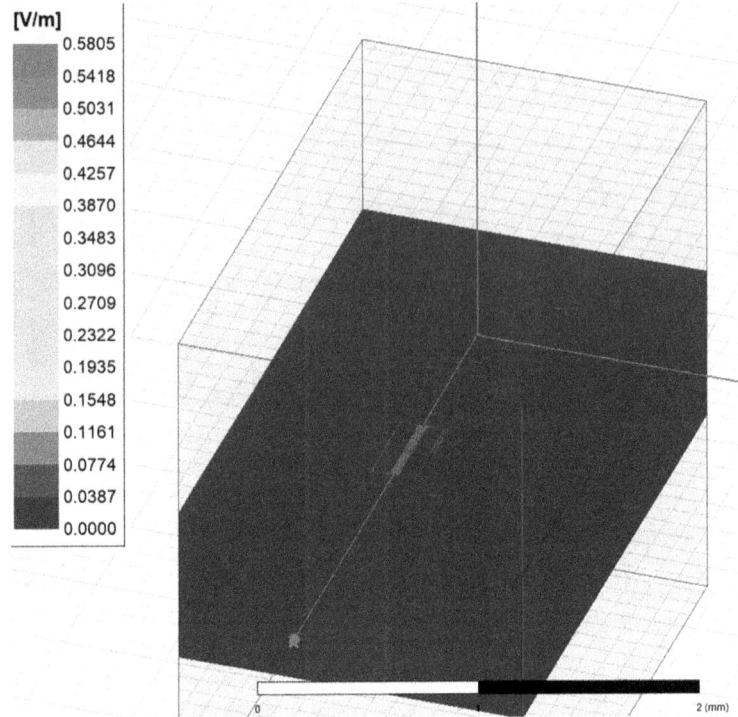

Figure 6-17 E-field on the chip's surface for the second eigenmode

```
'fock_trunc': 7,
'sweep_variable': 'Lj1'}
```

The energy and EPR analysis results are

```
energy_elec_all = 2.01926030136048 × 10^-25
energy_elec_substrate = 1.86157115120032 × 10^-25
EPR of substrate = 92.2%

energy_mag = 1.19184318501109 × 10^-25
energy_mag % of energy_elec_all = 0.6%
```

The code determines the EPR of the substrate to be 92.2%. With a Josephson inductance (L_J) value set to 13nH, the first eigenmode exhibits a frequency of 5316.63 MHz, while the second eigenmode resonates at a frequency of 6455.12 MHz. The Kerr nonlinear coefficient table is presented below.

The Table 6-2 provides the values of self-Kerr and cross-Kerr coefficients. The self-Kerr coefficients for the two transmons, where mode 0 couples to mode 0 and mode 1 couples to mode 1, are 353.30 MHz and 344.23 MHz, respectively. The dispersive cross-Kerr coupling between mode 0 and mode 1 is 1.04 MHz.

Table 6-2 Self-Kerr and cross-Kerr coefficients

	Mode 0	Mode 1
Mode 0	353.30 MHz	1.04 MHz
Mode 1	1.04 MHz	344.23 MHz

6.3.5 Double-Hanger Resonator (S Param)

This section discusses a simulation and analysis for a double-hanger resonator system with two transmon qubits. The geometry design comprises transmon qubits positioned on a chip, connected to hangers via meandered CPWs. The hangers are further connected to an open-to-ground structure at each end through a long horizontal CPW.

To create a layout for the above geometry design in GUI, we write a Python code with the main chip size set to 2 mm × 2 mm:

```
design = designs.DesignPlanar({}, True)
design.chips.main.size['size_x'] = '2mm'
design.chips.main.size['size_y'] = '2mm'

gui = MetalGUI(design)

from qiskit_metal.qlibrary.couplers.coupled_line_tee import
CoupledLineTee
from qiskit_metal.qlibrary.tlines.meandered import RouteMeander
from qiskit_metal.qlibrary.qubits.transmon_pocket import
TransmonPocket
from qiskit_metal.qlibrary.tlines.straight_path import
RouteStraight
from qiskit_metal.qlibrary.terminations.open_to_ground import
OpenToGround
```

Two transmon qubits, named Q1 and Q2, are positioned on the chip. Two hangers, TQ1 and TQ2, consisting of capacitively coupled transmission lines, are added to connect to the transmons.

```
options = dict(
    # Some options we want to modify from the deafults
    # (see below for defaults)
    pad_width = '425 um',
    pocket_height = '650um',
    # Adding 4 connectors (see below for defaults)
    connection_pads=dict(
        a = dict(loc_W=+1,loc_H=+1),
        b = dict(loc_W=-1,loc_H=+1, pad_height='30um'),
        c = dict(loc_W=+1,loc_H=-1, pad_width='200um'),
        d = dict(loc_W=-1,loc_H=-1, pad_height='50um')
    )
)

## Create 2 transmons
q1 = TransmonPocket(design, 'Q1', options = dict(
```

```
        pos_x='+1.4mm', pos_y='0mm', orientation = '90', **options))
q2 = TransmonPocket(design, 'Q2', options = dict(
        pos_x='-0.6mm', pos_y='0mm', orientation = '90', **options))

TQ1 = CoupledLineTee(design, 'TQ1', options=dict(pos_x='1mm',
                                                 pos_y='3mm',
                                                 coupling_length=
                                                 '200um'))
TQ2 = CoupledLineTee(design, 'TQ2', options=dict(pos_x='-1mm',
                                                 pos_y='3mm',
                                                 coupling_length=
                                                 '200um'))

gui.rebuild()
gui.autoscale()
```

We use two meandered coplanar waveguides (CPWs), meanderQ1 and meanderQ2, to connect the transmons to the respective hangers.

```
ops=dict(fillet='90um')
design.overwrite_enabled = True

options1 = Dict(
    total_length='8mm',
    hfss_wire_bonds = True,
    pin_inputs=Dict(
        start_pin=Dict(
            component='TQ1',
            pin='second_end'),
        end_pin=Dict(
            component='Q1',
            pin='a')),
    lead=Dict(
        start_straight='0.1mm'),
    **ops
)

options2 = Dict(
    total_length='9mm',
    hfss_wire_bonds = True,
    pin_inputs=Dict(
        start_pin=Dict(
            component='TQ2',
            pin='second_end'),
        end_pin=Dict(
            component='Q2',
            pin='a')),
    lead=Dict(
        start_straight='0.1mm'),
    **ops
)

meanderQ1 = RouteMeander(design, 'meanderQ1', options=options1)
meanderQ2 = RouteMeander(design, 'meanderQ2', options=options2)
```

6.3 EPR Examples in Qiskit Metal

```
gui.rebuild()
gui.autoscale()
```

Two open-to-ground structures, otg1 and otg2, are added at the ends of the horizontal CPW to provide grounding.

```
otg1 = OpenToGround(design, 'otg1', options = dict(pos_x='3mm',
                                                   pos_y='3mm'))
otg2 = OpenToGround(design, 'otg2', options = dict(pos_x = '-3mm',
                                                   pos_y='3mm',
                                                   orientation='180'))

gui.rebuild()
gui.autoscale()
```

A long horizontal CPW is formed by three straight CPWs—cpw_openRight, cpw_middle, and cpw_openLeft—connecting the transmons to the open-to-ground structures.

```
        ops_oR = Dict(hfss_wire_bonds = True,
                  pin_inputs=Dict(
                      start_pin=Dict(
                          component='TQ1',
                          pin='prime_end'),
                      end_pin=Dict(
                          component='otg1',
                          pin='open')))
       ops_mid = Dict(hfss_wire_bonds = True,
                  pin_inputs=Dict(
                      start_pin=Dict(
                          component='TQ1',
                          pin='prime_start'),
                      end_pin=Dict(
                          component='TQ2',
                          pin='prime_end')))
        ops_oL = Dict(hfss_wire_bonds = True,
                  pin_inputs=Dict(
                      start_pin=Dict(
                          component='TQ2',
                          pin='prime_start'),
                      end_pin=Dict(
                          component='otg2',
                          pin='open')))
cpw_openRight = RouteStraight(design, 'cpw_openRight',
options=ops_oR)
cpw_middle = RouteStraight(design, 'cpw_middle',
options=ops_mid)
cpw_openLeft = RouteStraight(design, 'cpw_openLeft',
options=ops_oL)

gui.rebuild()
gui.autoscale()
```

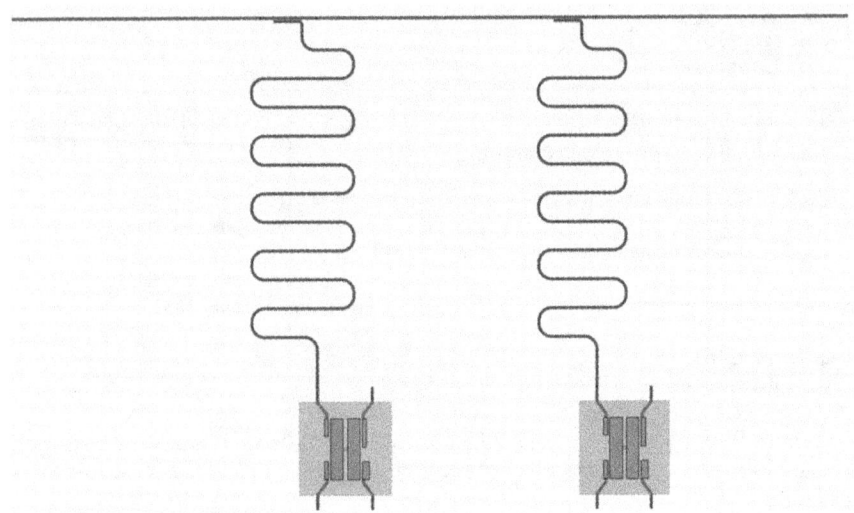

Figure 6-18 GUI design of the double-hanger resonator

The above code should give us the design as shown in Figure 6-18.

6.3.5.1 Setup
We select the intended analysis to run from the qiskit_metal.analyses.simulation collection. We also select the design to analyze and the tool to use for any external simulation.

```
from qiskit_metal.analyses.simulation.scattering_impedance import
ScatteringImpedanceSim
em1 = ScatteringImpedanceSim(design, "hfss")
```

For the DrivenModal simulation, we can use either of the methods mentioned below:

- Employ the user-friendly methods of em1.
- Directly control the simulation tool from the tool's GUI.
- Utilize the renderer method for simulation.

Here, we discuss the third method for this case.

6.3.5.2 Execute Simulation and Verify Convergence
We use the renderer from the analysis class to connect the design in HFSS. Now, we create and activate an eigenmode design called "HangingResonators." We also need to set the buffer width at the edge of the design to be 0.5 mm in both directions.

6.3 EPR Examples in Qiskit Metal

Execute the following commands to complete the above tasks:

```
hfss = em1.renderer
hfss.start()
hfss.activate_ansys_design("HangingResonators", 'drivenmodal')
hfss.options['x_buffer_width_mm'] = 0.5
hfss.options['y_buffer_width_mm'] = 0.5
```

6.3.5.3 Execute Simulation and Observe the Impedance

We now render the design from metal GUI to HFSS executing the code below. We assign lumped ports on the two CPW terminations. Here, pins cpw_openRight_end and cpw_openLeft_end are converted into lumped ports with an impedance of 50 Ohms. For this simulation, we don't render the junctions Q1 and Q2. There are a total of five parameters used in the rendering. The arguments in the code are given as

- The first parameter includes a list of all components to render.
- The second parameter consists of a list of pins (qcomp, pin) with open endcaps.
- The third parameter comprises a list of pins (qcomp, pin, impedance) intended for rendering as lumped ports.
- The fourth parameter has a list of junctions (qcomp, elt, impedance, draw_ind) to render as a lumped port.
- The fifth parameter consists of a list of junctions (qcomp, elt) intended to be completely excluded during rendering.

```
hfss.render_design(selection=[],
                   open_pins=[],
                   port_list=[('cpw_openRight', 'end', 50),
                   ('cpw_openLeft', 'end', 50)],
                   jj_to_port=[],
                   ignored_jjs=[('Q1', 'rect_jj'), ('Q2',
                   'rect_jj')],
                   box_plus_buffer = True)
hfss.save_screenshot()
```

The above code gives us the rendered image as presented in Figure 6-19.

To observe the impedance, admittance, and scattering matrices, we create a frequency sweep:

```
hfss.add_sweep(setup_name="Setup",
               name="Sweep",
               start_ghz=4.0,
               stop_ghz=8.0,
               count=2001,
               type="Interpolating")

hfss.analyze_sweep('Sweep', 'Setup')
```

In the next step, we plot the scattering (S), admittance (Y), and impedance (Z) parameters as a function of frequency. The interpolation type sweep starts from 4 GHz and ends at 8 GHz with a 2001 number of steps between them.

6 Energy-Participation Ratio Method for Quantization and Analysis

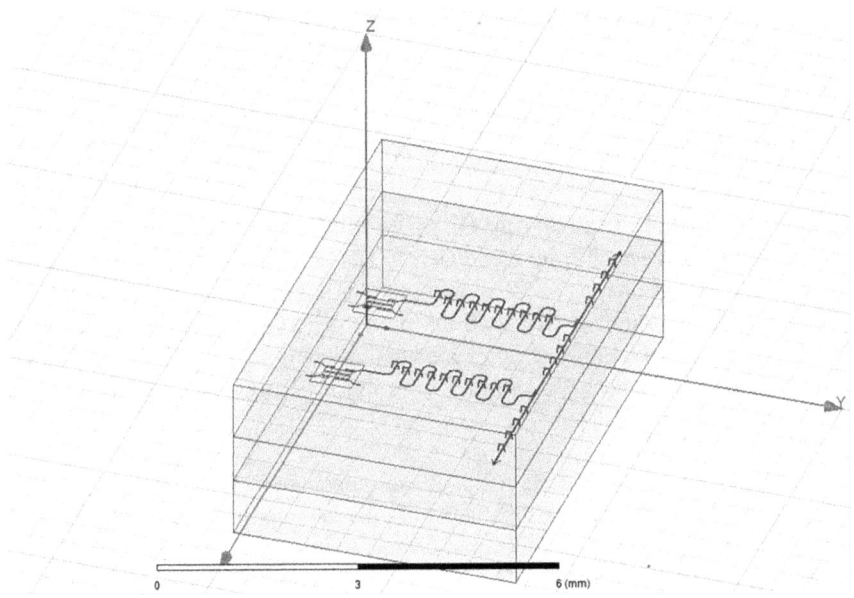

Figure 6-19 Rendered simulation of the double-hanger resonator

```
hfss.plot_params(['S11', 'S21'])
hfss.plot_params(['Y11', 'Y21'])
hfss.plot_params(['Z11', 'Z21'])
```

The results of the above code:

	S_{11}	S_{21}
4.000	$-0.143617 - 0.041106j$	$-0.276574 + 0.949311j$
4.002	$-0.143666 - 0.041021j$	$-0.275970 + 0.949483j$
4.004	$-0.143716 - 0.040936j$	$-0.275366 + 0.949654j$
4.006	$-0.143765 - 0.040851j$	$-0.274762 + 0.949826j$
4.008	$-0.143814 - 0.040765j$	$-0.274157 + 0.949997j$
⋮	⋮	⋮
7.992	$-0.037350 + 0.059355j$	$0.834663 + 0.546278j$
7.994	$-0.037260 + 0.059299j$	$0.835022 + 0.545741j$
7.996	$-0.037170 + 0.059244j$	$0.835381 + 0.545204j$
7.998	$-0.037080 + 0.059189j$	$0.835739 + 0.544667j$
8.000	$-0.036990 + 0.059133j$	$0.836097 + 0.544129j$

At the completion, we can disconnect from Ansys using the em1.close() command.

	Y_{11}	Y_{21}
4.000	$-0.000000 - 0.006918j$	$-0.000000 - 0.024393j$
4.002	$0.000000 - 0.006902j$	$0.000000 - 0.024388j$
4.004	$0.000000 - 0.006885j$	$0.000000 - 0.024384j$
4.006	$0.000000 - 0.006869j$	$0.000000 - 0.024379j$
4.008	$0.000000 - 0.006853j$	$0.000000 - 0.024374j$
⋮	⋮	⋮
7.992	$0.000000 + 0.034993j$	$-0.000000 - 0.041781j$
7.994	$0.000000 + 0.035040j$	$-0.000000 - 0.041820j$
7.996	$0.000000 + 0.035088j$	$-0.000000 - 0.041860j$
7.998	$0.000000 + 0.035136j$	$-0.000000 - 0.041900j$
8.000	$0.000000 + 0.035184j$	$0.000000 - 0.041939j$

	Z_{11}	Z_{21}
4.000	$-0.000000 - 12.573899j$	$0.000000 + 44.561044j$
4.002	$0.000000 - 12.544109j$	$0.000004 + 44.552788j$
4.004	$0.000001 - 12.514329j$	$0.000007 + 44.544553j$
4.006	$0.000001 - 12.484561j$	$0.000011 + 44.536341j$
4.008	$0.000002 - 12.454803j$	$0.000015 + 44.528149j$
⋮	⋮	⋮
7.992	$-0.000049 + 67.825480j$	$-0.000052 + 80.740443j$
7.994	$-0.000037 + 67.924162j$	$-0.000039 + 80.824275j$
7.996	$-0.000025 + 68.023050j$	$-0.000026 + 80.908315j$
7.998	$-0.000012 + 68.122145j$	$-0.000013 + 80.992565j$
8.000	$0.000000 + 68.221447j$	$0.000000 + 81.077025j$

6.4 Conclusion

The energy-participation ratio (EPR) method offers a robust framework for quantizing and analyzing superconducting circuits by accurately capturing the distribution of electromagnetic energy in quantum systems. This chapter provided a comprehensive overview of the EPR method, starting with the quantization of simple and general Josephson systems. It explored the integration of the EPR approach in Qiskit Metal, showcasing its versatility and practicality for circuit design and analysis. Through detailed examples—including single transmon qubits, CPW resonators, combined systems of qubits and resonators, and double-hanger resonators—the chapter illustrated the method's ability to extract key quantum parameters like eigenfrequencies, anharmonicities, and coupling coefficients. These insights establish the EPR method as a valuable tool for optimizing superconducting quantum circuits, paving the way for advances in quantum information processing and circuit design methodologies.

7 Modelling the Hamiltonian Transmon Qubit Cooper Pair Box in the Charge Basis

In the preceding chapters, we studied the properties of the transmon qubit and its quantization using various methods. In this chapter, we will discuss the post-quantization analysis of transmon qubit properties in the Cooper pair charge basis using the Hcpb (Hamiltonian Cooper pair box) class of qiskit-metal.

In the first section of the chapter, we carry out a theoretical discussion of transmon qubit properties in connection with the Cooper pair box. We observe that these properties have a crucial dependence on the E_j/E_c ratio (Josephson energy/charging energy ratio). We can analyze the dependence of several properties on E_j/E_c and decide a working regime of E_j/E_c for the optimum performance of the Transmon qubit. In the next section, we discuss the Hcpb class and its commands that can be used to solve the Hamiltonian of CPB and extract properties from it such as energy values (eigenvalues), wave function (eigenvectors), transition energies, anharmonicities, and dephasing time.

In Section 7.3, we systematically analyze the energy levels and wave functions of the transmon qubit, breaking down the modeling process into clear, step-by-step stages. To ensure reliable qubit operations, it is crucial to maintain sufficiently large anharmonicity, preventing unintended excitations to higher energy states. The charge dispersion characterizes how the qubit's energy levels vary with environmental offset charges and gate voltage, directly influencing the qubit's susceptibility to charge noise. Lower charge dispersion results in reduced frequency fluctuations due to gate charge variations. Both anharmonicity and charge dispersion are inherently tied to the ratio of E_j/E_c. In Section 8.4, we calculate charge dispersion and anharmonicity as a function of the E_j/E_c ratio and find the optimal range of the ratio for the transmon qubit operation. This task enables us to decide the physics properties of transmon such as E_j and E_c to get sufficient anharmonicity and reduced charge noise sensitivity when compared to conventional CPB. In this section, we also investigate charge-limited dephasing time T_2 as a function of E_j/E_c. The next sections of the chapter discuss Qutip simulation and back-calculation of physics properties.

7.1 Cooper Pair Box to Transmon Qubit

The transition from the charge qubit, known as the Cooper pair box (CPB), to the transmon qubit represents a significant advancement in superconducting qubit technology. The CPB qubit, while innovative, is highly sensitive to charge noise due to its strong dependence on environmental offset charges and gate voltages. This sensitivity limits its practical application, as charge noise causes fluctuations in qubit frequencies, thereby reducing coherence times. Although operating the CPB at "sweet spots" can mitigate linear noise sensitivity, higher-order effects of $1/f$ charge noise and quasiparticle poisoning still present challenges.

To address these limitations, the transmon qubit was introduced, leveraging a critical property of the Josephson energy-to-charging energy ratio E_J/E_C. In the transmon, this ratio is significantly increased compared to the CPB. This design choice leads to an exponential suppression of charge dispersion, thereby reducing the charge noise sensitivity of the qubit, while the anharmonicity decreases only algebraically. This trade-off is advantageous, as it minimizes charge noise effects without excessively compromising the anharmonicity needed for distinct qubit energy levels.

The circuit diagram of the Transmon qubit is presented in Figure 7-1. The transmon qubit is an extension of the traditional Cooper pair box design, and it consists of two superconducting islands coupled through two Josephson junctions, but isolated from the rest of the circuitry.

The DC-SQUID configuration enables the tuning of the Josephson energy through an external magnetic flux. The key difference between the transmon and the Cooper pair box (CPB) is the addition of a large shunt capacitance C_B between the two superconductors, along with a corresponding increase in the gate capacitance C_g.

The effective Hamiltonian can be simplified to match the form of the Cooper pair box (CPB) system, as expressed in Equation 2-59. In the transmon case, the

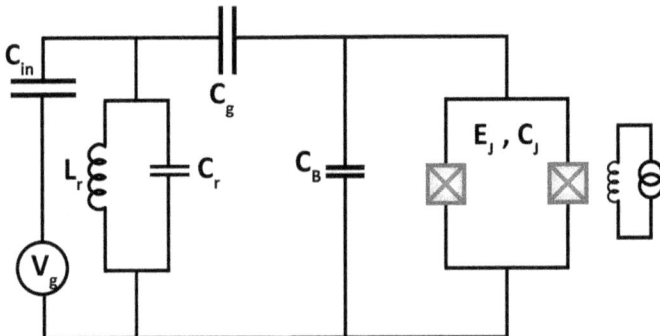

Figure 7-1 Circuit diagram of a Transmon qubit: two Josephson junctions with capacitance C_J and Josephson energy E_J, shunted by a large capacitance C_B and coupled via a gate capacitance C_g

charging energy, offset charge, and Josephson energy can be specified as follows:

$$E_C = \frac{e^2}{2C_\Sigma}, \quad n_g = -\frac{C_d \Phi_s(t)}{2e}, \quad E_j = \frac{\phi_0^2}{L_J} \tag{7-1}$$

Here, $C_\Sigma = C_J + C_B + C_g$. By introducing additional capacitance, the charging energy can be made significantly smaller than the Josephson energy. Unlike the CPB, the transmon operates in the $E_j \gg E_c$ regime.

7.2 Hamiltonian Model Cooper Pair Box (Hcpb) Class

The Hcpb class provides a fast and efficient way to model the Cooper pair box (CPB) Hamiltonian using a matrix-based approach. Using this class, the tridiagonal eigenvalue problem is solved on a charge basis. This class requires the user to input four arguments: E_J, E_C, n_g, and levels.

The Hcpb class can be called using the commnad below:

```
H = Hcpb(nlevels(int), Ej(float), Ec(float),
ng(float))}
```

This class requires four key input parameters:

- **nlevels (int)**: This parameter specifies the number of charge states considered for the CPB. The states are defined symmetrically around zero, ranging from $-$ nlevels to nlevels $+$ 1.
- **Ej (float)**: Represents the Josephson energy of the Josephson junction (JJ), which quantifies the energy associated with the tunneling of Cooper pairs across the junction.
- **Ec (float)**: Denotes the charging energy of the CPB, which arises due to the Coulomb repulsion of excess Cooper pairs on the island.
- **ng (float)**: Stands for the offset charge of the CPB and is expressed in units of Cooper pairs (2e). It typically varies between -0.5 and 0.5, with ng $= 0.5$ being referred to as the sweet spot, where the qubit is less sensitive to charge noise.

The following are the commands from this class that can be used to compute different properties:

1. **Hcpb.anharm()**: Compute the anharmonicity of the CPB.
   Function: Returns the anharmonicity defined as $E_{12} - E_{01}$.
   Return Type: float
2. **Hcpb.evalue_k(k)**: Return the eigenvalue of the Hamiltonian for level k.
   Parameters: k (int)—Index of the eigenvalue.
   Function: Provides the eigenvalue of the CPB Hamiltonian for the specified level.
   Return Type: float

3. **Hcpb.evec_k(k)**: Return the eigenvector of the CPB Hamiltonian for level k.
   Parameters: k (int)—Index of the eigenvector.
   Function: Provides the eigenvector of the $|k\rangle$ level of the CPB Hamiltonian.
   Return Type: array
4. **Hcpb.fij(i, j)**: Compute the transition energy (or frequency) between states $|i\rangle$ and $|j\rangle$.
   Parameters:
       i (int)—Index of state $|i\rangle$
       j (int)—Index of state $|j\rangle$
   Function: Calculates the transition energy E_{ij}.
   Return Type: float
5. **Hcpb.h0_to_qutip(n_Transmon)**: Wrapper around Qutip to output the diagonalized Hamiltonian truncated up to n levels of the transmon for modeling.
   Parameters: $n\_Transmon$ (int)—Number of transmon levels to truncate.
   Function: Returns a Qutip object for the diagonalized transmon Hamiltonian.
   Return Type: Qobj
6. **Hcpb.n_ij**: Compute the value of the number operator for coupling elements together in the energy eigenbasis.
   Parameters:
       i (int)—Index of state $|i\rangle$
       j (int)—Index of state $|j\rangle$
   Function: Calculates matrix elements corresponding to the number operator $n_{ij} = |\langle i|n|j\rangle|$.
   Return Type: float
7. **Hcpb.n_to_qutip(n_transmon[, thresh])**: Wrapper around Qutip to output the number operator (charge) for the transmon Hamiltonian in the energy eigenbasis.
   Parameters:
       $n\_transmon$ (int)—Number of energy levels to consider.
       $thresh$ (float, optional)—Threshold for small coupling terms (default: None).
   Function: Provides a Qutip object representing the number operator for coupling elements in the system.
   Return Type: Qobj
8. **Hcpb.params_from_freq_fixEC(f01, Ec, **kwargs)**: Find transmon E_J given a fixed E_C and frequency.
   Parameters:
       $f01$ (float)—Desired qubit frequency.
       Ec (float)—Charging energy (same units as $f01$).
   Function: Computes E_J for a given frequency and charging energy.
   Return Type: float
9. **Hcpb.params_from_spectrum(f01, anharm, **kwargs)**: Work backward from a desired transmon frequency and anharmonicity to extract the target E_J and E_C for design and fabrication.

Parameters:
  f01 (float)—Desired qubit frequency.
  anharm (float)—Desired qubit anharmonicity (should be negative).
Function: Updates the class parameters with computed E_J and E_C.
Return Type: (float, float)

10. **Hcpb.psi_k(k[, pts])**: Return the wave vector of the CPB Hamiltonian in the flux basis.
    Parameters:
      k (int)—Index of the eigenstate.
      pts (int, optional)—Number of points for approximation (default: 1001).
    Function: Returns the wave vector of the eigenstate $|k\rangle$ in the flux basis.
    Return Type: array

7.3 Modeling of a Transmon Qubit

To model a transmon qubit, we first import the key modules:

```
from qiskit_metal.analyses.hamiltonian.transmon_charge_basis
import Hcpb
from qiskit_metal.analyses.hamiltonian.transmon_CPB_analytic
import Hcpb_analytic
import numpy as np
import matplotlib.pyplot as plt
import pandas as pd
```

Here, with the Hcpb class, we also call the Hcpb_analytic class which uses that analytical method that gives the exact solution. We do this to compare the solution which we get using the matrix-based method.

7.3.1 Energy Level Computation

The qubit Hamiltonian (2-59) is solved exactly in the phase basis and the resultant. The eigenenergies are given by Koch et al. (2007):

$$E_m(n_g) = E_C a_{2[n_g+k(m,n_g)]}(-E_J/2E_C) \qquad (7\text{-}2)$$

Here, $a_v(q)$ represents Mathieu's characteristic value, while $k(m, n_g)$ is a function that appropriately arranges the eigenvalues. The analytical plots of the energy levels as a function of n_g are plotted in Figure 2 of Koch et al. (2007). Next in this section, we discuss plotting energy levels using the Hcpb class.

We use the a variable for the charging energy that ranges from -2.0 to $+2.0$. Then we define a normalization Hamiltonian (H_norm) that calls the Hcpb class. In this step, we define the $E_J = 1000.0$, $E_C = 1000.0$, $n_g = 0.5$, and nlevels $= 2$. For this exercise, we take equal charging and Josephson energy. Another normalization constant is defined which calls the H_norm to calculate the transition energies between the first and second states of the qubit at the degeneracy point where $n_g = 0.5$. We use the **Hcpb.fij**(i, j) command to find the energy difference.

```
# Define a range of offset charge (ng) values
a = np.linspace(-2.0, 2.0, 101)

# Define the CPB Hamiltonian with specified parameters:

H_norm = Hcpb(nlevels=2, Ej=1000.0, Ec=1000.0, ng=0.5)

# Calculate the normalization constant using the transition energy
norm = H_norm.fij(0, 1)
```

Next, we perform a sweep over the offset charge and compute the first three eigenvalues for a specified value of n_g. For this task, we first define the empty array named E0, E1, and E2 that stores the first three eigenenergies in the units of transition energy E_{01} as the values of n_g vary. Now, for a given value of offset charge (ng, represented by x), we need to calculate the CPB Hamiltonian using the previously assigned values of E_J and E_C. Then we calculate the eigenvalue using the **Hcpb.evalue_k**(k) command for three values of m and divide it by E01 we calculated earlier. Since we choose zero-point energy at the bottom of the m=0 level, to plot the energy levels, we deduct the minimum value for E0 from E0, E1, and E2 and plot them with the varying values of n_g.

```
# Initialize empty lists to store normalized eigenvalues for
energy levels 0, 1, and 2
E0, E1, E2 = [], [], []

for i in x:
    # Define the CPB Hamiltonian with nlevels=3, Ej=1000.0,
    Ec=1000.0, and varying ng
    H = Hcpb(nlevels=3, Ej=1000.0, Ec=1000.0, ng=i)
    E0.append(H.evalue_k(0)/norm)
    E1.append(H.evalue_k(1)/norm)
    E2.append(H.evalue_k(2)/norm)

# Define the minimum of E0 and set it as the reference
energy level (E=0)
floor = min(E0)

# Plot the normalized energy levels against ng
plt.plot(x, E0 - floor, 'k', label="m=0")
plt.plot(x, E1 - floor, 'r', label="m=1")
plt.plot(x, E2 - floor, 'b', label="m=2")

plt.xlabel("ng")
plt.ylabel("Em/E01")
plt.legend(title="Energy Level:", loc='upper right')
```

Using the code above, we obtain the energy level plot shown in Figure 7-2.

Figure 7-2 illustrates the plots of E_0, E_1, and E_2 as functions of the offset charge n_g for $E_J/E_C = 1.0$, consistent with Figure 2(a) in Koch et al. (2007). The y-axis

7.3 Modeling of a Transmon Qubit

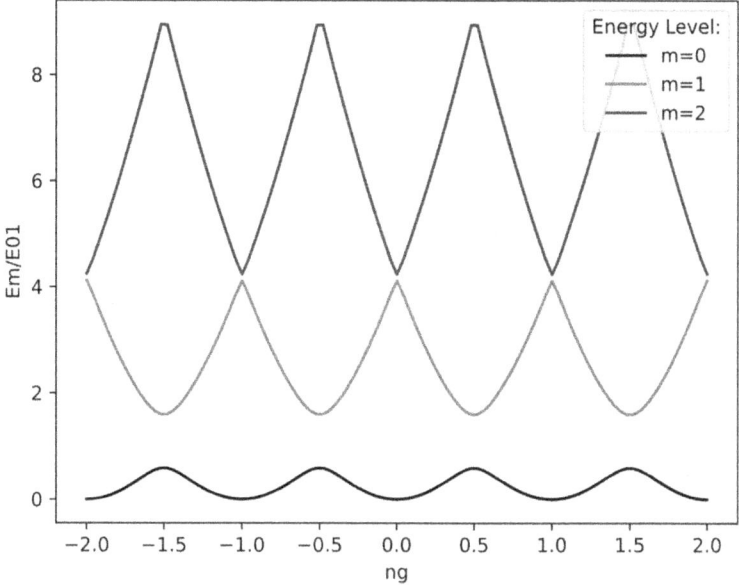

Figure 7-2 Eigenenergies Em (first three levels, $m = 0, 1, 2$) of the qubit Hamiltonian as a function of the effective offset charge n_g

shows the eigenenergies normalized by the transition energies, while the x-axis represents the offset charge n_g. The black, red, and blue curves correspond to the ground state, first excited state, and second excited state, respectively. At the sweet spot, $n_g = 0.5$, the plot has no slope, indicating minimal sensitivity to charge noise.

7.3.2 Comparison with the Analytic Expressions for Energy

Now that we learned the calculation of eigenvalues using the Hcpb class, we see how similar those values with the analytic solution using the "Hcpb_analytic" class. This class computes the transmon eigenvalues analytically by utilizing Mathieu characteristic values instead of a tridiagonal matrix–based approach. For Ej = 13971.3, Ec = 295.2, and ng = 0.0, we calculate and compare the ground state eigenvalue using both Hcpb and Hcpb_analytic.

```
# Define the CPB Hamiltonian using the Hcpb class.
H_CPB = Hcpb(nlevels=15, Ej=13971.3, Ec=295.2,
ng=0.0)

# Define the CPB Hamiltonian using the
Hcpb_analytic class.
# This approach uses exact (analytic) solutions
based on Mathieu characteristic values.
H_CPB_analytic = Hcpb_analytic(Ej=13971.3,
Ec=295.2, ng=0.0)

# Print and compare the ground state energy (E0)
from both numerical and analytic methods.
```

```
print("E0 (HCPB):", H_CPB.evalue_k(0))
print("E0 (HCPB analytic):", H_CPB_analytic.evalue_k(0))

# Calculate and print the percentage error between the two methods.
print("Error:", 100*(H_CPB_analytic.evalue_k(0)
- H_CPB.evalue_k(0)) / H_CPB_analytic.evalue_k(0))
```

We use the above code to calculate and compare the values for both cases. We also calculate the difference between them to find the error. The code gives the output as per below:

```
E0 (HCPB): -11175.114908534233s

E0 (HCPB analytic): -11175.114908534231

Error: -1.6277142726798518e-14
```

As we can see above, the calculated eigenvalues using the Hcpb class match the analytic values well with the numerical error. Hence, it is proved that solving the Hamiltonian using the matrix-based approach is an extremely robust and accurate way of treating the transmon qubit problem. Another part of the eigenvalue problem is the eigenvector of the wave-function calculation, which we will explore in the next section.

7.3.3 Wave function Plotting

For wave function plotting, we define a new Hamiltonian, this time with $E_J \gg E_C$ and a relatively small value of offset charge ng = 0.001 so that we have a nonzero slope. We first can calculate the transition energy between the ground and the first excited state as well as the anharmonicity with the following:

```
# Define the CPB Hamiltonian with specified
parameters:
H = Hcpb(nlevels=3, Ej=13971.3, Ec=295.2, ng=0.001)

# Print the transmon properties:
print(f"""
    Transmon frequencies
    omega01/2pi = {H.fij(0,1): 6.0f} MHz
    alpha/2pi = {H.anharm(): 6.0f} MHz
""")
```

We use the H.fij(0,1) and H.anharm() commands from the Hcpb class that return the transition frequency and anharmonicity of the qubit, respectively. The above code provides the output as mentioned below:

```
omega01/2pi = 5604 MHz
alpha/2pi = 11 MHz
```

7.3 Modeling of a Transmon Qubit

It is important to note that both the transition energy and anharmonicity are expressed in units of Megahertz (MHz). Next, we use the following code to plot the wave functions corresponding to the first three eigenstates of the transmon qubit:

```
import matplotlib.pyplot as plt

# Loop over the first 3 energy levels to plot wave functions
for k in range(3):
    # Get the wave function (psi) and phase (theta) for the
    eigenstate |k>
    psi, theta = H.psi_k(k, 101)

    # Plot the real and imaginary parts of the wave function
    summed together
    # The wave function is in either quadrature, but not both
    plt.plot(theta, psi.real + psi.imag, label=f"|{k}>")

# Set the x-axis label to describe the junction phase (theta),
wrapped in the interval [-pi, pi]
plt.xlabel("Junction phase theta (wrapped in the interval [-pi,
 pi])")

# Set the y-axis label to describe the real part of the
wave function
plt.ylabel("Re(psi(theta))")

plt.legend(title="Level")
```

In the above code, we use the H.psi_k(k, pts) that returns the eigenwavevector (ψ) of the CPB Hamiltonian in the flux basis. Here, k is the index of the eigenvector corresponding to the $|k\rangle$ eigenstate, and pts= 101 represents a number of points to approximate the wave vector in the interval $[\pi, \pi]$.

Following the above program, we obtain the wave function plot corresponding to the first three eigenenergy values as shown in Figure 7-3. On the y-axis, we have taken the real part of the wave function $\psi(\theta)$, and on the x-axis, we have the phase in the $[-\pi, \pi]$ interval. We can observe that the ground state $|0\rangle$ (marked in blue) and the second excited state $|2\rangle$ (marked in green) exhibit symmetric wave functions, implying that $\psi(\theta)$ holds the same value as $\psi(-\theta)$. In this context, the ground state energy is characterized by a symmetric Gaussian wave function. The first excited state (marked in orange) displays asymmetric behavior and follows the relation: $\psi(\theta) = -\psi(-\theta)$. By plotting more wave functions in the $[-\pi, \pi]$ region, we can observe that for every even energy level, the wave function is symmetric, while for every odd energy level, the wave function is asymmetric.

7.3.3.1 Verification of Orthonormality of the Wave functions

One of the characteristics of wave functions is that they should be orthonormal to each other since they are the eigenfunctions of the Hamiltonian. This implies that the inner product of any two wave functions should result in zero, confirming their orthogonality. To validate the orthonormality of the calculated wave functions, we take the first two eigenstates ψ_0 and ψ_1 and verify that their inner product is zero. It

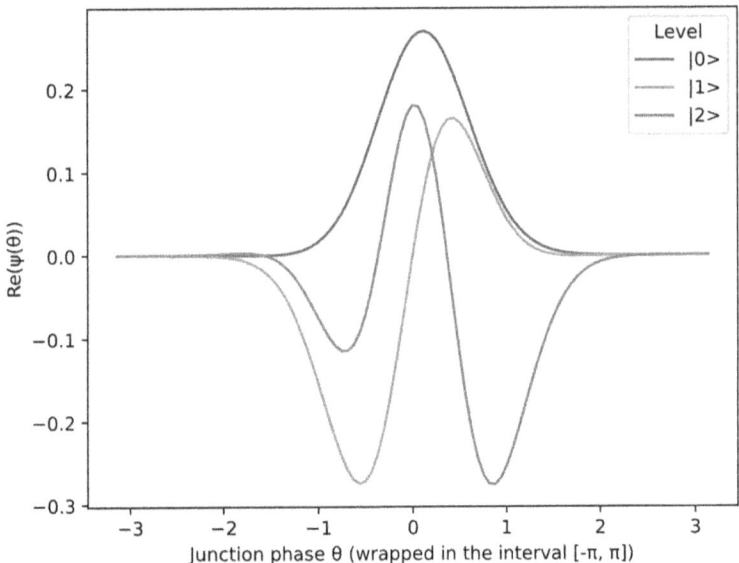

Figure 7-3 Wave functions of the transmon qubit

is important to highlight that, as the wave functions may be complex, the complex conjugate of ψ_1 must be taken into account.

```
# Compute the wave function (Psi) and phase (theta) for the
ground state (k=0)
Psii0, theta0 = H.psi_k(0)

# Compute the wave function (Psi) and phase (theta) for the
first excited state (k=1)
Psii1, theta1 = H.psi_k(1)

# Calculate and print the inner product between Psi0 and the
conjugate of Psi1
print(np.dot(Psii0, Psii1.conj()))
```

We use the "np.dot(i, j)" command to compute the dot product between ψ_0 and ψ_1, and the execution of this command yields the following values $(-2.2354805733859444e\text{-}09 - 3.4875983780408155e\text{-}17j)$.

As expected, the dot product is effectively zero, up to numerical precision. To further verify the unity of the wave function, that is, $|\psi(\theta)|^2 = 1$, we calculate the inner product of an eigenstate with itself.

```
print(np.dot(Psi0, Psi0.conj()))
print(np.dot(Psi1, Psi1.conj()))
```

We employ the above command to verify the unit amplitude for the $|0\rangle$ and $|1\rangle$ wave functions, and the obtained results are given as

(1+0j)
(1+0j)

We observe that we obtain $|\psi_0|^2$ and $|\psi_1|^2$ equal to 1, indicating that the total probability of finding an artificial atom in that energy level is 1.

7.4 Additional Analysis

In Section 7.3, we explored some basic functionality of the Hcpb class for computing energy levels and wave function of the Transmon qubit. In this section, we explore additional analysis options to calculate and observe the behavior charge dispersion, differences in the energy level, anharmonicity, and charge-limited dephasing time (T2). We analyze the dependence of all these properties on the physical of the qubit, for example, charging energy and Josephson energy.

7.4.1 Charge Dispersion

In the case of the transmon, sensitivity to charge noise is minimized by operating the system at the charge degeneracy point:

$$(n_g = 1/2).$$

At this point, the charge dispersion exhibits no slope, preventing linear noise contributions from affecting the qubit transition frequency. Using the tight-binding approximation, the dispersion relation $E_m(n_g)$ can be accurately approximated by a cosine function in the regime of large E_J/E_C.

$$E_m(n_g) \simeq E_m(n_g = 1/4) - \frac{\epsilon_m}{2} \cos(2\pi n_g) \tag{7-3}$$

where

$$\epsilon_m \equiv E_m(n_g = 1/2) - E_m(n_g = 0) \tag{7-4}$$

Here, ϵ_m represents the peak-to-peak value for the charge dispersion of the mth energy level. Using the expression of eigenenergies from Equation 7-3, the resulting charge dispersion is given by

$$\epsilon_m = (-1)^m E_C \frac{2^{4m+5}}{m!} \sqrt{\frac{2}{\pi}} \left(\frac{E_J}{2E_C}\right)^{\frac{m}{2}+\frac{3}{4}} e^{-\sqrt{8E_J/E_C}}. \tag{7-5}$$

The expression for ϵ_m is applicable in the regime where $E_J \gg E_C$. From Equation 7-5, it is evident that as the ratio E_J/E_C increases, the charge dispersion decreases exponentially, resulting in a qubit transition frequency that is highly stable against charge noise.

The peak-to-peak value of the charge dispersion for the mth energy level is given by the difference of the energies at ng $=0.5$ and ng $=0.0$ as mentioned in Equation 7-4. In this exercise, we want to see how the charge dispersion changes with varying values of E_j/E_c for different energy levels m. To plot the charge function in a unit of E01 (ϵ_m/E01) as a function of E_j/E_c for the first few energy levels, we can start by defining a value of charging energy $E_c = 100.0$. We then need to create empty lists for ϵ_0 to ϵ_4 to get the charge dispersion for $m = 0$–4.

```
# Define the charging energy (E_c) of the Cooper Pair Box (CPB)
E_c = 100.0

# Initialize Epsilon_0, Epsilon_1, Epsilon_2, and
Epsilon_3 correspond
# to charge dispersion  for energy levels m=0
through m=3
Epsilon_0, Epsilon_1, Epsilon_2, Epsilon_3 = [], [],
[], []

# Create an array of Ej/Ec ratios for the x-axis
x = np.linspace(1, 140, 101)
```

In the code above, the ratio E_J/E_C is represented as x, which we vary from 1 to 140 for each value of m. We then evaluate the expression for ϵ_m based on E_m and E_0. This is achieved using two separate Hamiltonians: one calculated at $n_g = 0.5$ and the other at $n_g = 0.0$. The results are normalized by the transition energy between the two lowest states, evaluated at the degeneracy point (E_{01}). Finally, we populate the list of ϵ_m values by running the model across the specified range of E_J/E_C ratios.

```
# Loop over each Ej/Ec ratio from the array 'x'
for i in x:
    # Calculate the Josephson energy (E_j) based on
    the current Ej/Ec ratio
    E_j = i * E_c

    # Define the CPB Hamiltonian at ng=0 (integer
    charge offset)
    Hamiltonian_0 = Hcpb(nlevels=15, Ej=E_j, Ec=E_c,
    ng=0.0)

    # Define the CPB Hamiltonian at ng=0.5 (half-
    integer charge offset, sweet spot)
    Hamiltonian_half = Hcpb(nlevels=15, Ej=E_j,
    Ec=E_c, ng=0.5)

    # Normalize using the transition frequency
    between levels 0 and 1 at ng=0.5
    Hamiltonian_norm = Hcpb(nlevels=15, Ej=E_j,
    Ec=E_c, ng=0.5)
    norm = Hamiltonian_norm.fij(0, 1)  #
    Normalization constant
```

7.4 Additional Analysis

```
# Calculate and store the normalized charge
dispersion for levels 0 to 3
Epsilon_0.append(abs(Hamiltonian_half.evalue_k(0) -
Hamiltonian_0.evalue_k(0)) / norm)
Epsilon_1.append(abs(Hamiltonian_half.evalue_k(1) -
Hamiltonian_0.evalue_k(1)) / norm)
Epsilon_2.append(abs(Hamiltonian_half.evalue_k(2) -
Hamiltonian_0.evalue_k(2)) / norm)
Epsilon_3.append(abs(Hamiltonian_half.evalue_k(3) -
Hamiltonian_0.evalue_k(3)) / norm)
```

These values can be plotted to visualize the exponential decrease in charge dispersion as E_J/E_C increases. The code below generates the output shown in Figure 7-4:

```
plt.plot(x, Epsilon_0, 'k', label="m=0")
plt.plot(x, Epsilon_1, 'b', label="m=1")
plt.plot(x, Epsilon_2, 'r', label="m=2")
plt.plot(x, Epsilon_3, 'g', label="m=3")
plt.yscale("log")
plt.xlabel("EJ/Ec")
plt.ylabel("Epsilon/E01")
plt.legend(title="Energy Level", loc='upper right')
```

In Figure 7-4, charge dispersion value ϵ_m normalized by transition energy E01 is taken on the y-axis. For increasing the value of E_j/E_c, we plotted ϵ_m/E01 in the log scale for different values of m energy levels. We can see that for each energy level m, the charge dispersion decreases exponentially as that value of ratio E_j/E_c increases. Physically, it represents that the transmon qubit operates in a regime where

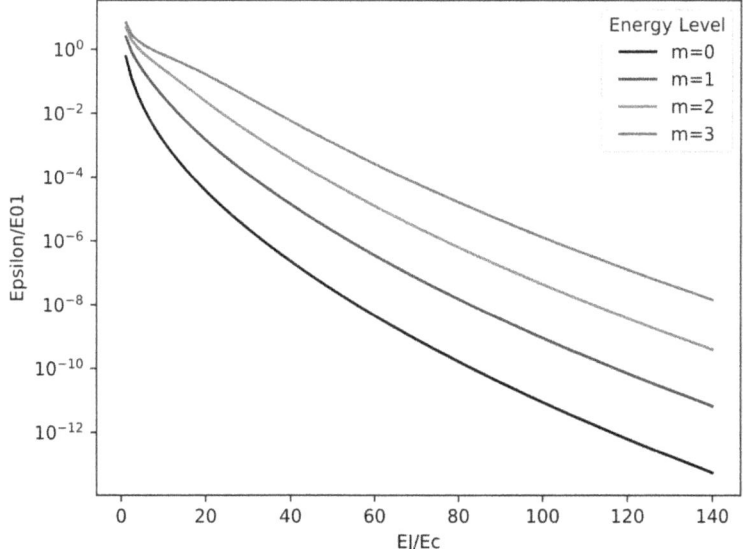

Figure 7-4 Charge dispersion ϵ_m as a function of the ratio EJ/EC for the lowest four levels

$E_J \gg E_c$, which means that we are aiming toward a point in the right-hand side of the plot where we obtain a decrease in the charge dispersion. We find that the exponential decrease in charge dispersion ϵ_m is approximately proportional to E_J/E_C.

We anticipated this type of behavior earlier with the analytical expression as per Equation 7-5. We can also notice that for a fixed value of E_j/E_c, the charge dispersion increases as we go from energy level $m = 0$ to $m = 3$. To understand this, we can refer to Figure 2-16 and notice that, as we climb up the cosine, the barrier to hop over from one well to another gets thinner, meaning that the tunneling probability for particles increases.

7.4.2 Energy Level Differences

Next, we calculate the energy difference between the m-th level and the ground state ($E_{m0} = E_m - E_0$) at the degeneracy point ($n_g = 0.5$) as a function of the E_J/E_C ratio. To perform this calculation, we first initialize empty lists for the energy levels (E_0 through E_3) and their corresponding energy differences (E_{00} through E_{03}).

```
E_0_0, E_1_0, E_2_0, E_3_0 = [], [], [], []
E0, E1, E2, E3 = [], [], [], []
```

To determine the values of E_{m0} at various E_J/E_C ratios, we perform a sweep over E_J/E_C from 0 to 140, using the variable x defined earlier. For each value of Ej/Ec, we construct the Hamiltonian and populate the E0, E1, E2, and E3 arrays with calculated eigenvalue at ng = 0.5. In the next step, we take the differences of the energy value with the ground state energy and store them in the E_0_0, E_1_0, E_2_0, and E_3_0 arrays. The energy level differences are normalized by the charging energy to ensure consistency with Figure 4(b) in Koch et al. (2007).

```
for i in x:
H = Hcpb(nlevels=15, Ej=i*E_c, Ec=E_c, ng=0.5)
E0 = H.evalue_k(0)
E1 = H.evalue_k(1)
E2 = H.evalue_k(2)
E3 = H.evalue_k(3)
E_0_0.append((E0 - E0)/E_c)
E_1_0.append((E1 - E0)/E_c)
E_2_0.append((E2 - E0)/E_c)
E_3_0.append((E3 - E0)/E_c)
```

These results can be plotted to observe how the energy level differences increase as the E_j/E_c ratio grows.

```
plt.plot(x,E_0_0,'k',label="m0")
plt.plot(x,E_1_0,'b',label="m=1")
plt.plot(x,E_2_0,'g',label="m=2")
plt.plot(x,E_3_0,'r',label="m=3")
plt.xlabel("Ej/Ec")
plt.ylabel("Em0/Ec")
plt.legend(title="Energy Levels", loc='upper right')
```

7.4 Additional Analysis

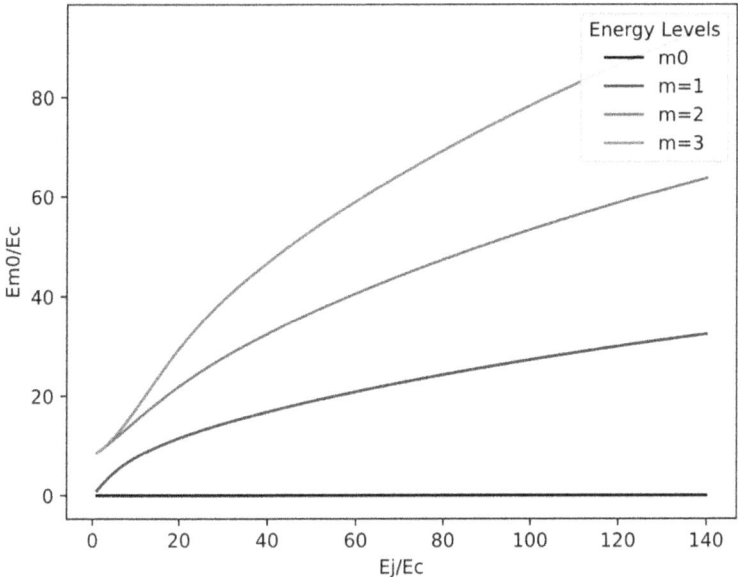

Figure 7-5 Energy level difference Em0 = Em − E0 at ng=0.5 as a function of the E_j/E_c ratio

The above code gives us the plot of normalized energy difference Em0 as a function of Ej/Ec for the first four eigenlevels. On the y-axis of Figure 7-5, we have Em0/Ec, and on the x-axis, we increase the value of E_j/E_c from 0 to 140. We see that the E_0_0 (marked in black) has a constant zero value. As we go from E_1_0 (marked in blue) to E_2_0 (marked in green) to E_3_0 (marked in red), we notice that the differences between each curve are not the same. This implies that the energy levels are not equidistant in the transmon qubit.

7.4.3 Anharmonicity

The significant improvement in charge noise insensitivity achieved by increasing $E_J \gg E_C$ comes at the cost of reduced anharmonicity. Adequate anharmonicity is essential to effectively simplify the many-level system into a qubit, as it determines the minimum duration of control pulses. The absolute and relative anharmonicity is defined as follows:

$$\alpha \equiv E_{12} - E_{01}, \qquad \alpha_r \equiv \alpha/E_{01} \qquad (7\text{-}6)$$

In this section, we focus on plotting the anharmonicity as a function of E_J/E_C using the Hcpb class. The ratio E_J/E_C is represented by x, which we vary from 0 to 80. We then initialize empty lists for α and α_r:

```
x = np.linspace(0,80,101)    #EJ/EC
alpha = []
alpha_r = []
```

Next, we sweep over x and compute the absolute anharmonicity for each value using the Hcpb.anharm() command. Following this, we calculate the relative anharmonicity (α_r) by dividing the output of Hcpb.anharm() by Hcpb.fij(0,1).

```
for i in x:
H_anharmonicity = Hcpb(nlevels=15, Ej=i*E_c, Ec=E_c,
    ng=0.5)
alpha.append(H_anharmonicity.anharm())
alpha_r.append(H_anharmonicity.anharm()/H_anharmonici
    ty.fij(0,1))
plt.figure(1)
plt.subplot(131)
plt.plot(x,alpha)
plt.xlabel("Ej/Ec")
plt.ylabel("alpha")
plt.subplot(133)
plt.plot(x,alpha_r)
plt.ylim(-0.2, 1.0)
plt.xlabel("Ej/Ec")
plt.ylabel("alpha_r")
```

We use the above code to plot the results, which gives us the following results:

Text(0, 0.5, 'alpha_r')

We observe that the anharmonicity initially decays inversely with E_J/E_C for small values of E_J/E_C, reaching a minimum just before $E_J/E_C = 20.0$. Beyond this point, it changes sign and gradually approaches zero as E_J/E_C tends toward infinity. This behavior closely aligns with the results shown in Figure 7-6. Unlike charge dispersion, the anharmonicity decreases following a weak power-law trend.

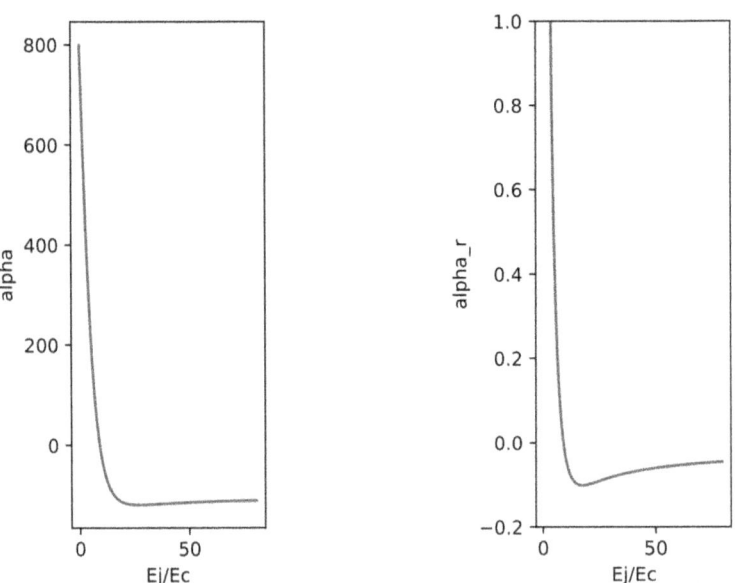

Figure 7-6 Absolute and relative anharmonicity as a function of the E_J/E_C ratio

7.4 Additional Analysis

As a result, there exists a range of E_J/E_C where the transmon exhibits significantly improved insensitivity to charge noise compared to the Cooper pair box (CPB) while maintaining sufficiently large anharmonicity.

For small values of E_J/E_C in Figure 7-6a, α scales as $9(E_J/E_C)^{-1}$. At $E_J/E_C = 9$, it changes sign, indicating that for larger energy ratios, the transition energy E_{12} becomes smaller than E_{01}. The relative anharmonicity exhibits a shallow local minimum around $E_J/E_C \approx 17.5$ and asymptotically approaches zero as $E_J/E_C \to \infty$.

7.4.4 Dephasing Time (T2)

Next, we examine the relationship between the differential charge dispersion, $\frac{dE_{01}}{dn_g}$, and the qubit's sensitivity to charge noise. Offset charge fluctuations contribute to qubit dephasing, impacting its coherence. For effective coherent control of the system, the pulse duration must be significantly shorter than both the relaxation time (T_1) and the dephasing time (T_2). The dephasing time, expressed in terms of the differential charge dispersion, can be given by

$$T_2 \sim \frac{\hbar}{A}\left|\frac{\partial E_{01}}{\partial n_g}\right|^{-1} \simeq \frac{\hbar}{A\pi|\epsilon_1|} \qquad (7\text{-}7)$$

Here, A is on the order of 10^{-4}. Since this expression is effectively the inverse of the charge dispersion for ϵ_1, we can directly compute T_2 as a function of E_J/E_C. To achieve this, we first create an array x for varying values of E_J/E_C from 0 to 100 and an empty array for the values of T_2 we intend to calculate.

```
# ratio of Ej/Ec varying from 0 to 80
x = np.linspace(0,80,101)

# empty list for T2
T2 = []
```

Next, we calculate the dephasing time (T_2) as a function of E_J/E_C. The eigenvalue output from the Hcpb calculation is in units of $E/h \sim$ MHz (10^6 Hz), which simplifies the calculation to $T_2 = \frac{1.0}{2\times(10^{-4})\times(10^6)|\epsilon_1|}$, where ϵ_1 is directly obtained from the Hcpb eigenvalue computation. To calculate ϵ_1, we follow the same procedure as before, evaluating two Hamiltonians, one at $n_g = 0.0$ and another at $n_g = 0.5$. For each value of x in the range of E_J/E_C, we compute ϵ_1 and utilize its inverse to determine the dephasing time T_2.

```
E_c = 1000.0
for i in x:
    Hamiltonian_half = Hcpb(nlevels=15, Ej=i*E_c,
        Ec=E_c, ng=0.5)
    Hamiltonian_0 = Hcpb(nlevels=15, Ej=i*E_c,
        Ec=E_c, ng=0.0)
```

```
    eps = abs(Hamiltonian_half.evalue_k(1) - 
        Hamiltonian_0.evalue_k(1))
    T2.append(1.0/(2.0*(1E-4)*(1E6)*eps))

plt.plot(x, T2)
plt.yscale("log")
plt.xlabel("Ej/Ec")
plt.ylabel("T2 (Sec)")
```

Text(0, 0.5, 'T2 (sec)')

We use the code above to plot the dephasing time T_2 as a function of E_J/E_C (see Figure 7-7). In the figure, the Y-axis represents the dephasing time T_2 on a logarithmic scale, while the X-axis shows the values of E_J/E_C. We observe that the dephasing time increases exponentially with increasing E_J/E_C, which is one of the key features of the transmon qubit. By increasing the E_J/E_C ratio, we reduce sensitivity to charge noise without significantly sacrificing anharmonicity, leading to a substantial improvement in dephasing time. This plot closely resembles Figure 5(c) of the paper by Koch et al. (2007).

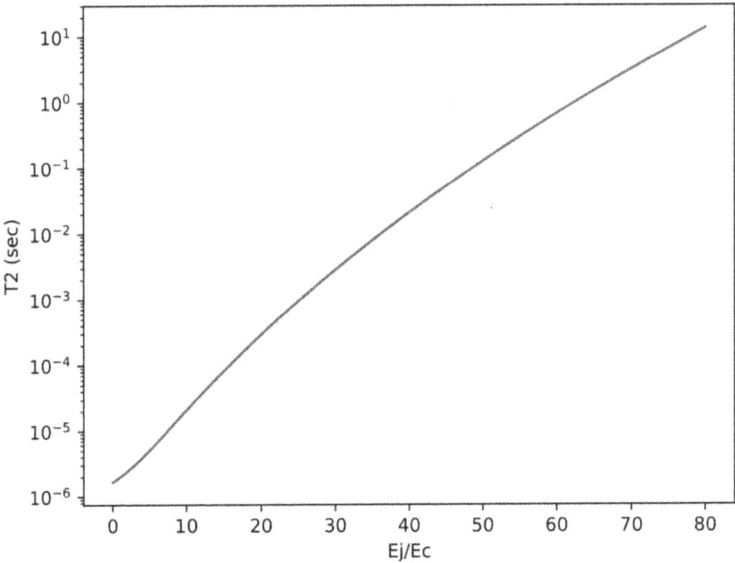

Figure 7-7 Dephasing time T2 due to charge fluctuation as a function of E_J/E_C

7.5 Qutip Simulation

In this section, we discuss getting the matrix form of the Hamiltonian using the Hcpb class. To obtain the diagonalized Hamiltonian truncated to n levels of the transmon, we use the following wrapper around Qutip:

```
H.h0_to_qutip(6)
```

The above command provides us with the following matrix:

```
Quantum object: dims = [[6], [6]], shape = (6, 6),
    type = oper, isherm = True
```

$$\begin{bmatrix} 0.0 & 0.0 & 0.0 & 0.0 & 0.0 & 0.0 \\ 0.0 & 3.243 \times 10^3 & 0.0 & 0.0 & 0.0 & 0.0 \\ 0.0 & 0.0 & 6.379 \times 10^3 & 0.0 & 0.0 & 0.0 \\ 0.0 & 0.0 & 0.0 & 9.40 \times 10^3 & 0.0 & 0.0 \\ 0.0 & 0.0 & 0.0 & 0.0 & 1.230 \times 10^4 & 0.0 \\ 0.0 & 0.0 & 0.0 & 0.0 & 0.0 & 1.507 \times 10^4 \end{bmatrix}$$

To obtain the matrix Hamiltonian above, we have truncated it up to six eigenlevels. As seen in the matrix, the diagonal elements are nonzero, while the off-diagonal elements are zero.

We utilize a Qutip wrapper to generate the transmon Hamiltonian's number operator (charge) in its energy eigenbasis. This operator is instrumental in calculating couplings with other components in the system. We use the following command to obtain the number operator:

```
H.n_to_qutip(6)
```

```
Quantum object: dims = [[6], [6]], shape = (6, 6),
    type = oper, isherm = True,
```

$$\begin{bmatrix} 0.0 & 1.424 & 1.060 \times 10^{-15} & 0.029 & 4.506 \times 10^{-16} & 0.001 \\ 1.424 & 0.0 & 1.979 & 1.296 \times 10^{-15} & 0.060 & 6.908 \times 10^{-16} \\ 1.004 \times 10^{-15} & 1.979 & 0.0 & 2.379 & 4.129 \times 10^{-15} & 0.100 \\ 0.029 & 1.268 \times 10^{-15} & 2.379 & 0.0 & 2.690 & 3.835 \times 10^{-15} \\ 4.509 \times 10^{-16} & 0.060 & 4.129 \times 10^{-15} & 2.690 & 0.0 & 2.936 \\ 0.001 & 6.908 \times 10^{-16} & 0.100 & 3.835 \times 10^{-15} & 2.936 & 0.0 \end{bmatrix}$$

We can use these matrices to plot the fluctuation in the number of Cooper pairs as a function of E_J/E_C for the first three energy levels. This requires calculating the variance in the number of Cooper pairs, defined as

$$\langle n^2 \rangle - \langle n \rangle^2,$$

where n represents the number operator calculated for energy level m.

First, we define the x-axis to represent $\frac{E_J}{E_C}$, ranging from 1 to 120. We then create empty lists to store the variances for the $m = 0$, $m = 1$, and $m = 2$ states. Additionally, we specify a value for E_C.

```
x = np.linspace(1,120, 101)
E_c=350.0
variance_0 = []
variance_1 = []
variance_2 = []
```

Next, we construct the Hamiltonian matrix and compute both $\langle n^2 \rangle$ and $\langle n \rangle^2$. We then calculate the square root of the difference between these two quantities for each value of E_J/E_C. Finally, the results are appended to the corresponding empty lists defined earlier.

```
for i in x:
    H = Hcpb(nlevels=15, Ej=i*E_c, Ec=E_c, ng=0.5)
    n_squared = H.n_to_qutip(6)*H.n_to_qutip(6)
    n = H.n_to_qutip(6)
    fluc0 = np.sqrt(np.real(n_squared[0,0] -
        (n[0,0])*(n[0,0])))
    fluc1 = np.sqrt(np.real(n_squared[1,1] -
        (n[1,1])*(n[1,1])))
    fluc2 = np.sqrt(np.real(n_squared[2,2] -
        (n[2,2])*(n[2,2])))
    variance_0.append(fluc0)
    variance_1.append(fluc1)
    variance_2.append(fluc2)
```

We can plot these variances as a function of E_j/E_c and verify that the resulting curves align closely with those presented in Figure 8 of reference Koch et al. (2007).

```
plt.plot(x,variance_0,'k', label="m=0")
plt.plot(x,variance_1,'r', label="m=1")
plt.plot(x,variance_2,'b', label="m=2")
plt.xlabel("Ej/Ec")
plt.ylabel("Variance")
plt.legend(title="Energy Levels", loc='upper right')
```

Physically, the plot in Figure 7-8 illustrates that the variation in the number of Cooper pairs is approximately 1 for the ground state and around 2 for the first excited state of the CPB when operated in the transmon regime with an $\frac{E_J}{E_C}$ ratio of 100. In summary, the transmon can be viewed as a CPB operating in the $\frac{E_J}{E_C} \gg 1$ regime, where charge fluctuations are on the order of unity.

7.5 Qutip Simulation

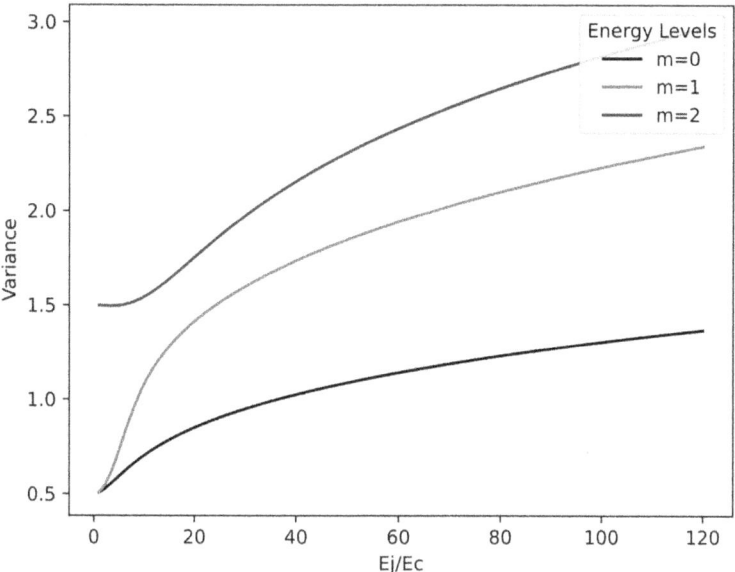

Figure 7-8 Variations in the number of Cooper pairs, n, as a function of $\frac{E_J}{E_C}$ for the first three energy levels of the transmon

We can investigate the evolution of the off-diagonal matrix elements of the Cooper pair box (CPB) Hamiltonian as a function of the $\frac{E_J}{E_C}$ ratio. To do this, we initialize four empty lists (m_{10}, m_{20}, m_{30}, and m_{21}), where $m_{ij} = \langle i|n|j \rangle$. Then, we iterate over the $\frac{E_J}{E_C}$ ratio, computing the off-diagonal matrix element for each value.

```
m_1_0 = []
m_2_0 = []
m_3_0 = []
m_2_1 = []

# For a given value of offset charge (ng,
represented by x) we will calculate the CPB
Hamiltonian using the previously assigned values of
E_J and E_C. Then we calculate the eigenvalue for a
given value of m.
for i in x:
    H = Hcpb(nlevels=15, Ej=i*E_c, Ec=E_c, ng=0.5)
    m_1_0.append(np.real(H.n_to_qutip(6)[1,0]))
    m_2_0.append(np.real(H.n_to_qutip(6)[2,0]))
    m_3_0.append(np.real(H.n_to_qutip(6)[3,0]))
    m_2_1.append(np.real(H.n_to_qutip(6)[2,1]))
```

The off-diagonal matrix elements can be easily visualized by plotting them as a function of the $\frac{E_J}{E_C}$ ratio.

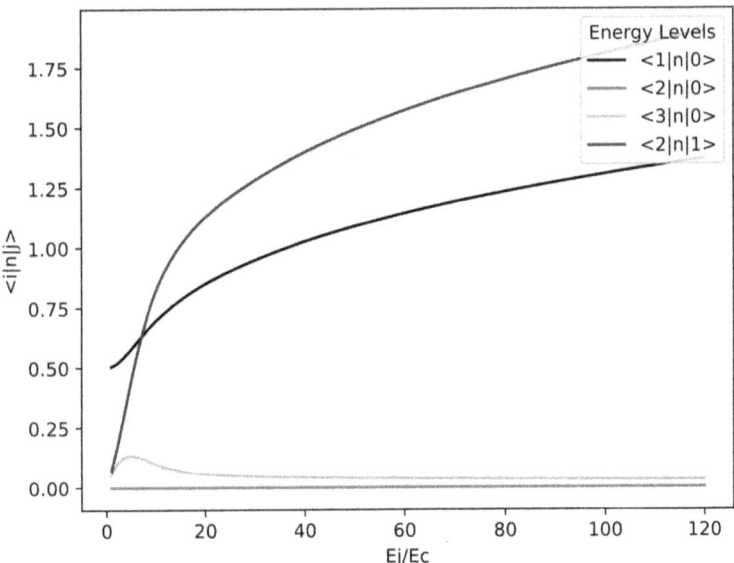

Figure 7-9 Off-diagonal matrix elements of the Cooper pair number operator as a function of the energy ratio EJ /EC (ng=1/2)

```
plt.plot(x,m_1_0,'k',label="<1|n|0>")
plt.plot(x,m_2_0,'r',label="<2|n|0>")
plt.plot(x,m_3_0,'y',label="<3|n|0>")
plt.plot(x,m_2_1,'b',label="<2|n|1>")
plt.xlabel("Ej/Ec")
plt.ylabel("<i|n|j>")
plt.legend(title="Energy Levels", loc='upper right')
```

The plot aligns closely with Figure 7-9 of the reference and highlights that, physically, the coupling between adjacent transmon states ($\langle 1|n|0\rangle$ and $\langle 2|n|1\rangle$) remains significant in the $E_J \gg E_C$ regime. In contrast, the coupling between non-adjacent states (e.g., $m = 0$ and $m = 2$) is negligible across all values of $\frac{E_J}{E_C}$.

7.6 Back-Calculation of E_J and E_c

We can employ the "Hcpb.params_from_spectrum" function to calculate the target E_J and E_C values for a given transmon frequency and anharmonicity. Specifically, we use the provided values of $E_J = 13971.3$ MHz and $E_C = 295.2$ MHz, corresponding to a transmon frequency and anharmonicity of $\omega = 5341$ GHz and $\alpha = -341$, respectively.

```
# 13971.3, Ec=295.2
omega, alpha = 5431, -341
E_j/E_c = H.params_from_spectrum(omega, alpha) # set
```

```
self.Ej, Cj
print(E_j/E_c)
print("transmon frequency:", H.fij(0,1),
"anharmonicity:", H.anharm())
```

The above code gives us the following output:

[13952.97584426 295.61920264]
transmon frequency: 5431.003285965414 anharmonicity: -340.9980226844036

In the first line of the result, the first value represents Ej, and second represents Ec. We can also calculate the value of Ej given the value of Ec and the transmon frequency. For this task, we use the Hcpb.params_from_freq_fixEC(f01, Ec) command that requires transmon frequency f01 and Ec as the input.

```
Ej = H.params_from_freq_fixEC(omega, 295.17)
print("Ej:", Ej)
```

For a fixed value of $\omega = 5431$ GHz and $E_C = 295.17$ MHz, the code computes $E_J = 14424.680512350775$ MHz. This result is close to the initial value of 13971.3 MHz that we started with.

7.7 Conclusion

This chapter delved into the modeling of the Transmon qubit, beginning with its origins from the Cooper pair box and the transition that mitigated charge noise sensitivity. The Hamiltonian of the Cooper pair box was formulated and extended to represent the Transmon qubit in the charge basis. Detailed numerical modeling was performed to compute energy levels, compare results with analytical expressions, and visualize wave functions. Further analysis included charge dispersion, energy level differences, anharmonicity, and dephasing time (T_2), highlighting their critical roles in qubit stability and coherence. Simulations using QuTiP provided insights into the system's quantum dynamics, while the back-calculation of E_J (Josephson energy) and E_C (charging energy) established parameter relationships essential for accurate modeling. This chapter thus provided a robust theoretical and computational foundation for understanding and optimizing the design and performance of Transmon qubits in practical quantum computing applications.

Manufacturing: Fabrication and Packaging of Qubits

Throughout the chapters, we explored several theoretical and practical applications of superconducting qubits, along with practical demonstrations of these concepts. Now, let us delve into the process of creating an integrated circuit and manufacturing superconducting qubits. Manufacturing plays a critical role in ensuring accurate simulations and real-time applications. If the qubits are not fabricated with precision, the resulting performance can deviate significantly from the expected outcomes. The challenge lies in producing these specialized qubits and maintaining their functionality at extremely low temperatures. However, these challenges are addressed through an advanced integration technique that we will be discussing in the subsequent sections. In the following section, we will examine how end-to-end manufacturing process is carried out and its impact on the fabrication of superconducting qubits.

8.1 Sputtering

Sputtering is the process in which microscopic particles are ejected from a surface when bombarded with energy particles. In other words, sputtering is a process where high-energy particles (usually ions) hit a material, knocking off its atoms, which then settle onto a surface to form a thin layer. This phenomenon can be seen to occur naturally in outer space, when the energetic particles released from the Sun during the coronal mass ejection damage the spacecraft orbiting around the earth. This results in the spacecraft getting damaged. Though sputtering can be seen as very harmful and damaging, when used in a proper controlled environment, it can also be used for precise etching and depositing thin film layers. This technique of sputtering is used in the process of creating superconducting devices and nanotechnology products.

Sputtering takes place when energetic ions collide with atoms of target materials used; this collision results in the transfer of energy, leading to the ejection of ions from the target materials. The transferred energy can be calculated using the relation

$$E_T = E_i \cdot \frac{4M_1 \cdot M_2}{(M_1 + M_2)^2} \tag{8-1}$$

where E_T is the transferred energy and E_i represents the incoming ion energy with M_1 and M_2 representing the incoming ion mass and target atom mass, respectively. If you notice Equation 8-1 closely, one can see that it is the most efficient when the target atom and incoming ion masses are nearly equal. During this scenario, when the target atom and incoming ion have nearly the same masses, the transferred energy is maximum and equal to the incoming ion energy.

One of the important parameters that helps in characterizing the effect sputtering is the sputtering yield. The sputtering yield defines the number of atoms ejected per incident ion and is provided by

$$Y = \frac{\eta \cdot E_T}{U} \tag{8-2}$$

where Y represents the sputtering yield, η shows the efficiency factor representing energy transfer to surface atoms, and U represents the surface binding energy of the target material, the minimum energy required to eject an atom. The sputtering yield is dependent on the angle of incident of the ion. The total yield of the system is dependent on the angle of inclination (θ), and it is said that

- $0° < \theta < 30°$: Decreased yield due to a low incident angle caused by reduced ion penetration and reduced collision between the incident ion and the target material
- $30° < \theta < 60°$: Relatively constant to slightly greater yield as the ion penetration depth and collision cascade stabilize over this range of incidence
- $60° < \theta < 90°$: Increases for these high incident angles as the ion penetration is deeper and creates more extensive collision with the target material

In an experimental setup, the sputtering yield can be calculated by the simple formula:

$$Y = \frac{N_{\text{eroded}} \times S}{N_{\text{bombarded}}} \tag{8-3}$$

where N_{eroded} represents the thickness of the eroded layer in atoms per surface area—in other words, the total erosion of the material that took place post the ions are bombarded onto the target substance. S represents the total surface area of the beam spot at the target—that is, the total area that the beam covers when in contact with the target—and $N_{\text{bombarded}}$ denotes the total amount of bombarded atoms onto the surface.

8.1 Sputtering

Sputter deposition is a technique used to deposit thin films onto surfaces through the process of sputtering. It falls under the category of physical vapor deposition (PVD), a method where material transitions from a condensed phase to a vapor phase and then back to a condensed phase as a thin film. In sputter deposition, energetic ion beams bombard a target material, causing atoms to be ejected and deposited onto a substrate, often a thin silicon wafer. These ejected particles, varying in energy and direction, resemble the chaotic dispersion of shattered glass fragments when hit by a ball. However, only a small fraction—about 1%—of these particles are ionized and possess sufficient energy to travel in a straight line toward the substrate.

During sputter deposition, the energetic ion beam is often composed of inert gases; these gases are known as sputter gas which causes the sputtering effect. Argon is commonly used as the sputtering gas due to its inert nature, but for more effective momentum transfer, the gas is often selected to have an atomic weight similar to the target material. For instance, neon is preferred for light elements, while krypton or xenon is suitable for heavier ones. The inert nature of these gases ensures that they do not react with the ejected ions, allowing them to deposit on the substrate. However, in specific cases where a chemical compound is required on the substrate, reactive gases may replace inert gases. This allows the ejected ions to chemically react with the sputtering gas, forming a compound that subsequently deposits onto the substrate.

Sputter deposition offers a wide range of customizable parameters, making it a versatile yet complex process. Alongside these parameters, various sputtering techniques are available to cater to specific requirements; we will be looking at these methods in the following sections.

8.1.1 Ion Beam Sputtering

Ion beam sputtering (IBS) is an extremely precise thin film deposition technique wherein a concentrated ion beam is directed toward the target material to cause sputtering, and the sputtered ions are deposited on the substrate, forming a thin layer film deposition. In this process, the target is present external to the source (ion beam). The high-energy ion beam in the source is generated using an ion source, which is a Kaufman ion source or a plasma source.

The Kaufman ion source is a type of hot filament ion source that uses a thermo-electron emitter cathode and grid extraction to produce a beam of ions. In this, the thermo-electron beam is generated by heating the graphite or tungsten filaments up to 1500 °C, which results in generating thermo-electrons. Following the generation of thermo-electrons, the ions are extracted from the plasma using a grid system, which consists of a cathode grid and an anode grid. The cathode grid is typically biased negatively to attract electrons, while the anode grid is biased positively to attract ions; this process is called grid extraction. This process helps in the formation of strong ion beams; the ion beam produced by this method has a broad energy distribution, typically ranging from a few eV to several hundred eV, depending on the operating conditions. The Kaufman ion source was invented by Harold R.

Figure 8-1 Ion beam sputter deposition setup used for thin film deposition

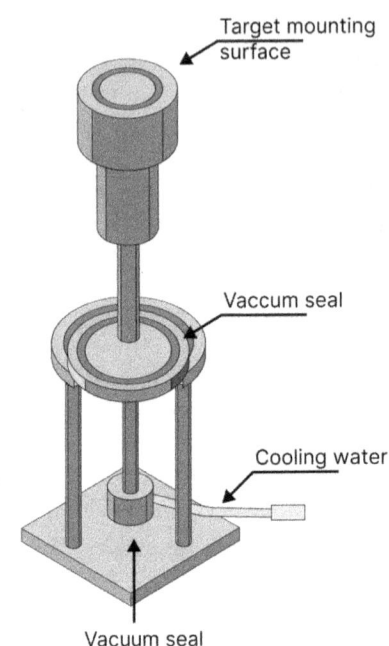

Kaufman, who is credited for the development of electrostatic ion thrusters for NASA during the 1950s and 1960s.

Figure 8-1 represents the fabrication setup used for the ion beam sputter deposit technique for thin film generation. Inside the ion beam sputtering, inert gases such as argon are used to create a stable ion stream. These inert gases are ionized by applying an electric field to a gas chamber, producing positively charged ions. These positively charged ions are accelerated using electric fields, achieving high kinetic energy. The kinetic energy of these positively charged ions can be controlled by varying the intensity of the electric field surrounding it. This stream of positively charged ions with high energy is bombarded onto the target material, causing sputtering. By varying the electric field intensity, the deposition conditions on the substrate are controlled. For high depositions, the intensity of the electric field is set to high, causing more sputtering in the target material and higher deposition; similarly, if the field intensity is set to low, the energy of the accelerated ions will be less, causing less sputtering and less deposition on the substrate.

The angle at which the ion beam is incident to the target plays a crucial role in the amount of deposition that will occur during sputtering and can be optimized as per the requirement by changing the angle of incidence. The sputtered particles travel through the vacuum chamber to deposit on the thin film substrate, which can be placed in line or at an angle to the target depending on the desired film characteristics.

Ion beam sputtering has a lot of advantages such as

- This process allows for precise control over the deposition parameters, such as ion energy, beam angle, and target material, enabling the fabrication of highly uniform films with precise thickness and composition.
- Reactive gases, such as oxygen or nitrogen, can be introduced to create compound thin films on the substrate such as oxides or nitrides of the target material; this type of sputtering where the sputter gas is changed with the reactive gas is known as *reactive sputtering*.
- This process is extremely precise and provides high control over film thickness and uniformity of the deposition on the substrate.
- This process operates in high vacuum chambers, resulting in less contamination of external sources or impurities during the decomposition process of the sputtered ions onto the substrate, producing near smooth films with low roughness, making them ideal for optical applications such as anti-reflective or reflective coatings.

8.1.2 Gas Flow Sputtering

Gas flow sputtering is a method where high-power pressure gases are used for the sputtering of atoms from the target material, which is then deposited on the substrate, forming a thin film. This process takes place inside a vacuum chamber where high-pressure inert gas is introduced for sputtering. Inert gases are used for nonreactive sputtering deposition, where only the target material is required for the deposition. This can be changed with some reactive gases if any compound deposition is required on the substrate film. Typically argon is used as the inert gas for sputtering, but depending on the target, the gas can be changed; if the target element has a lower atomic mass, then neon is preferred over argon, and, conversely, if the atomic mass of the target is higher, then krypton is preferred over argon for effective sputtering.

A strong electric field is applied between the target (cathode) and an anode; this causes the gas in the chamber to get ionized, creating a plasma. The plasma consists of positively charged ions and free electrons. The plasma gains significant energy from the strong electric field inside the chamber. This high-energy gas ion, or plasma, is directed toward the target material, causing the sputtering. Upon collision, these ions transfer momentum to the atoms in the target. When the energy transferred exceeds the threshold energy (binding energy) of the target material, it causes the atoms to get ejected, leading to sputtering.

The controlled flow of high-pressure inert gas is maintained inside the chamber, ensuring a uniform deposition of the sputtered ions on the substrate. When the gas molecules collide with the sputtered atoms, the energy of the sputtered atoms is reduced significantly, and they are scattered in random directions inside the chamber, leading to a more uniform distribution as there is no specific region where the concentration of the deposition will be more, resulting in a uniform deposition

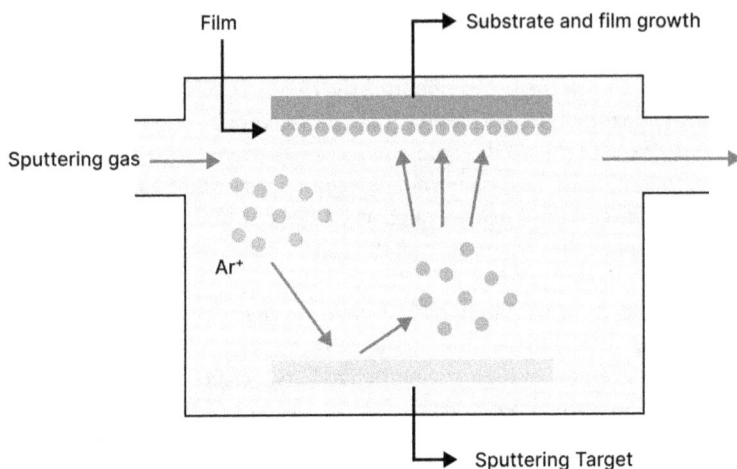

Figure 8-2 Gas flow sputter deposition setup used for thin film deposition

of the sputtered particles on the substrate. This method is effective even for complex and irregular shapes due to the random scattering of the sputtered atoms. The sputtered particles, after going through multiple collisions with gas molecules, eventually reach the substrate and deposit as a thin film. This random scattering of the sputtered ions makes this process extremely effective for coating large areas.

As discussed earlier, the deposition process on the substrate can be controlled by adjusting the gas flow rate or chamber pressure or by changing the inert gases for effective deposition on the substrate. Figure 8-2 demonstrates the fabrication setup of the gas flow sputter deposition technique with its various components. Gas flow sputtering provides multiple advantages, such as

- The sputtering effect is uniform and provides uniform film thickness over large areas and irregular shapes and geometries for the substrate.
- This process is extremely useful for large-scale applications, including industrial-scale production. Furthermore, this method is capable of depositing a wide range of materials, including metals, dielectrics, and compounds.
- This process includes effective material utilization due to controlled gas flow, which is why this process is most commonly used for thin film depositions for solar cells and energy storage devices.

Having discussed the two popular methods used in sputtering, let us now have a quick comparison of their functionalities. Table 8-1 provides a detailed comparison between the different types of sputtering discussed.

Table 8-1 Comparison between gas flow sputtering and ion beam sputtering

Gas flow sputtering	Ion beam sputtering
Uses a high-pressure inert or reactive gas to direct sputtered ions onto the substrate by inducing random collisions	Utilizes a focused and energetic ion beam to eject atoms directly from the target material for deposition
Collisions between sputtered ions and gas molecules lead to a random walk, guiding the ions toward the substrate	The ejected atoms follow a more deterministic trajectory, as the ion beam provides precise directional control
Typically involves higher chamber pressure due to the presence of sputtering gas	Operates under lower pressure since ion beams are generated in a controlled environment without requiring additional gases
The sputtering gas, such as argon or neon, plays a crucial role in influencing deposition dynamics	The ion beam itself is responsible for the ejection and subsequent deposition of atoms
Allows for the deposition of thin films through both physical and chemical processes, especially with reactive gases	Primarily focused on physical processes; chemical reactions are uncommon unless specifically designed
Commonly used for applications requiring uniform thin films over large areas	Suited for applications needing high precision and control, such as micro-fabrication and nanostructure creation

8.2 Evaporation

Evaporation, also known as thermal evaporation, is a technique that is widely used and, similar to sputtering, is a physical vapor deposition method, where the source material is heated until it reaches its evaporation point so that the material turns into its own gaseous form inside a vacuum chamber, and this resulting vapor is then condensed onto a substrate, depositing a thin layer onto the substrate.

A solid or a liquid substance (source) can be used as the material as per the required deposition onto the substrate film. When this material is heated to its evaporation temperature in a high vacuum chamber, the atoms or molecules of the substance travel to the substrate, where they form a uniform thin film and deposit themselves. The vacuum chamber helps in maintaining a low-pressure environment that ensures that the mean free path of travel of the vapor particles is long enough that it will avoid collisions, ensuring uniform deposition of the material. Figure 8-3 demonstrates the thermal evaporation process setup in detail.

The heating technique used for this type of deposition method is typically a resistive heating method, wherein a resistive material like tungsten or a molybdenum filament is heated precisely using a high-energy electron beam. The focused high-energy electron laser beam provides localized heating, ensuring that the filament is heated completely and the deposition takes place uniformly.

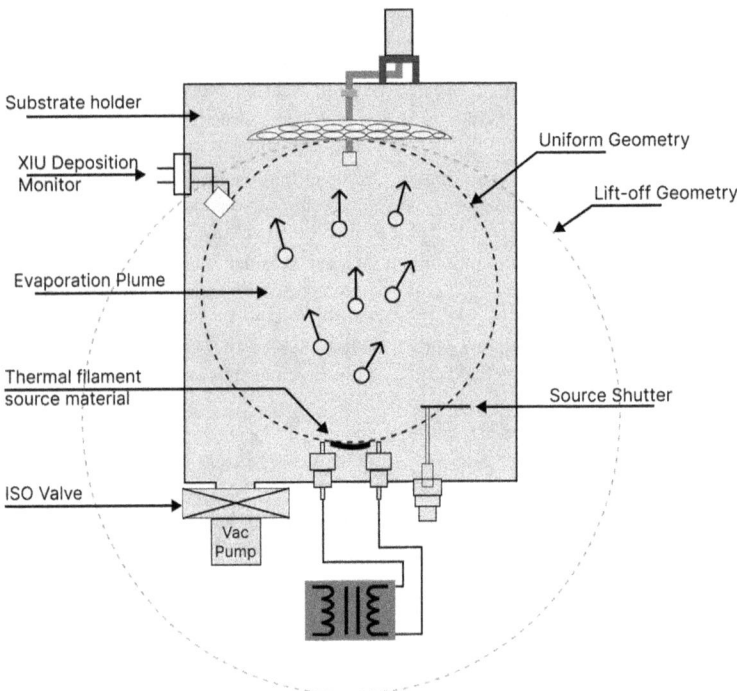

Figure 8-3 Thermal evaporation deposition setup used for thin film deposition

Let us look into a few equations that can help in understanding the process and calculating the values better. We can calculate the evaporation rate of the entire process using Equation 8-4.

$$R_e = \frac{\alpha P_{\text{vapor}}}{\sqrt{2\pi m k_B T}} \qquad (8\text{-}4)$$

where α is the evaporation coefficient of the material, which is typically closer to 1, and k_B is the Boltzmann constant. P_{vapor} is the vapor pressure of the material in Pascals at temperature T in Kelvin. So as we can deduce from Equation 8-4, vapor pressure of the source is directly proportional to the rate of evaporation. The vapor pressure of the source material at a specific temperature can be calculated using the Clausius-Clapeyron equation stated in thermodynamics relating the vapor pressure at a specific temperature with the absolute vapor pressure of the material.

$$P_{\text{vapor}} = P_0 \exp\left(-\frac{\Delta H_{\text{vapor}}}{RT}\right) \qquad (8\text{-}5)$$

where P_0 is the material's vapor pressure, ΔH_{vapor} is the enthalpy of vaporization, and R is the universal gas constant. Assuming an isotropic emission of the vapor

8.2 Evaporation

particles, the flux of the vapor can be calculated using the simple relation:

$$\Phi = \frac{R}{4\pi r^2} \tag{8-6}$$

where r represents the distance between the source material and the substrate where deposition will take place. Using this relation of flux obtained in Equation 8-6, the deposition rate can be calculated over a period of time t as

$$d = \Phi \cdot \alpha \cdot t \tag{8-7}$$

where d represents the thickness of the deposition over the period of time t, and α represents the sticking coefficient of the vapor particles with the substrate. The typical range of values for the sticking coefficient is $\alpha \in [0, 1]$, where 0 means that none of the evaporated vapor particles will stick with the substrate, whereas 1 means that all of the vapor particles will stick with the substrate, making a complete deposition. We can also calculate the deposition rate on the substrate forming a film, but before that we need to calculate the heat energy required for the evaporation of a material of mass m, and it is provided by the following relation:

$$Q = m \cdot \Delta H_{vapor} \tag{8-8}$$

where ΔH_{vapor} represents the enthalpy of vaporization. The power supplied to the system can be calculated as energy per unit time by taking the heat energy equation obtained from Equation 8-8 and calculating power with the following equation:

$$P = (Q + Q_{loss}) \cdot t^{-1} \tag{8-9}$$

where Q_{loss} represents the loss of heat energy in the process. This may be due to environmental factors or due to the loss in heating the filament. Using the power equation obtained from Equation 8-9, the deposition rate can be calculated by the following relation:

$$D = \frac{M \cdot \Phi}{A \cdot \rho} \tag{8-10}$$

where M represents the molar mass of the source material and ρ represents the density of the material. ϕ can be obtained from Equation 8-6, and P can be obtained from Equation 8-9.

Apart from thermal evaporation, the shadow evaporation technique is also commonly used for thin film deposition on the substrate. We will be discussing this technique in detail in the following section.

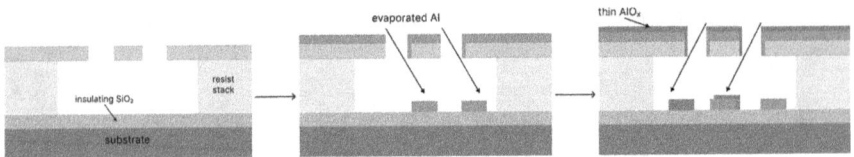

Figure 8-4 Shadow evaporation deposition setup used for thin film deposition

8.2.1 Shadow Evaporation

Shadow evaporation is a process of the thin film deposition technique that is especially used for creating complex and multilayered structures and thin and delicate patterns and is most commonly used for micro-fabrication and nano-fabrication. The shadow evaporation technique uses physical barriers placed between the evaporation source and the substrate. This barrier is referred to as "mask" in this process. This mask casts a shadow during the evaporation process by coming in between the vapor and the substrate, making the deposition only at certain places while blocking the rest. This helps in creating fine, thin patterns, which makes this technique extremely reliable for nanostructure fabrications. Figure 8-4 demonstrates the process of shadow evaporation used for the thin film deposition technique.

By changing the angle, position, and orientation of the mask, one can take physical control over the entire deposition process, allowing intricate patterns to be deposited onto the substrate. This technique helps in forming complex patterns without the need for any complex lithographic processes. Furthermore, one can change the angle of the mask to create multilayered structures with precise deposition. Since this process focuses on a particular region for the deposition of materials with high precision, it also allows the deposition of multiple different materials in specific regions with high precision.

The mask used for the process is often a suspended film or stencil that is prepared to cater to particular requirements based on the deposition pattern required. The mask is placed above the substrate inside the vacuum chamber, ensuring proper alignment with the mask openings. The evaporated material travels in a straight line in the vacuum, depositing on the exposed regions of the substrate.

We can represent the extent of shadow that the mask casts by this simple relation:

$$x_s = h_m \tan(\theta) \tag{8-11}$$

where h_m represents the distance between the mask and substrate, and θ represents the angle of mask with respect to the substrate. This method of evaporation technique provides quite a lot of benefits. Let's summarize the advantages of the shadow evaporation in the following:

- This technique proves to be extremely useful for fabricating microelectronic and nanoelectronic structures such as tunnel junctions and quantum dots. Further-

more, this technique is also useful for creating overlapping layers of superconducting materials.
- This technique is suitable for sequential deposition of multiple materials in distinct regions without cross contamination.
- This technique allows for depositing intricate designs with high precision and avoids the requirement for photolithography, reducing the complexity of the manufacturing process.

Having discussed all the fabrication steps and packaging methods for superconducting circuits with all the important parameters required for successfully completing the manufacturing process, there are some issues that arise in between them, causing faulty connections, such as the creation of unwanted Josephson junctions or the generation of strong magnetic fields inside the circuit, causing decoherence in the qubit due to supercurrents. We will be understanding these problems faced during manufacturing processes and the methods to rectify them in the following section.

8.3 Creation of Unwanted Josephson Junctions and Generation of Supercurrents

In superconducting qubits, Josephson junctions are typically formed by creating a weak link between two superconducting materials separated by a thin insulating barrier. These junctions are crucial for the operation of superconducting qubits, as they allow for the formation of superconducting loops and the control of supercurrents. Supercurrents are electric currents that flow without resistance in superconductors. The properties of supercurrents can be outlined as follows:

- In a superconducting state, electrons form Cooper pairs, which move through the lattice structure of the material without scattering off impurities or phonons (vibrations in the lattice). This lack of scattering leads to zero electrical resistance, allowing the supercurrent to flow indefinitely without energy dissipation. An in-depth theoretical definition of *phonons* is: "A type of quasiparticle in physics, a phonon is an excited state in the quantum mechanical quantization of the modes of vibrations for elastic structures of interacting particles." At extremely low temperatures, when the material reaches the point of superconductivity with absolute zero resistance, the vibrations of molecules between the two lattice points become minimal. This allows the Cooper pairs to easily slip past, maintaining the state of zero resistance.
- Supercurrents exhibit quantum coherence, meaning the phase of the Cooper pairs' wave function remains well-defined over macroscopic distances. This coherence is critical for the operation of superconducting qubits, where supercurrents flow through Josephson junctions to create and manipulate quantum states.
- The Meissner effect expels magnetic fields from the interior of the superconductor, leading to the formation of surface currents that screen the interior from

external magnetic fields. This property is crucial for maintaining the purity of the supercurrent flow without interference from external magnetic fields.

Supercurrents can flow across a Josephson junction (two superconductors separated by a thin insulating barrier) due to the tunneling of Cooper pairs. The current that flows across the junction is related to the phase difference between the superconducting wave functions on either side of the junction, as described by the Josephson relations:

$$I = I_c \sin(\phi) \tag{8-12}$$

$$V = \frac{h}{4\pi e} \frac{d\phi}{dt} \tag{8-13}$$

where I is the supercurrent, I_c is the critical current, ϕ is the phase difference, V is the voltage, and e is the electron charge.

While the transmission of supercurrents with zero electrical resistance facilitates easy data transmission, it poses several limitations. These include

- Supercurrents only flow at temperatures below the critical temperature of the superconducting material. Maintaining these low temperatures requires sophisticated cryogenic systems.
- Not all materials exhibit superconductivity, and the critical temperature varies significantly among superconducting materials. High-temperature superconductors (HTS) are an area of active research.
- While superconductors expel magnetic fields (Meissner effect), strong external magnetic fields can suppress superconductivity and disrupt supercurrents.
- Creating and maintaining high-quality Josephson junctions without defects is challenging, as discussed in the context of unwanted Josephson junctions in superconducting qubits.

These kinds of issues arise due to the creation of unnecessary Josephson junctions, which introduce problems in the performance and reliability of superconducting qubits. While the mathematical formulations are useful for designed Josephson junctions, the unintended ones can cause issues that only become apparent after the fabrication of the chip. Therefore, it is essential to avoid the creation of unnecessary and unwanted Josephson junctions. Below are some strategies that can help in avoiding the creation of such junctions:

- **Residues from Lithography and Etching**: Incomplete removal of photoresist or e-beam resist can leave residues that act as insulating barriers, forming unintended junctions. Over-etching can damage the substrate or create rough surfaces, leading to unintentional tunnel barriers.
- **Defects in Thin Films**: Imperfections in the deposition process, such as non-uniform thickness or contamination, can create areas that behave as weak links,

forming unintended Josephson junctions. Grain boundaries and dislocations in the superconducting films can also act as barriers.
- **Oxidation Control**: Non-uniform oxidation can create variations in the thickness of the insulating barrier, leading to unintended weak links. Over-oxidation can extend beyond the intended junction areas, creating additional barriers.
- **Patterning Issues**: Misalignment during lithography can cause overlaps or gaps in the patterns, leading to unintended junctions. Undercutting during etching can create narrow constrictions that behave as Josephson junctions.
- **Contamination**: Particles and contaminants from the environment or fabrication equipment can settle on the substrate, creating localized barriers that behave as unintended Josephson junctions.

8.3.1 Phonons

When discussing superconductors or even conductors, understanding the role of phonons is essential as they play a significant role in designing efficient circuits. Phonons are quantized lattice vibrations that occur between two lattice points. In condensed matter physics, it is understood that atoms in a material are connected to each other via spring-like forces, often referred to as interatomic forces. These forces are responsible for the transfer of energy, waves, magnetic fields, and heat throughout the solid. Phonons and electrons are the two primary types of excitations or elementary particles in solids.

While electrons govern the electrical properties of materials, phonons primarily determine the speed of sound within a material and its thermal properties—specifically, how much heat is required to change the material's temperature. In superconductors, when electrons interact, they tend to repel each other due to their like charges. However, at critical temperatures, these repulsive forces are mitigated by phonons, allowing the formation of Cooper pairs—pairs of electrons that are weakly bound together by these interactions. Phonons thus enable the creation of Cooper pairs, which are essential for superconductivity. Additionally, phonons exhibit quantum mechanical behavior, often described as *phonon tunneling*. At critical temperatures, phonons facilitate the process where Cooper pairs can tunnel through energy barriers, allowing the material to enter a superconducting state, where resistance vanishes.

Let us try to understand the influence of phonons mathematically and try to understand how these vibrations between the lattice points affect the wave traveling through it by calculating the dispersion relation for phonons. So, let us define the orientation in a crystal lattice between two points so that we can understand the interaction these points have with a traversing wave. A crystal lattice consists of atoms arranged in a periodic pattern. When atoms are displaced from their equilibrium positions, they experience restoring forces due to interatomic interactions, leading to lattice vibrations. In other words, just imagine when multiple balls are connected with strings in a tight formation; now, when you pull one of the balls, it will be pulled by other neighboring balls, which will lead to vigorous vibrations to reach the stable point again.

Consider a chain of N identical atoms of mass m separated at an equal distance of a, where a is called the lattice constant. Now let the displacement for the nth atom from its stable equilibrium position be given as $u_n(t)$; the equation of motion for the system turns out to be

$$m\frac{d^2u_n(t)}{dt^2} = \sum_m K_{nm}u_m(t) \qquad (8\text{-}14)$$

where K_{nm} represents the force constant between the nth and mth atoms. Now considering only the nearest atoms for simplifying Equation 8-14, it turns out to be

$$m\frac{d^2u_n(t)}{dt^2} = -C(u_n(t) - u_{n-1}(t)) - C(u_n(t) - u_{n+1}(t)) \qquad (8\text{-}15)$$

where C represents the spring constant between the nth atom and n^{n+1} and n^{n-1}. We are currently working with only a $1D$ chain, so for a series of atoms arranged in a single chain, it will have only two nearest neighbors, one to the left and one to the right. So simplifying Equation 8-15, we get

$$m\frac{d^2u_n(t)}{dt^2} = C(u_{n+1}(t) + u_{n-1}(t) - 2u_n(t)) \qquad (8\text{-}16)$$

Considering a wave traveling through this $1D$ lattice, let the solution of the plane wave be in the format

$$u_n(t) = Ae^{i(kna-\omega t)} \qquad (8\text{-}17)$$

where A is the amplitude of the plane wave, k is the wave vector, and ω is the angular frequency of the wave. Now finding the solution for the wave inside the crystal lattice which can be obtained by replacing the value of plane wave obtained from Equation 8-17 into Equation 8-16 and solving the differential, we get

$$-m\omega^2 Ae^{i(kna-\omega t)} = CA\left(e^{i(k(n+1)a-\omega t)} + e^{i(k(n-1)a-\omega t)} - 2e^{i(kna-\omega t)}\right) \qquad (8\text{-}18)$$

Simplifying Equation 8-18, we get

$$-\omega^2 = \frac{C}{m}\left(e^{ika} + e^{-ika} - 2\right) \qquad (8\text{-}19)$$

8.3 Creation of Unwanted Josephson Junctions and Generation of...

Now as per Euler's theorem, $e^{\pm ika} = \cos(ka) \pm i \sin(ka)$, substituting the value in Equation 8-19, we get

$$\omega^2 = \frac{2C}{m}(1 - \cos(ka)) \tag{8-20}$$

Simplifying Equation 8-20 by taking the square root on both sides and using simple trigonometric transformation $(2\sin^2\theta = 1 - \cos 2\theta)$, we get

$$\omega(k) = 2\sqrt{\frac{C}{m}} \sin\left(\frac{ka}{2}\right) \tag{8-21}$$

where $\omega(k)$ represents the dispersion relation due to phonons in a $1D$ chain. Similarly, dispersion relation can be calculated for a $2D$ square lattice structure too. For a square structure, there exist two directions of force contributors, along the x direction and y direction. The equation of motions turns out to be equal to

$$m\frac{d^2 u_{n,m}(t)}{dt^2} = C_x\left(u_{n+1,m} + u_{n-1,m} - 2u_{n,m}\right) \tag{8-22}$$
$$+ C_y\left(u_{n,m+1} + u_{n,m-1} - 2u_{n,m}\right)$$

where C_x and C_y represent the spring constants to x and y directions, respectively. The next step is to write the equation of the $2D$ plane wave solution, which turns out to be

$$u_{n,m}(t) = A e^{i(k_x n a_x + k_y m a_y - \omega t)} \tag{8-23}$$

Substituting the values of Equation 8-23 into Equation 8-22 and solving for it, we get the dispersion relation for a $2D$ square lattice to be equal to

$$\omega^2(k_x, k_y) = \frac{4C_x}{m} \sin^2\left(\frac{k_x a_x}{2}\right) + \frac{4C_y}{m} \sin^2\left(\frac{k_y a_y}{2}\right) \tag{8-24}$$

An isotropic system refers to a material or a solid that shows uniform and same properties from all directions; that is, properties such as thermal conductivity, electrical conductivity, optical properties, and mechanical properties remain the same despite the direction of measure. For isotropic systems, the $2D$ phonon dispersion relation obtained in Equation 8-24 can be reduced down to $C_x = C_y = C$, $a_x = a_y = a$.

$$\omega(k_x, k_y) = 2\sqrt{\frac{C}{m}} \sqrt{\sin^2\left(\frac{k_x a}{2}\right) + \sin^2\left(\frac{k_y a}{2}\right)} \tag{8-25}$$

Similar to how we calculated for $2D$ and $1D$, following the same steps, we can even calculate for a $3D$ cube too. A $3D$ cube will have another addition direction of force contributor for calculating the equation of motion through the z-axis. The equation of motion for a $3D$ lattice cube structure can be written as

$$m\frac{d^2 u_{n,m,l}(t)}{dt^2} = C_x\left(u_{n+1,m,l} + u_{n-1,m,l} - 2u_{n,m,l}\right) \\ + C_y\left(u_{n,m+1,l} + u_{n,m-1,l} - 2u_{n,m,l}\right) \\ + C_z\left(u_{n,m,l+1} + u_{n,m,l-1} - 2u_{n,m,l}\right) \tag{8-26}$$

Similarly, the plane wave solution can be represented as

$$u_{n,m,l}(t) = A e^{i(k_x n a_x + k_y m a_y + k_z l a_z - \omega t)} \tag{8-27}$$

Solving this, the dispersion relation for a $3D$ plane wave turns out to be equal to

$$\omega^2(k_x, k_y, k_z) = \frac{4C_x}{m}\sin^2\left(\frac{k_x a_x}{2}\right) + \frac{4C_y}{m}\sin^2\left(\frac{k_y a_y}{2}\right) + \frac{4C_z}{m}\sin^2\left(\frac{k_z a_z}{2}\right) \tag{8-28}$$

Understanding and calculating the dispersion relation is very important whenever manufacturing of devices comes into play. The dispersion relation helps in providing an equation and relation between the wave frequency (ω) and the wave vector (k) of the propagating wave in a medium. This relation helps us in providing a better understanding of how a wave is interacting and traversing inside the medium and provides a clear picture of the wave velocity and energy required to transfer the wave inside the medium alongside the thermal characteristics of the medium and sound propagation at the microscopic level.

8.3.2 Supercurrents and Magnetism

Once supercurrents are introduced in superconductors, the concept of magnetism arises. As Maxwell's laws of electromagnetism tell us, any moving charge generates a magnetic field. Therefore, supercurrents, with their high current densities, are expected to generate significant magnetic fields inside the superconductors. However, this phenomenon is not referred to as "supermagnetism," but rather the *Meissner effect*. As discussed earlier, the Meissner effect is one of the defining characteristics of superconductors. It describes the expulsion of magnetic fields from the interior of a superconducting material when it transitions below its critical temperature. Above the critical temperature, the current flowing through the conductor experiences resistance, causing it to generate a magnetic field inside the conductor. In simple terms, above the critical temperature, phonons (the vibrations of the crystal lattice) are tightly bound, preventing the formation of

8.3 Creation of Unwanted Josephson Junctions and Generation of...

Cooper pairs. When the temperature is reduced to the critical temperature of the superconductor, phonon vibrations decrease, allowing Cooper pairs to move through the material without resistance. As a result, the magnetic field is expelled from the superconductor—this is the Meissner effect.

The Meissner effect makes superconductors perfect diamagnets, with a magnetic susceptibility of $\chi = -1$, meaning that the magnetic field inside the superconductor is zero, regardless of the external magnetic field strength. The expulsion of magnetic fields from the superconductor occurs due to supercurrents generated on its surface. These supercurrents create a magnetic field that opposes and cancels the external magnetic field inside the bulk of the material. When an external magnetic field is applied to a superconductor, screening supercurrents are induced on the surface, generating a magnetic field that exactly cancels the applied field inside the superconductor.

The formation of supercurrents and the expulsion of magnetic fields can be understood energetically. In the superconducting state, free energy is minimized when the magnetic field is expelled, as maintaining a magnetic field inside a superconductor would require additional energy. The coherence of the superconducting wave function ψ ensures that the supercurrents flow in such a way that cancels the external magnetic field. This coherence is crucial for the establishment of the Meissner effect. The supercurrent is a current that flows without resistance due to the coherent motion of Cooper pairs. The current density J can be expressed in terms of the phase gradient of the macroscopic wave function as

$$J = \frac{n_s e^2}{m} A \tag{8-29}$$

where n_s is the density of Cooper pairs, e is the electron charge, m is the electron mass, and A is the magnetic vector potential. The macroscopic wave function can be expressed as $\Psi = |\Psi|e^{i\theta}$, where $|\Psi|$ represents the density of superconducting electrons, and θ is the phase of the wave function.

The London equations describe the behavior of supercurrents and their role in the Meissner effect. These equations indicate that the current density is proportional to the magnetic vector potential, thereby providing a unified description of supercurrents and the Meissner effect. Regarding the magnetic field inside the superconductor, while it does eventually drop to zero at the critical temperature, it does not do so instantly. Instead, it takes a certain amount of time for the field to decay, and this process is characterized by the *London penetration depth* (λ). The London penetration depth represents the characteristic length over which the magnetic field decays exponentially into the superconductor. For conventional superconductors, this length is typically on the order of tens to hundreds of nanometers. The change in the magnetic field as a function of depth is given by the following equation:

$$B(x) = B_0 e^{-\frac{x}{\lambda}} \tag{8-30}$$

where x is the depth below the surface, and B_0 is the magnetic field at the surface.

Addressing these challenges is important, and in order to achieve a smooth fabrication process, it is essential to keep these constraints in check by monitoring the entire fabrication process. In the following section, we will be discussing the importance of packaging in the manufacturing process. The packaging of these superconducting qubits is handled by an intricate process known as flip-chip technology.

8.4 Flip Chip

Flip-chip technology, also known as Controlled Collapse Chip Connection (C4), is a method for interconnecting dies—such as semiconductor devices, IC chips, integrated passive devices, and microelectromechanical systems (MEMS)—to external circuitry using solder bumps deposited onto the chip pads. C4 technology is a type of solder bump connection widely used in microelectronics and semiconductor packaging. It involves placing solder bumps on the active areas of a semiconductor chip, flipping the chip over, and aligning it with the target substrate (e.g., a circuit board). The solder bumps are then reflowed to form connections between the chip and the substrate. The term "controlled collapse" refers to the precise control over the collapse of the solder bumps during the reflow process, ensuring reliable and high-density interconnections in integrated circuits. The process of fabricating a flip chip is similar to conventional IC (integrated circuit) manufacturing, but with additional steps. Toward the end of the manufacturing sequence, the attachment pads undergo metallization treatments to enhance their solder receptivity. This involves applying specialized metal layers to the pads. Subsequently, a small solder dot is deposited on each metalized pad, and the chips are cut out from the wafer in the standard manner.

To integrate the flip chip into a circuit, the chip is inverted, bringing the solder dots into contact with connectors on the underlying electronics or circuit board. The solder is then re-melted through processes like thermosonic bonding or reflow soldering, establishing an electrical connection. This configuration introduces a small gap between the chip's circuitry and the underlying mounting. In many cases, an electrically insulating adhesive is used for *underfilling*, which enhances mechanical stability, creates a thermal bridge, and reduces stress on solder joints due to differential thermal expansion between the chip and the circuit board. The underfill effectively distributes thermal expansion mismatches, reducing stress concentrations in the solder joints and thus minimizing the risk of premature failure.

Various methods can be employed for attaching solder balls onto chips. Figure 8-5 demonstrates the method of employing these solder balls onto the chip. One approach involves separately manufacturing the solder balls and using a vacuum pick-up device to place them onto chips with flux-applied contact pads. Alternatively, electroplating can be used, where seed metals are initially deposited onto the wafer, enabling solder adherence during the electroplating process. The seed metals, deposited via sputtering, are selectively applied using a photoresist

8.4 Flip Chip

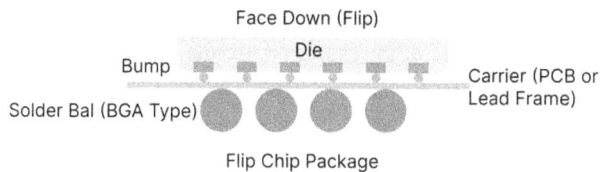

Figure 8-5 Flip-chip packaging process

mask. This entire process, known as *wafer bumping*, produces solder balls typically ranging from 75 to 500 microns in diameter. A notable advancement in high-speed mounting techniques occurred in 2008 through a collaboration between Reel Service Ltd. and Siemens AG, leading to the development of *MicroTape*. This innovation integrated a tape-and-reel process into assembly methods, enabling high-speed placement with a 99.90% pick rate and a placement rate of 21,000 components per hour using standard PCB assembly equipment.

Substrates manufactured with build-up film, such as Ajinomoto build-up film, follow a meticulous process. These substrates are created around a core, with film layers stacked on the core through vacuum lamination at elevated temperatures. After curing the film, laser vias are formed using CO_2 or UV lasers. The blind vias are then cleaned, and the build-up film undergoes chemical roughening with permanganate. Electroless copper plating is employed for copper deposition, followed by patterning the copper through photolithography and etching. This multilayered process is repeated for each layer of the substrate.

Flip-chip technology is integral not only to the packaging and manufacturing of conventional electronic circuits and integrated circuits but also plays a critical role in the fabrication of superconducting qubits. In the context of superconducting circuits, the flip-chip process is essential for creating high-fidelity qubit connections and ensuring efficient integration. In summary, let's briefly explore each step involved in the superconducting circuit manufacturing process and discuss the advantages and benefits it offers in enhancing the performance of quantum systems.

In quantum computing, flip-chip designs play a crucial role in the packaging and interconnection of quantum processors. Flip-chip technology allows for the precise placement and interconnection of quantum bits (qubits) on a chip, significantly improving the overall performance and scalability of quantum circuits. Below, we explore how flip-chip designs are utilized in quantum computing:

- **High-Density Interconnection**: Quantum processors often consist of an array of qubits, where the interconnection between these qubits is critical for the implementation of quantum gates and algorithms. Flip-chip designs enable high-density interconnections, allowing qubits to be placed in close proximity. This optimizes quantum gate operations by reducing the physical distance over which quantum information needs to travel.
- **Improved Signal Integrity**: Quantum information is extremely fragile and can be easily affected by environmental noise and interference. Flip-chip designs

offer a more controlled environment by allowing the qubit chip to be mounted precisely onto the substrate, thus minimizing the impact of external noise and improving signal integrity.
- **Enhanced Cooling**: Maintaining the quantum coherence of qubits requires extremely low temperatures, often achieved using cryogenic systems. Flip-chip designs facilitate effective cooling solutions by ensuring that the qubit chip maintains close contact with cooling elements, such as dilution refrigerators. This proximity enhances thermal conduction, crucial for preserving qubit coherence.
- **Reduced Inductance and Capacitance**: Parasitic elements like inductance and capacitance can degrade the performance of quantum circuits. Flip-chip designs minimize these parasitics by enabling direct connections between the qubit and the substrate without the need for traditional wire bonds, thereby reducing signal delays and losses.
- **Scalability**: As quantum computers evolve, there is a need to scale to larger numbers of qubits to solve more complex problems. Flip-chip designs provide a scalable solution, enabling efficient placement and connectivity of qubits as the size of quantum processors increases. This scalability is essential for the development of fault-tolerant quantum systems.
- **Precision Alignment**: The reliable execution of quantum gates and accurate qubit measurements require precise alignment of qubits with respect to control and readout components. Flip-chip technology ensures this precision, thereby enhancing the fidelity of quantum operations.
- **Integration with Classical Electronics**: Quantum computers often need classical control electronics for qubit manipulation and readout. Flip-chip designs enable seamless integration between quantum and classical components on the same chip, improving the overall efficiency and reducing latency in hybrid quantum-classical operations.
- **Minimized Crosstalk**: Crosstalk between qubits, where the state of one qubit unintentionally affects another, is a significant challenge in quantum computing. Flip-chip designs help reduce crosstalk by optimizing the placement and routing of qubits on the chip, thus enhancing qubit isolation.
- **Wafer-Scale Integration**: Flip-chip designs support wafer-scale integration (wafer-scale integration is a technology that allows large-scale integration of the integrated chips onto silicon wafers), allowing multiple qubits to be processed simultaneously during the fabrication process. This approach improves manufacturing efficiency and reduces costs, contributing to the practical realization of large-scale quantum processors.

8.5 Chip Fabrication Parameters

The preparation and fabrication process of superconducting qubits is critical, as even a few micrometers of deviation can result in the formation of an unwanted Josephson junction between two points, leading to false measurements and faulty chip designs. In this section, we will explore how such unwanted Josephson junctions can

8.5 Chip Fabrication Parameters

arise during the fabrication process. However, before initiating the fabrication of superconducting qubits, certain standards and measurements must be considered. The three most important parameters to assess are inter-chip spacing, chip tilt, and transition temperature. Let's dive into the details regarding these processes, how they can arise during fabrication, and how they can be mitigated.

8.5.1 Inter-Chip Spacing

Inter-chip spacing refers to the physical separation between the active regions of adjacent chips in a flip-chip assembly. It includes the distance between qubits or other functional elements on the chips' surfaces. This spacing is typically measured in micrometers (μm) or nanometers (nm) and plays a significant role in determining the performance and reliability of the quantum computing system. Inter-chip spacing is particularly important in quantum computing, where delicate quantum states are manipulated and preserved. This spacing is important as it reduces the qubit crosstalk and reduces the interference of electromagnetic waves traveling in adjacent transmission lines, which could lead to errors and decoherence.

The inter-chip spacing is typically determined by several factors. These constraints help mitigate the formation of unwanted Josephson junctions or unwanted couplers between two connection points. These factors include

- **Chip Size and Layout**: The dimensions of the chips involved in the assembly, including their width and length, are critical. Consideration of the arrangement of qubits or functional elements on each chip's surface ensures that each chip is placed optimally, which can help mitigate cross-connection issues during fabrication. Standard PCB (Printed Circuit Board) manufacturing processes can be employed for the optimal placement of the chips.
- **Minimum Spacing Requirements**: It is important to identify the minimum spacing required to maintain the desired level of interaction between qubits or functional elements. Quantum algorithms often rely on specific coupling strengths between qubits. Therefore, the spacing should be adjusted to either promote stronger coupling (for certain algorithms) or to reduce interaction for improved qubit coherence (in other cases).
- **Tolerances and Manufacturing Constraints**: Manufacturing tolerances imposed by fabrication processes must be considered. These include limitations in lithography resolution, alignment accuracy during assembly, and the availability of suitable packaging materials with thermal and mechanical properties. Lithography resolution determines the minimum feature size that can be reliably patterned on the substrate during the fabrication process.
- **Thermal Considerations**: Managing thermal dissipation is crucial. Smaller inter-chip spacing may lead to increased heat generation, which could degrade qubit performance. For superconducting qubits, maintaining a low operating temperature is essential. If the inter-chip spacing is too small and the coupling strength too high, the resulting temperature spike could push the chip temperature

beyond the optimal 4K threshold, risking decoherence. Therefore, balancing thermal management with inter-chip spacing is critical for ensuring the stability of qubits.
- **Simulation and Optimization**: Computational modeling and simulation tools can be used to analyze the effects of different inter-chip spacing configurations on qubit behavior and system performance. These tools help optimize the spacing to meet all performance and reliability criteria.

These criteria are essential for ensuring that the chips perform as expected. However, several other factors can influence the inter-chip spacing. The most notable factors are thermal considerations, qubit coupling requirements, and manufacturing defects that may arise during assembly. These micro- or nanoscale defects often go unnoticed but can result in faulty readings and degraded performance. Mitigation strategies include

- **Simulation Studies**: Computational models can simulate qubit behavior under different inter-chip spacing configurations, aiding in the selection of optimal designs for the quantum processor.
- **Experimental Validation**: Prototyping and testing various inter-chip spacings help validate theoretical predictions, ensuring that the design performs as expected before full-scale fabrication.
- **Iterative Refinement**: Continuous improvement through feedback from experimental results and theoretical advancements allows for the refinement of inter-chip spacing choices over successive fabrication iterations.

8.5.2 Chip Tilt

Chip tilt refers to the angular deviation of a chip from its intended alignment during the flip-chip assembly process. In semiconductor manufacturing, flip-chip assembly is a common technique used to connect integrated circuits (chips) to substrates or other chips, typically using solder bumps as interconnects. Proper alignment of the chips is crucial for ensuring reliable electrical connections and optimal device performance. Chip tilt can occur due to various factors during the assembly process and can have significant implications for the quality and reliability of the final product. The required inclination and the angle at which the chip is produced are crucial factors for the optimized use of the chip. Calculating chip tilt typically involves measuring the angular deviation of the chip from its intended alignment, which may require specialized equipment and techniques. The measurement of chip inclination can be performed by

- **Alignment Measurement Setup**: Set up a measurement system capable of accurately assessing the alignment of the chip relative to the substrate or reference plane. This may involve using optical alignment systems, coordinate measurement machines (CMMs), or specialized alignment stages.

- **Reference Plane Establishment**: Establish a reference plane against which the chip's alignment will be measured. This plane could be the substrate surface or another fixed reference point in the assembly setup.
- **Chip Tilt Measurement**: Use the measurement system to determine the angular deviation of the chip from the reference plane. This measurement may involve capturing images of the chip and substrate alignment, analyzing the position of fiducial markers or alignment features, or performing precision angle measurements.
- **Data Analysis**: Process the measurement data to calculate the chip tilt angle. This may involve comparing the positions of fiducial markers or alignment features on the chip and substrate, applying geometric calculations to determine angular deviations, or utilizing specialized software algorithms for alignment analysis.
- **Validation and Calibration**: Validate the accuracy of the tilt measurement system and calibration procedures by comparing measured results with known reference values or using calibration standards. Ensure that any sources of measurement error, such as optical distortion or mechanical misalignment, are accounted for and minimized.
- **Iterative Adjustment**: If chip tilt exceeds acceptable tolerances, make necessary adjustments to the assembly process, equipment setup, or substrate design to minimize tilt deviations. Iteratively refine the assembly procedure and measurement techniques to achieve optimal chip alignment.

It is important to note that accurately calculating chip tilt requires specialized equipment, expertise, and careful calibration procedures. Manufacturers may employ measurement techniques, including optical imaging, precision alignment stages, and sophisticated analysis software, to assess and control chip tilt during the flip-chip assembly process.

Many factors can influence the accuracy of chip tilt during the manufacturing process. Similar to inter-chip spacing, manufacturing defects contribute to random errors that can cause issues. Chip tilt can result from inaccuracies in the alignment process, where the chip is not precisely positioned relative to the substrate or other chips. Misalignments may occur due to imperfections in the assembly equipment, variations in the flatness of the bonding surfaces, or errors in the alignment procedure.

Another factor influencing chip tilt is thermal expansion and contraction. During the flip-chip bonding process, temperature gradients across the assembly can cause differential expansion or contraction between the chip and the substrate, leading to mechanical stress and deformation. Uneven heating or cooling can exacerbate these effects, resulting in non-uniform chip tilt.

Additionally, mechanical stress plays a major role in chip tilt. Excessive force or uneven stress distribution during the assembly process can distort the chip's position and lead to misalignment. The flexibility of the substrate or mounting surface can also influence chip tilt. Flexible substrates may deform under the bonding process's pressure, affecting the chip's alignment, while rigid substrates provide better support and stability, minimizing chip tilt.

To mitigate errors caused by chip tilt, several strategies can be employed:

- **Precision Assembly Equipment**: High-precision flip-chip bonding machines with advanced alignment capabilities minimize chip tilt during assembly, ensuring accurate positioning of interconnecting components.
- **In Situ Monitoring**: Real-time monitoring techniques, such as optical alignment systems or feedback-controlled assembly platforms, can detect and correct chip tilt deviations during bonding.
- **Flexure-Based Mounting**: Utilizing compliant mechanisms or flexible substrates helps accommodate minor misalignments caused by chip tilt, enhancing robustness against mechanical stress and thermal expansion.

8.5.3 Transition Temperatures

Transition temperatures are critical points in the thermal behavior of materials where significant changes occur in their physical or chemical properties. These transitions mark the boundary between different phases or states of matter, and they play a fundamental role in determining material behavior and functionality. Several types of transition temperatures are considered, including

- **Melting Point (Solid-Liquid Transition)**: The melting point is perhaps the most well-known transition temperature, representing the temperature at which a solid material transitions into a liquid state. At the melting point, the intermolecular forces holding the solid lattice together are overcome by thermal energy, allowing the material to flow and take the shape of its container.
- **Freezing Point (Liquid-Solid Transition)**: The freezing point is the temperature at which a liquid material transitions into a solid state. It is equivalent to the melting point but in the reverse direction. During freezing, the kinetic energy of the molecules decreases, causing them to arrange into a regular crystalline structure characteristic of the solid phase.
- **Boiling Point (Liquid-Gas Transition)**: The boiling point is the temperature at which a liquid material transitions into a gas phase. At this temperature, the vapor pressure of the liquid equals the atmospheric pressure (or the external pressure), allowing bubbles of vapor to form throughout the liquid, leading to vaporization.
- **Condensation Point (Gas-Liquid Transition)**: The condensation point is the temperature at which a gas transitions into a liquid phase. It is equivalent to the boiling point but in the reverse direction. Condensation occurs when vapor molecules lose thermal energy and come together to form a liquid.
- **Sublimation Point (Solid-Gas Transition)**: Some materials undergo sublimation, transitioning directly from a solid to a gas phase without passing through the liquid phase. The sublimation point is the temperature at which this transition occurs. Dry ice (solid carbon dioxide) is a common example of a substance that undergoes sublimation.

8.5 Chip Fabrication Parameters

- **Glass Transition Temperature (Tg)**: In amorphous materials such as polymers, glasses, and certain ceramics, the glass transition temperature (Tg) marks the transition from a rigid, glassy state to a more flexible, rubbery state. At Tg, the molecular mobility increases significantly, leading to changes in mechanical properties.
- **Curie Temperature (Tc)**: In magnetic materials, the Curie temperature (Tc) is the temperature at which they undergo a transition from a ferromagnetic or ferrimagnetic state to a paramagnetic state. Above Tc, the material loses its permanent magnetization.
- **Superconducting Transition Temperature (Tc)**: Superconductors exhibit a transition from a resistive state to a superconducting state at a critical temperature known as the superconducting transition temperature (Tc). Below Tc, superconductors display zero electrical resistance and expel magnetic fields.

Transition temperatures are typically determined experimentally using techniques such as differential scanning calorimetry (DSC), thermal gravimetric analysis (TGA), or differential thermal analysis (DTA). These measurements provide valuable information about material properties, phase stability, and thermal behavior, which are essential for various applications in fields such as materials science, chemistry, physics, and engineering. We will discuss these techniques in detail for a deeper understanding and analysis.

Transition temperature analysis plays a crucial role in solving and manufacturing flip-chips by extending the inter-chip and chip-tilt considerations. Temperature constraints are usually mitigated using transition temperature analysis, which facilitates a more accurate and effective assembly process. Let's explore how this transition temperature analysis is performed:

- **Differential Scanning Calorimetry (DSC)**: Differential scanning calorimetry (DSC) is a powerful analytical technique used to measure the heat flow associated with thermal transitions in materials as a function of temperature. It provides valuable information about phase transitions, reaction kinetics, purity, and thermal stability of materials. DSC works on the principle of comparing the heat flow into or out of a sample with that of a reference material, as both are subjected to the same temperature program. The difference in heat flow between the sample and the reference material is measured as a function of temperature. This differential heat flow reveals thermal events occurring within the sample.

    A typical DSC instrument consists of a sample holder, a reference holder, a furnace, temperature sensors, and a heat flow sensor. The sample and reference materials are placed in their respective holders, and both are subjected to the same temperature ramp. As the temperature increases, both materials absorb or release heat. The temperature difference between the sample and reference is measured by the heat flow sensor. When the sample undergoes a phase transition (such as melting or crystallization), it either absorbs or releases energy, resulting in a change in the heat flow detected by the sensor. The output of a DSC experiment is typically a plot of heat flow (or heat capacity) versus temperature. Peaks or valleys in this plot correspond to transitions in the sample. The transition temperatures can be determined by identifying the inflection points or peaks in the curve.

- **Thermal Gravimetric Analysis (TGA)**: Thermal gravimetric analysis (TGA) is a powerful analytical technique used to study the thermal properties of materials by measuring changes in mass as a function of temperature or time under controlled atmospheric conditions. TGA operates on the principle that the mass of a sample changes as a function of temperature due to physical or chemical processes such as decomposition, oxidation, dehydration, and desorption. In TGA, the sample is heated at a constant rate, and its weight change is continuously monitored over time. A typical TGA instrument consists of a balance (microbalance), a furnace, a temperature controller, a gas flow system (optional), and a data acquisition system. The sample is placed in a crucible, which is then loaded onto the balance. The balance continuously measures the sample's mass throughout the experiment.

  The sample is heated at a constant rate (ramp rate), while its mass is continuously monitored. As the temperature increases, the sample undergoes various thermal processes, leading to mass loss or gain. The change in mass is recorded as a function of temperature or time. The output of a TGA experiment is typically a thermogram, which is a plot of mass (or mass change) versus temperature (or time). From the thermogram, various parameters can be determined, such as onset temperature, peak temperature, rate of mass loss, and total mass change.

- **Differential Thermal Analysis (DTA)**: Differential thermal analysis (DTA) is a thermal analysis technique used to investigate phase transitions, chemical reactions, and other thermal phenomena by measuring temperature differences between a sample and an inert reference material as they are subjected to controlled heating or cooling. DTA operates on the principle of measuring the temperature difference (δT) between the sample and reference materials as they undergo controlled heating or cooling. Any endothermic (heat-absorbing) or exothermic (heat-releasing) processes occurring in the sample lead to temperature differences compared to the reference. The reference material typically exhibits known thermal behavior (usually inert), allowing the detection of temperature changes that are exclusively related to the sample's thermal events. Before the experiment begins, both the sample and reference materials are heated or cooled together from a starting temperature, establishing a baseline showing the temperature difference (δT) between the sample and reference under inert conditions. Once the baseline is established, the actual experiment begins, and both the sample and reference are subjected to controlled heating or cooling at a constant rate.

  As temperature changes occur, the difference in temperature between the sample and reference is continuously recorded. Endothermic processes (e.g., melting, evaporation) in the sample result in temperature decreases ($\delta T < 0$), while exothermic processes (e.g., crystallization, chemical reactions) lead to temperature increases ($\delta T > 0$). These thermal events are detected as peaks or valleys in the DTA curve. The output of a DTA experiment is typically a plot of temperature difference (δT) versus temperature or time. Peaks or valleys in the curve correspond to thermal events occurring in the sample, such as phase transitions or chemical reactions. The position (temperature), shape, and area of the peaks provide information about the nature and kinetics of the thermal events.

Inter-chip spacing, chip tilt, and transition temperatures are critical considerations in flip-chip fabrication for quantum computing, influencing qubit performance, reliability, and scalability. By optimizing these parameters through advanced manufacturing techniques and materials engineering, researchers can unlock the full potential of quantum computing technologies. In the previous sections, we have covered the basics of flip-chip and end-to-end manufacturing processes and gained a better understanding of how to fabricate and package a superconducting qubit.

8.6 Conclusion

In this chapter, we explored the methods of manufacturing superconducting qubits, starting from the discussion of the fabrication process, including sputtering and evaporation, to the packaging methods like flip chip. This chapter also addressed the issues that arise during the manufacturing processes, such as the creation of the unwanted Josephson junctions. As discussed, this chapter provided an important understanding of all the parameters essential for the manufacturing processes required to be submitted and taken into account while fabricating a superconducting qubit.

References

Barends, R., Kelly, J., Megrant, A., Sank, D., Jeffrey, E., Chen, Y., Yin, Y., Chiaro, B., Mutus, J., Neill, C., O'Malley, P., Roushan, P., Wenner, J., White, T. C., Cleland, A. N., and Martinis, J. M. (2013). Coherent josephson qubit suitable for scalable quantum integrated circuits. *Phys. Rev. Lett.*, 111:080502.

Bouchiat, V., Vion, D., Joyez, P., Esteve, D., and Devoret, M. H. (1998). Quantum coherence with a single cooper pair. *Physica Scripta*, 1998(T76):165.

Campbell, D., Kamal, A., Ranzani, L., Senatore, M., and LaHaye, M. (2022). Modular tunable coupler for superconducting circuits. *Physical Review Applied*.

Chen, Y., Neill, C., Roushan, P., Leung, N., Fang, M., Barends, R., Kelly, J., Campbell, B., Chen, Z., Chiaro, B., Dunsworth, A., Jeffrey, E., Megrant, A., Mutus, J., O'Malley, P., Quintana, C., Sank, D., Vainsencher, A., Wenner, J., White, T., Geller, M. R., Cleland, A., and Martinis, J. M. (2014). Qubit architecture with high coherence and fast tunable coupling. *Phys. Rev. Lett.*, 113:220502.

Friedman, J., Patel, V., Chen, W., Tolpygo, S. K., and Lukens, J. E. (2000). Quantum superposition of distinct macroscopic states. *Nature*, 406:43–46.

Hauke, P., Katzgraber, H. G., Lechner, W., Nishimori, H., and Oliver, W. D. (2020). Perspectives of quantum annealing: methods and implementations. *Reports on Progress in Physics*, 83(5):054401.

Koch, J., Yu, T. M., Gambetta, J., Houck, A. A., Schuster, D. I., Majer, J., Blais, A., Devoret, M. H., and Girvin, S. M. (2007). Charge-insensitive qubit design derived from the Cooper pair box. *Physical Review A*, 76(4):042319. https://doi.org/10.1103/PhysRevA.76.042319.

Manucharyan, V. E., Koch, J., Glazman, L. I., and Devoret, M. H. (2009). Fluxonium: single cooper-pair circuit free of charge offsets. *Science*, 326(5949):113–6. https://doi.org/10.1126/science.1175552.PMID:19797655.

Martinis, J. M., Devoret, M. H., and Clarke, J. (1985). Energy-level quantization in the zero-voltage state of a current-biased josephson junction. *Physical Review Letters*, 55:1543.

Minev, Z. K., Leghtas, Z., Mundhada, S. O., et al. (2021). Energy-participation quantization of josephson circuits. *npj Quantum Information*, 7:131.

Miyanaga, T., Tomonaga, A., Ito, H., Mukai, H., and Tsai, J. (2021). Ultrastrong tunable coupler between superconducting LC resonators. *Physical Review Applied*.

Nakamura, Y., Pashkin, Y. A., and Tsai, J. S. (1999). Coherent control of macroscopic quantum states in a single-cooper-pair box. *Nature*, 398(6730):786–788.

Rahamim, J., Behrle, T., Peterer, M. J., Patterson, A., Spring, P. A., Tsunoda, T., Manenti, R., Tancredi, G., and Leek, P. J. (2017). Double-sided coaxial circuit QED with out-of-plane wiring. *Applied Physics Letters*, 110(22):222602.

van der Wal, C. H., ter Haar, A. C., Wilhelm, F. K., Schouten, R. N., Harmans, C. J. P. M., Orlando, T. P., Lloyd, S., and Mooij, J. E. (2000). Quantum superposition of macroscopic persistent-current states. *Science*, 290(5492):773–777.

Vion, D. et al. (2002). Manipulating the quantum state of an electrical circuit. *Science*, 296:886–889.

Index

A
Action, defined, 13
Adaptive solver, 209
add_interaction() method, 217
Admittance matrix, 197–199
Agrangian formulation, 39
AliceReadoutResonator, 214
Amplifier, 184–185
AND gate, 9
Anharmonicity, 23, 145–146, 149, 228, 265, 272, 279–281
Annihilation operator, 40–41

B
Barkhausen criterion, 186
Bell entanglement, *see* Bell states
Bell states, 7, 95–96
Bipolar junction transistor (BJT) technology, 9–10, 185–186
Bit inversion gate, *see* NOT gate
Bob's operations, 98
Boiling point, 312
Bosons, 20
Bus resonator coupler, 170–173

C
Capacitance matrix, 188–191, 202–210, 212, 213, 216
Capacitive coupling, 165, 167, 171
Charge conservation, 45
Charge dispersion, 275–278
Charge qubit, 56–58
Charge vector matrix, 189
Charging energy, 158
Chi matrix, 216

Chip fabrication parameters
  concept, 308–309
  inter-chip spacing, 309–310
  tilt, 310–312
  transition temperatures, 312–315
Chip segmentation, 176
Chip tilt, 310–312
circuitGraph() method, 215
Circuit theory, 14
Classical circuits, 9–10
  advantages, 13
  oscillator, 11–12
Classical computing, 1, 3, 18
Classical Hamiltonian, 63–64
Classical oscillator, 11–12
Classic harmonic oscillator
  Hamiltonian formulation, 39–40
  Lagrangian formulation, 39
  Newtonian analysis, 38–39
Clausius–Clapeyron equation, 296
Clifford gate, 90
CNOT gate, *see* Controlled-NOT (CNOT) gate
Coaxmon qubit
  advantages, 74
  circuit design, 74
  defined, 73–74
Coherence times, 29, 31
Communication, 13
  measurement and classical, 98
Commutator notation, 40
Composite boson, 20
COMSOL multiphysics, 175
Concentric transmon qubit, 145–148
Condensation point, 312
Conjugate transpose of square root of X gate, 92–93
Constructive interference, 8

Contamination, 301
Control gate, 93–94
Controlled collapse, 306
Controlled Collapse Chip Connection (C4), 306
Controlled-controlled unitary (CC-U) gate, 91
Controlled-NOT (CNOT) gate, 7, 9, 87–88, 93, 102
Controlled-phase gate, 91
Control qubit, 87
Convergence, 177, 238–241, 247–248, 260–263
Cooling systems, 32
Cooper pair box (CPB), 56
    anharmonicity, 279–281
    charge dispersion, 275–278
    concept, 265
    dephasing time, 281–282
    E_J and E_c calculation, 286–287
    energy level differences, 278–279
    Hamiltonian model, 267–269
    Qutip simulation, 283–286
    transmon qubit, 266–267, 269–275
Cooper pairs, 19–20, 54, 56–57
Cooper pair tunneling, 21
Coplanar waveguides (CPWs), 124, 130–131, 258
    characteristics, 156–157
    components, 204
    connections, 155
    registers, 156
    resonator
        EPR analysis, 246
        finite element Eigenmode analysis, 243–245
        QiskitMetal GUI, 242–243
        refining convergence and EM field analysis, 245
    route meander, 139–142
CPhase gate, 91
Creation/raising operator, 41
Cross-Kerr coupling, 256–257
Crosstalk-aware pulse shaping, 33
Cryptanalysis, 104
Cryptography, 13
Curie temperature, 313

D

DC-SQUID configuration, 266
Decoherence, 33, 136
Degrees of freedom, 14
Dephasing time, 281–282
Deposition techniques, 162
Destructive interference, 8
Diamagnetism, 25–26
Differential scanning calorimetry (DSC), 313–314
Differential thermal analysis (DTA), 313–315
Direct coupler, 166–168, 173
    configuration, 213
    generic conductor set, 211–212
    modules, 210
    output, 218
    parameters, 213, 215
    registry, 211
    resonator, 214–215
    transmon capacitance matrices, 212
Direction routing, 133–136
Direct solver, 209
Dolan style Josephson junction, 158, 161–164
Double-hanger resonator (SParam)
    capacitively coupled transmission lines, 257–258
    CPWs, 258–259
    Eigenmode and impedance analysis, 260
    geometry design, 257
    GUI design, 260
    simulation and convergence, 260–263

E

Early quantum gates, 4–5
Eigenfield phasors, 225
Eigenmode analysis, 235, 260
    setup, 252–253
    setup with buffer adjustment, 253–256
Eigenvalue solver, 209
Elastance matrix, 200–201
Electric field distribution, 240–241, 245–247, 249
Electromagnetic analysis and quantization, 173–178
Electromagnetic fields, 239–241
Electromagnetic signal interference, 134, 136
Electromagnetic theory, 45
Encoding, 13
Endothermic processes, 314
Energy consumption, 32–33
Energy-level calculation, 201
Energy level computation, 269–271
Energy level differences, 278–279
Energy-participation ratio (EPR) model, 175
    concept, 221
    electromagnetic structures, 221
    QiskitMetal
        examples, 235–263
        quantum circuit in, 234–235

quantization (*see* Quantization)
Entanglement
　Bell states, 7
　defined, 3–4, 6–7
　quantum error correction, 4
EPR pairs, *see* Bell states
Error correction, 34, 96
Error reduction, 201
Etching, 300
Euler–Lagrange equation, 15, 39
Euler's theorem, 303
Evaporation
　defined, 295
　deposition, 295–297
　equation, 297
　heating technique, 295
　shadow, 298–299
　solid/liquid substance, 295
　vacuum chamber, 295

F
Fabrication process, 33
Falcon quantum processors, 33
Faraday's law, 26, 185
Faraday's law of induction, 45
Fault-tolerant quantum computing, 103
Fermions, 20
Field-effect transistor (FET), 185–186
Finite element Eigenmode analysis, 237–239, 243–245
Finite element method (FEM), 224–226
First-order perturbation theory, 66–67
Flip-chip technology, 306–308
Flux noise, 33
Fluxonium qubit
　advantages, 72
　design features, 71
　development, 71
　operational characteristics, 72
Flux quantum, 23–24
Flux qubit, 30–31, 58–60
Fourier transform, 40
Freezing point, 312
Frequency response, 177–178
Full-wave methods, 173–174, 177

G
Gas flow sputtering, 293–295
Gas-liquid transition, 312
Gaussian distribution, 52
Generalized coordinates, 14

GHZ state, *see* Greenberger–Horne–Zeilinger (GHZ) state
Ginzburg–Landau theory, 29
Glass transition temperature, 313
Gmon qubit
　advantages and features, 73
　circuit design, 72–73
Graphical user interface (GUI), 34, 116, 119–121, 204, 236–237
Greenberger–Horne–Zeilinger (GHZ) state, 7, 96–97
Grover's algorithm, 5, 8, 13, 78, 104–105
gui.autoscale(), 120
gui =MetalGUI(design), 119
gui.rebuild(), 120, 121
gui.screenshot(), 119

H
Hadamard gate, 6, 7, 9, 80, 84–85, 91, 95, 99, 100, 103, 105
Hamiltonian circuit
　analogy, 49
　conjugate variables, 49
　eigenvalues, 51
　fluctuations, 52
　generation, 46–48
　harmonic oscillator, 51–52
　ladder operators, 50, 51
　parts, 158–159
　phase space, 53
　raising/creation operator, 50
　uncertainty principle, 48, 53
Hamiltonian Cooper pair box (Hcpb), 267–269
Hamiltonian model, 16–17, 39–40
HangingResonators, 260
Harmonic motion, 38
Harmonic oscillator, 10–12
　classic, 38–40
　defined, 37–38
　quantum, 40–42
　qubit, 42–43
　solution, 66
Hcpb.anharm() command, 280
Heisenberg commutation relation, 48–49
Heisenberg uncertainty principle, 40–42, 48
H gate, *see* Hadamard gate
Hidden Markov model (HMM), 33
High-energy electron beam, 295
High-frequency structure simulator (HFSS), 124–125, 175–176, 244, 247, 248
High-temperature superconductors (HTS), 300
Hilbert space, 68, 216–217
Hybrid solver, 209

I

Identity gate, 85–86
Imaginary part, 198
Impedance matrix, 193–196
Impedance model, 175, 260
Inductive coupling, 163–165, 167, 201
Interatomic forces, 301
Inter-chip spacing, 309–310
Interdigitated transmon qubit, 148–152
Interference, 7–8, 13
Inverse capacitance matrix, 190
Inverse inductance matrix, 200–201, 216
Inversion about the mean, 104
Ion beam sputtering (IBS), 291–293, 295
Isotropic system, 303
Iterative solver, 209

J

Josephson dipole, 229, 230, 232
Josephson energy, 21, 56, 159
Josephson junction
    actual and approximated energy, 63
    charge qubit, 56–57
    configuration, 145
    definition, 20–23
    Dolan style, 158, 161–164
    electrostatic potential energy, 190
    flux qubit, 30, 58–59
    generation, 21
    Hamiltonian, 158–159
    irradiation, 24
    lumped-element linear inductor, 223
    Manhattan style, 158, 160–161, 164
    nonlinear inductive element, 53–54
    phase qubit, 29, 55
    properties, 159, 247–248
    structure, 158
    and supercurrents, 299–306
    transmon qubit, 28, 61–62

K

Kaufman ion source, 291
Kerr nonlinear coefficients, 250
Keysight Advanced Design System (ADS), 176
Kirchhoff's laws, 15, 45–47, 174–175

L

Lagrangian equations, 15
Lagrangian models, 13–15
Lamb shifts, 228, 231

LC oscillator circuit
    equation of motion, 45
    frequency and impedance, 45
    Hamiltonian circuit, 46–48
    lumped-element, 44, 45
    metal pads, 43
    physical layout, 43–44
    quantum Hamiltonian, 48–53
    time-dependent energy, 44
    time-invariant inductor, 43
    wave function, 52
LC tank circuit, 182–183
Legendre transformation, 46
Lenz's law, 26
Linear inductive element, 62
Linearized Hamiltonian, 231
Liquid-gas transition, 312
Liquid-solid transition, 312
Liquid-state nuclear magnetic resonance, 5
Lithographic patterning, 162
Lithography, 300
Logic gates, 9, 10, 80
    AND, 9
    CNOT, 87–88
    conjugate transpose of square root of X gate, 92–93
    control, 93–94
    CPhase, 91
    Hadamard, 84–85
    identity, 85–86
    NOT, 9, 87
    OR, 9
    Pauli gate, 86–87
    Reset, 87
    RX, 89
    R_{XX}, 93
    RY, 89
    RZ, 88–89
    R_{ZZ}, 93
    S dagger, 90
    S gate, 90
    square root of X gate, 92
    SWAP, 87, 94
    T dagger, 90–91
    T gate, 90
    Toffoli, 91–92
London equation, 26
London penetration depth, 305
Loss mechanisms, 178
Lumped oscillator model (LOM), 174–175
    advantages, 219
    auto_increase_solution_order, 207
    capacitance matrix and, 202–210
    components, 186

concept, 181–182, 187
direct coupler, 210–218
elements
    amplifier, 184–185
    LC tank circuit, 182–183
    oscillator frequency and stability response, 185–186
enabled, 208
freq_ghz, 208
matrices, 187–202
min_converged_passes, 208–209
min_passes, 208
name, 208
percent_error, 209
percent_refinement, 209
reuse_selected_design, 208
reuse_setup, 208
save_fields, 208
solution_order, 207
solver_type, 209

M

Machine learning, 33, 78
Magnetic flux, 23–24, 30, 53, 58, 223
Magnetism, 304–306
Manhattan style Josephson junction, 158, 160–161, 164
Mask, 298
Matrices
    admittance, 197–199
    capacitance, 188–191
    components, 187
    impedance, 193–196
    inverse inductance, 200–201
    mutual inductance, 199–200
    procedure, 187
    resistance, 191–193
    S-matrix, 201–202
Maxwell's equations, 176, 183
Meandered/serpentine geometry, 139
Mechanical stress, 311
Meissner effect, 24–26, 299–300, 304
Melting point, 312
Metrology, 96–97
Microelectromechanical systems (MEMS), 306
MicroTape, 307
Microwave analysis, 250
Mitigation strategies, 310
Multigrid solver, 209
Multi-qubit gate, 8–9
Mutual inductance, 164, 195, 199–200

N

Neutral atom qubits, 31–32
Newtonian analysis, 38–39
Noise resilience, 151
Non-Clifford gate, 91
Nonlinear Hamiltonian, 231
Nonlinear inductive element, 53–54, 62–63
NOT gate, 9, 87

O

Offset charge, 57
Ohm's law, 192, 197
Open-to-ground (OTG) structure, 243, 244
Operational amplifier (op-amp), 185–186
OR gate, 9
Orthonormality, 273–275
Oxidation control, 301

P

Paradigm-shifting revolution, 2
Parallelism, 13
Patterning issues, 301
Pauli gate, 9, 86–87
Pauli matrices, 16
Persistent currents, 26
Phase difference delta, 29
Phase qubits, 29–30, 55–56
Phase rotation gates, 100
Phase space, 48, 53
Phonons, 19, 299, 301–304
Phonon tunneling, 301
Photolithography, 178
Physical vapor deposition (PVD), 291
plot_bloch_multivector(), 78
plot_circuit_layout(), 79
plot_convergence method, 210
plot_histogram(), 78, 82, 83
plot_state_city(), 78
plot_state_qsphere(), 78
Poisson's equation, 189
Positive semi-definite (PSD), 188, 192, 194
Principle of least action, *see* Principle of stationary action
Principle of stationary action, 13
Python, 115–126

Q

qasm_simulator, 82
QComponents, 122
    CPW, 130–131
    CPW route meander, 139–142

direction routing, 133–136
pin, 130
QRoute, 130
routing at bent angles, 136–139
straight routing, 131–133
Qiskit
  documentation, 78
  draw(output) function, 81
  flowchart, 78
  histogram, 84
  logic gates, 84–94
  quantum circuits, 94–105
  transpiled circuit output, 82
  writing basic code, 77–84
  See also Qiskit Metal
Qiskit Metal, 34
  benefits, 107
  components, 120
  defined, 105–106
  designing, 106
  electromagnetic analysis and quantization, 173–178
  EPR analysis
    Ansys HFSS, Eigenmode analysis, 235
    circuit layout, 234–235
    combined transmon Qubit and CPW resonator, 247–250
    CPW resonator, 242–247
    double-hanger resonator (SParam), 257–263
    quantum Hamiltonian, 235
    single transmon qubit, 235–242
    transmon Qubit, 251–256
  full-fledged chip, 153–158
  functionalities
    chip, 124
    connection_pads, 124
    default values, 122–123
    HFSS, 124–125
    layer, 124
    loc_W and loc_H, 124, 125
    orientation, 123–124
    pos_x and pos_y, 123
    Q3D, 125
  GUI, 119–121, 204
  installation steps, 108–114
  Josephson junction, 158–163
  libraries, 115–118
  and Python, 115–126
  QComponents, 130–142
  QPins (*see* Quantum pins (QPins))
  qubit (*see* Qubits)
  superconducting qubit chip, 107
  typical structure, 106–107

qiskit_metal.analysis, 117
qiskit_metal.analysis.solvers, 118
qiskit_metal.designs, 116
qiskit_metal.Dict, 116
qiskit_metal.draw, 116
qiskit_metal.metal, 116
qiskit_metal.MetalGUI, 116
qiskit_metal.open_docs, 116
qiskit_metal.qlibrary.connectors, 117
qiskit_metal.qlibrary.couplers, 117
qiskit_metal.qlibrary.hangers, 117
qiskit_metal.qlibrary.passives, 117
qiskit_metal.qlibrary.qubits, 117
qiskit_metal.qlibrary.qubits.transmon_pocket, 116, 117
qiskit_metal.qlibrary.qubits.transmons, 117
qiskit_metal.qlibrary.splitters, 117
qiskit_metal.qlibrary.templates, 118
qiskit_metal.qlibrary.terminations, 117
qiskit_metal.qlibrary.tlines, 117
qiskit_metal.renderers.renderer_ansys, 117
qiskit_metal.renderers.renderer_blender, 117–118
qiskit_metal.renderers.renderer_gds, 118
qiskit_metal.toolbox_metal, 118
qiskit_metal.toolbox_python, 118
qiskit_metal.toolbox_python.attr_dict, 118
qiskit_metal.toolbox_python.transmon, 118
QRoute, 130
QRouteLead, 130
QRoutePoint, 130
Qscillator frequency, 185–186
Quality factors (Q-factors), 178
Quantization, 173–178
  coupled qubit and cavity system
    classical picture (FEM simulation), 224–226
    components, 222
    linear and nonlinear term, 223
    magnetic flux, 223
    maximum participation, 224
    minimum participation, 224
    quantum zero-point fluctuations, 226–228
    transmon configuration, 222
  general Josephson system
    composition, 230
    external controls, 230
    nonlinear elements, 229
    quantum Hamiltonian, 231–234
  inquiry, 222
Quantronium qubit
  design features, 70
  implementations, 70

operational principles, 71
schematic circuit diagram, 70–71
Quantum bit, *see* Qubits
Quantum circuits, 10
   advantages, 13
   counts/shots, 83
   Grover's algorithm, 104–105
   multi-qubit state preparation, GHZ states, 96–97
   oscillator, 12
   QFT, 100–101
   QiskitMetal, EPR analysis, 234–235
   Steane code, 101–103
   teleportation, 97–100
   two-qubit state preparation, Bell states, 95–96
Quantum computing
   circuits, 9–13
   CPWs, 131
   fault-tolerant, 103
   fundamentals, 5–9
   and history, 1–3
   representation, 2
   and superconducting circuits, 4–5, 17–19
   See also Quantum mechanics
Quantum error correction techniques, 33
Quantum Fourier Transform (QFT), 91, 100–101
Quantum gates, 8–10, 15
Quantum Hamiltonian, 48–53, 64–69, 231–234, 235
Quantum hardware, 5
Quantum harmonic oscillator (QHO), 40–42, 51–52
Quantum Key Sharing (QKS), 13
Quantum mechanics, 2, 3, 18
   Hamiltonian model, 16–17
   non-locality, 4
   Pauli matrices, 16
   Qiskit (*see* Qiskit)
   wave-nature duality, 5
Quantum oscillator, 12, 68
Quantum pins (QPins)
   chip, 130
   defined, 126
   features, 126–127
   gap, 130
   length, 130
   middle points, 130
   multiple input, 128–129
   net_id, 130
   normal vector, 130
   parent_name, 130
   points, 129
   single input, 127–128
   tangent vector, 130
   width, 130
Quantum simulations, 104–105
Quantum supremacy, 5
QuantumSystemRegistry, 213, 215
QuantumSystemRegistry.registry(), 211
Quantum teleportation, 97–100
Quasi-3D Extractor (Q3D), 125
Quasi-lumped oscillator model, 175
Quasi-static methods, 174
Qubit-cavity system, 221, 223
Qubit couplers
   bus resonator, 170–173
   defined, 163
   direct, 166–168, 173
   tunable, 168–170, 173
   types
      capacitive, 165
      comparison, 166
      inductive, 163–165
      resonator, 165–166
Qubits, 12, 18
   concept, 3–4
   couplers (*see* Qubit couplers)
   crosstalk, 33, 134
   electromagnetic environment, 201
   superconducting (*see* Superconducting qubits)
   types, 2
      comparison, 152
      concentric transmon, 145–148
      interdigitated transmon, 148–152
      Xmon, 142–145
Qutip simulation, 283–286

R

Reactive sputtering, 293
Readout errors, 33
Real part, 198
Reset gate, 87
Resistance matrix, 191–193
Resonator coupling, 165–166
Ring oscillators, 12
Rotating wave approximation (RWA), 66
Rotation gates, 9
Route meander
   advantages, 141–142
   asymmetry, 139
   challenges, 142
   fillet, 139
   routing, 140
   snap and prevent_short_edges, 139–140

total_length, 139
  Transmon qubits, 140–141
RoutePathfinder, 136, 138
RouteStraight() function, 133
Routing at bent angles, 136–139
RX gate, 89
R_{XX} gate, 93
RY gate, 89
RZ gate, 88–89
R_{ZZ} gate, 93

S
Scattering matrix (S-matrix), 201–202
Schrodinger's equation, 17, 41, 159
Screening currents, 26
S dagger gate, 90
Self-impedance, 193
Self-inductance, 193–194
Self-Kerr coupling, 256–257
S gate, 90
Shadow evaporation, 298–299
Shor's algorithm, 4–5, 29, 78
Single grounded transmon qubit, 142
Single-qubit gate, 8–9
Single transmon qubit, 235–242
  ERP setup, 241–242
  finite element Eigenmode analysis, 237–239
  GUI design, 236–237
  import required libraries, 235–236
  simulation, convergence and electromagnetic fields, 239–241
Solid-gas transition, 312
Solid-liquid transition, 312
Sputter gas, 291
Sputtering
  defined, 289
  deposition, 291
  experimental setup, 290
  gas flow, 293–295
  IBS, 291–293, 295
  transferred energy, 290
  yield, 290
Square root of X gate, 92
Stability response, 185–186
Steane code, 101–103
Straight routing, 131–133, 140
Sublimation point, 312
Superconducting circuits, 4–5, 17–19
  advantages, 31–32
  Cooper pairs, 19–20
  disadvantages, 32–34

EPR method (*see* Energy-participation ratio (EPR) model)
  flux quantum, 23–24
  Josephson junction, 20–23
  Meissner effect, 24–26
  realizing, 34
Superconducting quantum interference device (SQUID), 69, 72
Superconducting qubits, 5
  coherence times and error rates, 27
  defined, 26
  energy levels and quantum states, 15
  flux, 30–31
  nonlinear inductive element, 53–54
  phase, 29–30
  refinements
    coaxmon, 73–74
    fluxonium, 71–72
    Gmon, 72–73
    quantronium, 70–71
    Xmon, 69
  transmon, 27–28
  types
    charge, 56–58
    comparison, 61
    flux, 58–60
    phase, 55–56
  Xmon, 28–29
Superconducting transition temperature, 313
Superconductivity, 18–19
Superconductors, 18
  type I, 25
  type II, 25
Supercurrents
  Cooper pairs, 300
  limitations, 300
  and magnetism, 304–306
  phonons, 301–304
  properties, 299–300
  strategies, 300–301
Super diamagnetism, 25–26
Superposition, 6
SWAP gate, 87, 94

T
Taylor series, 62
T dagger gate, 90–91
T gate, 90
Theoretical foundations, 4
Thermal evaporation, *see* Evaporation
Thermal gravimetric analysis (TGA), 313–314
Thin films, 300–301
Tilted washboard potential, 55

Time-independent Schrödinger equation, 40
Toffoli gate, 9, 91–92, 105
Transition temperatures, 312–315
Transmon component, *see* Transmon qubit
Transmon cross, 142
Transmon Pocket, *see* Transmon qubit
Transmon qubit, 29–30, 58, 115, 140–141
    analytic expressions for energy, 271–272
    circuit diagram, 266
    classical Hamiltonian, 63–64
    CPB, 266–267
    defined, 27–28, 60–61
    direct coupler, 167
    Eigenmode analysis setup, 252–253
    Eigenmode analysis setup with buffer adjustment, 253–256
    energy function, 2D plane, 64, 65
    energy level computation, 269–271
    Josephson junction, 61–62
    junction inductance and capacitance, 251–252
    modules, 269
    nonlinear inductance representation, 62–63
    output value, 121–122
    pocket cavity and chip, 116–117
    quantum Hamiltonian, 64–69
    setup, 251
    wave function plotting, 272–275
        orthonormality, 273–275
Transpile function, 82

Transverse electromagnetic (TEM) mode, 131
Trapped-ion qubits, 31–32
Traveling Salesman Problem (TSP), 104
Tunable coupler, 168–170, 173
Turing machine, 3, 4
Type II superconductors, 25
Type I superconductors, 25

W

Wafer bumping, 307
Wafer-scale integration, 308
Wave function plotting, 272–275
Wave-nature duality, 5

X

Xmon qubit, 28–29, 142–145
    advantages and applications, 69
    circuit design and functionality, 69
    defined, 69
    features, 69
    schematic circuit diagram, 70

Z

Zero electrical resistance, 31
Zero-point energy (ZPE), 41–42, 52
Zero-point fluctuations (ZPF), 52, 226–228

GPSR Compliance

The European Union's (EU) General Product Safety Regulation (GPSR) is a set of rules that requires consumer products to be safe and our obligations to ensure this.

If you have any concerns about our products, you can contact us on

ProductSafety@springernature.com

In case Publisher is established outside the EU, the EU authorized representative is:

Springer Nature Customer Service Center GmbH
Europaplatz 3
69115 Heidelberg, Germany

www.ingramcontent.com/pod-product-compliance
Lightning Source LLC
LaVergne TN
LVHW010336260326
834688LV00036B/727